Re-reading Saussure

'Far and away the best book on Saussure's *Cours* that I know of . . . it offers a thorough-going re-thinking of Saussure, meticulously detailed, scrupulous, well informed . . . a fundamentally challenging text.'
                    Professor Gunther Kress, *Institute of Education*

Through a detailed re-reading of Saussure's work in the light of contemporary developments in the human, life and physical sciences, Paul Thibault provides us with the means to re-define and re-focus our theories of social meaning-making.

Saussure's theory of language is generally considered to be a formal theory of abstract sign-types and systems, separate from our individual and social practices of making meaning. In this challenging book, Thibault presents a different view of Saussure. Paying close attention to the original texts, including *Cours de linguistique générale*, he demonstrates that Saussure was centrally concerned with trying to formulate a theory of how meanings are made.

Re-reading Saussure does more than simply engage with Saussure's theory in a new and up-to-date way. In addition to demonstrating the continuing viability of Saussure's thinking through a range of examples, it makes an important intervention in contemporary linguistic and semiotic debate.

Paul J. Thibault is Associate Professor in English Language and Linguistics at the University of Venice, Italy.

Re-reading Saussure

The dynamics of signs in social life

Paul J. Thibault

London and New York

First published 1997
by Routledge
11 New Fetter Lane, London EC4P 4EE

Simultaneously published in the USA and Canada
by Routledge
29 West 35th Street, New York, NY 10001

Typeset in Garamond by Solidus (Bristol) Limited
Printed and bound in Great Britain by Biddles Ltd, Guildford and King's Lynn

British Library Cataloguing in Publication Data
A catalogue record for this book is available from the British Library

Library of Congress Cataloguing in Publication Data
Thibault, Paul J.
    Re-reading Saussure : the dynamics of signs in social life/
Paul J. Thibault.
    Includes bibliographical references (p.) and index.
    1. Saussure, Ferdinand de, 1857–1913. 2. Semiotics–Social
aspects. 3. Language and languages–Philosophy. 4. Linguistics.
    I. Title.
P85.S18T48   1996   96-2570
401'.41—dc20

ISBN: 0–415–10410–6 (hbk)
ISBN: 0–415–10411–4 (pbk)

This book is dedicated to my grandparents, and all they taught me in, through and around the signs we made together:

James Watman Lovell (1889–1985)
Mary Cleland Lovell, née Robertson (1895–1953)
Henri William Thibault (1900–83)
Dulcie Pearl Thibault, née Capewell (1904–66)

Contents

Figures

Tables

Preface

Is Saussure's semiological theory of language form and function of continuing relevance to theories of social meaning-making in the late twentieth century, or are the ideas that he developed in Geneva in the early part of this century superseded? This is the central question that informs this book. A re-reading implies an act of re-contextualization, a re-making. This is true both of other people's readings of Saussure, and of my own. Two main factors inform the genesis of the present book. Some years ago, while teaching courses in linguistics, semiotics and literary theory at the University of Sydney, I became convinced of the importance of encouraging students to read the major thinkers in their chosen fields of study, rather than to rely exclusively on secondary sources.

In the case of Saussure, this immediately raises issues concerning the historical, cultural and linguistic distance from the modern Anglophone reader. For example, how does one make sense of a set of texts that Saussure never actually wrote? Nevertheless, I remain convinced that the additional pedagogical and interpretative work that is required in order to overcome such inherent difficulties is immensely worth while. Rather than merely accepting the received doctrine, an active and dialogic engagement with the text renews the text itself, as well as our relations with it. Reading is not a process of passively 'decoding' someone else's thought. Nothing could be less Saussurean than the notion that pre-linguistic 'thoughts' or 'ideas' are simply packaged up in words by the writer, transmitted, and then passively decoded by the reader.

This brings me to the second of the two factors that I mentioned above. I started to make notes on my reading of Saussure during the preparation of the courses that I have referred to. Gradually, I became aware of my many disagreements with much conventional wisdom concerning Saussure. According to this conventional wisdom, Saussure sees the language system as formal and autonomous. He separates individual from society, and language from other non-linguistic sign systems. Society is an anonymous and coercive totality which is external to the individual. The speech practices of individuals are separate from, or external to, the language system. The former have no systematic relationship to the latter. The language system is a closed and static system which makes no contact with the world. Saussure is unable to explain variability and change in the linguistic and other signs that we use in social life. Language is a code by which the speaker 'encodes' and then transmits non-linguistic ideas and thoughts to the listener in the speech circuit; in turn, these are 'decoded' by the listener. The sign is not systematically shaped by its uses in concrete acts of meaning-making.

In this book, I shall reject all of these assumptions, which I take to be fundamentally mistaken. This does not mean that Saussure always presents us with fully worked out solutions to these issues. My point is that the conceptual framework which he gives voice to *is* able to provide solutions to all of the questions raised here, and in ways that are entirely self-consistent with the metatheory which Saussure proposes in order to explain how signs function in social life.

Our explanations and understandings of language are always refracted through the cultural categories and the technological metaphors of the dominant social groups in a given culture. Saussure and his interpreters are no exception to this. Thus, the Russian formalists, the Glossematics of the Copenhagen School lead by Hjelmslev, the structuralists, the Prague School of linguistics and semiotics, and the post-structuralists have all made seminal contributions to our understanding of Saussure, and to the further development of his thinking. In spite of the many important advances that have been made in linguistic theory and analytical practice, an adequate account of signs in social life has not been achieved.

Saussure's theory represents a fundamental shift away from the atomistic and objectivist focus on naturalistic explanations, isolable behaviours and physical cause and effect that prevailed in nineteenth-century studies of language. He is interested in meaning, pattern and the ways these are enacted, maintained and changed in a given society. In the past few decades, formal, pragmatic and cognitive models of language have tended to produce separate accounts of structure and meaning, rather than the conceptually unified account that Saussure outlined. The analytical focus in these recent developments has been on an asocial individual – usually an analytical projection of North American folk-theories of individual mind and behaviour.

This picture has now begun to change. Increasingly, there is a renewed recognition of the ways in which meanings are made through the social practices of a community. Language and other sign systems are resources for making meanings in and through particular social activities. In my view, this is precisely the path which Saussure set out to explore. These recent developments suggest that it is time to re-assess Saussure's project and what it can teach us today. My re-reading is in this spirit.

A reading is always a selective re-contextualization, to use a telling phrase of the British social theorist, Basil Bernstein. Saussure's *Cours de linguistique générale* (1915 [1971], hereafter *CLG*) is a canonical text in the history of twentieth-century linguistics and semiotics. A canonical text presents us with a very special problem of interpretation. Canonical texts get re-read, re-written and revised from generation to generation. *CLG* is no exception to this. That is, it has been progressively re-contextualized by the pedagogical and scientific practices of succeeding generations and schools of linguistic and semiotic thought. Increasingly, the canonical text becomes more implicit in the practices of each successor generation. There is not, of course, only one authentic and original way of reading Saussure. Rather, each generation tends to develop and specify a preferred reading of the canonical text. Consequently, different preferred readings are selectively filtered through the cultural and scientific themes and preoccupations of a given generation. This may then produce the effect of an increasing loss of direct engagement with the Saussurean texts.

The processes I have described in the previous paragraph are historical processes. They are, for this reason, irreversible. There can be no simple going back to what Saussure said or might have meant. With these considerations in mind, I should like to make two disclaimers concerning the aims of the present study. *Re-reading Saussure* is not a critical review of other, historically prior, readings of Saussure. Nor is it a work of historical or critical exegesis of the Saussurean texts and the background to these. My purpose, in trying to answer the question which I posed at the beginning of this Preface, is very different from either of these entirely legitimate activities.

Above all, I am concerned with the continuing relevance of the conceptual framework which Saussure outlines in *CLG* and elsewhere for a theory of social meaning-making, and how we might conceive of this in the late twentieth century. My *Re-reading* is, then, a critical intervention in and a re-working of the problems Saussure raises. However, my principal concern is to explore these problems in the light of contemporary developments. Thus, my engagement with Saussure's texts involves a constant effort of reconstituting their theoretical categories and the interrelations among these. My guiding principle is the study of the functioning of signs in social life that Saussure allows us to envisage in the early pages of *CLG*.

Linguists have not always taken up Saussure's concern with the linguistic sign. This is so of all of the formal and even many of the functionalist schools of twentieth-century linguistic thought. On the other hand, the seminal work of linguists and semioticians such as Louis Hjelmslev, Gustave Guillaume, André Martinet, Roman Jakobson, Sydney Lamb, Michael Halliday, Ronald Langacker and others all take up and develop the Saussurean notion of the sign, even when this term is not explicitly used.

Saussure's own intellectual endeavours stand in a rather peculiar relationship to the linguistic studies of his time. There was no canonical text to which he could defer in *CLG*. The edited text of *CLG*, as well as the later editorial efforts of Godel and Engler, may be seen as a heterogeneous set of textual records of a pedagogical practice and its reception by his students. It is a record of the making of a new theory of language. One of the central assumptions of this theory is that language may be described as a system of signs. Signs are the means by which speakers and listeners, readers and writers make and re-make meanings in social life.

On reading and re-reading Saussure I have been constantly struck by the open-ended and self-reflexive nature of his enquiry. We have 'before' us a constantly enquiring mind. Saussure calls into question not only many of the assumptions and practices which he inherits from the nineteenth-century traditions of the comparative philologists and the Neogrammarians, but also his own theoretical assumptions and analytical practices.

Saussure stands at the cutting edge in his field. To use Basil Bernstein's insightful expression, Saussure belongs to that domain of scientific practice that seeks the 'possibility of the impossible', or the 'unthinkable' (1990: 181). That is, he is concerned, above all, with the production and transmission, rather than the pedagogical reproduction, of a new order of scientific discourse about language. In trying to think the 'unthinkable' about language, Saussure opens up a new discursive space. This is the 'yet to be thought', which Saussure envisaged as the scientific study of *the functioning of signs within social life*' (*CLG*: 33; emphasis in original). The Saussurean texts are a constant reminder of the meeting point of 'order and disorder' which is, as Bernstein points out, a critical discursive site for the 'yet to be thought' and its further development.

A few words on the overall design of the present book would seem to be in order. This book comprises thirteen chapters. I have organized these into six parts on thematic grounds. In Part I, I discuss the metatheoretical issues that I believe to be central to our understanding of Saussure's project. These concern the constructed, rather than given, nature of the object of study, Saussure's rejection of empiricism and positivism, and his constructivist epistemology of language form. In Part I, I also raise the question as to what Saussure might have meant by a 'social psychology' of signs in social life.

The two chapters in Part II look at the notion of *langue*, or the language system. This is one of the most central components in Saussure's theory. The discussion in these chapters concerns both the 'static' and the temporal perspectives on this. It also deals with the methodological and ontological status of *langue* as, dually, object of study and historically changing and socially shared resource for the making of meanings. The constitutive place of both the individual and society in this framework also comes under scrutiny.

Part III focuses more closely on the individual in relation to both *parole* and the overall speech circuit. I argue for the need to re-think the relationship between individual and society and to accord a more central place to the individual in Saussure's framework. I also reject the view that the circuit is a transmission or code model of communication. Instead, I argue that it is an important precursor of more recent ecosocial theories of human social meaning-making. It is the means by which individuals are linked both to each other and to the system of *langue* in and through jointly created signifying acts.

Part IV takes up one of Saussure's most fundamental theoretical notions – linguistic value. The system of values in *langue* is, I argue, a system of contextualizing relations. It is the means by which language users construct and construe meaningful relationships between semiotic forms and the world. I also discuss the economic underpinnings of linguistic value in relation to the category of linguistic work.

Part V focuses on the linguistic sign and the question of signification. I consider the stratified nature of meaning-making and the internal nature of the relation between signifier and signified from this point of view. Signs are not simply pre-given entities. Instead, they are made in and through contextualized uses of the system of values.

In Part VI, I explore and extend Saussure's notion of the 'mechanism of the language system'. I discuss how a theory of contextualization may be built on this basis. The frequently misunderstood notions of arbitrariness and motivation in signs are also discussed in this connection. Through a number of textual analyses of both linguistic and non-linguistic modalities of semiosis, I consider how Saussure's theory already 'contains' the critically important notions of schematicity, prototypicality, intertextuality, meta-semiosis and grounding (indexicality), all of which have been so important in much recent discussion. Overall, the three chapters in Part VI seek to explore and extend the possibility of a science of signs in social life in relation to these notions.

There are three main absences in the present study. These are: (1) Saussure's phonological theory; (2) the issue of writing in relation to speech; and (3) the place of the body–brain complex in Saussure's theory. The reason for these gaps is very simple. During the preparation of the present book, a further study also crystallized around these three sets of issues. For this reason, I have preferred a more extended discussion in a separate, forth-coming book entitled *The Signifying Body*.

In the present book, I shall mainly draw on *CLG*. However, I also refer to the *Sources manuscrites* edited by Robert Godel (1957), and to the *Edition critique* of *CLG* edited by Rudolph Engler (1967), as well as to the other sources referred to below. A note on my use of the original French text of *CLG*, along with the two currently available English-language translations by Wade Baskin (1959) and Roy Harris (1983), also seems in order. Where it seems useful to do so, I have indicated the French term in square brackets, along with the appropriate page reference to the Payot edition. All quotations taken from the original French-language editions of *CLG*, and any other non-English-language sources, have been translated by myself, unless otherwise specified.

On a number of occasions, I refer directly to the English-language translations of *CLG* in order to draw attention to specific terminological or other problems. None of the two English language translations is ideal, in my view, and I strongly recommend the original French text. Tullio de Mauro's Italian translation and critical commentary are admirable. Indeed, linguistic folklore has it that Roman Jakobson considered the De Mauro translation to be the finest translation of *CLG* available in any language! I am in no position to take this on board as my own opinion. I have at all stages assumed an English-speaking reader.

In the interests of terminological consistency, I have usually used the French terms *langue* and *parole*, rather than English-language translations. Generally speaking, I take *langue* to refer to the language system; *parole* refers to specific instances of language in use. On occasion, I also use English-language glosses on these two terms. In the chapters which follow, I develop a more precise set of distinctions in connection with these terms.

A number of individuals have provided me with material, moral and intellectual support, and wonderful discussion and friendship throughout the preparation of the manuscript and the development of my thinking on the issues discussed therein. In particular, I should like to mention John Alexander, Jennifer Biddle, Paul Bouissac, Isa Bussi, Kristin Davidse, Norman Fairclough, Elio Gatti, Francisco Gonzálvez García, Michael Halliday, Morag Harris, Ruqaiya Hasan, Noel King, Gunther Kress, Blair McKenzie, Monique Le Corre, Marc Lorrimar, Bob Lumsden, Michael O'Toole, Maria Pavesi, Federico Pellizzi, Fred C. C. Peng, Cate Poynton, Carlo Prevignano, Susanna Shore, Theo van Leeuwen, Jay Lemke, Jim Martin, Kieran McGillicuddy, Bill McGregor, Steve Muecke, Winfried Nöth, Clive Thomson, Terry Threadgold and Eija Ventola. To Claire L'Enfant, Julia Hall and Alison Foyle at Routledge, all of whom were involved at various stages in the preparation of the manuscript, my very special thanks for making this project possible, as well as for their constant advice and professional help. Morag Harris read the entire manuscript and made many valuable comments and suggestions. My daughter, Ilaria, generously allowed me to use a number of her texts in some of the textual analyses that follow. Through her example, I have learned more than I could otherwise have known about the making of signs in social life.

Bologna and Venice, November 1995

Acknowledgements

The author and publishers are grateful to the copyright holders for permission to reproduce the following material: Figure 13.11, from *Quaderno di Lavoro 5* by Sergio Danieli © 1981 Giunti, Florence: by kind permission of the publisher; Appendix 'Putting in the ribbon', from *User's Guide. LX-800 9 Pin Dot Matrix Printer* by Seiko Epson Corporation © 1986 Seiko Epson Corporation Nagano, Japan; Figure 13.16, 'Execution' by C. Morris/Black Star/Colorific!

While the author and publishers have made every effort to contact copyright holders of material used in this volume, they would be grateful to hear from any they were unable to contact.

Part I

Constructing a science of signs

Chapter 1

Defining the object of study

1 STAKING OUT A SCIENCE OF THE LINGUISTIC SIGN

Commentators such as Jonathan Culler (1976) and Terence Hawkes (1977) have tended to emphasize the Copernican revolution, as Roy Harris (in Saussure 1983: ix) puts it, which was inaugurated with the posthumous publication of Saussure's *CLG*. Saussure's achievement, according to this view, lies in his systematic elaboration of a general science of signs, or a semiology. In *CLG* these principles are, of course, elaborated with respect to language, which Saussure envisaged as just one part of a more comprehensive study of '*the life of signs in social life*' (*CLG*: 33; emphasis in original). Thus, Saussure stakes out the citizens' rights of this future science of semiology right from the outset. Further, Saussure does not view this science of semiology as an autonomous science. 'It would', he claims, 'form part of social psychology, and consequently of general psychology' (*CLG*: 33). I shall return to this last point in Chapter 2, section 4.

It is doubtful that Saussure intends the terms 'social psychology' and 'psychology' to mean exactly what we understand by these notions in their contemporary sense. Saussure does not take this point any further. Instead, he undertakes a quite precise division of labour. He leaves it up to the psychologist 'to determine the exact place of semiology' (*CLG*: 33) in the overall field of human knowledge. The more specific and delimited task of the linguist, Saussure continues, 'is to define what it is that makes the language system [*la langue*] a special type of system within the totality of semiological facts' (*CLG*: 33). In making this claim, Saussure effects an important strategic move; it is a move which is both political and theoretical in its implications. Linguistics becomes constituted as an 'autonomous' realm of scientific enquiry at the very moment when language is constituted as an object of scientific enquiry in its own right:

> Why is it that semiology is not yet recognized as an autonomous science, having like all the others its own object? This brings one full circle: on the one hand, there is nothing more suitable than the language system for allowing the nature of the semiological problem to be understood; but, in

order to pose it in an appropriate way, it has almost always been approached as a function of something else, from other points of view.

There is first of all the superficial conception of the general public: it sees the language system as nothing more than a nomenclature (see p. 97), which suppresses all research on its true nature.

(CLG: 34)

Saussure is intent on shifting the study of language from the purely instrumental basis which had prevailed, and as a result of which language had been a means for studying something else, to language as an object of systematic enquiry in its own right (Chapter 2, section 6).

Many commentators have taken this to mean that for Saussure the concrete social and historical production and use of signs is split from the science of semiology which he envisages. However, Wlad Godzich (1984: 19) has suggested that Saussure's notion of social psychology may constitute the locus of a renovated science of signs in social life. In this book, I shall attempt to demonstrate that Saussure's conception of the sign is entirely compatible with such a project. It is also an essential starting point for a theory of signs in social life. In the next section, I shall discuss two models of scientific enquiry which have hitherto influenced our understanding of Saussure.

2 TWO THEORETICAL MODELS FOR READING *CLG*

The commentators whom I named above reflect the more recent structuralist reading of *CLG*. Structuralism developed as a full-fledged movement in the human sciences, first in France, then elsewhere, in the period which runs from the 1950s to the 1970s (Thibault, in press a). Its intellectual and historical roots go back to the Russian formalists, who were active in the Soviet Union in the 1920s and 1930s. This entailed a specific reading of *CLG*. Further, the general principles which Saussure elaborated for language were extended beyond language to a wide variety of other signifying systems: kinship, the mass media, popular culture, gastronomic codes, fashion, narrative and so on. This also entailed a particular conception of 'theory'. Taking a particular reading of Saussure's concept of *langue* as their model, the structuralists sought a conceptual framework in which the mechanisms which are postulated as lying 'behind' and causing the observed phenomenon might be studied. Such generative mechanisms would then constitute the explanation of the phenomenon.

A theory, so defined, assumes an ontology of the causal mechanisms which underlie and generate the observed phenomenon. The ontological basis of theory, in this sense, resides in the notion that the language system (*langue*) defines the general conditions of possibility of human subjectivity and experience. This presupposes, as Ian Hunter (1984) has argued, that a continuous and totalizing conception of human experience is founded on the general conditions of possibility afforded by *langue*.

The structuralist reading of Saussure made this ontology very much its own. Structuralism, however, takes the matter still further. The structuralists claim that signifying systems and their principles of organization represent the very conditions of possibility of the ways of perceiving, experiencing and acting of the individual members of a given social or cultural order. Lévi-Strauss (1972) quite explicitly locates these systems and rules in the pre-given and universal structures of the human mind. Consequently, the constructive role of individual and social activity is marginalized. In structuralism, there is no account of signs-in-use. Structuralism remains a formal theory of abstract and decontextualized *systems* of signs. It posits essentially *a priori* structures and categories of mind very much after the fashion of Immanuel Kant (1970 [1781]). These are categories which exist prior to individual human experience and which allow individuals both to recognize and to categorize the world, as well as to impose a rationality upon it.

There is also another sense in which *CLG* can be read as a theory of the language system. This has received less attention from the structuralists, although it has been central in the development of the various structural–functional theories of language which *CLG* also foreshadowed. In this second sense, a theory is an open set of necessarily related propositions. These serve to express the relationships among the various concepts of the theory. From this point of view, Saussure, in an admittedly programmatic and incomplete way, maps out a blueprint for the structural–functional description of the internal design features of a given language system, or its grammar. He seeks to interpret the basic constituent units, their interrelationships and their functional values in the grammar of a given language.

3 INTERNAL VERSUS EXTERNAL LINGUISTICS

Saussure's initial problem is really very simple: what methods must the linguist use and what analytical decisions must he or she take in order to separate language from other related phenomena in the process of studying the internal design features of language itself? Instead of using language as a means or instrument for investigating non-linguistic phenomena, this requires that language and its internal systems of relations themselves become the object of study (section 1 above). It is sometimes mistakenly thought that Saussure proposes a static and closed model of language. But this is to mistake an essentially *methodological* decision about how to delimit the study of the language system with Saussure's comprehensive knowledge of historical, geographical and dialectal factors, which are ever present in *CLG*. For example, Saussure, in terms not dissimilar to the 'centripetal' and 'centrifugal' tendencies which Mikhail Bakhtin (1981 [1975]) observed in the language practices of a community, wrote: 'In the whole of the human masses two forces simultaneously act unceasingly and in opposite ways: on the one hand, the particularistic spirit, the "parochial spirit"; on the other, the force of "intercourse", which creates communication among men' (*CLG*: 281).

Saussure sets about defining this new science in terms of a basic distinction between an 'internal' 'linguistics of the language system [*langue*]', and an 'external' 'linguistics of speech [*parole*]' (*CLG*: 36–9). He gives theoretical prominence to the first of these as a way of delimiting the object of study. In Saussure's view, the language system is a system of terms related by the purely negatively defined differences that distinguish any given term from the others in the same system (Chapter 3, section 3). The primary task of the linguist is to study the internal principles of organization of the language system, so defined. 'External' linguistics, which is seen by Saussure as 'secondary' to the more 'essential' internal linguistics (*CLG*: 37), is concerned, on the other hand, with individual and social *uses* of language. These include, as Saussure points out, the study of language in relation to: (1) its historical development; (2) social institutions such as church and school; (3) the literary development of a language; and (4) political history (*CLG*: 41).

Now, the dichotomous view of the relationship between the two components of this distinction remains to this day the dominant reading of Saussure. Moreover, linguists and semioticians who have taken up this reading have tended to assume that Saussure's distinction between an 'internal' linguistics of *langue* and an 'external' linguistics of *parole* amounts to a description of the concrete reality of language. In actual fact, the distinction between *langue* and *parole* belongs to a theory of *linguistics*. It is not inherent in the concrete reality of language (Coseriu 1981: 18). I think this is a serious misreading of Saussure, which has given rise to a confusion between methodology, on the one hand, and ontology, on the other. A careful reading of Saussure does not necessarily lead to the rigid set of dichotomies which have predominated in subsequent thinking about these issues. One of the purposes of this book is to propose an alternative reading of this relationship.

Saussure is very clear about the methodological problem which confronts him. Here he is at the very outset of *CLG* attempting to come to grips with the problem of defining the language system (*langue*) as the object of study:

> Language [*langage*] at each instant implicates at the same time an established system and an evolution; at each moment, it is an institution in the present and a product of the past. It seems at first glance very simple to distinguish between this system and its history, between what it is and what it was; *in reality, the relationship which unites these two things is so close that it is difficult to separate them.*
>
> (*CLG*: 24; my emphasis)

The separating of the two is not in the 'reality' of the concrete and living language (*langage*), but in the methodological perspective which the linguist adopts in order to analyse this. Saussure does not ontologically split language (*langage*) in two. Instead, linguistic theory, as Saussure defines it, makes a methodological and, hence, epistemological distinction between *langue* and *parole*. This is abundantly clear in the opening chapter of the later discussion dedicated to synchronic linguistics:

> delimitation in time is not the only difficulty that we encounter in the definition of a state of the language system [*état de langue*]; the same problem poses itself in regard to space. In brief, the notion of a state of the language system can only be approximate. *In static linguistics, as in the majority of the sciences, no demonstration is possible without a conventional simplification of the data.*
>
> (*CLG*: 143; my emphasis)

The process nouns *delimitation, demonstration* and *conventional simplification* in this quote amply suggest that Saussure is not talking about language *per se*. Instead, he is referring to the theoretical and descriptive activities which the linguist performs in the process of transforming – cf. 'delimiting', 'approximating', 'demonstrating' and 'simplifying' – the data into terms compatible with his science of a 'static linguistics'. Figure 1.1 extends and develops the diagram whereby Saussure himself proposes 'a rational form which linguistic studies must take' (*CLG*: 139).

Saussure analytically separates *langage* ('the [Japanese, English or French, etc.] language') into two components: (1) *langue*, or the language system, which is the resource systems that language users draw on and deploy in order to make meanings in specific contexts; and (2) *parole*, or 'speech', which is 'the sum of what people say', comprising '(a) individual combinations, dependent on the will of the person who speaks, and (b) acts of

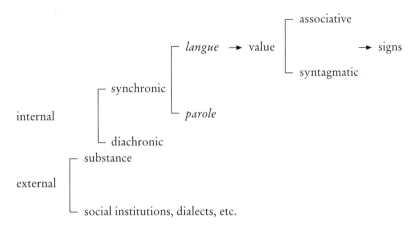

Figure 1.1 Defining the domain of the object of study; internal and external linguistics

phonation, which are equally voluntary, necessary for the execution of these combinations' (*CLG*: 38; Chapter 2, section 3). Saussure claims that *langue* is 'social in its essence and independent of the individual' (*CLG*: 37). Does this mean, then, that *parole* is for Saussure purely individual, random, subjective and voluntaristic? Or is *parole*, on the other hand, patterned and socially constrained? Generally speaking, *parole* has been interpreted as being a mere 'rag-bag', as Holdcroft (1991: 52) puts it, of random and accidental features. I shall develop alternative arguments in Chapter 5.

According to some scholars, these distinctions derive from the socio-logical theory of Emile Durkheim. In *The Rules of Sociological Method* (1982 [1902]), Durkheim proposes a 'morphological' definition of the 'social fact'. It has been claimed that this anticipates the concept of *langue* as a purportedly anonymous and coercive social phenomenon which is external to the individual (e.g., Hodge and Kress 1988: 19). Thus, Saussure's assertion that 'The language system [*langue*] itself is not a function of the speaking subject. It is the product which the individual registers passively' (*CLG*: 30) is given as evidence of this. In my view, the supposed 'passivity' of the individual has quite a different theoretical sense. I shall discuss this in Chapter 5. Compare this to what Durkheim has written:

A social fact is any way of acting, whether fixed or not, capable of exerting over the individual an external constraint; or which is general over the whole of a given society whilst having an existence of its own, independent of its individual manifestations.

(Durkheim 1982 [1902]: 59; emphasis in original)

Importantly, Saussure asserts the 'interdependence' of *langue* and *parole*. He also insists on 'the absolute nature of the distinction between the two'. In so doing, he avoids hypostatizing *langue* as something independent of the social collectivity itself:

Without doubt, these two objects [*langue* and *parole*] are closely linked and one presupposes the other: the language system is necessary so that *parole* is intelligible and produces its effects; but the latter is necessary so that the language system can be established; historically, the fact of *parole* always comes first. How would one know how to associate an idea with a verbal image, if one didn't first discover this association in an act of *parole*? On the other hand, it is in listening to others that we learn our mother tongue; it gets stored in our brain only on the basis of innumerable experiences. Finally, it is *parole* which causes the language system to evolve: it is the impressions received while listening to others which modify our linguistic habits. *Langue* and *parole* are, then, interdependent; the former is at the same time the instrument and the product of the latter. But all of this does not stop them from being two absolutely distinct things.

(*CLG*: 37–8)

Saussure clarifies at the outset that the distinction between *langue* and *parole* is one between two 'objects of study', and not between two independently existing realities. The distinction exists in the methodological approach which the linguist adopts. It is not inherent in the reality of the living language, which Saussure designates with a third term, *langage* (see above). He argues in the above passage that: (1) a language system is a necessary condition of any signifying act in *parole*; (2) the system is, however, 'established', or analytically reconstructed, only on the basis of concrete uses of language (*parole*); (3) the speakers of a language learn to construe meaningful relations between 'ideas' and 'verbal acoustic images' not on the basis of an abstract language system as such, but through historically and socially specific signifying acts; (4) the individual child's construction and internalization of the language system occur in and through his or her participation in concrete uses of language in *parole*; (5) social uses of language are the starting point for change in the system, and not the other way round; (6) linguistic contact with others can change our linguistic practices; (7) the 'absolute' distinction Saussure wishes to maintain between *langue* and *parole* does not mirror the very different and dynamic reality described in points (1)–(6), and which are fully acknowledged by Saussure. Instead, it refers to a precise set of methodological aims.

What, then, is the point of the distinction between *langue* and *parole*? Saussure does not develop his thinking about the 'interdependence' of *langue* and *parole*. However, the fact that he acknowledges this interdependence indicates that he is aware of the arbitrary nature of the boundaries separating them. There is ample evidence on reading *CLG* to show that Saussure was a more subtle and flexible thinker than the dichotomous reading has hitherto allowed for. The main point of the distinction is to allow the linguist to focus on and to describe the meaning-making resources which *langue* provides for its users. However, Saussure does not develop the theoretical links between this perspective and a theory of signs-in-use. Such a link is, of course, essential for a theory of signs in social life. In this book, I shall suggest ways as to how this link might be theorized.

4 SAUSSURE'S OBJECTIFICATION OF GRAMMAR

In Chapter 1 of the 'Introduction' to *CLG*, Saussure cites one of the achievements of the German school of Neogrammarians as being their refusal to view language as 'an organism developing of its own accord' (*CLG*: 19). Later, Saussure likens the organization of language into 'groups of signs' to 'the functioning of a machine' (*CLG*: 177). These metaphors are of more than casual significance.

Saussure's scientific project necessarily requires a degree of abstraction which neither the traditions of comparative and historical linguistics nor the Neogrammarians had achieved. A genuine science of language must be able to distance itself from the immediate and sensual reality of everyday linguistic praxis. Saussure accomplishes an important step in this direction. This may seem a paradoxical and contradictory step for a phenomenon (language) which is so immediately and intimately connected to everyday human activity. The point is that the resulting process of objectification is a necessary step in the attainment of a mediated distancing from our commonsense ways of thinking and talking about our own linguistic praxis. This does not aim at an alienating and sterile formalism. Rather, the aim is a more complexly mediated scientific account which does not remain trapped in our everyday, immediate experience of language and our commonsense explanations of this (Chapter 2, sections 10 and 11).

5 INTRINSIC VERSUS EXTRINSIC CRITERIA: SAUSSURE'S CRITIQUE OF HISTORICAL LINGUISTICS

In Chapter 1 of *CLG* Saussure refers to a number of problems which his attempt to found a science of *langue* on semiological principles has inherited from his nineteenth-century antecedents. The problems are both theoretical and methodological in nature. Saussure makes a series of revealing observations on the work of the nineteenth-century comparative philologists, and in particular the work of August Schleicher (*CLG*: 16–17).

The first problem which Saussure draws attention to is the assumption made by the comparative philologists that change in a given language system is continuous with the passing of time. As I shall show in Chapter 4, Saussure demonstrates the essentially *discontinuous* nature of language change. It is not analogous to the 'evolutionary' phases of growth, which plants, in Saussure's example, are assumed to undergo. A second problem is the question of the model of causality which is implicit in this same line of reasoning. According to the historical linguists, the prior phase of the vowel change referred to in Saussure's discussion somehow 'causes' the succeeding stage. A third problem is Schleicher's assumption, as Saussure's discussion of Greek and Sanskrit vowel alternation shows, that the two languages in question are spatio-temporally co-ordinated. Saussure concludes his discussion by noting the lack of 'any necessary parity among the grammatical effects which develop in one or the other language' (*CLG*: 17).

The erroneous reasoning which Saussure alludes to in this remark concerning Schleicher's analysis has to do with the latter's assumption that the two sets of results – the systems of vowel alternation in, respectively, Greek and Sanskrit – are susceptible to direct observation. But, Saussure points out, it is only through a model of the grammar of the language system in question that the linguist can construct a conceptual framework for investigating any specific phenomenon. The mistake which the comparativists made was to assume, in the absence of any conception of the language system, that the reality of the language could be represented by a direct appeal to the so-called 'facts'.

Saussure objects to Schleicher's analysis of the Greek and Sanskrit vowel systems because it makes reference to some absolute standard in relation to which the vowels from the two systems are to be measured. In a coherent general linguistics, Saussure argues, there can be no absolute descriptive standard. Instead, the terms which are internal to a given language system are defined on the basis of their relationships to one another, rather than with reference to extrinsic criteria. Saussure shows that all semiological systems and their study are relative in this sense. That is, the terms that constitute a given system are defined by their relations to each other, as well as by the particular metatheoretical criterion which the linguist arbitrarily chooses as the reference point for the analysis (Chapter 2, sections 1 and 7).

Saussure's metatheory is concerned with the general problem of co-ordinating the analysis of the language system and of other sign systems for the purpose of establishing the general principles which govern these. The methodological criteria for doing so must be specified with reference to the value-producing relations among the terms that are internal to a given system (Chapter 2, section 9). Saussure's insistence on intrinsic criteria lies at the heart of his instructive objections to Schleicher's methodology. Schleicher adopts *extrinsic*, rather than intrinsic, criteria of analysis; that is, he appeals to criteria which are defined independently of the value-producing relations that are intrinsic to the given language system. He adopts a classical Newtonian epistemology. Such an epistemology relies on the reductionist criterion of a single, ultimate standard, seen as fixed and determinate.

Saussure's intrinsic theory is based on a very different general assumption: that is, the description of linguistic phenomena must include a statement about the relations that link the explanation to the context(s) in which the phenomena occur. Such a theory rejects the assumption that there are universal criteria and descriptive formalisms that necessarily apply to all language systems. Instead, it assumes that each system defines its own terms and the relations among them. This is a consequence of Saussure's view that a given language system, at a given moment in time, is the historical product of the social work which has produced it (Chapter 8, section 6). In such a view, there can be no *a priori* specification of the analytical criteria, nor of the relevant terms and their relations in the system. This is what Saussure's epistemological relativism means. In this perspective, nothing is necessarily fundamental with respect to anything else. Or, if you like, everything intrinsic to a given system is, potentially, fundamental precisely because everything is a value in that system. Consequently, the co-ordination of different frames of reference is achieved by appealing to intrinsic criteria that define the specific object of study, rather than by imposing extrinsic criteria on this. This is the problem Saussure poses in his definition of a 'synchronic reality':

What is a synchronic *reality*? What concrete or abstract elements of the language system can be so called?

Take for example the distinction among the parts of speech: on what does the classification of words into substantives, adjectives, etc. rest? Is it done on the basis of a purely logical, extralinguistic principle, applied to the grammar from outside, like degrees of latitude and longitude on the globe of the world? Or does it correspond to something which has its place in the language system and is conditioned by it?

(*CLG*: 152)

The analogy with the lines of latitude and longitude is telling. Saussure has recourse to a mathematical–geometrical formalization, yet his social-semiological metatheory does not, in the final analysis, rest on this. The problem Saussure poses has to do with the adequate means for observing and analysing a given synchronic reality in a given language system. He is concerned with making metatheoretical statements about social-semiological terms and relations, not mathematical ones. A synchronic state of *langue* is an analytical abstraction from the concrete reality of *langage*. In this sense, it is an idealization. The linguist strives to make a complete statement about this idealization, rather than about the heterogeneity of *langage* in any direct way. This is what observational closure means: it is necessary to assume the invariance of any given synchronic state in order to be able to make coherent analytical statements about the language system. The principle of observational closure is, then, a methodological requirement concerning *langue* as object of study: 'The language system is a system in which all of its parts can and must be considered in their synchronic solidarity' (*CLG*: 124).

'Synchronic solidarity' refers to the way in which all of the terms that comprise a given synchronic state of *langue* are interdependent. They are, for this reason, mutually defining. The requirement of 'intrinsic completeness' must not, however, be confused with the formal completeness of mathematical systems. Saussure uses mathematical formalizations as a tool of his analysis. He does not, however, derive axioms concerning the nature of social-semiological relations and structures in *langue* from these. Thus, his use of mathematical formalization does not entail a reduction of social-semiological phenomena to the properties intrinsic to the mathematical formalism. The role of the latter is heuristic, not ontological. I shall return to further aspects of this question in section 7 below.

In Saussure's view, the work of the Neogrammarians in the latter part of the nineteenth century represented a significant step forward with respect to their predecessors, the comparative philologists. In particular, the Neogrammarians developed a truly historical perspective on language. Language, according to the Neogrammarians, is the product of the collective psychology of a community. Yet, and in spite of the impressive progress made by the Neogrammarians, the 'fundamental problems of general linguistics', as

Saussure (*CLG*: 19) puts it, remained unsolved. This issue will be the subject of the next section.

6 THE SCOPE OF LINGUISTICS AND ITS RELATION TO OTHER DISCIPLINES

What, precisely, are these 'fundamental problems' to which Saussure alludes? Saussure outlines his own response to this question in Chapter 3 of *CLG*. But before doing so, he demonstrates, in Chapter 2, the very wide scope of the new science of linguistics. Linguistics, Saussure argues, is concerned with 'all manifestations of human language [*langage*]' (*CLG*: 25). The programme which Saussure sets out for achieving this has a number of subcomponents. These are as follows:

- historical;
- typological;
- universal laws;
- metatheoretical.

Saussure also makes clear that linguistics, while aspiring to its own autonomy, 'has very close connections with other sciences'. The methodological autonomy which Saussure specifies in the following quotation does not mean, as I shall show below, that language is independent of social and cultural factors:

> The language system [*la langue*], on the contrary, is a whole in itself and a principle of classification. Henceforth, we give it first place among the facts of language [*langage*], we introduce a natural order in a totality which lends itself to no other classification.
>
> (*CLG*: 25)

Saussure's project is, to be sure, centrally concerned with a series of metatheoretical questions about the specificity and the intrinsic nature of the language system. However, Saussure does not reify this object of study – the language system – as an independent domain of cause and effect (Chapter 2, section 1). On the contrary, he raises fundamental and far-reaching questions concerning the praxis of linguists when they make and use linguistic theories (Chapter 2, section 7). In Saussure's view, linguistics is a radically inter-disciplinary and self-reflexive enterprise:

> Finally, what is the use of linguistics? Very few people have clear ideas on the matter; this is not the place to establish them. But it is obvious, for example, that linguistic questions interest everyone, historians, philologists, etc. who have to do with texts. Even more obvious is its importance for culture in general: in the life of individuals and societies, language is a factor more important than any other. It would be inadmissible if its

study were to remain the business of a few specialists; in fact, everyone is concerned with it in one way or another; but – paradoxical consequence of this interest in it – there is no domain in which more absurd ideas, mirages, fictions have arisen.

(*CLG*: 21–2)

The radical shift in the study of language which Saussure inaugurates is more clearly delineated in Chapter 3 of *CLG*. This has a number of very far-reaching implications which are variously methodological, epistemological and ontological in character. These will be discussed in due course. In the next section, I shall explore the implications of Saussure's claims concerning the constructed nature of the object of study.

7 THE OBJECT OF STUDY IS CONSTRUCTED, NOT GIVEN

Saussure calls into question the notion that the object of the new science of linguistics can be defined in naturalistic terms as a pre-given and irreducibly physical object. Instead, he proposes that the object of linguistic study be seen as constituted on the basis of what might be termed its epistemological, rather than ontological, objectivity:

Other sciences operate on objects given in advance and that one can then consider from different points of view; in our domain, [there is] nothing of the sort. Someone utters the French word *nu* ['naked']: a superficial observer will be tempted to see in it a concrete linguistic object; but a more careful examination will in turn allow three or four perfectly different things to be found, according to the way in which it is considered: like the sound, like the expression of an idea, as corresponding with the Latin *nudum*, etc. Far from the object preceding the point of view, one would say that it is the point of view which creates the object, and in any case nothing tells us in advance that one of these ways of considering the fact in question is prior to or superior to the others.

(*CLG*: 23)

The object of study in linguistics is not the immediately given phenomenon. Rather, it is constructed and constituted in and through a specific conceptual and epistemological framework, and a specific set of analytical procedures. Epistemology is the term philosophers use to talk about how knowledge of the world comes about. Epistemologists ask questions such as the following: What point of view is being taken up to talk about a given phenomenon? How do we acquire knowledge about something?

Saussure's discussion of the French word *nu* shows that much more than the description, in naturalistic terms, of the physical phenomenon of the sound uttered is at stake. In order to make his point, he delineates a number of different possible viewpoints which could be used to talk about this word.

Saussure shows how a different object of study emerges according to the particular conceptual and epistemological framework which is used to describe it. In other words, there is, as I shall show below, a plurality of different, though complementary, conceptual frameworks which may be used to acquire knowledge of the word *nu*.

Saussure's solution to this plurality of frameworks is strikingly similar to the theory of quantum mechanics which was developed by the physicists N. Bohr (1935, 1948) and W. Heisenberg (1966, 1976) in the first half of the twentieth century. There is no evidence in *CLG* of any direct connection between the work of these physicists and Saussure's thinking. Nevertheless, the epistemological construction of the object of study is a foundational principle in both quantum mechanics and in Saussure's semiological meta-theory.

Physicists Bohr and Heisenberg and Saussure all agree on the constructed nature of the object of study. Neither the object of study, nor the conceptual framework used to study it, nor the analytical procedures adopted are independent of one another. Furthermore, Bohr's conception of both the arbitrariness and the intrinsic irrationality of the processes of observation with respect to that which is observed are strikingly similar to Saussure's insistence on the arbitrary and irrational nature of the language system in relation to the individual language user (Chapter 7, section 8). Saussure's arbitrariness principle refers, in part, to the fact that the internal design of the language system does not depend on the will or the purpose of the individual language user (Chapter 9, section 2). Instead, the internal characteristics of the language system both constrain and enable what language users can do with language on any given occasion. For this reason, the social is internal to the language system in Saussure's account. On the other hand, society and the individual belong to ontologically separate domains. This important point will be discussed in Chapter 3, section 8.

Saussure's rejection of the naturalistic conception of the object of study also means that he rejects the idea that this object, and the point of view, or the conceptual framework which the linguist adopts for talking about it, are disjoined. In Saussure's view, the two interact to produce the object of study. In this, Saussure is at one with the fundamental postulate of quantum mechanics that there is no radical disjunction between the observed phenomenon and the process of its observation and analysis.

Saussure's next move is, once again, in striking synchrony with a further fundamental postulate of the quantum mechanics of Bohr and Heisenberg. Like these physicists, Saussure adduces a notion of 'complementarity' in the study of linguistic phenomena. In this regard, he proposes four dualities which are central to his definition of 'the linguistic phenomenon' (see *CLG*: 22–3). These are:

1   the correspondence between the acoustic impressions perceived by the
    ear as syllables, etc. and the sound produced by the vocal apparatus;
2   the correspondence between the sound, as a complex acoustico-vocal
    unity, and the idea, as a complex physiological and mental unity;
3   the correspondence between the individual and the social aspects of the
    language system;
4   the correspondence between the established language system and its
    diachronic evolution.

The four dualities presented here are not dichotomies; rather, they are all
complementary aspects of the 'global totality of language' (*langage*), seen
from these four points of view. Each of the four complementarities will be
discussed in detail later in this book: the first is the focus in Part II; the second
in Part III; the third in Parts IV and V; and the fourth will be dealt with in
Part III.

In all four cases, the complementarities are internal to the language system.
Saussure's solution to the question of the 'corresponding faces' which
linguistic phenomena present to the theorist is to point out that the
contradictions which seem to manifest themselves in the object of study
(language) are, in actual fact, contradictions which are intrinsic to the
epistemological framework itself. That is, to the way the various facets of the
object of study are defined. This solution is, of course, in keeping with the
prior thesis of the jointly constructed nature of the observed phenomenon
and the means used to describe it. With his notion of 'complementarity',
Saussure draws attention to the ways in which the object of study, language,
cannot be explained or described exhaustively or completely by any one
framework. Instead, a plurality of complementary frameworks characterize
the *internal* properties of the metatheory which is to describe the object of
study in all its complexity and diversity.

How does Saussure resolve this problem? Before discussing this, here are
Saussure's own words on this question:

> There is, according to us, only one solution to all these difficulties: *it is
> necessary in the first instance to place oneself on the terrain of the language
> system [la langue] and to take it as the norm for all the other manifesta-
> tions of language [langage]*. In effect, among all of these dualities, the
> language system alone would appear to be susceptible to an autonomous
> definition and provide the mind with something satisfying to hold onto.
>
> (*CLG*: 25; emphasis in original)

Saussure goes much further than merely proposing a radical re-thinking of
the conceptual and methodological problems which beset the comparative
philologists and the Neogrammarians. As the above quotation shows very
clearly, he seeks to demonstrate that it is only by means of the notion of the
language system (*langue*) that the linguist can re-think (1) the relationships

among the otherwise disparate conceptual frameworks and theoretical languages which the various facets of the linguistic phenomenon entail, and (2) the relationships among the various theoretical objects and the theoretical languages used to talk about them. In other words, the language system provides a conceptual framework which allows the linguist to deal with all of the various points of view which Saussure invokes in relation to the French word *nu*. *Langue*, as Saussure points out, is 'a principle of classification' in this sense (*CLG*: 25; section 6 above).

The notion of the 'language system' does not mean that all possible ways of talking about language can be reduced to a single, totalizing framework (Chapter 2, section 1). Saussure means something quite different. In actual fact, he sets out to define and delimit the scope of linguistics in relation to other domains of enquiry. The complementary facets of the four sets of phenomena which he outlines in Chapter 3 of *CLG* may be explained by means of the principle of the *ontological stratification* (Bhaskar 1979: 16) of the language system (Chapter 13, sections 11–14). In other words, any given level of reality in the language system, and the phenomena which belong to that level, are describable and explainable in a conceptual framework which is specific to the units and relations on that particular level. The concept of ontological stratification means that the language system is a multilevel reality, and that this stratification is both social and historical in character. The issue becomes one of showing how the units and relations on any given level, or stratum, are produced in relation to those on 'higher' and 'lower' levels. Thus, the four sets of linguistic phenomena which Saussure refers to in Chapter 3 are ontologically stratified in relation to each other, as shown in Figure 1.2.

Each level, or stratum, in the hierarchy of relationships which is represented in Figure 1.2 expresses a relationship in the hierarchy of units, structures and relations which constitute the 'reality' of that particular stratum in the language system. Such a hierarchy is not representable as a closed formalism on account of the open-ended nature of the hierarchy itself (Lemke 1984b: 73). For this reason a formally complete theory of language is not possible. In taking the study of the language system (*langue*) as primary, Saussure shows how a theory of this, while unable to avoid self-reference, must avoid internal inconsistency (Lemke 1984b: 72).

It does so by allowing self-reference between the linguist's notion of the language system, which is always a theoretical construct, and any specific stratum in the system which the linguist wishes to focus on. When Saussure says that 'all other manifestations of language' must be related to the language system, he is drawing attention to the fact that the system is always immanent in what we do with language. That is, in all of its manifestations and uses, including the linguist's theoretical descriptions of it. For this reason, the study of language cannot remain the business of a few 'specialists' (*CLG*: 21). Rather, Saussure's goal, as I shall show in Chapter 2 (sections 7, 9 and 10) is

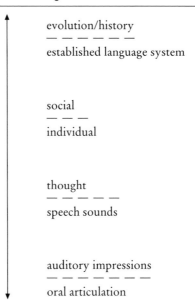

evolution/history

— — — — — —

established language system

social

— — —

individual

thought

— — — — —

speech sounds

auditory impressions

— — — — — — —

oral articulation

Figure 1.2 Ontological stratification of the language system

to produce linguists who make and re-make theory in their praxis. Theory is not an end in itself, but a tool of our praxis as theorists and users of language. The point is that we can only ever use our limited and partial, yet complementary, conceptual frameworks to analyse and to intervene in any of the specific levels of reality which constitute the overall phenomenon of language. For the reasons outlined above, the conceptual framework which we use to do so will always be necessarily partial and incomplete. These issues will be further explored in Chapter 2.

Chapter 2

Saussure's social-semiological metatheory

1 THE UNITARY CHARACTER OF SOCIAL-SEMIOLOGICAL THEORY

In this chapter I shall argue that Saussure attempts to construct a unitary or self-consistent, rather than a totalizing, social-semiological metatheory. The Italian linguist Raffaele Simone (1992b: 169) has pointed out that in *CLG* Saussure attempts to show that the language system, or *langue*, is just one instance of a more general class of semiological systems. Saussure aims to develop a theory of the language system which is founded on a more general social-semiological theory of sign systems of all types (Simone 1992b: 171). The metatheory which Saussure proposes is general in the sense that the theoretical terms and the relations among these are intended as a means for talking about languages of all types. That is, specific languages are seen as instances of a more general class of social-semiological system.

A social-semiological system is a structured system comprising the resources which social agents use to make meanings in systematic and socially recognizable ways in a given culture. These resources include, for instance, the typical lexicogrammatical patterns and relations of the language system. They also include the resources for making meanings in other semiotic modalities such as the visual image, the human body, music and other non-linguistic forms of social meaning-making. Saussure is interested in developing the theoretical categories which are useful and relevant in the interpretation of the intrinsic design features of sign systems of all types, both linguistic and non-linguistic. In this sense, it may be said to be a unitary project; it aims to develop a unified conceptual framework for talking about *all* types of social sign systems. It does not, however, seek to explain all phenomena in this framework. In this sense, Saussure's is not a totalizing project. Instead, he restricts the domain of enquiry to the general class of specifically social-semiological systems. As I shall show later, Saussure is very careful not to reduce these to some more essential biological or physical substrate. Nor does he attempt to explain, for instance, the biophysical aspects of articulation and audition in social-semiological terms.

The unitary nature of Saussure's conceptual framework also means that notions such as sign, signifier, signified, signification, *langue* ('language system'), *parole* ('speech'), syntagmatic relation, associative relation, function, unit, value, difference and others are *metatheoretical* categories. They are not descriptive categories which are used to describe any specific language system, such as Japanese or Pitjantjatjara or Italian; rather, they specify the ways in which all language systems have design features in common which characterize them as belonging to a more general class of social-semiological system. This is very different from saying that the same descriptive categories can be applied to all languages. The descriptive categories refer to specific languages. The metatheoretical categories, on the other hand, specify the general characteristics that languages in general and other sign systems have in common in order to be included in the domain of social-semiological metatheory. For example, Saussure (*CLG*: 152–3) makes the point that the traditional notions such as adjective, verb and substantive (noun), which were proposed by grammarians in the analysis of the 'parts of speech', are, in effect, descriptive categories based on logical notions which have been applied to European languages. These descriptive categories are applied to certain classes of words in these languages. However, they are 'defective', in Saussure's view, because they do not tell us anything about the 'inner' semiological basis of language in general as a type of sign system. The 'parts of speech' are extralinguistic logical categories which grammarians have used in the interpretation of specific European languages (Chapter 1, section 5).

2 THE SPECIFICITY OF *LANGUE*: AVOIDING THE ERRORS OF REIFICATION AND VOLUNTARISM

Reification

Saussure also suggests that the metatheoretical, rather than the descriptive, categories he proposes are applicable to sign systems other than language (section 13 below). The fact that *langue* is the focus in *CLG* does not mean that it is the model for all other sign systems, as we shall see below; rather, it is Saussure's point of entry into a theoretical problem which is far more general in scope. Saussure's starting point is the fact that the language system (*langue*) is a social institution along with many others. However, it is distinguished from other social institutions in important ways:

> We have just seen that the language system [*langue*] is a social institution; but it is distinguished in several ways from political, juridical and other institutions. In order to understand its special nature, it is necessary to come up with a new order of facts.
>
> (*CLG*: 33)

When Saussure appeals to the 'special nature' of the language system, he draws attention to the need to study both the intrinsic characteristics, or design features, of the language system, as well as those features which language has in common with all other social-semiological systems. Saussure does *not* say that *langue* is the model for all other sign systems (see also Chapter 13, section 17). This is a common misconception (e.g., Sebeok 1977: 182). It has lead to a number of misunderstandings concerning the way in which Saussure conceives of the relationship between the language system (*langue*) and the other sign systems in a given society. I shall return to this point. Nor does Saussure seek to isolate the language system from the other sign systems which we use to make meanings (section 13 below). Instead, Saussure invokes 'a new order of facts', which he outlines as follows:

> One may then conceive of *a science which studies the life of signs within social life*; it would form a part of social psychology, and consequently of general psychology; we will call it *semiology* (from the Greek *semeîon*, 'sign'). It would teach us what signs consist of, what laws govern them. Since it does not yet exist, one cannot say what it will be, but it has a right to exist, its place is given in advance. Linguistics is just one part of this general science; the laws which semiology will discover will be applicable to linguistics, and the latter will in this way be related to a well defined domain in the totality of human facts.
>
> (*CLG*: 33; emphasis in original)

What, then, is the nature of this 'new order of facts' which Saussure inaugurates here? Earlier in the same chapter, Saussure had observed that the language system is both 'a whole in itself' and 'a principle of classification' (*CLG*: 25). In other words, the language system is, dually, an 'autonomous' object of study, as well as a metatheoretical means whereby the object of study is conceptualized and analytically constituted (Chapter 1). Saussure also makes it clear that *langue* does not exist independently of the practices of social meaning-making which are deployed by social agents in any given community. In this way, he avoids the error of *reification*.

He also points out that *langue* defines the conditions of possibility of these same practices of meaning-making. *Langue* is a second-order reality which exists independently of language users' adequate or inadequate conceptualizations of it. Thus, *langue* is 'a whole in itself' in so far as it constitutes the totality of the social-semiological resources which social agents draw upon and deploy in the necessarily joint production of meanings in specific social contexts. From this perspective, *langue* designates a level of social reality which does not exist independently of what language users do with language in particular contexts (Chapter 1, section 3). By the same token, language users may not normally be consciously aware of the language system when they use its resources to make meanings in particular contexts.

Langue is also a 'principle of classification'. It is an analytical construct which the linguist uses to describe and explain specific regularities and typical patterns of language use in a given community. Saussure is doing two things here. First, he shows that specific and observable regularities in actual patterns of language use provide the linguist with a basis for analytically deriving some more general 'principle of classification'. The linguist abstracts this from many different historically specific instances of language use. In making this claim, Saussure shows that the actual language practices which the linguist observes and the 'principle of classification' which he or she derives from this occur on two distinct levels of abstraction. This explains why Saussure, after having introduced the crucial distinction between *langue* and *parole*, makes the following claim about the former:

> The language system [*langue*] is not a function of the speaking subject, it is the product which the individual registers passively; it never presupposes premeditation, and reflection only comes into it for the activity of classification which will be discussed later.
>
> (*CLG*: 30)

Saussure's claim concerning the 'passive' nature of the speaking subject's relationship to the language system has aroused some misunderstanding: for example, Holdcroft (1991: 29) takes this to mean that for Saussure 'language [*langue*] is passive'. The passage I have just cited does not bear this interpretation out. In my view the issue is a different one. Saussure's point is that a level of social reality (*langue*), which is not normally available in its totality to the conscious awareness of language users, cannot be reduced to our necessarily partial and local conceptualizations of it. That is why it is important to insist on the two orders of abstraction referred to above.

Langue, seen as a 'whole in itself', exists independently of the necessarily partial conceptualizations which agents have of it. It is in this sense that *langue* is a 'product which the individual registers passively'. The point of Saussure's argument is this: the language system exists independently of our partial conceptualizations of it at the same time that it is able to change independently of any particular conceptualization of it.

Second, Saussure draws attention to the fact that *langue*, seen as a self-reflexive 'principle of classification', is a conceptual framework which the linguist constructs in order to define and delimit the object of study. In this way, Saussure seeks to avoid the errors of both reification and voluntarism. For Saussure, *langue* is a socially and historically specific system of value-producing differences. The view of language as a device for labelling and naming a pre-given real world of natural kinds, on the other hand, transforms this social and historical reality into nothing more than a set of reified ideas which exist independently of words (*CLG*: 97). That is, 'ideas' exist independently of the socially and historically specific meaning-making practices and the semiotic forms which constitute and define a given language system and its relations to the world. This is why Saussure, in arguing against this particular reification, claims that the commonsense or folk-theoretical view of language as a nomenclature has hindered progress in the development of a truly adequate conceptual framework for talking about *langue*. I shall discuss more fully the implications of Saussure's critique of this view below.

Voluntarism

Another target of Saussure's critique is the related error of *voluntarism*. Saussure's proposals for a second-order or metatheoretical perspective on *langue*, based on social-semiological principles, also contests the voluntaristic reduction of language to a form of social institution which 'depend[s] more or less on our will' (*CLG*: 34). This also explains the passing criticism Saussure makes of the notion that language is a form of contract which is based on the freely arrived-at consent of its users (*CLG*: 104). For the same reason, Saussure considers it necessary to go beyond the American linguist, William Dwight Whitney's, designation of words as arbitrary and conventional. Here is what Whitney wrote on this matter in the context of his discussion concerning the way children learn the meanings of signs:

> In the true and proper meaning of the terms, then, every word handed down in every human language is an arbitrary and conventional sign: arbitrary, because any one of the thousand other words current among men, or of the tens of thousands which might be fabricated, could have been equally well learned and applied to this particular purpose; conventional, because the reason for the use of this rather than another lies solely in the fact that it is already used in the community to which the speaker belongs.
>
> (Whitney 1979 [1875]: 19)

Whitney, in Saussure's view, correctly grasped the conventional character of linguistic signs, but he did not go far enough in revealing the specifically social-semiological features which are intrinsic to *langue*. This also means that Whitney did not fully overcome the problem of the voluntaristic reduction of *langue* to a form of conventional contract among the individuals who use the language (*CLG*: 26: 110; see also Prampolini 1994: 21).

The errors of, respectively, reification and voluntarism which Saussure critiques are founded on two forms of substantive reductionism. In the first case, the view of language as a labelling device reduces the value-producing relations of the language system to a highly ideologically constrained rationalization of the way language is used. In this view, there is a direct and unmediated connection between words and the objects, etc. 'out there' in the real world. Language is simply used to name, label or otherwise refer to these. This embodies the assumption that language is a transparent and non-semiotic medium which simply reflects or refers to the extralinguistic reality which exists outside it. Language, in this view, plays no role in the construction of the social reality of its users.

In the second case, the social-semiological character of the language system is reductively explained in terms of the conscious aims, purposes and intentions of *individual* language users. This issue will now be discussed.

3 *PAROLE* AND THE INDIVIDUAL

Saussure has sometimes been accused of repressing the role of the individual in the social processes of meaning-making (e.g., Hodge and Kress 1988: 16–17). I do not think this is an adequate account of the place of the individual in Saussure's theory. It is precisely the task of another important term, *parole*, in Saussure's theory to allow a place for the individual, and in two important ways: first, individuals are endowed with causal powers in so far as human actions are characterizable in terms of will, purpose, individual intelligence and intentionality; second, individuals are biological beings who are endowed with neuroanatomical and neurophysiological capabilities. In the context of a discussion on the reasons for distinguishing *langue* and *parole*, Saussure makes the following observations on the latter:

> *Parole* is on the contrary an individual act of will and intelligence in which it is necessary to distinguish: 1. the combinations by means of which the speaking subject uses the code of the language system with a view to expressing his personal thoughts; 2. the psycho-physical mechanism which allows him to externalise these combinations.
>
> (*CLG*: 30–1)

But Saussure does not make the mistake of reducing social-semiological structures, forms and relations to individual ones, however. The former are the domain of *langue*, not *parole*. Saussure's point is that individual language users, in acts of *parole*, use the social-semiological resources of *langue* to express their thoughts, to achieve their purposes and intentions, and so on. Notions such as individual will, purpose and intention are forms of explanation which characterize the individual's participation in linguistic interaction from the point of view of the individuals who use the language. Similar arguments may also be made concerning the neuroanatomical capabilities which are the biological substrate of the individual's use of the language system.

A social-semiological system such as *langue* is not comprised of a simple aggregate of individual acts of *parole*. The forms of explanation which are pertinent to the description of the individual's use of language are *not* pertinent to the description of a social-semiological system such as *langue*. They are two distinct, though interrelated, orders of phenomena. A social-semiological system is a structured system of *both* the semiotic resource systems (e.g., the lexicogrammar of a language) and the *typical* patterns of their use in a given community (Chapter 3, sections 6–8). The latter refers to the typical ways of saying, writing and acting with language, its discourse genres, semantic registers, text types and the social activity-structure types with which language is used in regular and typical ways. All this is the domain of the language system, or *langue*. In making the analytical distinction between *langue* and *parole*, Saussure understands very well that change and stability in the language system cannot be explained, theoretically speaking, in terms of the ontologically distinct domains of the individual's psychological dispositions or neuroanatomical capabilities (Chapter 3, section 5).

4 RE-LINKING *LANGUE* AND *PAROLE*: TOWARDS A DISCURSIVE SOCIAL PSYCHOLOGY

The possibility of a theoretical link between the domains of *langue* and *parole* is suggested, however, when Saussure claims the nascent science of semiology to be a part of social psychology (*CLG*: 33). Saussure does not spell out exactly what he means by this term. However, it is not difficult to reconstruct, on the basis of Saussure's own discussion, the likely relations between semiology and social psychology. The former is defined as 'a science which studies the function of signs as part of social life' (*CLG*: 33). It is concerned with the internal organization of signs and 'the laws which govern them' (*CLG*: 33). Saussure also claims that *langue* exists virtually 'in the brains of an ensemble of individuals' (*CLG*: 30). In other words, *langue*, for Saussure, also has its material instantiation in embodied social beings. If *langue* were no more than this, then we would have a species of 'downwards' reductionism. That is, the social-semiological system of *langue* would reduce to the neuroanatomical and neurophysiological capabilities of the individual *qua* biological organism. But *langue* is also, and most centrally, the system of typical patterns of language use. These are not reducible to the individual precisely because they are both generic, rather than specific, and transindividual in status.

Saussure also remarks that psychology does not make contact with the sign. The latter is *both* social and semiological in character (*CLG*: 34). Instead, the perspective of psychology is limited to aspects of individual execution in *parole*. In modern terms, the discipline of psychology endeavours to solve problems concerning the cognitive resources which a person must have in order 'to be able to make a complete contribution to the social activities in which he engages' (Harré 1979: 140; see also Van Dijk 1992). Traditional social psychology has relied on a view of enduring internal mental states and dispositions which are specific to the individual. Recent developments in social psychology, along with the newly emergent domain of enquiry called 'discursive psychology', are challenging this conception (Potter and Wetherell 1987; Edwards and Potter 1992; Harré and Gillett 1994). Saussure's subsuming of semiology, or the study of the role of signs in social life, under the rubric of a still more general 'social psychology' suggests the possibility of a way out of this impasse. In effect, Saussure does away with commonsense, individualistic conceptions of the social. This does not mean, however, that the individual does not have an important place in his overall theory. He simply acknowledges the ontological hiatus between individual and society and develops his theory accordingly (Chapter 3, section 5). Saussure's conception of the individual will be the focus in Chapters 5 and 6.

In Saussure's view, *langue* is an analytical reconstruction of both the social-semiological resource systems of a given speech community and their typical patterns of use. 'Typical' does not reduce to 'individual', which is the domain of *parole*. Social psychology, as Saussure conceives it, may provide a theoretical bridge between the 'internalized' templates of the typical patterns of social meaning-making which individuals draw upon in the joint construction of social occasions of discourse, and the actual real-time performance of these. If the 'internalized' templates correspond to the virtual existence of *langue* in the brains of a given social ensemble of individuals, then the only way to describe these templates is by means of an adequate and explicit account of the typical patterns of language use in a given community. In this way, the virtual capabilities of language users may be linked to actual instances of discursive interaction. Social psychology, in Saussure's view, may be a way of relating specific semiotic performances and the participants in these to the typical patterns of language use (*langue*) in relation to which the former have the meanings they do (Chapter 3, sections 6–8).

5 THE SPEAKING SUBJECT AND THE INDIVIDUAL

Saussure makes a crucial distinction between 'the speaking subject' (*le sujet parlant*) and 'the individual' (*l'individu*). Saussure's use of this first term provides the basis for an alternative formulation of the relation of the individual to the (transindividual) system of *langue*. The notion of 'speaking subject' shifts the terms of the discussion away from what Michel Foucault (1974 [1969]): 194) has referred to as 'the psychological problem of an act of consciousness' to the analysis of 'the formation and transformation of a body of knowledge' (*ibid.*). Saussure indicates that both the maintenance and change of the language system do not depend on individual acts of consciousness. Instead, they depend on changes in some wider system of social-semiological structures and relations. Speaking subjects participate in these, but the relevant system of relations is not reducible to the actions of individuals. The advantage of Saussure's term 'speaking subject' is that it allows for an alternative formulation of the relationship between the speaking subject and the language system. Such a formulation is not based on individual acts of consciousness. These belong to *parole*. Instead, it is based on the typical speaking and listening positions which subjects may or may not occupy in the typical language-using practices of the community. Saussure's lack of interest in individual consciousness as the basis for a theory of the language system stands in marked contrast to many of the mentalistic tendencies in linguistics in recent decades. The reasons for Saussure's non-individualistic premises may be summed up as follows.

1 *Langue* is not reducible to *parole*, though the latter can only exist by virtue of the former. Saussure makes the following point: '*Langue* does not exist without the individual; yet *langue* does not depend on him but on the collectivity' (Saussure 1967: 42). In other words, *langue* is only ever instantiated in acts of *parole*. However, individuals, in *parole*, always draw upon and deploy the available resources in *langue*. In any given act of *parole*, *langue* is irreducibly present.

2 Change in the language system is not reducible to individual or collective acts of consciousness. Instead, it must be described in relation to innovations in the speech practices of *parole* and the ways in which these may bring about transformations in the language system itself. Such transformations are diachronic events. Saussure, in speaking of the distinction between 'synchronic' and 'diachronic', has formulated the notion of a diachronic event as follows:

> It is in this way that the synchronic 'phenomenon' has nothing in common with the diachronic one; the one is a relationship among simultaneous elements, the other the substitution of an element by another in time, an event.

> (*CLG*: 129)

Saussure subscribes to an evolutionary model of change. Such a model is concerned with historically significant events. The 'events' he refers to here constitute radical and unpredictable mutations in the evolving social-semiological system, rather than regular and predictable developmental stages, seen as natural and universal.

3 Speaking subjects, as defined above, are not determined by a monolithic and totalizing language system which is external to them (see also paragraph 1 above). Saussure does not say this. Instead, he draws attention to what he calls the *idiosynchronic* (*CLG*: 129) nature of the language system. That is, a language system is further subdivided into its various subsystems, viz. its 'dialects and subdialects' and, by implication, its semantic registers and discourse genres (Chapter 4, section 4). The recognition of this fact opens the way to a formulation of speaking subjects in terms of the continuities and the discontinuities, the intersections and the mixings of the various strategic interrelations which occur among the typical patterns of language use which constitute a given language system;

4 *Langue* is 'the product of social work' (Saussure 1967: 46). In other words, the language system is constantly produced and re-produced in and through the language-using practices of the community. These practices are the social work whereby the language system is maintained and changed. An important consequence derives from this: the language system can only exist by virtue of the speech practices which the system itself makes possible. That is, *langue*, as Saussure points out, is itself a product of the social–linguistic work of the users of the language. This also means that *langue* has no independent existence in relation to *parole*. Thus, language users do not only fashion their speech practices in and through the resources which *langue* makes available to them; they also make and re-make the very resources and conditions through which *parole* itself is possible. This further implies that *langue* is not, and cannot be, independent, or autonomous, with respect to the speech practices of *parole*. *Langue*, I pointed out earlier, is not an aggregrate of individual acts of *parole*; nor is it, on the other hand, a mere aggregrate of the semiological resources and the typical patterns of language use which make up a given speech community. Instead, it is a system of globally patterned social-semiological relations and practices.

The *idiosynchronic* character of *langue* means it is not an organic or harmoniously functioning totality. The typical patterns of language use in a community – its dialects, subdialects, semantic registers, discourse genres – are *not* equally shared or accessed by all language users. Instead, they are differentially distributed and accessed, not in relation to categories of speaking subjects *per se*, but in relation to each other. The point is that not all of the dialects, registers and so on in a given community will intersect with each other with equal probability (Lemke 1984c: 10). *Langue* is a complex and uneven unity of these various subsystems, their intersections and disjunctions.

6 THE THEORETICAL GOALS OF SOCIAL SEMIOLOGY

The science of semiology which Saussure proposes is a metatheory of 'the nature of signs and the laws governing them'. Saussure continues: 'The task of the linguist is to define what makes the language system [*la langue*] a special system in the ensemble of semiological facts' (*CLG*: 33). The radical shift in perspective which Saussure advocates entails the development of a social-semiological metatheory. Such a project has two main goals: first, it must account for the ways in which *langue* is an instance of the more general type of social-semiological system which the metatheory describes; second, it must demonstrate its own relations to the specific object of study, *langue*. Neither of these conditions can be met if *langue* is considered exclusively from extrinsic viewpoints – 'as a function of something else' (*CLG*: 34) –

rather than as an object of metatheoretical reflection in its own right (Chapter 1, section 1).

Further, 'the order which [synchrony] defines is precarious, precisely because it is not imperative' (*CLG*: 131). In other words, the structures and relations of a given language system (*langue*) are not permanent, necessary and unchanging; rather, they are subject to historical and social transformation (section 5 above). Saussure also insists on the social nature of the language system. This is why, for example, he considers the workings of the vocal apparatus to be of secondary importance (*CLG*: 35). There are a number of important conclusions to draw from these claims. Because *langue* is both social-semiological in nature and liable to change, so, too, is the social-semiological metatheory which the linguist uses to talk about it. It follows from this that the metatheory itself is neither autonomous nor permanent with respect to the object of study.

7 SOCIAL-SEMIOLOGICAL METATHEORY

What type of theory of language does Saussure attempt to give voice to in *CLG*? Is it a formal theory? Does it constitute a basis for talking about other, non-linguistic, sign systems? According to Simone, Saussure's aim is to produce 'not a linguistic theory, but a semiological metatheory' (1992c: 191). Simone draws on Carnap's distinction between 'object-language' and 'meta-language' to develop this point, as follows:

> In the case of linguistics, which is the theory of language, the object-language is linguistics itself, the meta-language [is] that of the theory of linguistic theory. Linguistic theory applies to the observed data of language the available theoretical notions with the aim of constructing models of the functioning of natural language. But the theoretical notions which linguistics makes use of are elaborated at a higher level of abstraction, that of the meta-language, which establishes the use, the domain of applicability, and so on, of the notions.
>
> (Simone 1992c: 192–3)

Earlier in the same article, Simone draws attention to the emphasis which Saussure, in his correspondence with the French linguist, Antoine Meillet, had placed on 'showing the linguist what he does' (Simone 1992c: 176). That is, Saussure is interested in the *practices* of the linguist. Simone's interpretation of this point is concerned, above all, with *epistemological* questions. In other words, Simone interprets Saussure's metatheory as a way of knowing and establishing facts about language. There is no denying that this is an important aspect of Saussure's project. Yet, Simone's interpretation plays down the emphasis that Saussure constantly places on the practices of the linguist who makes and uses linguistic theory. I shall now explore this in some detail.

According to Simone, 'the problem resides then principally in constructing a method which is appropriate to the object of linguistics, the language
system' (1992c: 177). Simone emphasizes the appropriate form which the
theory must take if it is to constitute an adequate scientific reflection on the
object of study. In adopting this line of reasoning, Simone, perhaps
unwittingly, reproduces the action–reflection split which is such a hallmark
of logical positivism. I do not think that this is an adequate characterization
of Saussure's theoretical enterprise. Simone frequently draws attention to
Saussure's preference for mathematical formalization (Chapter 1, section 5).
This aspect of Saussure's theorizing is somewhat downplayed in the 'official'
version of *CLG*. It emerges with greater clarity in Engler's critical edition of
CLG (1967) and in Godel's *Sources manuscrites* (1957).

Nevertheless, Simone's interpretation tends, overall, not to do justice to
Saussure's constant concern with 'what the linguist does'. In my view,
Saussure is interested in the social praxis of constructing and giving voice to
a particular scientific community of linguists. He is not, then, concerned with
purely formal criteria for their own sake. This is an important change of
emphasis. Saussure's efforts are directed to the theoretical practices which
characterize a particular community of theorists, and which distinguish this
from other such communities in relation to the designated object of study.
Simone's view is interesting because it privileges a specifically logical-
positivist account of the relations among metatheory, theory and 'object' of
theory. His use of the Carnapian distinction discussed above is significant in
this connection.

8 SAUSSURE'S ONTOLOGY OF SYSTEM AND STRUCTURE: AN ALTERNATIVE TO LOGICAL POSITIVISM

As the above passage from Simone shows, this particular reading of
Saussure's metatheoretical project, in line with logical positivism, is founded
on the distinction between logical or mathematical formalization and
axiomatization, on the one hand, and the category of experience, on the
other. The former is taken to be independent of experience and empirical
facts; the latter is tied to the 'observed data'. These are the two poles of a
particular model of rationality which has predominated in the human and
social sciences in the nineteenth and twentieth centuries. The function of this
model is to attempt to eliminate human subjectivity as a possible source of
interference from both the 'objective' domain of experience and from the
axiomatic system, or calculus. The system of axioms aims to predict all
propositions which are a logical consequence of – that is, are deducible from
– the system of axioms which constitute the metatheory.

A central problem, however, arises in the logical positivists' attempt to
exclude self-reference from the formal axioms of the metatheory. In other
words, a given theoretical proposition is predicted by the metatheory if, and

only if, it is deducible from the axioms of the metatheory. Yet the moment the metatheory includes propositions about itself it is subject to internal inconsistencies which can only be overcome by a radical change of perspective. This can only be achieved if the assumptions of logical positivism are rejected. In Simone's reading, the aim of Saussure's meta-theory is to produce a linguistic theory, suitably formalized, of the 'observed data'. But *CLG* is not primarily concerned with the analysis and classification of observed data. Saussure, to be sure, analyses a large number of specific examples. But these 'objects' are already preconstituted by a specific theoretical point of view. They cannot be reduced to empirical regularities, positivistically defined. Saussure makes no such claim about the examples he discusses. Further, *parole* is neither a mere source of linguistic data, nor is it reducible to the category of rule-governed behaviour or action. There are good reasons for making this point: namely, the concept of *parole* is a theoretical re-description of that which is specific and unique in the individual's use of the language system on concrete occasions; it does not refer to that which is typical or regular. *Parole* does not, then, reduce to the notion of 'observed data', passively sensed as empirical regularities in the speaking subject's experience. It, too, is a theoretical category which stands in a specific and constitutive relation to *langue* (Chapter 5, section 3).

Saussure does not appeal to empirical regularities or to an ontology of linguistic behaviour. Instead, he proposes an ontology of social-semiological relations and structures. That is, he is interested in the systemic conditions which make *parole* possible. In this connection, the following passage is most revealing:

> By entity, we intend the object which presents itself. In the language system [*langue*], taken as it is, there are neither given units nor entities. In order to find it, an effort is necessary. We are badly placed for that, since the phenomenon of the language system is interior and complex. A positive operation is necessary and all of our *attention* in order not to be misled.
>
> (Saussure 1967: 235; emphasis in original)

This passage is taken from Saussure's discussion of 'The concrete entities of the language system'. He is concerned with the ways in which such entities may be established and delimited by specific analytical procedures. Such entities are not simply given in *langue*. Instead, a constructive or analytical effort on the part of the linguist is required in order to establish what the entities are. Saussure also draws attention to the 'interior and complex' character of *langue* itself. This is a consequence of two important factors: first, the analytical effort of the linguist is directed to the internally stratified nature of the language system (Chapter 1, section 7), rather than to external linguistic events or behaviour; second, this analytical effort and the categories derived from it are contingent upon and are determined by the internal properties of the object of study, *langue*.

Saussure's is a non-positivistic ontology of the language system and its structural possibilities. Simone's mistake is to reduce this ontology to one based on empirical regularities and their description according to appropriately established discovery procedures. Saussure draws attention to the practical difficulties of the task to hand: 'we are badly placed for this'. In so doing, he also reveals that much of the 'interior and complex' character of *langue* is not transparently available to the conscious understanding and awareness of social agents. Both a 'positive operation' and 'all our attention' are required in order not to be 'misled' by factors which would hinder the attainment of this kind of understanding. Saussure's ontology of structure is founded on the open-system character of the language system. As such, the language system cannot be reduced to the empirical regularities of observed linguistic performance or behaviour. Saussure's tacit acceptance of the open-system character of *langue* has two major implications. First, *langue* is transcendentally real. It is not, therefore, reducible to the empirical regularities of 'observed data', as I said above. Second, it is, by the same token, constituted as an object of study in and through the metatheoretical categories of the linguist.

Simone, I have argued, gives voice to a positivistic ontology of 'observed data'. He sums up his interpretation of Saussure's correspondence with Meillet (Saussure 1961 [1894–1911]) as follows:

> In this perspective, the Saussurean aspiration (presented in the letter to Meillet) of showing to the linguist what he does, does not only mean reforming the concrete cognitive work of the linguist himself, but, more appropriately, providing this task with an adequate theoretical framework, giving him as a basis a battery of theoretical notions which allow him to account for the peculiarity of his object of study.
>
> (Simone 1992c: 184)

Simone emphasizes the importance of an 'adequate theoretical framework'. In adopting this point of view, Simone takes it for granted that the goal of the linguist is the development of theory. The implications of Saussure's desire to 'show the linguist what he does', while not ignored, are relegated to a secondary role. In my reading, on the contrary, the Saussurean discourse is more centrally concerned with the development of an alternative conception of the relation between theory and practice. I shall return to this point in the following section. Before doing so, I should like to conclude the discussion on the relations between theory and object of theory with some further observations.

Simone (1992c: 181) has drawn attention to Saussure's interest in mathematical formalization. As I pointed out before, this interest emerges far more clearly in the *Sources manuscrites* edited by Robert Godel than in the 'official' edition of *CLG*. Simone explains Saussure's use of mathematical formalization as an attempt to achieve an appropriate level of isomorphism between language system and linguistic theory:

> that which renders in some way necessary the appeal to mathematics (and specifically to algebra and to geometry) as a model for the construction of a linguistic science is the insight, matured, as is well known, over a long period of time, into the systemic character of the language system. Now, given the requirement, constantly put forward by Saussure, for constructing for linguistics a method which is directly modelled on its object, the language system, it follows as a consequence that the formal schema of the language system, its systematicity, must also be valid as the formal schema of linguistics.
>
> (Simone 1992c: 181)

Simone outlines a specifically structuralist reading of Saussure. The emphasis is on the formal model or schema. The function of such a model is to reduce a complex and indeterminate reality to a series of repeatable and controllable operations. The relationship between the model and 'reality' is one of *representation*. This presumes that there is an empirical correspondence between model and reality, or between the formal axioms and the observed data. In such a view, the social activity – the work – of the theorist, or the theorist–community, in constituting a given object of study is not accounted for. Questions of both social praxis and human subjectivity are left out.

9 LINGUISTIC PRAXIS AND THE PROBLEM OF SELF-REFERENCE

Does Saussure provide us with the possibility of an alternative account? I believe there is ample evidence to suggest that he does. The key to understanding what such an alternative might look like lies in the notion of *self-reference*. Thus far, I have devoted considerable attention to the logical positivist reading of Saussure. I have done so because it is this reading which has subsequently become the predominant one in all of the human sciences. Logical positivists attempt to achieve a representational fit between the formal model and the observed data. They also assume that a formal theory, in order to be self-consistent, must not include propositions about itself (Lemke 1984b: 72; Chapter 1, section 7). The theory asserts only those propositions which are deducible from the axioms and postulates of the controlling metatheory. Self-reference, as Lemke (1984b: 72) points out, would undermine the internal self-consistency of such a system, as I said before. Now, a social-semiological theory of the kind Saussure proposes can neither avoid nor restrict self-reference (Lemke 1984b: 72). In order to 'escape from the strictures of formalism', Lemke, drawing on the historical examples of Marx and Freud, points out that these theorists 'were concerned with *practice* first, and theory only as a tool of *action*, whether of revolution or therapy' (1984b: 72). Lemke continues:

> The Gödelian dilemma arises only when we forget that the aim of science is in fact to produce scientists who *use* theories, make and remake them. It is not the theory of SSSs [social-semiotic systems] which must be our goal, but the praxis of SSS-theorists, for which theory is an adjunct.
>
> (Lemke 1984b: 72–3)

There is ample evidence in both the official and critical editions of *CLG* to support the view that Saussure was not interested in producing a formal linguistic theory *per se*. Saussure's teachings in Geneva aimed to produce a community of social-semiological theorists. The various published editions of Saussure's Geneva lectures provide us in actual fact with a textual record, or a series of interrelated textual records, of the acquisition of the pedagogic discourse of linguistics which Saussure gave voice to in his lectures at the University of Geneva. They are a composite textual record of the classroom practices of teaching the new scientific discourse of linguistics and its reception by the students who attended and made the notes on which the published texts and other source material are based.

In my view, *CLG* is a textual record of a progressive and necessarily incomplete attempt, on the part of Saussure and his students, to negotiate the ways in which the praxis of the linguist is itself included in the domain of the linguistic theory being constructed. This is a consequence of the fact that the activities of the linguist *qua* theorist are themselves meaning-making activities which the linguist performs on the object of study – language. Thus, the activities of the community of social-semiological theorists are not outside the domain of the theory. They are not, in other words, outside the particular social-semiological system which is being theorized; rather, they and their activities as linguists or semiologists are a constitutive part of it. The theoretical categories of the linguist necessarily interact with the object of study (Thibault 1991: Ch. 3).

Saussure faces up to the fact that a social-semiological theory can neither avoid nor restrict self-reference, as Lemke has expressed it. It must, however, avoid internal inconsistency. Saussure makes some penetrating observations on the ways in which traditional grammarians fail to do so. This is evident in his critique of the traditional grammarians' notion of the 'parts of speech'. Saussure concludes his critique on the ways in which traditional grammarians go about establishing linguistic units as follows:

> Thus linguistics works unceasingly on concepts forged by grammarians, whose real correspondence to factors constitutive of the language system one has no certain knowledge of. But how can we know? And if they are phantoms, what reality do we oppose to them?
>
> In order to be free from illusions, it is necessary first of all to be convinced that the concrete entities of the language system do not present

themselves to our observation of their own accord. It is in seeking them out that one makes contact with the [linguistic] reality; starting from there, one is able to elaborate all of the classifications which linguistics needs in order to organize the facts which come into its scope. On the other hand, to found these classifications on something other than the concrete entities – to say, for example, that the parts of speech are factors of the language system simply because they correspond to logical categories, – is to forget that there are no linguistic facts independent of a phonic substance divided into meaningful elements.

(*CLG*: 153)

Saussure's critique rests on the way in which traditional grammarians have appealed to substantive, extralinguistic categories in order to classify words into nouns, adjectives and so on. To do so, traditional grammarians represented the open-system character of the language system as a closed system of formal categories derived from logic. These are extrinsic, rather than intrinsic, categories (Chapter 1, section 5). Saussure, in contrast, addresses the issue of the open-system character of *langue*. A given unit in the language system is not established on the basis of criteria which are external to the system. Instead, linguistic units are established on the basis of the functional values which arise from a given unit's position, relative to other units, in the overall system to which it belongs. Saussure shows how a given instantiation of a linguistic sign always expresses some higher-order relationship of values in the overall system of types. The system, in other words, contextualizes particular linguistic units as potentially or actually significant on the basis of the hierarchies of values which are internal to the system itself:

The idea of unit would perhaps be clearer for some if one spoke of meaning-making units [*unités significatives*]. But it is necessary to insist on the term: *unit*. Otherwise, one risks getting used to a false idea and believing that there are words existing as units and to which a meaning [*une signification*] is added. It is on the contrary the meaning which delimits words in thought.

(Saussure 1967: 248)

Meaning, Saussure points out, is not something pre-given, which is then added on to a linguistic unit. Rather, the value-producing differences in a given language system construe significance in the material units in the phonic sequence:

What are values formed from? This differs according to the basis of each system; there is only one constant thing about it which is that values are never simple units, and they are so less than ever in the language system where a material unit cannot even be delimited independently of its value.

(Saussure 1967: 248)

There can be no *a priori* representation of the relevant system of relations. Saussure insists that this cannot be established independently of the praxis of a given community of theorists. Nor can it be adequately represented by a closed formal theory. For Saussure, theory is not an end in itself. The aim of theory is to produce linguists who make and re-make the theory in their own scientific praxis. Theory informs and guides practice; it is not an end in itself. This comes across very clearly in Saussure's discussion of the procedures the linguist applies in order to establish the appropriate analytical divisions in the speech chain:

> In order to verify the result of this operation and to be sure that one is dealing with a unit it is necessary that, in comparing a series of phrases in which the same unit is found, one should in each case be able to separate the latter from the rest of the context while ascertaining that the sense [*le sens*] authorizes this delimitation. Take the two phrases: *lafǫrsdüvâ* (*la force du vent*) and *abudfǫrs* (*à bout de force*): the same concept coincides with the same phonic segment *fǫrs*: therefore it is clearly a linguistic unit. But in *ilmǝfǫrsaparle* (*il me force à parler*), *fǫrs* has a completely different sense: it is then another unit.
>
> (*CLG*: 146–7)

Saussure shows here the connection between the praxis of the linguist and the necessarily open-ended nature of the language system. The latter contextualizes the former: that is, the linguist's analytical practices are included in the domain of the social-semiological system which is the object of study. In the above example, Saussure shows how the linguist establishes whether the various occurrences of *fǫrs* are the same linguistic unit or not. He does so by demonstrating that the linguist's own analytical practices are connected to and are contextualized by the wider social-semiological system of which the linguist's own analytical practices are a constitutive part.

Saussure draws attention to the ways in which the relationship between the linguist's analytical practices and the object of study is anything but the mere representation of observed data by a neutral or objective observer. Both the 'data' and the linguist's analytical techniques are contextualized by the value-producing relations of the language system in question. The issue is the relationship between a material occurrence of a given sound sequence – that is, the phonic sequence *fǫrs* – and the 'concept' which is assigned to it by the terms or categories in the language system in determinate and specifiable contexts. This relationship depends on the global context in which a given material event occurs. There is not, then, a physical–material event *per se* and a meaning which is then attached to it *a posteriori*. Saussure does not assume that the former is more real to start with and that it is only subsequently that it is transformed into an object of knowledge by a process of representation. Instead, the 'concept' co-varies with the given material event in systemically specifiable context types (Chapter 9, section 5).

The analytical procedure of delimitation which Saussure illustrates in this passage further implies that a given physical–material event may or may not enter into the hierarchy of contextualizing relations – the system of values – which define the meaning system of a given community. Thus, in a given context type *fǫrs* enters into a relationship with a given 'concept' and with another in some other context type. Nor are physical–material events simply givens which are then interpreted through a grid of pre-existing linguistic categories. Saussure's point is that both linguists and, more generally, the users of a given language *construct* meaningful relationships between classes of physical–material events and the values which are produced by the language system of that community. Furthermore, they do so in ways which enact and define recognizable context types in that community. Context in such a view is the larger meaningful whole which results from the cross-coupling of the functional values of the language system to material (phonic) events in what Saussure calls the 'concrete real' (see below).

In the above passage Saussure does not limit himself to a description of the contextualizing relations between physical–material events and the system of values of a given language system. The passage cited is also an act of self-observation. Saussure, before his Genevan students, reflects on the nature of the linguist's own praxis in relation to the object of study. This act of self-observation may be described in the following way: Saussure attempts to observe his own praxis as a linguist through his own pedagogical praxis in the classroom. In so doing, he seeks to render explicit for his students the metarules which govern both the linguist's own analytical procedures as well as his or her relationship to the chosen object of study. This means that he self-reflexively connects his own activities as a linguist to the wider meaning system of the community in question. While doing so, he also draws attention to the ways in which the linguist's own praxis is itself contextualized by the same meaning system. As I said before, the linguist does not stand 'outside' or 'above' the relevant system of relations. There is no such thing as a neutral or value-free observation point in Saussure's conception. There are a number of additional points that I should now like to make in this connection.

First, Saussure makes no reference to the subjective consciousness of the analyst. More accurately, he operates a particular kind of pedagogical discourse in the sense defined by Basil Bernstein (1990: 183). The specialized competences which are transmitted in the Saussurean discourse are the techniques of linguistic analysis proposed by Saussure. This is what Bernstein refers to as the *instructional* discourse. The instructional discourse is embedded, as Bernstein points out, in a *regulative* discourse. The latter is 'a discourse of social order' (1990: 183) which regulates and controls the instructional discourse. This may be revealed by an informal analysis of the discursive strategies at work in the paragraph under discussion here, and cited above. Briefly, these are as follows.

Initially, Saussure states the consequences which would result from the correct application of the procedures in question here. This is the function of the first main discursive move in Saussure's discussion, viz. 'In order to verify ...'. Saussure next specifies both the nature of the specialized competences in question here and how they are to be applied so as to obtain the desired results. This move is signalled by the complex modality 'it is necessary ... that one should be able to ...' (*il faut qu' ... on puisse ...*). In this move, Saussure, the teacher, both specifies the conditions necessary for the exercise of the given competency as well as delegates it to the apprentice linguists in his student audience. That is, Saussure positions himself as the agent who has the authority and the knowledge to transmit the specialized competences of linguistic analysis to his students.

Second, Saussure shows how the knowledge which the linguist acquires about language is not obtained through a relationship between the consciousness of the individual linguist and an already given object of knowledge. The object of knowledge is constructed (Chapter 1, section 7). This occurs through the contextualization of the given physical–material event through some restriction of the overall possibilities of the meaning system which the members of a community operate in their praxis. Saussure understands that self-reference, or autorecursion, quite the contrary to producing internal inconsistency in the theoretical framework, is the very basis on which the object of study is constructed. Saussure's problem is as follows: how can the potentially infinite regress of contexts which a social-semiological analysis generates both be represented as well as brought under control for the purposes of any given analysis? His analysis of the sound sequence *fɔrs* suggests the levels of contextualization proposed in Figure 2.1.

The first level of analysis which Saussure describes is that of the two distinct senses (*sens*) which may, depending on context, co-vary with the phonic sequence *fɔrs*. I have labelled these two distinct senses *force₁* and *force₂*. At a still higher order in the hierarchy of contextualizing relations proposed in Figure 2.1, these two distinct senses of *fɔrs* are recognized as occurring in distinct context types in the meaning system of the community of language users in question. The specific examples *la force du vent* and *à bout de force* are prototypical instantiations of these two context types (Chapter 13, section 8). The final level in the proposed hierarchy of contextualizing relations is that of the analytical operations of the linguist.

```
((phonic /        force₁) // meaning system)) analytical
  sequence: fɔrs  force₂     of users:          operations of
                             context₁           linguist:
                             context₂           unit₁
                                                unit₂
```

Figure 2.1 Hierarchy of contextualizing relations in the analysis of *fɔrs*

These operations are immanent in the practices of the community of social-semiological theorists, rather than in the practices of the community of language users. This is a necessary distinction because the analytical units in the theory may not be explicitly recognized, if at all, by the community of language users. This does not mean that the two perspectives are unrelated to each other. Both perspectives are immanent in the overall meaning system in and through which they are contextualized. Saussure has this to say on the distinction between the categories which are mainly implicit in the meaning system of language users and the explicit categories which the theorist seeks to establish in order to explain the former:

> everything that is significant to some degree appears to [speaking subjects] as a concrete element, and they distinguish it infallibly in discourse. But it is one thing to perceive this rapid and delicate play of units, and another thing to account for it in a methodical analysis.
>
> (*CLG*: 148)

There is nothing directly given in the materiality of the phonic sequence which allows either speaking subjects or linguists to establish what the relevant units and meanings are. Saussure makes the point that meaning is not 'in' the given sequence; it is not passively sensed as already given in the perception of this. Instead, a significance is attributed to the sequence in and through the contextualizing operations which are performed on it. Saussure demonstrates in the following passage that words (and other grammatical units) are not simply given by the language system:

> Let us take *mois* ('month'). Let us admit straightaway that *moi* ('me', 'myself') and *mois* ('month') are different for us, although one can talk at length about this in order to distinguish them and say that there already was a combination of sound and idea in this distinction: that is to say that *moi* and *mois* are not directly given to us as distinct units. Are *mois* ('month') singular and *mois* ('months') plural the same word? If they are, *cheval* ('horse') and *chevaux* ('horses') are the same word. But then in order to find a unit in them, it is necessary to take neither *cheval* nor *chevaux*: but that which results as the average of the two: we make an abstraction, we take as a unit something which is no longer given directly, which is already the result of an operation of the mind.
>
> But there is another resource. If I take another basis, the continuity of discourse [*la continuité du discours*], I am taking the word as forming a section in the chain of discourse and not in the totality of its signification. There are in effect these two ways of considering the word.
>
> (Saussure 1967: 238)

Two important issues emerge in this passage. These are Saussure's antipositivism and his constant emphasis on the praxis of the linguist. Saussure's emphasizing of these two factors effects an important shift from the presumed givenness of the material event (the phonic sequence) and from the subject who immediately apprehends this event in sense perception, as I explained above. Instead, the more schematic units which result from 'making an abstraction' can only be derived by means of a conscious analytical effort (Chapter 7, section 6). He also shows how the ways in which social agents construe meanings in some phonic sequence are immanent in the global system of contextualizing relations (*langue*) of some community. Mind (*l'esprit*) is not separate from this, but is immanent in it.

Saussure's conception of linguistic praxis makes it possible to provide a conceptually unified answer to the following two questions: what and how is it possible to mean in a given speech community? Furthermore, he poses these questions in ways which are relevant to both the community of language users *and* to the community of social-semiological theorists in a unitary way. In Saussure's account, what one can know, experience and do in a given community are not distinct from what one can *mean* in that community:

> In order to account for what [an abstraction] is, a criterion is necessary. This criterion is in the consciousness of each one of us. That which is in the awareness [*le sentiment*] of speaking subjects, that which is experienced [*ressenti*] to some degree is meaning [*la signification*], and one can say therefore that the concrete real [*le concret réel*], not at all so easy to grasp in the language system [*la langue*] = that which is experienced, which is in turn = that which is meaningful [*significatif*] to some degree. That which is meaningful is translated by a delimitation of a unit, it is meaning which creates it, it does not exist in advance: there are no units which are there to receive a meaning.
>
> (Saussure 1967: 239–40)

The physical–material domain – 'the concrete real' – is not, according to Saussure, something which is already given and available to sense perception. Saussure argues that the speaking subject's conscious awareness and experience of the 'concrete real' is equivalent to that which is meaningful in a given community. The 'concrete real' does not simply pre-exist meaning; it *emerges* in and through the meaning-making activities of speaking subjects (Chapter 7, section 4). The 'concrete real' is construed, re-construed and de-construed in and through the meaning-making practices of social agents in a given community. Saussure does not say that this is a uniquely individual act. Nor is his notion of consciousness in the above passage the unique property of the individual *per se*. In Saussure's account, consciousness, awareness and experience depend on and are constituted in and through social acts of meaning-making (*signification*). These always require a higher-order meaning system which defines them.

Meaning, Saussure argues, is always the *social* product of the language system. However, this is not an all-or-nothing matter. There are 'degrees of awareness and of meaningfulness' (Saussure 1967: 239). Meanings are gradable. It is not the case that there are absolute distinctions between one term and any other in a given language system. More usually, the terms and categories in the language system are distinguished as graded continua, rather than as sharply defined categorical distinctions (Chapter 7, section 6). Thus, the graded nature of meaning and, hence, of awareness means that many entities, events, and so on in the 'concrete real' are not easily or unproblematically assimilable to a *langue*-based system of types *per se*. The 'making sense' of some phenomenon in the 'concrete real' is, necessarily, a partial and provisional achievement. The partial and provisional nature of this achievement is a consequence of the socially constituted and relative nature of the value-producing differences in *langue*.

I have already pointed out that Saussure's goal is not to develop a formal theory *per se*. His real interest lies in constructing a linguistic praxis which may be used to shape and guide the theoretical and analytical activities of the community of social-semiological theorists. In the earlier discussion of the two meanings of *fɔrs*, we saw this linguistic praxis in action. In that analysis, Saussure makes explicit the normally 'hidden' and implicit ways in which meanings are made in particular contexts. He also shows how these meanings are immanent, not in the phonic sequence *per se*, but in the interaction between this and the meaning-making practices of both language users and linguists. Further, there are limits which the meaning system itself imposes on the agents who use it. Normally, language users are not entirely aware of these limits, which remain implicit in their practices (Silverstein 1981; Thibault 1991: Chs 2–4). However, it is important that they be made explicit and explained by the linguist's metatheory. A theory which confines itself to the most explicit categories and practices, as is the case with the view of language as a nomenclature, cannot account for the complex and stratified reality of the language system.

10 THE OPEN AND INCOMPLETE CHARACTER OF THE THEORY

I have already drawn attention to the self-reflexive character of Saussure's theory-making. Saussure neither emphasizes nor seeks formality and completeness in the process of making theory. This is different from the intrinsic completeness that I referred to in connection with the synchronic analysis of a given 'state' of the language system in Chapter 1 (section 4). What he does emphasize is the open and contingent nature of the process of theoretical enquiry. He constantly analyses and critiques his own analytical procedures and theoretical assumptions, as well as those of others. What interests Saussure is the social-semiological basis of all meaning-making. Theory, for Saussure, is not, then, a means for describing a body of already given 'facts' which serve either to prove or to disprove the theory; rather, Saussure emphasizes the unstable and the non-given nature of *both* the object of study – language – and the theory itself. This instability is evident in the way in which Saussure privileges meaning over any notion of the 'concrete real'. The point is that the latter does not and cannot have significance other than that which the meaning-making practices of some culture construe for it. This does not mean that meanings exist *sui generis*. Saussure's point is quite different. In showing that material events have the meanings they do by virtue of the specific contextualizing relations which are immanent in *langue*, he also shows that meaning is only made when the contextualizing relations in *langue* and the 'concrete real' are cross-coupled in particular signifying acts.

Moreover, the theories we construct for talking about and describing the 'concrete real' are themselves acts of meaning. Saussure has good reasons for privileging the meaning system over and above what he calls the 'concrete real'. Therefore, *langue* is both relative and non-substantive. He explains why in the following passage. This passage concludes a discussion in which Saussure compares the object of study in linguistics to that in other scientific disciplines (e.g., zoology, astronomy), whose object is given in advance:

> Language [*le langage*] on the other hand has fundamentally the character of a system which is founded on oppositions (like a game of chess with different combinations of forces attributed to the different pieces). The language system [*la langue*] being complete in the opposition of certain units and having no other substrate – the language system consists of these units only! There is in the language system only the interplay of these units in relationship to each other.
>
> (Saussure 1967: 241–2)

The language system is not reducible to some more substantive substrate. However, the fact that it is 'complete in the opposition of certain units' in no way implies that it is a closed and autonomous system; rather, there is no pre-given or more real non-semiotic order of things to which the language system is reducible. Some may see in this a disturbing relativism. Certainly, Saussure's conception is relativistic to the extent that all social-semiological systems, of which *langue* is just one case, are both socially made and historically changing. This means that they are culturally specific.

It does not follow from this, however, that all (theoretical) points of view are equally valid. Such a view would lead to a form of irrationalism which is not present in Saussure. Saussure puts a great deal of effort into putting forward rational criteria as to why his social-semiological approach is to be preferred to other schools of linguistics, past and present. One such criterion is the important observation that abstract grammatical entities, or categories, are not 'free-floating' entities. They are always cross-coupled with some material substrate on which the system itself confers a semiotic value:

All these things [the abstract grammatical entities] exist in the language system, but as *abstract entities*; their study is difficult, because it can never be known exactly if the awareness of speaking subjects goes as far as the grammarian's analysis. But the essential thing is that *the abstract entities always rest, in the final analysis, on concrete entities*. No grammatical abstraction is possible without a series of material elements which serve as their substrate, and it is to these elements that one must always return in the final analysis.

(CLG: 190; emphasis in original)

The non-substantive basis of *langue* does not mean that the material world has been eschewed. The relative and value-producing character of the system of oppositions in *langue* reminds us that meanings change. Also, there are potential alternative ways of making meaning and, therefore, of constructing theories about the material world itself. This also means, as we saw earlier, that the ways in which we act on, selectively attend to and are aware of the material world depend on the socially made meanings we use to interpret it. That is why Saussure, in turning his own theory back onto his own analytical procedures and theoretical assumptions, is careful to point out that there are no linguistic units, no linguistic facts and no conceptualizations of the language system that are independent of the meaning system of some community. This comes out very well in the following passage, where he refers to the complexity of both linguistics and its object of study:

> Linguistics is not at all simple in its principles, in its method, in its research as a whole, because the language system is not. In the first place, it is the contrary of what it appears: the language system (language?) appears to us very close at hand; perhaps it is too close . . .: spectacles by which and through which we grasp other objects. This is an illusion. The language system offers the most disturbing contrasts and paradoxes to those who want to understand it in one respect or another.

(Saussure 1967: 244)

In drawing attention to the complex and paradoxical nature of the language system, Saussure also shows how any partial view which does not account for this will only impose limits on the complexity and the paradoxes, rather than comprehend and explain them. One such view is that which sees language as an unproblematic lens on an 'outside' reality. Saussure provides a way out of the impasse caused by the imposition of such limits on the system. That is, he emphasizes the constructive role of meaning, rather than a closed and already given object-world which language simply 'reflects'.

11 LANGUAGE, MEANING AND REALITY: LANGUAGE IS NOT A NOMENCLATURE

A meaning system, such as the language system of a given culture, is already an implicit theory of reality for the members of that culture. However, rather than say that meaning is simply the object of the theory, Saussure turns this logic upside down and says that the linguist uses meaning itself as a tool in his or her own praxis. In other words, the meaning system of a given community, in so far as the linguist refracts his or her own praxis through this, can be used self-reflexively to analyse and criticize the linguist's own analytical practices.

This is precisely what those theories which take into account only the most explicit and 'official' categories and relations fail to do. Saussure singles out the folk-theory of language as a nomenclature for special mention in this connection. In modern terminology, this is what is known as the referential theory of language. In this view, language is a means for naming things 'out there' in the real world. The basis of Saussure's critique of this particular commonsense view of language is this: in attending to only the most explicit and nameable categories, a nomenclaturist or referential theory of language form and function fails to account for the more implicit meaning relations which the theorist must be able to analyse in order to understand the nature of language *qua* system, rather than as a collection of words for labelling entities in extralinguistic reality:

> ... when the language system is studied as psychologists, philosophers, or even the general public study it: in effect, they consider the language system to be a nomenclature and they thereby suppress the reciprocal determination of values in the language system which arise from their very co-existence.
>
> All variables depend on each other: will one determine in this way what *jugement* ('judgement') is in French? It can only be defined by what surrounds it, both to say what it is in itself, and to say what it is not. It is the same if one wants to translate it into another language. In that case, the need to consider the sign, the word, in the overall system would be evident. Similarly, the synonyms *craindre* ('fear', 'be afraid of'), *redouter* ('fear', 'dread') only exist next to each other: *craindre* would be enriched by all of the content of *redouter* as soon as *redouter* ceases to exist. The same goes for *chien* ('dog'), *loup* ('wolf') as long as they are considered as isolated signs.
>
> (Saussure 1967: 50)

The value of any given term in the language system depends on the many often implicit relations it enters into with other terms. From the point of view of the system, these relations contextualize any given term in the system. Saussure also refers to translation from one language system to another. This raises the question of the ways in which translation, as well as other forms of intercultural contact, bring two distinct meaning systems into a contingently new relationship with each other. It is never a simple question of directly transferring a word to its 'equivalent' in the language of the translation. Saussure's observations suggest that the translator must take into consideration the systemic value a given word has in both the language it is to be translated from and that into which it is to be translated. The 'reciprocal determination of values' in the system is always immanent in the practices of language users, including translators. However, the translator is in a peculiar position whereby his or her praxis is contextualized, not by the two languages taken separately, but by the newly contingent joint system which results from their interaction in the praxis of the translator.

Saussure's point is that a social-semiological theory of *langue* must avoid the substantivist reductionisms that he finds in some philosophers' and psychologists' explanations of language. The view that language is a nomenclature is one such reductionism. Saussure is concerned with the way in which this view of language reduces the reciprocal determination of values in the system to a metaphysical doctrine of reference. That is, the explanation of the internal workings of the system is reduced to the observable fact that one of the uses of language-in-context is to talk about entities, states of affairs and so on in the world. No one, including Saussure, would deny that this is one of the functions which language serves. The problem arises, however, when it is assumed that this reduction of the complexities of the language system to just one of its uses itself constitutes an explanation of the system. In addition, this positivistic, and hence non-semiotic, conception of the relationship between language system and the material world, assumes that this relationship consists in the establishment of true or false claims about the correspondences between discrete entities, states of affairs and so on in the world and discrete, segmentable units of language form. Such theories take only the most explicit and nameable (lexicalized) categories as their basis. They are reductionist in two senses: first, the complexities of the language system are explanatorily reduced to just one use of language – the referential or naming function; second, meaning is not seen as internal to language form itself, but to the real-world categories which language simply 'reflects' or 'refers' to.

The view of language as a nomenclature 'suppresses', as Saussure puts it, 'the reciprocal determination of values in the language system'. He points out that this theory is deeply embedded in both the scientific (philosophical, psychological) and commonsense views of language. A principal assumption is the dualism of words and things: that is, words 'stand for' things in the real world; the things are more real to start with. A number of closely related dualisms cluster around this one. These include words and actions, form and meaning. In both cases, the dualistic way of thinking fails to appreciate the fact that the two terms in these two pairs are constitutively inseparable.

Now, Saussure is not simply interested in demonstrating the scientific inadequacy of this commonsense view. The paragraph I have cited above also shows Saussure's concern for the ways in which such commonsense views shape and guide our social practice. But it is not a simple matter of overturning this view, or of revealing its inadequacies with a superior scientific account. The commonsense view is so effective because it has become so thoroughly naturalized in everyday thinking and doing. It embodies an ideological assumption to the effect that the entities, states of affairs and so on in the material world exist independently of the meanings which the 'reciprocal determination of values' in the language system allows its users to make. The real world just *is*, independently of what we do to it in and through language.

Saussure's social-semiological metatheory resists this commonsense view. It also resists the limitations which the nomenclature view imposes on our understanding of language. Saussure tries to make explicit the systemic basis of language. This means more than simply providing a truer account of the complexities and paradoxes of the language system. In showing that language does not simply reflect or label a pre-given and non-semiotic real world, Saussure's social-semiological theory reveals that language users make the world in which they live in and through the value-producing potential of the language system itself. To limit an explanation of language to the notion that some classes of words (nouns) 'stand for' things 'out there' is to 'suppress' the ways in which social agents deploy the 'reciprocal determination of values' so as to construct the social world itself. This does not mean that language does not, in part, function to classify objects, events, happenings and so on in the material world. It does; but it is wrong to think that it does so on the basis of a direct and unmediated link between word and object. Saussure's argument is that the value-producing resources which are internal to a given language system cross-couple with the 'concrete real'. Further, the ways in which it does so are specific to particular cultures. It is these culturally specific cross-couplings which produce the consciousness, awareness and experience which agents have of phenomena in the 'concrete real'.

The view that language is a nomenclature privileges propositional meaning and the referential or 'naming' function of language. For this reason, it is a unifunctional view of language form. Propositional meaning is assumed to be constant when these forms 'refer to' or 'name' the same kind of real-world entity. The latter are the categories referred to in extralinguistic reality. Meaning inheres in these rather than in the language forms used to refer to them. In this way, meaning, which is external to language, is opposed to language form. In 'suppressing' both the reciprocal determination of values and the constitutive role of semiotic forms in the processes of meaning-making, the view of language as nomenclature also 'suppresses' the many simultaneous and overlapping functions which language and other semiotic forms enact in context (see Halliday 1979 and Silverstein 1987 for two recent accounts).

12 THE INDIVIDUAL CANNOT CONSTITUTE THE BASIS OF A THEORY OF *LANGUE*

I suggested earlier that it is not simply a matter of Saussure's replacing an erroneous commonsense view by a truer scientific one. Saussure draws our attention to the way in which a substantive and monofunctional account of language form and function supports the view of a merely conventional 'correspondence', legislated in advance, between word and object, rather than a socially constructed and semiotic one. Importantly, Saussure's struggle to give voice to an alternative theory constitutes a continual reflection on the praxis of the linguist. Most of Saussure's contemporaries in the field of linguistics, with the notable exception of Whitney, ignored or downplayed the social nature of language. Saussure sought to change this view. By the same token, he also sought to change the practices of linguists themselves while, at the same time, allowing linguistics to find its place in relation to other language-related studies (Chapter 1, section 6). His social-semiological metatheory is, then, more than just an attempt to re-conceptualize the object of study. In understanding that this is not given to start with, Saussure endeavoured to re-constitute the practices whereby this object is constructed.

Saussure's argument turns on the need to replace the individual as the basic unit by one based on the social-semiological properties and relations which characterize *langue*. This comes through clearly enough in the continuation of the paragraph which I cited above:

> In the second place, one is led, when one wishes to increase our knowledge of the sign, to study its workings in the individual, to analyse the mental and physical operations that one can grasp in the individual.
>
> Why is the individual chosen? Because it is more within our reach, [it] depends on our will.
>
> Thus, this is only the execution of the sign, it is not its essential character (any more than the execution of a sonata by Beethoven is the sonata itself).
>
> In the third place, when one recognizes that it is necessary to consider the sign socially, one is tempted at first to take into account only that which seems to depend most on our will; and one limits oneself to this aspect thinking that one has hit upon what is essential: it is this which makes one speak of the language system [*la langue*] as a contract, an agreement.
>
> That which eludes our will (social and individual) in the language system, that is the essential character of the sign and it is less apparent at first sight.
>
> (Saussure 1967: 50–1)

Saussure rejects the view that *langue* is, in the final analysis, a collection of individual speakers. In so doing, he avoids two specific reductionisms. First, he recognizes that *langue* possesses social-semiological properties and relations that are irreducible to the physical and mental operations which are necessarily involved when a given individual participates in acts of *parole*. Saussure does not, then, assign any causal role to these operations *vis-à-vis langue*. Second, in refusing to equate the study of language with the study of the workings of the vocal apparatus, Saussure refuses to reduce the social-semiological character of *langue* to some more physicalist or naturalistic basis.

In Saussure's view, it is the very neglect of the study of *langue* which has hindered the development of a social-semiological account of the sign. The focus on the individual has proved to be the single main reason for this failure. Saussure has been generally misunderstood on this point. Specifically, and under the early influence of Meillet's (1921) sociological reading of the concept of *langue*, Saussure has been accused of reifying the social as an anonymous and coercive supra-individual entity (see also Annibale 1978: 17–26 for a useful discussion). Meillet's influential reading has had the unfortunate effect of imposing a Durkheimian account of the social onto the notion of *langue*. The effects of this reading continue to the present day.

The notion of *parole* lends no support to the view that the individual is simply acted upon by external social forces. This would imply that society acts upon and affects individuals as inert and passive entities. But individuals have internal complexity and potential. According to Saussure, individuals, in *parole*, have both 'will' and 'intelligence', and are capable of linguistic innovation. The identity and structural integrity of the individual are generated in and through the interaction of the individual's internal complexity and potential with the social-semiological resources of *langue*. Saussure's point is that the individual is *not* determined by *langue*. Instead, the individual is *non-determinate*. The individual's behaviour is not in strict conformity with the social-semiological resource systems of *langue*. Individuals draw on and deploy these in the joint construction of social meanings in *parole*. Their linguistic activity is not causally determined by *langue*.

Saussure's theory implicitly rejects the Newtonian discourse of physical cause and effect as a model of human social meaning-making. According to the Newtonian discourse, the behaviour of an entity which has no internal means of self-regulation in relation to its environment is simply shaped by the actions of external forces and fields. This view is valid for the world of inanimate entities. Yet individuals are not closed, atomistic entities. They are not simply acted upon by external forces which cause their motion. This does not mean, on the other hand, that individuals behave in unstable and random ways. In rejecting the view that society simply acts on the individual as an external and coercive force, Saussure, in his attempt to construct a unitary social-semiological theory of *langue*, endeavours to show how individual speaking subjects, who are situated at the intersection of both social-semiological factors in *langue* and biophysical ones in *parole*, are regulated, not by external mechanical forces, but by social meanings.

13 *LANGUE* IN RELATION TO OTHER SOCIAL SIGN SYSTEMS

In attempting to bring about this shift, Saussure stresses the centrality of a unitary social-semiological discourse. That is, one in which it is possible to construct the links between typical linguistic practices (*langue*) and the other meaning systems which are specific to a given culture. These include non-linguistic signifying acts such as 'rites' and 'customs':

> The nature of the sign can only be seen, then, in the language system, and its nature consists of phenomena that are least studied.
>
> It is for this reason that one does not see at first glance the particular necessity or the utility of a semiological science, that is, when the language system is studied from generic, philosophical points of view; when one studies other things with language.
>
> If the sign is considered in this light, aspects which had never been suspected will appear, in studying rites, etc.; and it will be seen as part of a common study, that of the particular life of signs, semiology. It may then be claimed that the language system is not the only [system] of its kind, but that it is surrounded, in a circle of that which is rather broadly referred to as *social institutions*, by a certain number of phenomena that must be studied along side it.
>
> Anything which increases the distance between the language system and any other semiological system, although it may seem more important at first sight, must be put aside as least essential in order that the nature of [the language system] may be studied: thus the play of the vocal apparatus; there are semiological systems which have no use for it, which are based on completely different principles.
>
> But why hasn't it yet been recognized as a science in its own right, defined by its object just like the others? It must be said that in assimilating rites, customs, etc. as other signs, these rites, etc. will appear in a different light, and perhaps in this light their unity will better be seen and the need to unify them in and for semiology will be felt.
>
> (Saussure 1967: 51–2)

I have already argued that Saussure's call for a unitary social-semiological science of signs is not a totalizing one. Semiology, so conceived, does not try to explain everything. Yet the study of 'rites' and 'customs' suggests that the linguistic semiotic is also contextualized by its relations to other, non-linguistic forms of social action. Saussure may tend to view these from the standpoint of language, but the remarks cited above show his awareness of the fact that language is always contextualized in relation to other semiotic modalities in the enacting and making of social life. Saussure seeks a unitary conceptual framework which can bridge the ideologically constructed gaps that have worked to keep the study of language separate from the study of other social sign systems and the wider social and cultural structures, processes and relations these enact. He explicitly recognizes that the object of such a theory is not given in advance, but is constituted in and through the social practices of theory construction:

> whatever is the exact way to draw a circle around the language system, it is evident that we have before us a rather particular social action of man in order to constitute a discipline. And all of these facts will be the object of a discipline, of a relevant branch of the sciences of psychology and sociology.
>
> (Saussure 1967: 48)

Saussure proposes that such a unitary theoretical discourse come under the rubric of a 'general psychology' (section 1). In this way, all of the relevant facts can be brought together in a single conceptual framework. Such a framework can reveal the systematic relationships between the language system (*langue*) and the other sign systems in a given society. The language system is neither formal nor autonomous. It is 'intrinsically' social-semiological in character, as well as sharing systematic relationships with the other social sign systems in a given society. Saussure recognizes that there can be no adequate theory of a social-semiological system unless it takes into account these two facts.

Now the special attention which Saussure devotes to the language system in the development of his social-semiological metatheory requires some comment. It does not follow that *langue* is accorded any privileged ontological status in comparison with the other non-linguistic sign systems. Rather, this is the result of an arbitrary methodological choice:

> But it must be said right away that the language system [*la langue*] will occupy the principal compartment in this science; it will be the general model. But this will be casual: theoretically, [the language system] will only be *one* particular case of [the general model].
>
> (Saussure 1967: 48; emphasis in original)

The precise way in which Saussure proposed to 'draw a circle around the language system' in order to define and delimit it and his theoretical reasons for doing so will be explored in the following chapter.

Part II

Langue as social-semiological system

Chapter 3

Saussure's three conceptions of the language system

1 *LANGUE* IS A SYSTEM FOR MAKING MEANINGS

I should like to begin this chapter by reflecting on the implications of the title which Saussure applies to the first subsection of the chapter on linguistic value in *CLG*. The title of this subsection is 'The language system as thought organized in phonic substance' (*CLG*: 155). For Saussure, the language system is a system for making meanings in and through its regular lexicogrammatical patterns. It is not a system of forms *per se*; rather, the basis of the system is 'thought', and how this is expressed in and through a system of phonic and conceptual differences. This is a direct consequence of Saussure's claim that value is internal to the language system (Chapter 7). Saussure, in adopting this view, rejects the notion of a formal and autonomous syntax, along with the epistemological assumptions of such a view. His point is that the values which emanate from the system arise as a result of the differential relations among the terms in the system. The language system is value-producing and, hence, meaning-making. With these preliminary considerations in mind, I should like to explore in the next section the differences between formal theories of language form and Saussure's social-semiological theory of the linguistic sign.

2 FORMAL AND SOCIAL-SEMIOLOGICAL THEORIES OF LANGUAGE FORM: A COMPARISON

Initially, I should like to concentrate on some further implications of the theoretical priority that Saussure assigns to the notion of *value* and, hence, to the meaning-making potential of language form, rather than to meaning or to form *per se*. The notion of value will be fully discussed in Chapters 7 and 8. Meaning and form are not constitutively separable in Saussure's account of the sign. Saussure's is not a formal theory of the language system, or of the forms that constitute this. Saussure's account of language and other semiotic forms is a *social-semiological* one. A formal theory, on the other hand, is, by definition, non-semiological. I shall now discuss why this is so.

What claims does a formal model make about the relationship between language form and meaning? How does Saussure's theory differ from such claims? To answer these questions, I shall briefly consider the following definition of a generative grammar by the American linguist, Noam Chomsky. This definition serves as a good guide to the kinds of formal models of syntax which predominated in linguistics during the 1960s:

> knowledge of a language involves the implicit ability to understand indefinitely many sentences. Hence, a generative grammar must be a system of rules that can iterate to generate an infinitely large number of structures. This system of rules can be analysed into the three major components of a generative grammar: the syntactic, phonological, and semantic components.
>
> The syntactic component specifies an infinite set of abstract formal objects, each of which incorporates all information relevant to a single interpretation of a particular sentence.
>
> (Chomsky 1965: 15–16)

In Chomsky's view, syntax is abstract, formal and autonomous with respect to its semantics. The latter is mapped onto the syntax by means of rules of interpretation: that is, syntax in this view is a set of forms to which meanings are then added in order to 'interpret' the forms. Chomsky illustrates this with reference to the sequence of formal items which make up a sentence such as *I persuaded a specialist to examine John* (1965: 22). Chomsky characterizes this sequence as follows: Noun Phrase – Verb – Noun Phrase – Sentence. In Chomsky's account, it is the linear sequence of grammatical class items – Noun Phrase, Verb Phrase and so on – which constitutes the syntactic structure of the sentence. In Saussure's terms, Chomsky takes the *linear* sequence of formal class items as primary in the description of the grammatical structure of the sentence: that is, the grammatical structure of the sentence is specified as the relations among the nodes that indicate the formal class items which enter into the constituency structure of the sentence. The structure of the sentence is specified as a set of phrase structure rules: for example, [Sentence] = [Noun Phrase] + [Verb Phrase] + [Noun phrase], and so on. The rules, so defined, generate the grammatical structures of the language.

In Chomsky's formal model, syntactic structure is heavily based on the linear sequencing of formal class items on the syntagmatic axis. The structures so generated by the rules of the grammar are then 'interpreted' by the semantic component. Semantics is located in a separate 'component'. This semantic component serves to interpret the formal strings of class items in the syntactic structures that are generated by the rules of the language. In this sense, the syntactic component is 'autonomous': the grammatical structures which are generated by the phrase structure rules are purely formal sequences of constituents (grammatical class items). The structural relations that these enter into in the sequence have no intrinsic semantic or functional value. The formal class items do not, in other words, make meaningful distinctions in the structure of the whole to which they belong. Instead, they are 'interpreted' by a separate semantic component. Grammatical form, so conceived, is autonomous with respect to semantic function.

Saussure's position is radically different from this. By the same token, it must be said that Saussure's position has often been assimilated to the view that the language system is formal and autonomous. I shall now consider in what ways Saussure proposes a radical alternative to the formal view of grammar. Saussure's focus on *langue*, or the language system, aims to study the lexicogrammatical resources which speaking subjects draw on and deploy in order to make meanings in specific contexts. That is, he is interested in describing the systems of grammatical choices with which any given form contrasts in a structured system of other 'associated' forms (*CLG*: 179). Saussure interprets these choices as intersections of syntagmatic and associative relations. This is what he calls the 'mechanism of the language system' (Chapter 11). The theoretical priority that Saussure assigns to the language system means that the linear sequencing of formal items *per se* is secondary.

Instead, it is the system of differences in *langue* which is the fundamental principle of organization. The phonic and conceptual terms in *langue* make possible the organization of 'thought' and its expression in language form. The system of phonic and conceptual differences are interpreted as typical syntagmatic and associative relations and selections. That is, they are organized in the language system according to these two principles. A given linguistic form is interpreted as a configuration of functional values from the two orders of difference. The lexicogrammatical forms that are associated with particular configurations of functional values are systemically motivated by these (Chapter 12). In Saussure's theory, form and function are inseparable (Chapter 13, section 1).

3 TERMS, NOT SIGNS, ARE THE BASIC BUILDING BLOCKS OF THE SYSTEM

Let us take the distinction between [SINGULAR] and [PLURAL] in English in order to explain what a term is in Saussure's account. Throughout this book, I shall use small capitals and square brackets as a notational convention in order to express the fact that these are abstract terms, or features, in some associative group (or subsystem) which is recognized in the English language. The associative group, which I shall gloss with the superordinate term [NUMBER], may be represented as in Figure 3.1. The conceptual term [PLURAL] is defined purely negatively in virtue of the fact that it differentially contrasts with the other term, [SINGULAR], in the associative group, [NUMBER], in English. Terms are, then, purely negative and relational. They have no positive defining characteristics. The fact that in English the term

Figure 3.1 Associative group [NUMBER], showing associative solidarity between the conceptual terms [SINGULAR] and [PLURAL]

[PLURAL] is realized by morphemes such as the plural suffix in plural nouns such as *boys* is not relevant to the definition of the conceptual term itself at this particular level of schematicity. There is an associative solidarity between the two subordinate terms in this group because they are related to each other by virtue of their sharing the common superordinate term, [NUMBER]. It is this relation which constitutes the common associative link between them. A given associative group is, from the system point of view, a hierarchy of contextualizing relations. Thus, [SINGULAR] and [PLURAL] are contrasting terms on the same level in the hierarchy. They are also related to each other by the shared link they have with the higher-level term [NUMBER].

Terms contrast with each other in a given hierarchy of contextualizing relations in the system of differences. The term [PLURAL] has the value it does in English by virtue of the way it contrasts with the other term, [SINGULAR], in the associative group, [NUMBER]. Saussure's theory seeks, above all, to specify the differential relations whereby a given associative group of terms may be established. That is, the terms which constitute the system of differences are assumed to be primary. In turn, the way terms configure in particular structures to form signs is specified by a description of the ways in which the two orders of difference – phonic and conceptual – which constitute the language system are combined in the making of linguistic signs (see below).

Similarly, the phonic terms [VOICED] and [VOICELESS] differentially contrast with each other in relation to the superordinate term [VOICE] in their associative group, as in Figure 3.2. Again, phonic terms are purely negative and differential. It is only when a given selection of these configures to produce a particular phoneme that these have positive value. Phonic terms belong to the analogue, rather than digital, domain of phonic differences. The difference between [VOICED] and [VOICELESS] refers to the presence or

Figure 3.2 Associative group [VOICE], showing associative solidarity between the phonic terms [VOICED] and [VOICELESS]

absence of periodic vibration of the vocal cords in articulation. Phonic terms, like their conceptual counterparts, do not occur singularly. Specific combinations of these specify the phonemic categories of a given phonological system. While there are biophysical limits on the range of phonic terms that are present in human articulation, each language system selects and combines these in distinctive ways to create its own phonological system. Phonic terms have both phonic and conceptual value in the overall sign. In the sign, a phoneme symbolically construes both (1) phonic differences in the analogue continuum of articulation as phonological values on the stratum of the signifier at the same time that (2) it construes conceptual differences as morphological values on the stratum of the signified. This may be illustrated by the significance of the selection of [VOICED] and [VOICELESS] in distinguishing verb from noun in pairs such as *breathe* and *breath* or *bathe* and *bath* (Prakasam 1987: 284–5).

I do not assume the terms to be fixed or universal semantic primes or primitives in the way that the idea of 'componentiality' suggests (see Langacker 1987: 86–7 for discussion). The terms belong to the historically changing and socially made system of pure values. They are always relative in this sense. The system of *langue* is the product of the social and linguistic work of its users. It follows that the terms themselves and the relations among the terms in a given system may change as the speech practices of the community, in time, change. They do not refer to fixed or universal cognitive or perceptual categories that language simply reflects (cf. Bierwisch 1970); rather, they are the basic categorical distinctions that are assembled into language forms relative to specific contextual requirements. On this basis the language system provides the means whereby analogue differences in the flux of bodily process (articulation) and perceptual experience are categorically re-construed as digital distinctions in language form. Analogue differences are continuous and non-discrete. They refer to 'differences of magnitude, frequency, distribution, pattern, organization' (Wilden 1980 [1972]: 169). The digital refers to the domain of discrete, bounded and categorical distinctions.

Let us consider a more concrete illustration of the way in which terms from the phonic and conceptual orders are cross-coupled in the making of signs.

The word *boys* may be specified both in relation to the conceptual terms which configure in this sign as well as the phonic terms which also configure to signify the former. This is shown in Figure 3.3. A sign, such as the English word *boys*, is interpreted as a configuration and cross-coupling of terms from the two orders of difference in the language system. This is what Saussure's semiological account of the sign means. That is, terms from the two orders of difference are selected and combined so as to form the two distinct layers (strata) of structure whose combination produces a given sign. One layer is not 'autonomous' or independent of the other. The relationship of symbolic construal which Saussure postulates as linking the two strata is a two-way or reciprocal one (Chapter 9, section 1). Saussure called these two strata *signifier* and *signified*. In Figure 3.3, the phoneme /z/ symbolically construes the conceptual meaning [PLURAL] in this sense. Together the two layers of organization form a composite symbolic structure, which Saussure called the *sign* (Chapters 9 and 10). Each of the two strata in this relationship is interpreted as a configuration of terms from the two orders of difference. I shall now explain this with reference to the example in Figure 3.3.

In *boys*, the stratum of the signified comprises the grammatical structure [[BASE NOUN: *boy*] + [MORPHEME: PLURAL SUFFIX]]. This sequence of formal grammatical class items motivates the intersection in this grammatical structure of the conceptual terms shown in Figure 3.3. That is, the terms specify the functional values which the class items in this grammatical form have by virtue of their entering into its structure. The grammatical structure of the word is interpreted as the intersection of the terms which are selected from their respective associative groups. For example, the lexical item *boy* is interpreted as the intersection of the conceptual terms which I have glossed as [THING: ANIMATE; HUMAN; MALE; YOUNG]. That is, the lexical item *boy* represents the simultaneous intersection of these terms, which have been selected from the system of conceptual differences in English. Likewise, the selection of the term [PLURAL] in English, which is a choice in the associative group [NUMBER], is signified by a particular grammatical item, the plural morpheme suffix [S].

Terms are not meanings; rather, they derive from the system of pure differences. This is independent of and logically prior to any specific context of meaning-making. A given form is always a motivated combination of a selection of terms from one or more associative groups. It is this intersection of terms which systemically motivates a particular form. This is evident in the

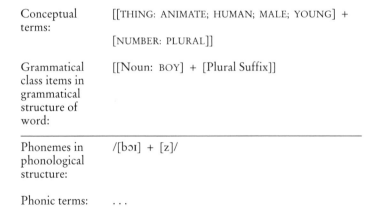

Conceptual terms:	[[THING: ANIMATE; HUMAN; MALE; YOUNG] + [NUMBER: PLURAL]]
Grammatical class items in grammatical structure of word:	[[Noun: BOY] + [Plural Suffix]]
Phonemes in phonological structure:	/[bɔɪ] + [z]/
Phonic terms:	. . .

Figure 3.3 Combination of terms from Saussure's conceptual and phonic orders of difference in the formation of the sign *boys*

word *boys*. The word *boy* is a result of the intersection of the terms which specify this particular lexical item. In the same way, the plural morpheme suffix is the intersection of the term [PLURAL]. However, neither [PLURAL] nor [SINGULAR] occurs as an isolated formal unit in the grammar of English. The plural morpheme suffix is always part of a composite grammatical structure, such as the noun *boys*. It does not occur on its own. Furthermore, terms such as [SINGULAR] and [PLURAL] occur in a variety of different grammatical environments in English. For example, [PLURAL] occurs in the verb *go* in *we go* on the basis of the principle of number concord between subject and verb. It also occurs in deictic elements such as *these* and *those*. In each of these examples, the term [PLURAL] is intersected with other terms from other associative groups to motivate the grammatical forms in question. I shall discuss the issue of motivation more fully in Chapter 12.

In the case of *boys*, it is the intersection of the terms from both of the associative groups in question here which motivates the grammatical form of this word. The intersection of terms in a form specifies the grammatical meaning of that form. A conceptual term, considered on its own, is simply a conceptual difference which is made in the system of 'pure values'. Grammatical form, on the other hand, is motivated by the way terms are selected and combined from the two orders of differences in the making of a given sign.

The same basic argument also applies to the system of phonic terms. The phonemes /b/, /ɔ/, /ɪ/, and /z/ combine to form a composite phonological structure [/bɔɪ/ + /z/] on the stratum of the signifier. Phonemes are phonological class items which have particular phonological and, hence, functional values in the syntagmatic structures into which they are integrated. Each of the phonemes in this structure is, in turn, an intersection of terms from the 'order' of phonic differences in the phonological system of English. These combine to realize the phonemes of the language. For example, the phoneme /d/ in /dɒg/ is comprised of the following phonic terms which configure to instantiate this particular phoneme. Thus: [+VOICE; +APICAL; +OBSTRUENT].

Saussure, as I pointed out above, claims that *langue* is a system of 'pure values' (*CLG*: 155). It is constituted by the two orders of difference – phonic and conceptual – referred to above. Saussure points out that '*this combination produces a form, not a substance*' (*CLG*: 157; emphasis in original). That it, it is the combination of terms from the two orders of difference which produces the linguistic sign. The sign in its totality is, then, a form comprising two layers of structural organization, as shown in Figure 3.3. It is quite wrong to suppose that in Saussure's account the signifier *per se* is a form which expresses or carries a meaning, or signified. Both strata in the sign's internal construction contribute a layer of meaning and structure to the whole.

Saussure does not reify meaning as something distinct from and separable from the forms which create meanings. On the other hand, this is exactly what many recent accounts of meaning have done. In pursuing the logic of the view that syntactic forms are 'autonomous', meanings of all kinds have been delocated from language form and relocated, variously, in separate semantic or pragmatic components. The resulting reification of meaning or function – 'semantic' or 'pragmatic' – as something separate from form tends to ignore the constitutive priority of the forms in and through which meanings are made. Meaning is treated as something which exists independently of and even prior to the forms which construe their meanings. It is important that this fundamental difference between Saussure's social-semiological conception of the sign and formal accounts be clarified from the outset. Only when this is done can we understand the radical implications of Saussure's project. These implications may be posed in the form of the following question: *how can the internal organization of the language system* [*langue*] *be related to the processes of social meaning-making in a unified and principled way?* In my view, this is the unifying thread which links the various parts of Saussure's social-semiological metatheory. It is a central aim of this book to explore and develop the ways in which Saussure's theory tries to answer this question.

4 SAUSSURE'S FIRST PERSPECTIVE ON *LANGUE*: THE SYSTEM OF PURE VALUES

The system of 'pure values' is 'absolutely arbitrary' (*CLG*: 180–4) because, at this level of schematicity, the terms which constitute the system make no contact with either form or substance (Chapter 12). The purely negative basis of the differential relations among the terms means that there exist no formal or substantive criteria which might motivate them in any positive way. Terms have schematic content, but neither form nor substance. I shall henceforth designate this most abstract conception of *langue* in Saussure's account by means of the numerical subscript, as in *langue*$_1$. In this section, I shall discuss the implications of this first perspective on *langue*.

It is too easy to take the sign as a given and, consequently, to miss the real import of Saussure's claim. That is, the fundamental linguistic fact is not the sign, nor even the relations among the signs in some system. The fundamental linguistic fact for Saussure is the distribution of 'ideas' or conceptual distinctions among the *terms* in a given language system (Godel 1957: 246). Godel points out that in *CLG* the order of exposition may suggest that the relation of signifier to signified in the sign is, logically speaking, prior to the relations among the terms in the language system. In actual fact, as Godel shows, the contrary is true. The sign is no more than the fixing of a value to some term, relative to the other terms in the system. This raises the important question as to the relationship between the theoretical notions of term and sign in Saussure's theory.

The terms which comprise the language system have no positive value because they have not, and cannot have, logically speaking, form or substance. That is why they are purely negatively defined and relational differences. A sign, which is a form with positive value, arises only when the two orders of differences are cross-coupled. Consequently, signs are less schematic entities than are terms in the overall hierarchy of contextualizing relations. What, then, is the relationship among terms and signs? I shall answer this as follows.

Terms, I suggested above, are purely schematic categories. This means that they are of a higher order of both generality *and* abstraction with respect to the signs they combine to make. Thus, terms are superordinate categories with respect to signs. Terms are said to be schematic in the sense that they specify only the most criterial features of the category in question. A sign is a more specific instantiation, to varying degrees of nearness or farness, of the schematic criteria specified by the terms (Langacker 1987: 68; Chapter 7, section 6).

The observations contained in the preceding paragraph help to assign Saussure's notion of *term* to its rightful place in his overall conception of the language system. The relationship I have proposed above between 'term' and 'sign' depends most crucially on Saussure's observation that difference is not an all-or-nothing matter. In his *Harvard Manuscripts* Saussure makes the following pertinent remark: 'Awkward term difference! because it admits of degrees' (Saussure 1994: 77). In this highly significant observation, Saussure draws attention to the fact that the ways in which a given sign instantiates the more schematic categories (the terms) is not necessarily a clearcut issue. Signs instantiate the schematic terms to varying degrees of nearness to or farness from the criteria specified by the schema: that is, to varying degrees of prototypicality (Chapter 13, section 8). Saussure's conception of the two orders of difference which constitute the language system is, at this very high level of abstraction, a *topological* one. Saussure does not use this term, but that is what the system of 'pure values' amounts to. A topology is a mathematical concept. It designates a set of criteria for establishing degrees of sameness or difference among the various instantiations of a given higher-order category. Degrees of sameness or difference mean degrees of farness from or nearness to the features which are established as being schematic, or criterial, for some category.

Now, Chomsky's well-known critique of *langue* as 'merely a systematic inventory of items' (1965: 4) is not very helpful. This has led to a great deal of misunderstanding of the true significance of Saussure's notion. Saussure's topological conception of the language system means that the terms in a given system are situated in a topological space which is defined by the relations among the terms themselves. Such a space is an analogue continuum. Those signs which most closely conform to the schematic criteria specified by the terms are represented in this space as being closer to the schematic term; those which are less alike are further away. What is important is the choice of criteria – the schematic terms – that define similarity or difference along some functionally relevant dimension in the two orders of difference.

From the point of view of this system of 'pure values', the combination of an 'idea' with a 'sound' in order to produce a sign may be represented as a definite point in the topological space. This space is produced by the differential relations among all of the value-producing terms in the system. A given sign may be represented as groupings of points in various relations of nearness to and farness from this ideal point, which is represented by a term. Thus, a sign, in this view, is specified in and through the functional values of the terms which are selectively mapped onto it. That is, a given sign represents the values which cluster at some point in the topology relative to the schematic criteria specified by the terms.

It follows from the above argument that any given physical–material event – for example, a vocalization, body movement and so on – may or may not be assimilable to any regular schema established by the topology. These criteria are conventional and, for this reason, value-producing. A given physical–material event may not be a difference which is in any way salient according to the value-producing criteria of the system of differences: that is, it may not be assignable a value by the system of differences. In assigning a value to some event, this is assimilated to the system of contextualizing relations in *langue*, and in ways that the members of a given culture will recognize as significant.

Let us consider a concrete example to illustrate this argument. In English, the schematic term [PLURAL] is realized in the grammar of the noun by a morpheme suffix, as in the words *cats*, *dogs*, *horses* and *oxen*, by internal modification of the morpheme, as in *feet*, or by the zero morpheme, as in *sheep*. In English grammar, the schematic term [PLURAL] may be realized as a plural noun suffix by a morpheme whose possible phonological shapes are shown in Figure 3.4. The value of the term [PLURAL] may be distributed across any of the phonemes shown in Figure 3.4 in order to produce a linguistic sign of 'plurality' in English.

Let us consider the word *dogs* in a little more detail. In this discussion I want to explore a little further what it means to say that *langue*, seen as a

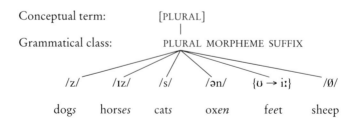

Figure 3.4 Phonemic realizations of schematic term [PLURAL] in English plural nouns

system of 'pure values', is comprised of the differential relations among terms which have no positive value. At this level of schematicity, *langue* is an empty calculus. It has no contact with either linguistic form or substance. This follows from the fact that in Saussure's theory, form arises only through the cross-coupling of the two orders of difference in the making of signs (see above). Therefore, the two orders of difference, when considered separately, are represented as an 'empty' and purely schematic calculus comprised of the purely topological relations among terms in an analogue continuum of pure difference. I shall now illustrate this in relation to the noun *dogs*.

This word is an instance of the grammatical class 'noun'. (I am putting aside the question of 'plurality' for the moment.) The grammatical class noun may be specified in relation to the superordinate term [THING]. That is, all instances of the noun class will exhibit, to varying degrees, the schematic criteria specified by this term. [THING] is the most superordinate term in the hierarchy of contextualizing relations which specifies what a noun is. At this level of schematicity, the term [THING] in the conceptual order may, potentially, be realized by a schematic phonological unit, specifiable as [...] (Langacker 1987: 81). Following Langacker, the phonologicial unit is, at this level of schematicity, 'empty'. It is impossible to specify which phonic terms may belong to such an empty structure. Thus, the grammatical class [NOUN] can be analysed in relation to the terms which derive from the two orders of difference, as shown in Figure 3.5.

The level of schematicity which is illustrated in Figure 3.5 is very high indeed. The terms which enter into this relationship have schematic content, but not specific content. In a plural noun such as *dogs*, the schematic conceptual term [THING] combines with the schematic conceptual term [PLURAL] to form a grammatically more complex unit. The purely schematic nature of the terms in this structure means that it is impossible to assign anything other than schematic status to the terms from the phonic order of difference that these combine with. Figure 3.6 illustrates this as it does not refer to an actual sign relation. It shows the schematic terms which can be specified in relation to the two orders of difference. At this level of

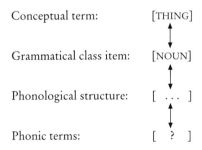

Figure 3.5 Schematic representation of grammatical class [NOUN]

$$[[\text{THING}] + [\text{PLURAL}]]$$

$$[[\ \ldots\ ] + [\ \ldots\ ]]$$

Figure 3.6 Schematic combination of terms; phonic and conceptual orders

schematicity, the conceptual values [THING] and [PLURAL] combine to form a composite schematic structure on the stratum of the signified. However, the purely schematic status of this structure means that no corresponding integration of terms from the phonic order can be specified. For this reason, the stratum of the signifer is an 'empty' specification.

It is now necessary to relate Saussure's most schematic conception of *langue*₁ to two further perspectives which he develops in his overall theorization of *langue*. I shall now discuss the second of these.

5 SAUSSURE'S SECOND PERSPECTIVE ON *LANGUE*: THE SYSTEM OF REGULAR LEXICOGRAMMATICAL PATTERNS

Saussure's second definition of *langue* may be found in the chapter on syntagmatic and associative relations. This definition entails a less schematic conception of the language system than was the case in *langue*₁. The focus is no longer the differentially defined terms in a system of 'pure values'. Instead, *langue*₂, as I shall henceforth designate this second definition, focuses on the regular and typical ways in which associative and syntagmatic solidarities are formed in the language system (Chapter 11). Saussure notes that 'the notion of syntagm is not only applied to words, but to groups of words, to complex units of every size and type (compound words, derivatives, parts of sentences, entire sentences)' (*CLG*: 172). On this basis, some commentators (e.g., Holdcroft 1991: 100) have interpreted Saussure as claiming that the sentence belongs to *parole*. But this interpretation over-looks the dialogic nature of Saussure's argument, which is constructed, not as Saussure's own view, but as that of some alternative view which Saussure then proceeds to argue against. This is evident in the following passage:

> Here an objection could be made. The sentence [*la phrase*] is the most typical type of syntagm. But it belongs to *parole*, not to the language system [*langue*] (see p. 30); does it follow from this that the syntagm is a matter of *parole*? We don't see it like this. The distinctive character of *parole* is freedom of combination; it is necessary therefore to ask whether all syntagms are equally free.
>
> (*CLG*: 172)

The first part of this paragraph consists of a point of view which Saussure clearly distances himself from. This is Saussure's representation of a point of view which he does not himself hold in its entirety. The second part of the paragraph, beginning with *We don't see it like this*, signals Saussure's response to this other point of view. The question that Saussure focuses on here is whether syntagms belong to *langue* or to *parole*. Saussure does not actually say that sentences belong to *parole*. What he says is that the latter is distinguished by 'freedom of combination'. Such combinations are the means whereby the 'speaking subject utilises the code of the language system with a view to expressing his personal thought' (*CLG*: 31). These combinations pertain to the concrete operations of *parole*. Syntagms, on the other hand, designate a more abstract type of relation among groups of signs in *langue$_2$*:

> it is necessary to attribute to the language system [*langue*], and not to *parole*, all types of syntagms constructed on regular patterns. In effect, as there is nothing abstract in the language system, these types only exist if it [the language system] has registered a sufficiently large number of specimens. When a word such as *indécorable* ('undecoratable') appears in *parole* ... it presupposes a determinate type, and this in turn is only possible through the recollection of a sufficient number of similar words belonging to the language system (*impardonnable* ('unpardonable'), *intolérable* ('intolerable'), *infatigable* ('indefatigable'), etc.). It is exactly the same for sentences and groups of words established on regular models; combinations such as *la terre tourne* ('the earth rotates'), *que vous dit-il?* ('what does he say to you?'), etc. respond to generic types, which in turn have their basis in the language system in the form of concrete recollections.
>
> (*CLG*: 173)

Syntagms, in this perspective, refer to regular and typical patterns and structures in the language system. They do not refer to individual combinations in *parole*. The question Saussure poses in the above passage is how syntagms are related to the language system. The syntagms he talks about are not outside the system of *langue* to start with. Instead, they are regular and typical syntagmatic patterns which specify how particular sets of choices in the associative groups are instantiated. That is, they specify how particular intersections of choices motivate language form in the typical syntagmatic patterns in *langue*. A given instance in *parole* is always contextualized in and through these typical syntagmatic patterns in *langue*.

Parole is the active dimension where the individual can exercise 'freedom of combination'. But 'freedom of combination' does not mean random or unsystematic. When a speaking subject instantiates an act of *parole*, he or she is not simply acted upon or causally determined by the language system. In *parole*, the speaking subject actively draws on the resources of *langue* on the basis of their past experience of the 'regular models' which this provides. He or she does so in ways that are appropriate to the contingencies of the situation. The 'freedom' that Saussure speaks of is not unlimited. Instead, the speaking subject's meaning-making activities in *parole* are both enabled and constrained by the possibilities afforded by the language system, and their past experience of this. This in turn affects their ability to control and to predict its regularities. In making this step, Saussure provides a crucial link between the abstract system of 'pure values' in *langue*₁ and the way in which this provides the basis for producing the typical lexicogrammatical forms of the language in *langue*₂.

Saussure concludes this discussion of syntagmatic relations by returning to his earlier concern with the question of 'freedom of combination' in *parole*, as distinct from regularity and typicality in *langue*:

> But it must be recognized that there is no boundary clearly distinguishing a fact of the language system, registered by collective usage, and a fact of *parole*, which depends on individual freedom. In many cases, it is difficult to classify a combination of units, because one or the other factors have converged to produce it, and in proportions which are impossible to determine.
>
> (*CLG*: 173)

Are the two points of view really opposed? Has Saussure simply failed to resolve a theoretical dilemma here? I would answer 'no' to both of these questions. I shall now show why.

The solution to this apparent problem may be expressed in terms of the ontological hiatus between society and the individual in Saussure's account. I shall argue that this is fundamental for understanding Saussure's distinction between *langue* and *parole*. Roy Bhaskar (1979: 43–4) has characterized this ontological hiatus in terms of the 'duality of structure' and the 'duality of praxis'. I shall draw on Bhaskar's distinction to make the following observations on *langue* and *parole*. In so doing, I shall make a distinction between the 'duality of the language system' and the 'duality of linguistic praxis'.

Thus, the language system (*langue*), constitutes the conditions of possibility whereby language users draw on and deploy the resources of the system to make meanings. In this sense, *langue* is both constraining and enabling. The 'duality of the language system' may be expressed as follows: (1) the language system is a necessary condition for language activity to occur in *parole*, yet (2) the system is itself the continually reproduced social and historical outcome of these same activities. The 'duality of linguistic praxis' may be expressed as follows: *parole* is both (1) the conscious production of linguistic tokens in order to attain the immediately perceivable and fully conscious goals, purposes and intentions of language users, and (2) the means whereby the unconscious reproduction and, occasionally, the transformation of the systemic possibilities of *langue* itself occur. Table 3.1 presents some selected quotations from Saussure which illustrate his awareness of the two dualities discussed here.

Saussure's awareness of these two dualities has a number of important

Table 3.1 Duality of language system and duality of linguistic praxis in Saussure's distinction between *langue* and *parole*

Duality of language system; langue	Duality of linguistic praxis; parole
I 'the language system is necessary in order that *parole* is intelligible and produces all of its effects' (*CLG:* 37)	I 'but [*parole*] is necessary in order that the language system be established; historically, the fact of *parole* always comes first' (*CLG:* 37)
	'it is *parole* which makes the language system evolve: there are the impressions received from others which modify our linguistic habits' (*CLG:* 37)
II 'Among all of the individuals so linked by language [*le langage*], a sort of mean will be established: all will reproduce – doubtless not exactly, but approximately – the same signs linked to the same concepts' (*CLG:* 29)	II '*Parole* . . . is an individual act of will and intelligence, in which it is useful to distinguish: 1. the combinations by which the speaking subject utilises the code of the language system with a view to expressing his personal thoughts; 2. the psycho-physical mechanism which allows him to externalise these combinations' (*CLG:* 31)

implications. These are both methodological and ontological. The distinction Saussure makes between *langue* and *parole* is a *methodological* one. This is necessary in order that the object of study and the procedures for studying it may be established. However, the distinction Saussure makes between society and the individual is an *ontological* one. Saussure does not conflate these two sets of distinctions. It is important that they be kept apart in order that the relations between the social-semiological system and the individuals who use its resources may be reconstructed. I shall show in due course that the individual is neither external to nor opposed to the language system in Saussure's account.

Saussure does not claim that *langue* and *parole* are simply opposed to each other. The distinction does not reduce to a simple dichotomy. Instead, these two theoretical notions are co-articulated in relation to each other in a theoretically much more complex and interesting way. Saussure's point is that the properties possessed by *langue*, which is a transindividual social-semiological system, and the properties possessed by individual language users in acts of *parole* are, ontologically speaking, very different. This means that Saussure's concern with, on the one hand, 'freedom of combination' and, on the other, the regularity and typicality of syntagmatic patterns can now be explained. There is no contradiction between the two points of view. Syntagmatic relations are concerned with the questions of 'what goes with what?' That is, with which other units does a given unit combine in order to form some larger structural whole. Saussure's recognition that very many syntagms conform to 'regular models' (*patrons réguliers*, p. 173) shows that there are always, in a given speech community, limits on what language users can do in and through language (and other semiotic) forms in that community. If this were not the case, and if the only principle were that of individual 'freedom of combination', then there would be no possibility of making meaning at all. In other words, there are typical syntagmatic patterns which are socially shared and used in regular ways by the members of a given speech community.

By the same token, there is also a degree of elasticity or lability in the system of possible combinations. This ensures that syntagmatic combinations which are not typically made *can* be made. The possibilities of combination are not, then, totally fixed or determinate. The notion of regularity does not imply this. There is always the possibility of new combinations, and some of these may be recognized as 'creative' or 'innovative' in the community.

Saussure's notion of individual 'freedom of combination' is not, however, an individualistic one. In attributing syntagmatic 'freedom of combination' to the will and intelligence of the individual language user, Saussure recognizes that purposefulness and intentionality are constitutive characteristics of human action, including linguistic action. Yet, individual intentions and purposes are always mediated by a system of social possibilities for acting and meaning. Such a system is both enabling and constraining of these possibilities. In other words, purposefulness and intentionality are not wholly explainable in terms of the individual *per se*. This is so because all instances of language use necessarily entail the use of a system which is the condition for any given act to occur. Individuals do not have the freedom to produce any combinations they please. Creative and innovative uses of language are always transformations of the available social-semiological resources.

The language system is also based on what Saussure refers to as *associative relations* (see Chapter 11 for a full discussion). Syntagmatic relations specify which units combine with which, and how they do so, in order to form some larger-scale structural whole in, say, the grammar of the language. Associative relations refer, in part, to the sets of alternatives in relation to which a given unit has its meaning. Syntagmatic and associative refer to two distinct, though interrelated, dimensions of contextualization in the language system (Chapter 11).

Langue$_2$ is not concerned with the abstract terms from the two orders of difference. The focus is on the typical ways in which grammatical units of all sizes, from morpheme to sentence, (1) constitute regular patternings in the language system and (2) derive from regular patterns of contrasting terms in some associative group (e.g., the associative group [NUMBER] discussed in

$$[[\text{CAT}] + [\text{PLURAL}]]$$

$$/[\text{ kæt }] + [\text{s}]/$$

Figure 3.7 Composite linguistic sign *cats*

section 3). *Langue*₁ is concerned with the schematic terms in a system of 'pure values'. *Langue*₂, on the other hand, is concerned with typical and regular syntagmatic and associative groups. In other words, it is concerned with sign types, rather than instances. Sign types are the typical lexicogrammatical forms which are available to the users of a given language for the making of meanings. For instance, the noun *cats* is a composite sign which is formed by combining the complex signified [[CAT] + [PLURAL]] with the composite signifier [/kæt/ + /s/]. Figure 3.7 illustrates this. The sign types in *langue*₂ have a degree of positive value because they are specifiable formal patterns in the language system. Unlike the terms in *langue*₁, the sign types in *langue*₂ are not founded on entirely negative and differential principles. This is so because the combination of a signifier with a signified in the making of a sign type in *langue*₂ necessarily entails a specification of the phonological or graphological units whose combination signifies a given grammatical unit. It should be emphasized that this is an abstract level of phonological or graphological representation. It does not refer to the materiality of articulation, which is the domain of *parole* (Hjelmslev 1942: 41).

6 SAUSSURE'S THIRD PERSPECTIVE ON *LANGUE*: THE SYSTEM OF TYPICAL MEANING-MAKING PRACTICES

Saussure calls our attention to a third definition of *langue* when he refers to the 'collective habits' of a given speech community. I shall refer to this definition of the language system as *langue*₃. *Langue*₃ is concerned with the typical patterns of language *use* in a given community. Whereas *langue*₂ is concerned with 'regular forms' or 'regular models' (*CLG*: 173) of lexicogrammatical patterns, independently of the text types and discourse genres in which these are used, *langue*₃ specifies the meaning potential of the system relative to the ways in which this potential is typically used in particular context types. This does not mean, however, that *langue*₃ is concerned with specific instances of language-in-use; rather, it is concerned with the typical and regular ways in which the lexicogrammatical resources of *langue*₂ are assembled and deployed in the formation of the typical semantic registers, discourse genres and text types of some community. Saussure is much less explicit about this third, least schematic, notion of *langue*.

The official edition of *CLG* does not give much space to the notion of *langue₃*. *Langue₃* is most closely approached when Saussure emphasizes the internally social-semiological character of the language system. Before this can be adequately described, Saussure argues that it is necessary to recognize three fundamental properties of the language system. These are (1) 'the ensemble of linguistic habits which allow a subject to understand and to make himself understood' (*CLG*: 112); (2) the internally social-semiological character of the language system; and (3) the historical dimension of the language system.

In Saussure's view (1) alone is not sufficient to describe the workings of *langue* because it leaves out of consideration the 'social reality' of *langue*. The focus in (1) is too restrictively that of the speaking subject who interacts with other speaking subjects. But this focus on individual speaking subjects who interact with each other is not sufficient to explain *langue*. Here is the reason Saussure gives:

> But this definition still leaves the language system outside of social reality; it is in fact an unreal thing, since it includes just one aspect of reality, the individual aspect; a *speaking mass* is required in order that a language system may exist. At any moment, and contrary to appearances, this does not exist outside of the social fact, because it is a semiological phenomenon. Its social nature is one of its internal characteristics; a complete definition of it places us before two inseparable things, as the diagram shows.

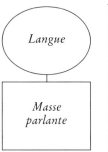

But in these conditions, the language system is viable, not living; we have only accounted for the social reality, not the historical fact.

3. Since the linguistic sign is arbitrary, it seems that the language system, so defined, is a free system, able to be organized as one pleases, uniquely dependent on a rational principle. Its social character, considered in itself, is not exactly opposed to this point of view. Doubtless, the collective psychology does not operate in a purely logical way; it is necessary to account for everything that affects reason in the practical relations among individuals. And yet, what stops us from regarding the language system as a simple convention, able to be modified according to one's interests, is

not this. It is the action of time, which is combined with that of the social force; outside of duration [*durée*], the linguistic reality is not complete, and nothing can be concluded.

(*CLG*: 112)

Speaking subjects do not 'freely' use a set of social conventions. Nor is *langue* conceptualized as the sum of the interactions among subjects. Saussure poses a much more far-reaching problem. A social-semiological system which is based on the freely interacting wills of its individual members is a contradiction in terms. It does not and cannot explain the fact that such a system remains relatively stable in time. The three factors mentioned above are all *internal* characteristics of the language system. Individuals do not use the system according to their will. They do, however, mutually regulate each other in their interactions on account of the mediating function of *langue*: 'each individual participates in [the language system] all the time, and that is why it is unceasingly subject to the influence of everyone' (*CLG*: 107). The language system (1) both endures and is continually reproduced in historical time at the same time that (2) the activities of the subjects who participate in it are responsible for (1), by virtue of the mutually regulating effects of their interactions with each other. Saussure's solution is to cross-couple the internally social-semiological nature of *langue* with its existence in historical time (Chapter 4, section 6). In so doing, he provides a link between the activities of individual subjects and the *typical* systems of social-semiological relations and practices in which subjects participate. In this way, Saussure shows how the actions of individuals are defined by the social-semiological relations and practices of *langue*, rather than by individual or collective acts of will. It is this system of relations and practices – what Saussure calls the 'speaking mass' – which endures in historical time, rather than the specific interactions among individuals, or the individuals themselves.

Langue₃ is, then, based on the typical systems of social-semiological relations and practices in some community. Saussure's notion of the 'speaking mass' (*la masse parlante*, p. 112) captures the idea that what endures in historical time are not the interactions among individual speaking subjects *per se*, but the higher-order relations among the *typical* systems of practices specified by *langue₃*. What determines the internal social-semiological character of *langue* are the typical social-semiological relations and practices of the 'speaking mass'. In this way, actual instances of interaction among individual speaking subjects on some occasion can be related to the typical systems of social-semiological relations and practices in and through which the former have their meaning. Table 3.2 sets out the principal ways in which the three definitions of *langue* differ from each other.

The three definitions of *langue* do not refer to three distinct language systems. Rather, they designate three theoretical perspectives on the language

Table 3.2 The three perspectives on *langue* compared

Unit of analysis	Distribution potential	Degree of specificity (delicacy)	Value or meaning?	Basis of semiotic relation
Langue$_1$ Phonic and conceptual terms in the two orders of difference	Equi-probable distribution of terms in system of pure values	Schematic categories	Pure values (formal system meaning) of terms	Negatively defined pure differences; no positive values; no cross-coupling of two orders of difference
Langue$_2$ Sign types; typical lexicogrammatical forms and patterns (morpheme to sentence)	Probabilities inherent in associative and syntagmatic solidarities and relations	Prototypical instances of forms ('regular models')	Meaning potential of forms as systemic resources	Opposition and contrast of forms in syntagmatic and associative groups; relative positive values of these; typical cross-couplings of signifiers and signifieds
Langue$_3$ Text types	Probabilities specified to text type	Typical instantiations, uses, of forms according to text type	Meaning potential specified to text type	Typical co-patternings of forms; typical cross-couplings with other semiotic modalities and material domain

system as a whole. As Table 3.2 shows, the difference among them lies in the degree of schematicity: *langue*$_1$ represents the highest order of schematicity (i.e., abstraction and generality); *langue*$_3$ the lowest.

7 ILLUSTRATION OF THE THREE PERSPECTIVES ON *LANGUE*: A TEXT ANALYSIS

To illustrate the differences among the three levels of abstraction, I shall briefly consider the following text (see Appendix for a copy of the original).
    The clause-level segmentation of the text now follows.

Putting in the ribbon
1   Check that the printer is not connected to the power supply.
2   Take off the dust cover.
3   Gently but firmly move the print head to its middle position.
4   Tighten up the ribbon by turning the feeding knob in the direction of the arrow marked on the cartridge – this will make it easier to insert it into the printer.
5   Push the cartridge firmly into position, making sure it fits over the ribbon feeder knob. To find the knob, look down into the printer: it is an upright black plastic knob, towards the left.
6   Use a pencil, paper-clip or your fingers to guide the ribbon between the print head and the ribbon mask, making sure that the ribbon is not creased or folded.
7   Check that the ribbon is tight by turning the feeding knob anti-clockwise.
8   Move the print head backwards and forwards along the carriage to check that the ribbon is installed correctly.
(*User's Guide. LX-800 9 Pin Dot Matrix Printer*, Nagano, Japan: Seiko Epson Corporation, 1986, pp. 12–13)

This text is an instance of the instructional genre. Most of the clauses in the text select for imperative mood. Imperative mood is the most typical, or the most probable, mood selection in texts of this type. However, imperative mood is not the most frequent mood selection in the English language as a whole. The most frequent mood selection, overall, is [INDICATIVE: DECLAR-ATIVE]. In this sense, instructional texts skew the probabilities of the MOOD system in the grammar of English. How may these observations be related to the three levels of abstraction in *langue* which I have proposed?
    The terms which belong to a given associative group in *langue*$_2$ are not related to each other as pure differences *per se*; rather, the terms in the same associative group systematically *contrast* with each other. On the other hand, the term [IMPERATIVE], which originates from the MOOD system in the grammar of English, merely differs from the term [PLURAL], which belongs to the NUMBER system. Both of these terms belong to the system of 'pure

values' in the conceptual order of differences in English. However, [IMPER-ATIVE] systemically contrasts with [INDICATIVE] in the MOOD system in the grammar of English, just as [SINGULAR] systemically contrasts with [PLURAL] in the NUMBER system. In any given associative group, such as MOOD or NUMBER, the contrasts among the terms in these groups are *systematic*. Each term contrasts with the others according to criteria of *relative* sameness and difference. This is what I take to be at the basis of systemic motivation (Chapter 12). The terms in a given associative group systematically contrast with each other. The contrasts among them motivate, from the systemic point of view, the relations among them. For example, [IMPERATIVE] and [PLURAL], seen as terms in the overall system of 'pure values' (*langue₁*) in English, simply differ from each other. There is no specific systemic relationship which motivates this difference as a systematic contrast. On the other hand, the contrast between [SINGULAR] and [PLURAL] is systemically motivated. These two terms do not simply differ from each other. By virtue of their belonging to the same associative group, they both share the same superordinate term [NUMBER]. This fact means that the contrast between the two subordinate terms is systemically motivated on the basis of the relations of relative sameness and difference between them in the particular con-textualizing hierarchy to which they belong.

The basic MOOD system in English may be represented as in Figure 3.8, which presents the MOOD system in English as an associative group of contrasting terms. These terms are the basic mood selections in English grammar. Reading from left to right, Figure 3.8 tells us: first choose either [INDICATIVE] or [IMPERATIVE]; if [INDICATIVE] is chosen, then choose either [INTERROGATIVE] or [DECLARATIVE]; if [INTERROGATIVE] is chosen, then choose either [WH-] or [YES/NO], and so on. The choices which result from this associative group are as follows:

1   [INDICATIVE; INTERROGATIVE; WH-] ↓ Wh^Finite
2   [INDICATIVE; INTERROGATIVE; YES/NO] ↓ Finite^Subject
3   [INDICATIVE; DECLARATIVE] ↓ Subject^Finite
4   [IMPERATIVE] ↓ Predicator

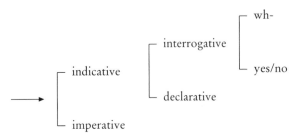

Figure 3.8 English MOOD system, seen as an associative group in which the terms are systematically contrasted with each other

The items specified in the square brackets are the terms, or features, which are selected in order to realize a given option in the network. In the formalism of the network, they specify a left-to-right pathway through the network until a terminal point has been reached. Terminal points are the parts furthest to the right of the network. The notational convention of the downwards arrow, '↓', specifies the formal grammatical realization of the terms (features) in square brackets. Thus, the selection of the terms [INDICATIVE; INTERROGATIVE; WH-] is formally realized by the grammatical structure specified as *Wh^Finite*. This notation means that in the grammatical structure in question the wh-element is followed by the Finite element. An example of this type of grammatical structure is the clause *who* (wh-) *is* (Finite) *he?* The clause *who is he?* is, then, a prototypical instantiation of a particular type of lexicogrammatical structure, viz. *Wh^Finite*, in the English MOOD system (Chapter 13, section 8). It is an example of Saussure's 'regular models' of syntagmatic relations (Chapter 11, section 2).

What is the status of the conceptual terms with respect to grammatical form? The selection, or intersection, of the terms [INDICATIVE; INTERROGATIVE; WH-] in the grammatical structure *Wh^Finite* may be said to correspond to the functional values which motivate that particular grammatical form in relation to some aspect of its overall meaning. In this sense, the form *Wh^Finite* is the grammatical instantiation of the configuration of terms [INDICATIVE; INTER-ROGATIVE; WH-]. The terms motivate the form in question. From the point of view of *langue₁*, terms are pure values; however, from the point of view of *langue₂*, the particular selection of conceptual terms which configure in and motivate a particular form may be said to be the *grammatical* meaning which that form has in the associative group to which it belongs. This grammatical meaning is really a part of the meaning potential which the form has as a sign type, in some associative group, independently of any specific context-of-use. I shall discuss further implications of this in relation to the specific meaning a selection obtains in acts of *parole* in Chapter 5.

An associative group such as the one illustrated in Figure 3.8 belongs, formally speaking, to *langue₂*. It specifies the associative solidarities among the terms in a particular associative group. There is an associative solidarity among, for example, the terms [INDICATIVE; INTERROGATIVE; WH-] and [INDICATIVE; DECLARATIVE]. This is the case in two ways: (1) both of these sets of terms share, or have in common, the superordinate, or schematic, term [MOOD]; and (2) the two sets of terms systematically contrast with each other by virtue of the relations of relative sameness and difference among them. That is, it is possible to show which terms the two selections have in common, as well as which terms differentiate them. In this case, both selections share the term [INDICATIVE], but are differentiated by the contrast among the more specific terms that each selects.

But what about *langue₃* in relation to the text? I have already pointed out that the text is an instance of the discourse genre 'instruction'. This is a fact of *langue₃*. I have also pointed out that in the texts which are assignable to this category of discourse genre there is a relatively high probability that selections in [IMPERATIVE] mood will predominate. In the text, there are ten clauses which independently select for MOOD in the way specified in Figure 3.8. Eight of these select [IMPERATIVE]; two select [INDICATIVE; DECLARATIVE]. These are typical features of the instructional genre. This analysis is far from exhaustive or detailed. I am merely trying to indicate the kinds of factors which might be relevant to *langue₃*.

I have also said that *langue₃*, which is concerned with the typical systems of meaning relations and practices, is the point at which it becomes necessary to specify the typical ways in which the linguistic semiotic enters into functional solidarities with other semiotic modalities. Texts which belong to the instructional genre, in its written or printed form, typically combine with the graphological and visual semiotic systems of layout and graphic display in specifiable ways. That is, it is possible to specify typical ways in which the linguistic, graphological and visual semiotic systems combine in this genre of text. This could include, for instance, choices of font type and size for assigning relative priority to some parts of the text. It could also include the tendency to feature a vertical column in which the different stages of the text follow each other in a numbered sequence which indicates the order in which the specified activity is to be carried out. A further feature could be the way in which graphs, illustrations and diagrams co-pattern with the linguistic semiotic. All of these are typical features of the instructional genre in the sense that there is a relatively high probability of their co-occurring in regular ways in texts of this type.

8 LINKING THE INDIVIDUAL TO THE LANGUAGE SYSTEM

A reasonably clear definition of *langue₃* may also be found in the notes to the second course compiled by Robert Godel. These were based on the notes of three students, A. Riedlinger, F. Bouchardy and L. Gautier, who attended Saussure's Geneva lectures (Saussure 1957). These may be compared to the comments Saussure makes in *CLG*, and which I cited in section 6 above:

> This institution is above all a *convention*, but that which immediately distinguishes the language system [*la langue*] from all other conventions is the fact that it is supported by thousands of signs, used millions of times, everyday. Thus, it is an extremely complex system on account of the number of pieces that it deploys.
>
> For this reason, the language system is an ensemble of conventions necessarily adopted by the social body [*le corps social*] so as to enable the language faculty [*la faculté du langage*] to be used by individuals. The language faculty is a fact distinct from the language system, but one which cannot be put into practice without it.
>
> (Saussure 1957: 10)

What is especially interesting about this statement is the way in which Saussure intersects the social and conventional nature of the language system with the individual's use of his or her language faculty. *Langue₃* makes contact with individual use. This does not mean that the former is reduced to the latter, or vice versa. Saussure's point is very different. Again, Saussure shows that the language system is not comprised of individual speaking subjects, or of individual uses of signs; rather, *langue₃* is a system of social conventions which are adopted by the 'social body', rather than by individuals *per se*. Once again, Saussure draws attention to the way in which *langue₃* is a system of typical (conventional) social-semiological relations and practices. Individual speaking subjects alone do not use these in a direct, unmediated way. Instead, Saussure points out that an 'ensemble of conventions' is 'adopted by the social body'. He does not, therefore, say that individuals use conventions *per se*. Two critically important questions are at issue here. First, the 'ensemble of conventions' provides a means of linking individual uses of language to the typical systems in and through which the former have the meanings they do. Second, Saussure does not reduce the language system to the individual's language faculty; rather, the 'social body' mediates between the 'ensemble of conventions' and the individual's use of his or her language faculty in specific acts of *parole*. There is, then, no direct or unmediated link between the social conventions of *langue₃* and the individual's use of his or her language faculty in the instantiation of acts of *parole*. These last are always mediated by and connected to a system of meaning-making conventions. The social and individual dimensions of this relationship are schematized in Figure 3.9.

Figure 3.9 illustrates the two principles of the duality of the language system and the duality of linguistic praxis, which I discussed in section 4. The 'ensemble of conventions' is the global system of typical meaning-making resources in a given community. It is an analytical construct which specifies how the various text types, discourse genres and so on are related to each other, how they are distributed, and which categories of speaking subject have access to them. Saussure's 'social body' or 'social mass' specifies the ways in which the global system of relations is maintained in and through the typical relations and practices which characterize the social life of the community. This level of analysis also functions to mediate between the level of individual acts of *parole* and the typical formations which these instantiate. Individual acts of *parole* position speaking subjects in ways which both reproduce and, potentially, alter the systems of typical relations and practices. In turn, individuals, in acts of *parole*, are the intersection of the individual as, dually, a biological organism with specific neuroanatomical and neurophysiological, etc. capabilities (e.g., the vocal apparatus) and as a participant in concrete instances of social interaction.

The arguments discussed in the previous paragraph indicate Saussure's understanding of the socially shared basis of meaning-making (*parole*).

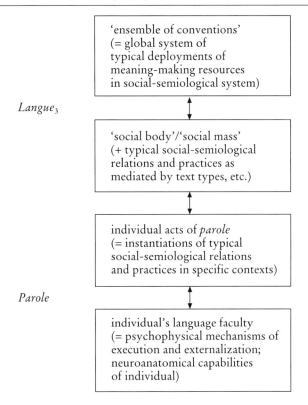

Figure 3.9 Social and individual dimensions of the links between *langue* and
    parole

Meaning-making is not a matter of individual decision or will *per se*. Without
the individual's connection to the typical, or conventional, social-
semiological relations and practices of the community, the individual cannot
participate in the meaning-making practices of that community. Individuals
participate in acts of *parole*, but this is not dependent on the individual's
language faculty alone. This faculty can only dispose individuals to participate in *parole*. Acts of *parole* are always instantiations of, and are always
mediated by, the typical systems of the 'social body'. That is, acts of *parole*
do not stand in a direct and unmediated relationship to the 'ensemble of
conventions'. Individuals *qua* individuals cannot directly access this or act
upon it. As Saussure points out, the language faculty can only be put into
practice when there is a language system which connects individuals to the
system and to each other through the mediating effects of the system.

    This should also help to clarify just what Saussure means by the
individual's 'passive' relationship to *langue* (Chapter 2, section 1). Individuals are 'passive' from the point of view of *langue*. The individual alone

cannot directly act on and change the system of *langue*. This does not mean that individuals are reducible to 'functional slots' in an anonymous and coercive social structure. Saussure's argument is more subtle and merits closer attention. His point is this: the individual cannot directly act upon the system. The potential which the system affords is distributed, not across individuals on the basis of some sort of legislative contract or gentleman's agreement, but across the typical systems of value-producing relations and practices in the language system. For this reason, Saussure explicitly rejects the idea of an originary legislative contract or agreement among free individuals as the basis of the language system:

> The false method [for talking about language] consists in regarding the language system as a legislation, after the manner of the philosophers of the 18th century, as dependent on our will; now the language system, even more than legislation, must be submitted to far more than one can produce it; there is in the language system little [possibility of] initiative.
>
> The original contract gets confused with that which happens all the time in the language system (with the continuous creation of signs), with the permanent conditions of the language system: if one sign is added to the language system, the meaning [*signification*] of the others decreases proportionally. Reciprocally, if by some remote chance only two signs were chosen at the beginning, all meanings would be distributed [*réparties*] over these two signs. One would have designated one half of phenomena, and the other, the other half.
>
> (Saussure 1957: 22)

Change in the language system is not, and cannot be, explained on the basis of individual acts of will or consciousness. Rather, change occurs in the whole system of value-producing relations. Nevertheless, individual speaking subjects both participate in the dynamics of these processes as well as deploy the social-semiological resources of the system in the pursuit of their own projects. The place of the individual and his or her relation to *parole* in Saussure's account will be taken up and discussed in Chapters 5 and 6. In this chapter, I have been concerned, above all, with the 'static' or synchronic dimension of the language system as a resource for the making of meanings. In the next chapter I shall turn my attention to the temporal dimension of *langue* as a dynamic and historically evolving system.

Chapter 4

The time-dependent nature of *langue*
The dialectic of synchrony and diachrony

1 SYNCHRONIC AND DIACHRONIC LINGUISTICS

Saussure's distinction between *synchronic* and *diachronic* linguistics introduces the problematic of the time-dependent nature of the language system. This distinction closely relates to the one he makes between *langue* and *parole*. This is a consequence of Saussure's methodological decision, at the outset of *CLG*, to separate the study of *langue* from *parole*.

Saussure (*CLG*: 138) speaks of the necessity for the linguist to make a second methodological choice. The linguist now stands at a second 'crossroads'. In one direction this leads to diachrony; in the other to synchrony. This second methodological choice is absolutely dependent upon the first. Diachrony refers to the 'succession in time' of linguistic facts (*CLG*: 117). Synchrony refers to the linguist's 'projection' from these of a system of value-producing terms. This constitutes the reality of language at any given moment, from the point of view of the user. Saussure does not dichotomize synchrony and diachrony. Instead, the two perspectives are interdependent: both are necessary in order to explain the dynamics of the language system.

2 THE PROBLEM OF LANGUAGE CHANGE: SAUSSURE'S ACCOUNT

Saussure's distinction between synchrony and diachrony has had a powerful influence on structuralism. Latter-day commentators have written of the 'radical distinction' (Saussure 1983: x) which Saussure made between the two perspectives. This has led to a number of misunderstandings. For instance, Saussure does not claim that historical or diachronic facts are 'irrelevant' to the study of *langue* (cf. Culler 1976: 30–1). And, in speaking of the 'momentous' importance of this distinction, Terence Hawkes claims that a given language system (*langue*) 'has a wholly valid existence *apart* from its history, as a system of sounds issuing from the lips of those who speak it now' (1977: 20). Saussure does not actually say this. Let us now see what Saussure's position is.

Saussure (*CLG*: 117) makes a careful analytical distinction between the perspective of 'the speaking subject' and that of the linguist. For the former, the 'succession in time' of linguistic facts, in the specifically historical sense, is non-existent. The speaking subject has before him or her a state (*il est devant un état*, *CLG*: 117). The task of the linguist 'who wishes to understand this state' is to treat as a *tabula rasa* everything which, historically speaking, produced this state: that is, the linguist must ignore its diachrony. Saussure says: '[the linguist] can only enter into the consciousness [*conscience*] of the speaking subject by suppressing the past. The intervention of history can only falsify his judgement' (*CLG*: 117). However, Saussure does not say that *langue* exists apart from history. Nor does he say that the speaking subject has no sense of the history of the language. The point is that the language user does not recapitulate the history of a given form every time he or she uses it. Clearly, any language user is in possession of an historically informed metalinguistic awareness. This may range from the scholarly to the folk-etymological to the personal-biographical. Saussure repeatedly emphasizes in *CLG* both the concrete and the time-dependent nature of the linguistic system (*langue*).

Saussure makes two very different claims from the point of view cited above. First, he says that the speaking subject who uses a particular language system is, under normal circumstances, unaware of the history of that system, in the sense just given. The speaker of modern English does not need to be aware of Old English in order to speak to and understand other speakers of modern English. Second, he says that in order to study this system, the linguist must 'suppress the past'. In other words, the linguist's adopting of the synchronic perspective and the consequent 'suppressing' of diachrony is an analytical and methodological decision. It derives from the logically prior decision to privilege *langue* as the object of study. Saussure does not say that the language system exists 'apart from history'. On the contrary, he constantly emphasizes history, change, evolution and flux as inherent properties of the dynamics of the system. It is no accident that Saussure devotes a major proportion of *CLG* – Parts III–V – almost exclusively to questions of diachrony. However, the methodological and theoretical priorities which Saussure assigns to *langue* and, hence, to synchrony, mean that the linguist must become an agent who works to 'suppress' the agency of history itself.

Saussure was steeped in the very traditions of historical and comparative linguistics to which a certain structuralist reading would oppose him. Indeed, Saussure spent most of his professional career working on problems that belong to those traditions. An attentive reading of the relevant parts of *CLG* will show that Saussure, far from excluding diachrony, attempts to re-formulate the question of linguistic change. He does so in ways which are radically different from the substance-based models which characterized the approach of the Neogrammarians.

Saussure does not oppose linguistic change, or the time-dependent nature of linguistic phenomena, to a 'static', synchronic conception. Instead, he seeks to re-integrate the two perspectives. This obliges Saussure to devote considerable space to the development of the very perspective which was missing in the linguistic traditions he inherited from the nineteenth century. This new development was the *langue*-based and synchronic perspective that is so central to the constitution of the object of study. Saussure does not oppose linguistic change to synchrony; rather, he opposes his new model of language change to the one which the Neogrammarians had formulated. This in itself is a remarkable accomplishment in intellectual re-conceptualization. Saussure, it should not be forgotten, had studied as a Neogrammarian at Leipzig, which was a major centre for this school of linguistics, in the very early stages of his career.

3 SAUSSURE AND THE HISTORICAL AND EVOLUTIONARY LINGUISTICS OF THE NEOGRAMMARIANS

Saussure's reaction to the linguistic ideology of the Neogrammarians is by no means an isolated chapter in intellectual history. It was part of a more general reaction against the positivistic and naturalistic tendencies of science in the nineteenth century. These include Emile Durkheim's sociology, Bergson's vitalism and Husserl's phenomenology. During the period in which he gave his course in general linguistics in Geneva, Saussure inserted himself into a more general reaction against the scientific practices of the preceding century. Indeed, the distinction between synchrony and diachrony goes back to the sociologist August Comte's distinction between 'static sociology' and 'dynamic sociology' (Coseriu 1981: 17). The same distinction already existed in the work of the linguist François Duclos in the late eighteenth century. This is also true of the linguists André Bello and K. Heise.

The linguistics of the nineteenth century represents a decisive break, from many points of view, with that of the preceding century. This does not mean that the linguistics which Saussure and others pioneered in the early twentieth century is a direct continuation of the eighteenth-century tradition. Saussure (*CLG*: 118) points out that the Port-Royal grammarians were prescriptive and normative in orientation. He (*CLG*: 119) makes explicit the links he sees between his conception and that of the eighteenth-century grammarians. Theirs was a synchronic conception, but it was one which, according to Saussure, called for new theoretical directions.

What was it in the linguistic ideology of the Neogrammarians that Saussure reacts against? Around the beginning of the nineteenth century, Bopp inaugurated the tradition of comparative and historical linguistics. This was mainly concerned with the Indo-European group of languages. Its most notable achievements were the study of the Classical, Romance and Germanic languages. Its linguistic ideology was informed by the Romantic movement.

Around 1870 the school of linguistics known as the Neogrammarians arose. Its founder was the German linguist August Schleicher. Other notable exponents included Antoine Meillet in France and G. I. Ascoli in Italy. The linguistic ideology of the Neogrammarians was strongly positivistic. A number of principles characterized their approach.

First, the Neogrammarians were interested in individual facts. This was in keeping with the scientific atomism of positivism. Saussure, on the other hand, is interested in making significant generalizations about the internal organization and time-dependent dynamics of the language system. That is why he gives priority to the study of *langue* rather than to that of *parole*. Saussure understands that the earlier diachronic perspective was more interested in 'facts', defined in positivistic terms, rather than in the internal systemic organization of language. Diachronic facts, for Saussure, are 'particular' and do not constitute a basis for making significant generalizations about the language system (*CLG*: 134). It is only through the conceptual framework provided by the language system that such problems may be dealt with.

Saussure illustrates this point with respect to the synchronic opposition between the singular and plural forms *Gast* ('guest') and *Gäste* ('guests') in modern German (*CLG*: 122). The plural form *Gäste* replaces the historically prior form *gasti*. It is, Saussure explains, the synchronic opposition which is significant. The replacement of the earlier plural form by the present one does not in itself amount to a significant opposition in the language system.

Second, the approach of the Neogrammarians was substance-based. They considered individual facts as if they were things-in-themselves. They were interested in 'facts' as material entities. They had no interest in the functions these had in some grammatical form, or in the system of values which gives rise to these functions. For example, Saussure (*CLG*: 194) points out that historical phonetics was only interested in the material dimension of the sound of the word. That is why it is a substance-based approach. It excluded considerations of grammatical form and function. Regarding this approach, Saussure makes the following observation:

> To study the history of the sounds of a word, one can ignore its functional role [*sens*], taking into account only its material envelope, thereby segmenting it into its phonic parts without inquiring as to whether it has a meaning [*signification*].
>
> (*CLG*: 194)

Saussure does not simply leave things as they then stood, however. Most importantly, he goes on to point out: 'Words change meaning [*signification*], grammatical categories evolve' (*CLG*: 194). Up to this point in my discussion, Saussure has delimited an absolute distinction between the substance-based diachronic phonetics he seeks to replace and the new orientation he proposes in its stead. This may suggest that he sees an absolute cut-off between synchrony and diachrony. But Saussure inserts the question of *meaning* into the problematic of time. This is a logical consequence of the centrality of the sign in his theoretical framework. In so doing, he raises the question of the *relationship* between the diachronic and the synchronic perspectives. These are mutually exclusive only when the diachronic perspective remains, as it was for the Neogrammarians, substance-based. Such was also the case where the older historical phonetics was concerned. The question of meaning brings Saussure to the point of acknowledging the *interdependent* nature of the relationship between the two perspectives. As he says:

> And if all the facts of associative and syntagmatic synchrony have their history, how can the absolute distinction between diachrony and synchrony be maintained? This becomes very difficult the moment one leaves pure phonetics.
>
> (*CLG*: 194)

Saussure does not suggest that there is an absolute distinction to be made. Instead, he attempts to reformulate the relationship between synchrony and diachrony according to new principles. These principles are both meaning-based and systemic. They are another reason as to why he gives so much prominence to *langue*.

Third, the perspective of the Neogrammarians was an evolutionary one. They were interested in the historical evolution of the facts they studied. This much is evident in Saussure's discussion of historical phonetics. The Neogrammarians considered linguistic, and especially phonetic, change to be generated by necessity. They attributed a certain 'fatalism' to linguistic change. Very often this was couched in organic and racial terms: for example, the Italian Neogrammarian Goidànich has referred to 'the imperfect function of the organs of hearing and of the oral apparatus: *they are for this reason fated*' (1938: 43; emphasis in original). Goidànich and many other Neogrammarians believed that every racial group was in possession of a genetically inherited articulatory ability. Phonetic changes, in this view, were due to racial factors. This meant that they were also independent of the innovations which individual speakers introduced into the language. Particular racial groups had distinctive articulatory and hearing traits and capacities. It was these that caused phonetic change. Goidànich did not hesitate to postulate a hierarchy of languages according to their acoustic–articulatory traits; at the top of which he placed, after Latin, Italian.

Saussure makes it clear that what he calls linguistic 'laws' (*CLG*: 129–30) are neither prescriptive nor imperative. Instead, they are statements about general tendencies in the language system. Saussure does not directly refer to the Neogrammarians in this part of his discussion; however, his explicit refutation of either moral or causal necessity as an explanation of change in *langue* makes it clear that he has them in mind. Saussure is not explicit on this point, but the 'heteroglossic' opposition in *CLG* to the discourse of linguistic 'fatalism' is clear enough (see below). According to Saussure, a synchronic law

> is imposed on individuals by the constraints of collective usage . . ., but we do not envisage here an obligation on the part of the speaking subjects. We mean that *in the language system* [*langue*] no force guarantees the maintenance of the regularity of any given point. Simple expression of an existing order, the synchronic law registers a state of affairs; . . .
>
> (*CLG*: 131)

Saussure understands a synchronic law to be a statement of a statistical or probabilistic tendency which the language system manifests. It is a statement of distributional principles. These are, by definition, always systemic in character. He then acknowledges 'a dynamic factor' which pertains to diachrony (*CLG*: 131). This dynamic factor produces certain effects and gets certain things done (*un effet est produit, une chose exécutée*, p. 131). Yet, Saussure refutes any teleological, or causal, explanation of diachronic facts, which, according to him, have 'an accidental and particular character' (*CLG*: 131).

Fourth, the Neogrammarians explained the facts which they identified on naturalistic grounds. The founder of the Neogrammarians, the German August Schleicher, took the then science of glottology to be a natural science. Thus the Neogrammarians sought to explain linguistic change on the basis of naturalistic (e.g., racial and articulatory) factors, rather than on historical and cultural ones. Not all Neogrammarians took this view. For those who did, like Goidànich, languages were transmitted, genetically speaking, from one generation to the next.

Saussure (*CLG*: 202–3) explicitly rejects such racially motivated explanations. Again, he does not name the Neogrammarians, but his references to the notion of 'an Italian [vocal] organ' and 'the German mouth' make it clear that he has the views of the Neogrammarians in mind. In so doing, Saussure also shows the distance he has travelled from the reductively materialist explanations of the Neogrammarians. The next section will discuss the nature, the extent and the importance of the theoretical advances Saussure makes.

4 SAUSSURE'S REFORMULATION OF SYNCHRONY AND DIACHRONY

Saussure's critique of historical phonetics does not mean that he seeks to replace the diachronic perspective with a synchronic one; rather, Saussure attempts to re-think in a radically new way the relationship between the two. The Neogrammarians had an organismic and evolutionary view of linguistic change. They described individual, or group, linguistic behaviour on the basis of physiological traits. In modern terms, this would be a sort of *typological* description. The 'facts' which they described were the traits which a given (racial) group exhibited in some particular historical moment. The Neogrammarians had no means of showing how the 'facts' at any one moment related to the 'facts' at prior moments, or to possible future moments. The reason for this failing, aside from those already mentioned, lies in the total absence in their description of any conception of the language system. Additionally, their view of language change was a finalistic, or teleological, one. In actual fact, the Neogrammarians' view of language change better corresponds to a linear succession of synchronic moments. These are orientated to some ideal future state.

Saussure rejects both the Neogrammarians' lack of a systemic (*langue*-based) conception and their finalism. A careful reading of the relevant chapters in *CLG* shows that he has coherently worked out theoretical positions on both of these points.

First, Saussure makes it absolutely clear that 'diachronic facts do not in any way have as their goal the marking of a value by a new sign' (*CLG*: 121). On the following page, he adds that diachronic change 'is extraneous to all intentionality' (*CLG*: 122). A new sign does not come into being with the express purpose of creating a new value in the system. Saussure's explanation is radically different. When he says that 'a diachronic fact is an event whose *raison d'être* lies in itself' (*CLG*: 121), this means that such diachronic facts do not come into being because of some final goal-state towards which the system is striving. Instead, the system changes because of cultural and functional factors which are specific to that particular 'diachronic fact' (see also Coseriu 1981: 128).

Second, Saussure, in emphasizing the language system, places a lot of value on the *continuity* which underlies change. The Neogrammarians emphasized the 'facts', seen from a positivist point of view. These facts were substance-based and, hence, non-functional. It was a view which foregrounded the differences from one historical state of the language to another. Change was discontinuous. Saussure sees change in quite different terms:

> the system is never directly modified; in itself it is immutable; only certain elements are altered without regard to the solidarity which links them to the whole ... it is not the whole which has been replaced nor has one system engendered another. But one element in the first has been changed and this has been sufficient to bring another system into being.
>
> (*CLG*: 121)

In other words, a given change does not lead to anything so radical as the total replacement of one system by another. Saussure views change as passing through a number of historically definable stages. The system is the theoretical constant against which change can be measured. But if change were no more than a temporal succession of discrete moments, or diachronic facts, then there would be no basis for describing the systemic continuity which is always the background to change. The concept of the system provides just such a model for studying how change occurs against a background of systemic stability and continuity.

In the final analysis, Saussure says that it is the system itself which changes and not isolated facts which are external to it. Only a synchronic model of the system can, seemingly paradoxically, provide the basis for a study of system change. Further, Saussure's use of the concept of system is not totalizing in its implications. It would be more accurate to say that he is talking about particular subsystems of a given language. These change against the background of the wider system of which they are subcomponents. Saussure's own examples make this clear. Thus, the phonemic opposition between the German singular and plural forms *Gast* and *Gäste* is a synchronic fact. It refers to one significant opposition in one associative group, or subsystem, of the German language. It is a part of that subsystem of phonemic oppositions which constitute the difference in meaning between the singular and the plural morphemes in a given subclass of noun in modern German. The replacement of the historically prior plural form *gasti* by the modern one *Gäste* is a change which occurs against a stable background of systemic oppositions in other parts of the language system. We do not suddenly have a completely new system. Instead, it is in some sense the 'same' system, but changed in some particular way.

Throughout *CLG*, Saussure constantly demonstrates his profound awareness of change and of its implications for the language system. This goes hand in hand with Saussure's emphasis on the fact that variability always occurs against a background of invariability:

> Time, which assures the continuity of the language system [*langue*] has another effect, apparently in contradiction with the first: that of altering more or less rapidly linguistic signs and, in a certain sense, one can speak at the same time of the immutability and of the mutability of the sign.
>
> (*CLG*: 108)

In a footnote to his translation of *CLG*, Roy Harris comments that this serves to 'emphasise the fact that a language changes even though its speakers are incapable of changing it' (Saussure 1983: 74–5n.). But the point is, rather, Saussure's awareness of the dialectic between the two perspectives: the linguist can only talk about variability against a background of invariability. Both variability and invariability, like the related distinction between synchrony and diachrony, are *analytical* constructs. Saussure is constantly attentive to the need not to reify these. He clarifies this very point by comparing the 'relation between the historical reality [of language] and a state of the language system [*langue*], which is a projection of the former at a given moment' (*CLG*: 125).

Saussure makes two points here. (1) A synchronic and *langue*-based perspective is no more than an analytical re-construction of the given historical reality at some point in time. Saussure, in other words, does not confuse the two in the way many of his latter-day commentators have done. (2) The system is the point of entry into, and the basis for, the study of its own temporal–historical dynamics, rather than the other way round. That is why Saussure then adds: 'It is not in studying ... diachronic events that one will come to know the synchronic states' (*CLG*: 125). This is so not because Saussure insists on a rigid dichotomy between synchrony and diachrony, but because this distinction involves two distinct levels of abstraction. The first – the diachronic events – refers to the temporal dynamics of the language system in historical time. This cannot be the object of study in any direct, unmediated way. The second – a given synchronic state – is an analytical abstraction, or a 'projection', from any given moment in the first. The two belong to two logically distinct orders of abstraction. This does not mean, however, that these belong to two ontologically distinct realms. It is the second which interests Saussure as the primary object of study. The two perspectives are analytically, rather than constitutively, separable. Rather, synchrony and *langue* are necessary as analytical abstractions: they function to stabilize and define the object of study. This is always an analytical operation. It is only in this way that the linguist can study the dynamics of variability and invariability and synchrony and diachrony.

How does the linguist perform these operations? Saussure is very clear on this point: 'Synchrony has only one perspective, that of the speaking subjects, and its entire method consists of gathering evidence from them' (*CLG*: 128). In other words, *langue* is an analytical abstraction which the linguist derives from the evidence which 'speaking subjects' provide in *parole*. Yet the object of study is not the data which are so collected in any direct empirical way (Chapter 2, sections 7–8). The linguist reconstructs a 'synchronic projection' of the language system on the basis of the evidence collected. It is this which is the object of study for Saussure. In stating this premise, Saussure formulates one of the central axioms for many of the most important developments in twentieth-century linguistics.

The concept of the language system is neither totalizing nor unchanging. Saussure points out that alterations

> never occur to the whole system, but to one or the other of its elements, they can only be studied as being external to the system. Doubtless, each alteration has its effect on the system; but the initial fact has affected one point only.
>
> (*CLG*: 124)

The 'facts' belong to concrete, historical reality; the system to the linguist's synchronic projection from this.

Why, then, does Saussure insist on the simultaneous 'autonomy and interdependence' (*CLG*: 124) of the synchronic and diachronic perspectives? Why does he also point out that 'absolute immobility' (*CLG*: 193) of the linguistic system does not exist? This is not the result of an equivocation on Saussure's part; rather, it stems from his awareness that it is speech (*parole*) which is the agency of change, and not the system *per se*:

> *everything which is diachronic in the language system [langue] is only so through speech [parole]*. It is in speech that the seed of all changes is found: each one of them is in the first instance launched by a certain number of individuals before entering into usage.
>
> (*CLG*: 138; emphasis in original)

Saussure observes shortly afterwards:

> An evolutionary fact is always preceded by a fact, or by a multitude of similar facts in the sphere of speech [*parole*]; this does not invalidate in any way the distinction established above, rather, it confirms it. For in the history of all innovations one always comes across two distinct moments: (1) that when [the innovation] arises among individuals; (2) that when [the innovation] has become a fact of the language system [*un fait de langue*], outwardly identical [to the first moment], but adopted by the collectivity.
>
> (*CLG*: 138–9)

Only a few pages earlier, Saussure had observed that the synchronic study of the language system does not take as its object of study everything which is simultaneous. Instead, it is concerned with

> only the set of facts which correspond to each language system [*langue*]; to the extent to which it is necessary, this separation will extend to dialects and subdialects. In fact, the term *synchronic* is not sufficiently precise; it should be replaced by ... *idiosynchronic*.
>
> (*CLG*: 128)

With specific reference to 'phonetic change', Saussure also notes the contribution of *material* factors to the processes of change. Such changes are, more often than not, 'tied to determinate conditions; in other words, it is not the phonological type which changes, but the phoneme when it occurs in certain environmental conditions and conditions of stress' (*CLG*: 199).

What do all of these diverse observations add up to? Saussure does much more than merely locate the starting point for system change in *parole*. What he calls the *idiosynchronic* nature of system change acknowledges that dialects and subdialects and, by extension, semantic registers, sociolects and creoles, all play their part in the processes of change. Further, each of these has its own systemic specificity. There is not one single, homogeneous language system. Instead, there is, to use Saussure's own term, an *idiosynchronic* interplay of various subsystems. In other words, a language comprises this interplay of its various subsystems. The systemic properties of each of these means that the system has the potential to change in many different possible ways. Change always occurs in and through the particular functions which the various subsystems serve in the speech practices (*parole*) of the community.

The notion of idiosynchrony shows, then, that variation and heterogeneity are intrinsic characteristics of *langue*. Change can occur in both the lexicogrammatical means of expression and in the material phonetic means of realizing this. Material change of the second kind does not directly affect the meaning-making resources of the grammar. The first involves change in the actual speech practices of speaking subjects. This is the kind of semantic variation that is associated with the different kinds of contexts in which meanings are made in a given community. This is why Saussure locates the 'seed' of change in the practices of *parole*. *Parole*, as the instantiation of the system in particular contexts, represents the interface between the system and the material environments with which language-in-use is always cross-coupled. Idiosynchronic variation in the language system is organized in relation to the systematic and, hence, non-random, relations between the semantic variation that is associated with different context types in a given culture. The material features and the social practices that are typically associated with these contexts systematically co-vary with the semantic variation referred to here. In the absence of a fully articulated theory of *parole*, Saussure does not develop these implications. Nevertheless, idiosynchronic variation at the level of the system can allow for this dialectic between changes in the social practices of *parole* and the internal re-organization of the system itself.

Further, this variation in the meaning potential of the system has a history. This is why the interpretation of a text from the past can never simply restore some prior state of the language system. Instead, the act of interpretation necessarily entails a constant synchronic and diachronic dialectic between the text and all successor states of the system which link the modern reader to the text. The reader can neither restore the 'original' synchronic state of the language nor ignore the intervening diachronic evolution of the system. Rather, the modern reader's own synchronic state, in 'containing' its precursor states, provides the reader with a much expanded semantic potential for the reading of, say, poetic texts from historically prior states of the language (see Birch 1987 for a revealing discussion).

Saussure does not in principle exclude the material dimension of *parole* from the processes of language change. This is certainly so as far as phonological change is concerned. *Parole* is always both a semiotic and a material activity. Now, Saussure, to be sure, does not bring all of these observations together into some more coherent overall statement about *parole*. Doubtless this is due to at least two factors. First, *parole*, for Saussure, is a source of evidence from which the linguist may deduce theoretical statements about *langue*. It is not, then, the principal object of study in Saussure's approach (Chapter 1, section 3). Second, the prior linguistic traditions which Saussure inherited simply had not developed a science which studied in a systematic way social occasions of linguistic (and other) interaction (cf. text linguistics, discourse analysis, pragmatics and so on). Saussure was the inheritor of both the normative synchronic grammars of the eighteenth century and the positivistic conceptions of the linguistic facts, historically defined, which characterized the efforts of the historical and comparative linguists and later the Neogrammarians in the nineteenth century. Ethnography was at the level of 'travellers' tales'. Saussure can hardly be blamed for these limitations, which circumscribed the whole field of linguistics, as it then stood. This does not, of course, alter the fact that these inherent limitations – both historical and theoretical–methodological in character – meant that Saussure was only able to glimpse, rather than systematize, the fact that change always begins in specific contexts (*parole*) before it has deeper and more persistent consequences for the system. Saussure's great achievement is to have conceptualized the fundamental role of the language system (*langue*) in this dynamic.

5 THE TOPOLOGICAL NATURE OF *LANGUE* AND ITS TEMPORAL DYNAMICS

Saussure's achievement is to have provided the basis for a *topological* model of system change. He never uses this term, but, translated into modern terminology, that is what he is saying. Change is not a matter of a mere temporal succession of 'diachronic facts'. Instead, the linguist can describe a given language system on the basis of the probabilities that are intrinsic to it. This is a way of describing the relative frequency of the various possible values of each of the terms in the system. Historically prior states of the system are described in terms of shifts in the distribution patterns of these terms and, hence, their values. On this basis, the linguist can re-construct the actual (or hypothetical) intermediate stages through which the system has passed. In Part III, Chapter 1 of *CLG*, Saussure discusses numerous examples of sound changes which illustrate this principle of re-construction.

Significantly, the topological character of the system dynamics comes more to the fore when Saussure moves on to the terrain of grammar. Saussure understands that the linguist's re-construction of a given system is always an idealization (Chapter 1, section 5). Topologically, the values which the system represents are distributed in clusters around 'ideal' points. The historical developments which lead to change in the system mean that the location of this idealized point, around which a given set of values cluster, may shift. One possible result is that a given system may split into two new systems. Another is that two previously distinct systems may merge so as to form a new one.

As an example of the second kind of change, Saussure (*CLG*: 196) shows how the French future form *prendrai* ('I will take') is the result of a synthesis of the historically prior elements *prendre* ('to take') and *ai* ('I have') on the stratum of the signified. These two elements belonged to two distinct associative groups before they merged to create the new form. A second synthesis concerns the phonetic level. In this case, the two accents of the original two groups are reduced to one in the new form: *préndre aí* → *prendraí*. A given change of this kind can alter the topological character of the system along some parameter or other. Unlike the Neogrammarians' emphasis on the 'historical facts', Saussure understood that such a topological model of the system is necessary so that the linguist can re-construct the intermediate stages through which the system passed prior to any given synchronic state.

Systems *per se* do not change of their own accord. The system, Saussure shows, constitutes a potential in two dialectically related senses. Speakers may use this potential in order to speak according to current norms. They may also use it to create new forms and meanings. Saussure brings out this point in his discussion of analogy. Analogy, to be sure, is a grammatical process. But there is an important theoretical point at issue here:

> Thus one whole part of the [analogical] phenomenon is completed before one sees the new form appear. The continual activity of language [*langage*] in analysing the units already given contains in itself not only all possibilities of speaking in conformity to usage, but also all analogical formations. It is, therefore, a mistake to believe that the generative process only occurs at the moment in which the creation arises; its elements are already given [by the language system].
>
> (*CLG*: 227)

In the following chapter, Saussure poses the question as to how such innovations enter the linguistic system. He makes the point that not all such innovations enjoy 'this good fortune' (*CLG*: 231). He gives the example of children's language. The linguistic innovations of children may not be salient or distinctive, or they may not have a regular pattern which corresponds to 'adult' criteria of the language system. Saussure points out that analogy is 'a principle of renovation and conservation' (*CLG*: 235), that is, of *both* change and stability. In making this point, he hits upon the importance of distributional criteria in system change. New linguistic forms and meanings do not simply come into being *ex nihilo*. Saussure points out that it is the distributional properties of the system which shift:

> in the enormous mass of analogical phenomena which represent several centuries of evolution, almost all of these elements are conserved; they are only distributed differently.
>
> (*CLG*: 235)

The important point to emerge in this discussion is that while *parole* is the 'seed' of change, it is not isolated, individual or context-specific innovations which in themselves lead to system change. Such innovations may be necessary to get the whole process going. But it is only when these innovations ramify, or spread, across many different contexts that the distributional characteristics of the system will, in time, alter. The system of *langue* describes differences which are distributed in a topological space. This is the system's meaning-making, or value-producing, potential. This potential alters in significant and perceptible ways only when the speech practices of *parole* bring about a shift in the distributional probabilities of the value-producing terms in the system.

In Part IV, Chapter 3 of *CLG*, which is entitled 'Causes of geographical diversity', Saussure spells out the topological basis of his model in more detail. To do so, he proposes a simple theoretical situation. He imagines a language which is spoken in one place and which is taken to another geographical location by a group of colonists. Initially, the two groups speak the same language, a. Over time, there will be significant lexicogrammatical and phonological differences in both groups. Figure 4.1 reproduces Saussure's own diagram and shows the divergent evolutionary pathways which the initially identical language of the two groups undergoes in the course of time. Time, Saussure argues, is the crucial factor, not geographical location. Saussure's diagram illustrates the possible future pathways which the future development of the initial system may take. The starting point is the difference between the language of first focus (F) and the language of second focus (F'). The three pathways represent further differentiation and/or specification of a common precursor, or initial, system a. The linguist can use any particular pathway in order to reconstruct the various intermediate stages which occurred during the historical development of the system. In this way, it is possible to construct a basis for understanding what the differentiated pathways have in common. The fact that the three pathways all, to some extent, share common elements means that it is possible to postulate a basis for comparison across otherwise seemingly different systems. The topological basis of the description makes this possible. Saussure makes the point that the study of the processes of differentiation illustrated in Figure 4.1 cannot be one-sided. The innovations which take place in both of the languages are of equal importance (*CLG*: 271).

This leads to Saussure's discussion of a second diagram, which is shown

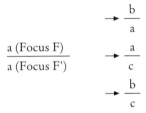

Figure 4.1 Innovation in two languages due to time factor

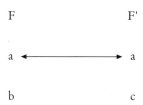

Figure 4.2 Geographical differentiation from an original linguistic situation

in Figure 4.2. This shows an initial system a, which has, over time, become the two distinct systems, b and c. Again, time, Saussure argues, is the principal agent in this process of progressive linguistic differentiation. What Saussure calls '*the change itself*' (the particular change which occurs) and 'the instability of the language system' are both time-dependent (*CLG*: 272).

Saussure shows the time evolution which occurs when the topological space, a, splits into two new spaces, b and c. A topological space describes a non-random distribution of value-producing terms relative to a given system. The differentiation of the initial system, a, into the two diverging systems, b and c, means that two new topological spaces come into being. Each of these has its own distributional characteristics. The topological character of the system means that this is inherently unstable, or *dynamical*. Minor perturbations or variations in some initial state may be amplified. In turn, this leads to the creation of new evolutionary pathways, which diverge from the precursor state. The situation Saussure describes here is very close to that of the theory of thermodynamic systems (sections 6 and 10 below).

6 TWO PERSPECTIVES ON DIACHRONIC ANALYSIS

In Part V of *CLG*, Saussure distinguishes two perspectives on diachronic analysis. The first is 'prospective' (*prospective*, *CLG*: 291). It consists of a simple recounting of the events from their starting point in the past and, thence, forwards to some future moment. This method is based on the documentary evidence one has at one's disposal. The second is 'retrospective' (*rétrospective*, *CLG*: 291). This perspective requires the linguist to 'go back in the flow of time by means of retrospection' (*CLG*: 292). It involves 'a reconstructive method which is based on comparison' (*CLG*: 292). Saussure gives priority to the second perspective. The point is that the linguistic forms which the linguist uses to re-construct some 'original' form are themselves subject to change. The critical factor in the retrospective method is continuity of change. Saussure emphasizes the 'absolute continuity of development' (*CLG*: 296) of a language system. The comparative basis of the retrospective method means that the linguist can see which forms provide a common basis for comparison. In this way, the linguist can re-construct the stages which lead from the precursor system to its successors. In other words, change is continuous because a given linguistic form passes through a whole series of intermediate stages which the linguist can re-construct. It is important to establish such principles of continuity across systems. Change always takes place against a background of stability. Saussure understands that the system is, at any given moment, the result of a constant dialectic between synchronic and diachronic factors. On this basis, the language system always embodies principles of both stability and change, simultaneously.

Saussure does not, however, reify the processes of re-construction:

> The aim of reconstruction is not to restore a form for its own sake ... but to crystallise, to condense a series of conclusions that one believes to be right, according to the results that one was able to obtain at that moment; in a word, to register the progress of our science.

$$(CLG: 301)$$

The linguist's re-construction can tell us something about the possible histories of the system: that is, the possible histories which are 'contained' in a given synchronic state. In actual fact, it is only the linguist's 'synchronic projection' which corresponds to such a 'state'. The concrete, historical reality of language, as Saussure well understands, is dynamical. The source of both change and stability has a systemic basis. Any given value-producing term in the system may participate in the processes of either change or stability.

There is a still deeper reason why Saussure prefers the retrospective re-construction of the flow of time to the prospective one. Each of these new systems, as shown in Figures 4.1 and 4.2, has its own internal system-time. The prospective viewpoint is a mechanical and external recounting of a linear succession of 'facts'. The retrospective point of view grasps the topological nature of the system. Internal system-time is the series of intermediate stages the system itself has to go through before it gets to the particular synchronic state which is under consideration. This internal time admits of a global history of the system. This depends, in turn, on the topological nature of the system. The prospective type of re-construction depends, on the other hand, on a linear re-construction through the documentation of a series of 'facts' which were not previously known to the linguist. The dynamics of the system would consist of a linear succession of such 'facts'. It is the task of the linguist to discover these. Each 'fact' is a discrete and local moment in the history of the system. That is why it is a purely synchronic, though *non-*systemic, point of view.

The notion of a system-internal time means that time is not a purely mathematical abstraction. Time in this abstract sense is not and cannot be a causal force which acts on the language system so as to change it. Saussure does not view time as a vector. He denies time a physical, causal role for the simple reason that time does not have an independent existence of its own. It is not an independent variable; it is, rather, constituted by its relations with what Saussure calls 'the social force' (*CLG*: 113; Chapter 3, section 5). For this reason, *langue* is not a 'simple convention' consisting of the practical relations among individuals.

Saussure would appear to have taken on board an important lesson from Einstein's relativity theory: there is no absolute 'entity' time. Time is an abstraction from real, concrete social events. For this reason, it is simply inaccurate to talk in terms of 'the state of system x at time t'. Saussure does not do so. This kind of reasoning really means something like 'the state of language system x when the social dimension is in time t'. The social dimension constitutes a concrete frame of reference which avoids focusing on the purely formal and mathematical at the expense of the concrete and the social. Time, if viewed as a purely mathematical abstraction, is causally vacuous. It is, Saussure shows, only when it is embedded in a frame of reference of concrete social-semiological processes that it is causally efficacious. Once again, Saussure demonstrates the importance he attaches to the social-semiological processes which are intrinsic to *langue*, rather than to formal, mathematical abstractions *per se*. This means that the synchronic states of the system are always frame-dependent. Units of time are always local, rather than global. The reference frame always consists in the concrete social forces that are intrinsic to the system and its history. If, by contrast, time were disjoined from social factors, then it would amount to an 'absolute' and, hence, extrinsic standard of measurement (Chapter 1, section 5). But time and the social are, for Saussure, intrinsically cross-coupled in the internal dynamics of *langue*. This means that the system's social and temporal qualities are defined in relation to its value-producing terms and their interrelations.

Retrospective reconstruction views probability as internal to the system. This implies the intrinsically time-orientated and dynamical systems described by thermodynamics (Prigogine and Stengers 1985). The dynamics of *parole* introduce elements of instability into the system itself. *Parole* perturbs *langue*. In so doing, *parole* brings new probability features into the description of the system. Such features may take the form of newly relevant or newly salient patterns of difference. The inherent instability of the system has to do with the non-deterministic and irreversible nature of its dynamics. The system does not already contain its possible futures. Instead, it *irreversibly* 'moves' from present to future.

7 SYSTEM DYNAMICS AND SAUSSURE'S CHESS ANALOGY

In both the game of chess and in any given state of the language system the chess pieces and the terms, respectively, derive their values only through their differences with respect to all the other constituent elements in the entire system of relations. It is not simply the number of terms which makes a system more or less complex, but the ways in which these relate to, or cross-couple with, each other. The more cross-couplings there are, the more complex the system and the less predictable its future dynamics (Lemke 1993: 252).

On this basis, Saussure is led to a second observation: 'the system is only ever momentary; it varies from one position to the next' (*CLG*: 126). Does this contradict his notion of a 'state' of the language system? Surely not. A synchronic 'state', as I have pointed out, is a methodological 'projection'; it is an analytical construct of the linguist. It is not an ontological claim about the very different reality of the time-dependent dynamics of change in the language system. Saussure's point is that both chess and *langue* are systems in which the complex cross-couplings of pieces and terms, respectively, increase in complexity and diversity in time. In this way, new combinatorial possibilities are created. Further, this increase in complexity proceeds irreversibly from past to future.

The language system is not inherently 'static'. To think that this is the case amounts to a profound misunderstanding of what Saussure intends by the term 'static'. His point is that it is the dynamical behaviour of the system in time which maintains it in any given state. This is why, as Saussure observes, the system so defined is only ever a 'momentary' one which is in reality constantly changing from one moment to the next. The system is extended in time and only exists in time. That is, it is only definable along its complete evolutionary trajectory. Again, does not the 'static' point of view contradict this? Only if the point of view adopted assumes that any given synchronic state can be described in terms of its immediately prior states, rather than its complete evolutionary trajectory.

In Saussure's extended analogy, neither the observer who has 'followed the whole game' nor the 'curious person who comes to inspect the state of play at the critical moment' (*CLG*: 127) is essentially better off than the other. They are only able to observe particular prior states of the game on the basis of a presumed continuity of states from 'before' to 'after'. This fact is based on the way in which a given prior state enables one to predict the successor states. But, Saussure argues, such changes, even while they may act upon 'isolated elements' (*CLG*: 126) in particular subsystems, have unforeseeable repercussions upon the entire system of relations. Thus, a language system may shift in unpredictable ways from one state to another. For this reason, it is impossible to predict change in any precise way; any given change may create new states which are less symmetric in time. This is why any given move in the game of chess may 'revolutionize the whole game and have consequences even for the pieces not in question' (*CLG*: 126). It is not possible to foresee all the consequences of any given move because a given 'change of values' (*CLG*: 126) may provoke random fluctuations whereby the system re-organizes itself as a new stable state in one of its possible less symmetric, further from equilibrium, states.

In saying that the change belongs to neither the 'preceding' nor the 'resulting' state of the chessboard, and in affirming that 'the states alone are important' (*CLG*: 126), Saussure suggests, by analogy, that the language system may become newly stable in one of the possible global states which the system has itself created in and through its interactions with its semiotic environments, viz. the players in a game of chess and the speech practices of *parole*. This illustrates the phenomenon referred to as *bifurcation* in modern theories of complex, dynamic open and evolving systems (Prigogine and Stengers 1985: 169–70; Lemke 1993).

Saussure also argues that the system is only *ever* 'momentary' and that the system's values depend above all on an 'unchanging convention, the rules of the game, which exists before the beginning of the game and persists afterwards' (*CLG*: 126). The point is, I believe, that the system and its instantiations are 'embedded' in a stable, regulating environment with which it exchanges matter, energy and information (Lemke 1993: 254). From the diachronic point of view, the environment of the language system is the system of cultural practices of a community, its matter-energy flows, and the ways in which the typical cross-couplings of these entrain and organize the latter (Lemke 1993: 262). The environment shapes and guides the system and its development by virtue of these same transactions. Thus, the distinction between the 'momentary' character of the system and the 'unchanging' character of its environment needs to be understood in this sense. Changes in the system are not completely random. The environment provides an external source of information and regulation which selects the possible developmental pathways of the system (Lemke 1993: 257). This is the principle known as 'epigenesis' in modern biology and systems theory. However, when Saussure says that the 'unchanging' conventions of the game of chess are analogous to the conditions which regulate change in the language system, this should not be taken literally to mean that the environment of the system never changes. Instead, it refers to the rate of change relative to the scalar perspective which is adopted. The implications of Saussure's chess analogy will be further explored in sections 8–10 below.

8 SAUSSURE'S MORPHOGENETIC THEORY OF LANGUAGE CHANGE

Saussure's account of systemic change is a *morphogenetic* one. The concept of *morphogenesis* is contrasted with that of *morphostasis* in systems theory. I shall now explain briefly the significance of these two terms before exploring their relevance to Saussure's account of change in the language system.

'In morphostasis', Wilden (1980 [1972]: 355) writes, 'there is either maintenance of structure, or the elaboration of preprogrammed structures, or the replacement of one structure by a homologous structure.' Morphostasis implies that the essential norms of the system do not change in spite of changes of the kind Wilden refers to. Morphogenesis, on the other hand, involves 'the elaboration of new structures through systemic activities' (*ibid.*). Saussure does not use these two terms. However, there can be no doubt that the historical and evolutionary (diachronic) perspective which he adopts on system change is a morphogenetic one. Saussure's position here differs significantly from that of the comparative philologists, who saw language change in morphostatic terms. This is revealingly elicited by Saussure in his discussion of Schleicher in the first chapter of *CLG* (Chapter 1, section 5).

Schleicher talks about the changes in the Greek and Sanskrit vowel systems as if these involved continuing processes of selection and combination according to the norms of the system of, say, Proto-European. In Schleicher's model, changes in the vowels involve the continuous temporal re-coding of these norms. It is as if the system or the subsystem in question undergoes a continuous developmental trajectory along some pre-given pathway. This is a morphostatic conception.

Saussure's conception of evolutionary or historical change is, by contrast, genuinely morphogenetic. The innovations which individuals initiate in *parole* are projected onto the systemic organization of *langue*. This leads in time to the re-structuring, or the transformation, of the system. It involves some transformation in the goal-seeking activities of the system itself, and in ways which are distinct from the precursor 'states' of the system. My use of quotation marks around the word 'state' serves to remind one of the methodological status of Saussure's usage. In a brief, though illuminating, comment on his own use of this word, Saussure evidences his own self-reflexivity concerning the metatheoretical status of the terms he uses:

> In political history one distinguishes *epoch*, which is a point in time, and *period*, which encompasses a certain duration. However, the historian speaks of the Antonin epoch, the epoch of the Crusades when he considers a set of characteristics which have stayed constant during this time. One might say that static linguistics is concerned with epochs; but state [*état*] is preferable; the beginning and the end of an epoch are generally marked by some more or less sudden revolution which tends to modify the state of established things. The word state stops one from thinking that anything similar happens in the language system.
>
> (*CLG*: 142)

Saussure carefully distinguishes change in a given 'state of the language system' (*état de langue*) from 'epochal' change. Change in a language system may occur either very slowly or very suddenly. The point is that such change involves the elaboration and emergence of new levels of organization which are *internal* to the system. 'Epochal' change refers, instead, to *external* or 'accidental' factors which perturb the system from the outside.

Saussure goes to some trouble to point out that there is no direct relationship between change in the historical and political context of a language and the internal dynamics of the language system (*CLG*: 206–7). Saussure does not, however, say that there is no relationship. Wilden, I believe, has misunderstood this point in his critique of Saussure's theory of diachrony:

> no PROCESS of changing complexity in an evolutive or historical sense can be discerned in language change. There is simply a peaceful transition from one set of rules to another set, assisted by noise generated internally and externally. Language complexity bears no relation to social complexity. And if social changes or invasions by other groups accelerate or set off linguistic change, the change from one linguistic code to another remains a pure epiphenomenon with no theoretical value as a MODEL of history. All such change is morphostatic; it is in no real sense whatsoever 'historical' or 'dialectical'.
>
> (Wilden 1980 [1972]: 340–1)

In my view, Wilden's criticism of the diachronic model is misconceived. The kind of 'epochal' historical and political upheavals to which Saussure draws our attention are more likely to produce, in the short term, a rapid turnover of lexical items. But the kind of change Saussure is talking about goes well beyond this. It involves the 'inner-most' layers of the language system, or its grammar. The grammatical systems of a language change only very slowly compared to either lexis or the sound system. Wilden seems not to have understood that systemic change in the grammar of a language takes place much more slowly than do the 'social changes', 'invasions' and 'political upheavals' which I have mentioned here. For Saussure, both time and the social are internal to the systemic organization of language as a social-semiological system (*CLG*: 112–13; Chapter 3, section 5). Therefore, it makes no sense to say, as does Wilden, that change is a 'pure epiphenomenon' in Saussure's diachronic model. This brings me back to the relevance of *parole* to the present argument.

Saussure correctly points out that the 'seed' of language change lies in the dialectic between *langue* and *parole*, or between system and instance (Halliday 1992: 20). When Saussure claims that 'epochal' change, such as the political upheavals he refers to, are 'external' factors, he means that there is no direct, unmediated causal relationship between such events and the long-term re-organization of *langue* as a species of dynamic, open, adaptive and evolving system.

I argued in Chapter 2 that Saussure is interested, above all, in developing a social-semiological metatheory of the language system: that is, he is primarily interested in the principles which underlie the internal structuring and dynamics of *langue*. According to the structuralist reading, *langue* is a closed and self-regulating system. This influential reading of *langue* is totally inadequate. In my view, Saussure, who is generally considered to be the founder of twentieth-century structuralism, is not a structuralist in the classical sense; rather, he is an important precursor of the much more recent epistemological developments in the theory of dynamic open systems. This theory, which was first developed in the physical and life sciences, is, in recent years, having important consequences for the social sciences as well, as evidenced in the work of René Thom, Jean Petitot and Jay Lemke. In other words, I contend that Saussure participated in an emerging new theoretical dialogue between the social-semiological and the biophysical dimensions of meaning-making. Unfortunately, the structuralist reading of Saussure, with its emphasis on morphostasis and self-regulation, rather than morphogenesis and adaptiveness, truncated this dialogue until its re-emergence became possible in the light of a number of more recent developments.

Now Saussure, to be sure, lacks an adequate metalanguage for giving voice to the language of matter, energy and information exchange between *langue*, seen as a social-semiological system, and its physical and social environments. Saussure did not have at his disposal the developments in cybernetics, systems theory, information theory and the recent ecosocial view of cultural systems (Lemke 1993). The important point here is that Saussure's is a non-causal theory of system change. It is also a relational and dynamical one. That is, change is not driven by the logic of efficient, unilinear causes. Cause does not precede effect. Instead, Saussure proposes a teleonomic, or goal-seeking, model in which the effect precedes the cause (Wilden 1981: 27). In such a perspective, the relevant system factors concern questions of meaning potential, absent or latent contextualizing relations, difference and constraint (Wilden 1980 [1972]: 337).

Saussure demonstrates a profound awareness of the dynamical dimensions of *langue*. Of course, Saussure does not use these terms. The metalanguage of dynamic open systems was not available to him. Nevertheless, that is the direction in which his description of the process of system change goes in his account of transactions between *langue* and innovation in *parole*. *Langue*, I have argued, is enacted and maintained on the basis of the regularities and structural stabilities which are reconstituted in and through specific occasions of use. *Parole* is the point of contact between the system and its environments. This is manifested in the fact that *parole* represents the point of intersection between social-semiological forms and physical–material processes. As I shall show later, this is the case with respect to both signifier and signified in the sign (Chapter 7, section 4). *Langue*, as a species of dynamic open system, both maintains its overall stability and integrity and, in the longer term, changes on account of the continual transactions between it and its environments in acts of *parole*.

These transactions between the system and its material and social environments serve to maintain the overall system of differences. Thus, Saussure's methodological distinction between *langue* and *parole* does not mean that the one is independent of the other. The ontological hiatus between the social and the individual dimensions of the analysis is real enough. However, this distinction must not be conflated with that between *langue* and *parole*. Both of these perspectives are necessary for explaining the overall dynamics of the system. *Langue* is a metastable and dynamic open system (Lemke 1984b: 63; 1993). It is a dynamic and open system because of the continual transactions of matter, energy and information which it engages in in order to maintain its own structural integrity. It is a metastable system because these same transactions serve to maintain it in an approximately invariant state from one moment to the next in spite of the many dynamical processes involved.

The point of Saussure's critique of 'epochal' historical and political upheavals as the basis of a theory of system change now becomes clearer. In this form of explanation, the basic assumption is that the language system is stable unless perturbed by outside factors. Saussure's point is radically different. It is that the linguistic work which is enacted by individuals in very many acts of *parole* serves to maintain the overall 'metastability' of the language system. By the same token, innovations in the speech practices of *parole* may, under favourable conditions, bring about changes in the system itself. *Parole* represents the point of contact where the system continually adapts to the contingencies of its environments. This means that *parole*, far from being an ancillary factor, is a necessary component in the explanation of both stability and change in the language system in historical time (Chapter 5, section 5).

Saussure sees 'the global totality of language' as comprising both *langue* and *parole* (Chapter 5, section 3). *Langue* and *parole* are analytically, though not constitutively, separable parts of this totality. Both perspectives are necessary in the overall conceptualization of the phenomenon of language. *Langue* in this perspective is always immanent in acts of *parole*. It is only through the contextualizing (value-producing) relations of *langue* that acts of *parole* are defined: 'the language system is necessary so that *parole* is intelligible and produces all its effects' (*CLG*: 37). In so far as *parole* is the material enactment of semiotic form, it follows that the contextualizing relations of *langue* are not external to *parole*. Instead, they are internally and systematically related to it.

9 *LANGUE* AND *PAROLE* AND THE RENEWAL OF THE LANGUAGE SYSTEM: PHONETIC CHANGE AND GRAMMATICAL ANALOGY

At various points in *CLG*, Saussure observes that the practices of *parole* serve both to renew the language system (*CLG*: 152) and to change it (*CLG*: 138). He makes a distinction between the changes which these *langue–parole* transactions produce (1) in their local environments and (2) in the wider system (*CLG*: 138–9). Saussure describes the first as 'a fact, or rather a multitude of similar facts in the domain of *parole*' (*CLG*: 138–9). He describes the second as 'an evolutionary fact' (*CLG*: 138). The second is consequent upon the first. This distinction means that system change has consequences for both the unique historical–biographical individuals who participate in *parole*, as well as for the longer-term dynamics of the system. On the basis of this distinction, Saussure formulates a number of very powerful principles for theorizing the dynamics of both stability *and* change in *langue*. I have gathered together and summarized these as follows.

1 Local variation and change in *parole* are regulated by higher-order principles of synchronic identity (Chapter 13, sections 4–6). That is, there is a system of recognizeable and structurally stable semiotic forms. The structural integrity of these is maintained in spite of many small variations in their material enactments from one occasion of use to another (*CLG*: 150–3). In other words, the system incorporates principles for its own internal self-regulation.

2 The language system itself, and not only acts of *parole*, builds possibilities of change into its own internal dynamics. This internal lability is illustrated by the very wide range of potential and, hence, not-yet-realized possibilities that are immanent in the system of differences. Saussure provides two very clear examples which testify to this principle of systemic self-deregulation. The first of these has to do with phonetic change:

> the phonetic phenomenon is a factor of disturbance. Wherever it does not create alternations, it helps to loosen the grammatical ties that link words to each other; the sum of forms is increased unnecessarily; the linguistic mechanism becomes obscure and complicated inasmuch as the irregularities born of the phonetic change prevail over the forms grouped under general types; in other words inasmuch as absolute arbitrariness prevails over relative arbitrariness.
>
> (*CLG*: 221)

Revealingly, Saussure calls these processes of phonetic change 'a factor of disturbance' (*un facteur de trouble*). Phonetic change is an example of *systemic* self-deregulation. This explains the importance which Saussure ascribes in this passage to the system-internal perspective of 'absolute arbitrariness' (Chapter 12, section 1). Phonetic change is a 'factor of disturbance' in the sense that it functions to ensure that the language system does not achieve a state of total stability, or self-regulation. In the process of prising apart the grammatical links among words, new patterns and combinations may emerge. In other words, phonetic change is a source of 'lower'-level novelty and mutation. Change of this kind is essentially random and, hence, unpredictable. The important point is that it is not an exogenous factor which perturbs the system from the outside. On the contrary, it is a 'factor of disturbance' which is built into the internal dynamics of the system. The microprocesses of phonetic change work to de-regulate the general system of types and, hence, to change them.

The de-regulatory effects of phonetic change, if unchecked, would lead to a state of entropy. However, the randomness of these 'lower'-level mutations is counterbalanced by the lexicogrammatical process Saussure calls *analogy*. Unlike the randomness of phonetic change, analogy preselects according to an already established regular model in the system. Saussure explains analogy as follows:

> Fortunately the effect of these transformations [phonetic change] is counterbalanced by analogy. It is concerned with all the normal modifications of the exterior aspect of words which are not phonetic in nature.
>
> Analogy supposes a model and its regular imitation. *An analogical form is a form made in the image of one or more forms according to an established rule.*
>
> (*CLG*: 221; emphasis in original)

Analogy presupposes some higher-order principle of organization which derives from the general system of types. This means that the system itself provides diachronic antecedents or precursors for the new forms created by analogy.

Saussure's discussion of phonetic change and analogy draws attention to the impossibility of a purely synchronic model of *langue* as a social-semiological system. The reason for this is very simple, as Saussure himself demonstrates through his numerous examples. Both lower-level phonetic change as well as higher-level lexicogrammatical processes of analogy draw attention to the fact that the social uses of language in the practices of *parole* do not simply replicate the system of general types in *langue*. Instead, new patterns and combinations which do not conform to the criteria established by the type may emerge. In showing this, Saussure reveals two fundamental characteristics of the language system: first, the emergence of new patterns requires a dynamic model of the system itself; second, system change can only be explained through the combined effects of innovation-in-time. These two points lead me to propose a third general principle on the basis of Saussure's explanation of the processes which contribute to both stability and change in the language system. This third principle may now be added to the previous two, discussed above:

3 The structure of *langue* must be described by taking into account the practices of *parole* which occur in specific historical times and places. The linguistic work which is expended in *parole* produces and re-produces in time the synchronic 'states' of the language system.

I started this section by drawing attention to the importance which

Saussure attaches to *parole* as the 'seed' of all change in the language system. The emphasis is on the dynamics of the speech practices which work to alter and to renew the language system. *Parole*, I have shown, is often taken to refer to the individual's use of language. However, Saussure is careful not to give it an individualistic interpretation. For example, he does not locate either meaning or innovation in the 'mind' of the individual. *Parole* does not refer to the individual's performance of some putatively asocial cognitive competence. Language change does not, then, originate in the consciousness of the speaking subject, but in real-time innovations in speech practices. Saussure avoids locating change in what Foucault has referred to as 'the founding function of the subject' (1974 [1969]: 12).

In opposition to the 'founding function of the subject', Saussure shows that the site of change is always specific acts of *parole* (*CLG*: 138). *Parole* does not refer to the consciousness of the individual language user. It is Saussure's term for the specific social occasion of linguistic interaction, which is always 'executed' by two or more historical–biographical individuals in some jointly enacted 'complex unity' (Chapter 5, section 1). Saussure identifies two 'moments' in the overall process of system change. These are as follows:

> in the history of all innovation one always encounters two distinct moments: 1. when it arises among individuals; 2. when it has become a fact of the language system, externally identical, but adopted by the collectivity.
>
> (*CLG*: 139)

Saussure's point is twofold. (1) In specific acts of *parole* individuals may create new combinations or new relations among combinations and in ways which give rise to newly contingent meaning-relations on specific occasions. In this first 'moment', these new combinations achieve their initially local effects because they contrast with the already established patterns of socially significant differences. (2) The overall system of relations is altered if the new practice is taken up by a sufficiently large number of individuals to the extent that it enters into and, hence, alters the previously established system of differences in *langue*.

Saussure's discussion of the transition from *ich was* to *ich war* in German demonstrates this. Individual innovations in *parole* tend to be unique re-combinations of the typical patterns in *langue*. Analogy is a good example of this. Generally speaking, linguistic innovation, if it is to be successful, cannot be confined to a single biographical individual. It has to be taken up and repeated by a sufficiently large number of individuals in a given speech community. Saussure's point is that the system of types in *langue* can be said to have changed only when it is possible to specify a community of language users for whom the innovation has, in a second 'moment', become typical.

In German, the transition from *ich was* to *ich war* came about because the new form, initially used by a restricted number of individuals, became in time socially significant for the speech community as a whole. The new form thus came to make a difference in the system of differences. In opposition to the sovereign role of consciousness, to use Foucault's term, Saussure's decentring of the individual speaking subject reveals the relational character of all meaning. For a 'fact of evolution' (*CLG*: 138) to arise, it is essential that the speech practices in *parole* construe new patterns of relations or new significances for existing patterns. Saussure's separation of this process into two 'moments' shows that what may initially seem to be purely contingent and accidental 'facts of *parole*' do, nevertheless, become noticed by language users. Obviously, those which go unnoticed will have no effect on the system and will sooner or later pass into oblivion. The point is that an innovation which is noticed and adopted by a large enough number of individuals on enough social occasions has the potential to alter the system of differences: that is, to become a 'fact of *langue*'. At this point, the entire system of value-producing relations is in some way altered.

10 SYSTEM DYNAMICS AND EVOLUTIONARY CHANGE IN *LANGUE*

In section 8 above I argued that Saussure's theory of the dynamical transactions between *langue* and *parole* is a morphogenetic one. My contention is that Saussure's description of linguistic innovation in *parole* and evolutionary change in *langue* closely resembles the theory of thermodynamic states in its basic epistemological assumptions. I shall now explore this possibility in some detail. A system which is in a state of global thermodynamic equilibrium may change as the result of local fluctuational instabilities leading to local non-equilibrium states. Saussure's description closely resembles that class of thermodynamic situations that are irreversibly associated with the making of constraints. The arrow of time goes in the direction of increasing systemic order. It is a level of description which designates so-called self-organizing systems.

Saussure's notion of a 'synchronic law', or 'a principle of regularity' (*CLG*: 131), is close to the notion of a system at thermodynamic global equilibrium. The evolution of systems operating at global equilibrium means that local degrees of freedom change as the result of the breaking of local constraints. Saussure explains his notion of a synchronic law as follows:

> The synchronic law is general, but it is not imperative. Doubtless, it is imposed on individuals by the constraints of collective usage (see p. 107), but we do not envisage here an obligation with respect to speaking subjects. We mean only that *in the language system* no force guarantees the maintenance of this regularity when it prevails on some point. Simple expression of an existing order, the synchronic law records a state of

affairs.... And the order that it defines is precarious, precisely because it is not imperative.

(CLG: 131)

The second thermodynamic law states that all local constraints are susceptible to fracture at some time-scale of analysis. When Saussure points out that a 'synchronic law is precarious, precisely because it is not imperative' he draws attention to the ways in which local instabilities in *parole* generate microlevel fluctuations that are continually regulated by the global stability requirements, as defined by the second law. Synchronic laws are 'precarious' precisely because, under certain conditions, the microlevel instabilities may amplify, resulting in global instabilities, and the emergence of a new global order.

In the theoretical language of thermodynamics, a microlevel fluctuation constitutes a spontaneous deviation from a globally defined equilibrium state. Viewed globally – that is, from the perspective of the 'existing order' – the fluctuation appears as a transition from a more probable to a less probable state. However, when viewed globally (i.e., diachronically), or from the perspective of the instability, the fluctuation, which Saussure identifies as a 'dynamic factor' (*CLG*: 131), moves in the direction of a more probable local state. As Saussure puts it, 'an effect is produced, a thing is carried out' (*CLG*: 131). Saussure rightly resists talking in terms of diachronic laws because of the essentially spontaneous nature of such deviations. Diachronic events, Saussure points out, 'always have an accidental and particular character' (*CLG*: 131).

Saussure expresses the tendency of fluctuation to depart locally from the global equilibrium of the system in terms of the competition between innovations in *parole* and the system of already established general types in *langue*. Instability, or local fluctuation in *parole*, is a natural and intrinsic process that competes with the entropy processes defined by the second law of thermodynamics. Thus, local fluctuations in *parole*, which correspond to Saussure's first 'moment' in the appearance of an innovation, are a consequence of stability defined at the synchronic level. Thermodynamically, the system cannot simultaneously satisfy the requirements of local and global stability. If the requirements of global stability are met, it must exhibit microlevel instabilities, or innovations in *parole*, which result in fluctuations. If the system satisfies local stability requirements, it must exhibit global instability. That is, 'evolutionary development', as Saussure calls it, takes place, resulting in transition phases when local instabilities become incorporated into the global organization of the language system.

Thermodynamically, the system tends towards globally stable states whereas, and according to the requirements of statistical mechanics, particular microlevel fluctuations in *parole* tend towards locally stable states, or diachronic effects. Saussure's description of this dialectic between synchronic and diachronic factors, in line with thermodynamic theory, shows how the overall behaviour of a language system is organized by the constant dialectic between global and local stabilities.

Saussure's account of this dialectic represents a break with the Newtonian paradigm in which interactions are dominated by force exchanges. That is, in the Newtonian paradigm, all phenomena are reducible to descriptions of the state of a system and the extrinsic force which acts on it to bring about a change of state. This paradigm has provided the basis for approaching the problem of causality not only in physics, but in all other domains of enquiry in both the natural and the social sciences. Thus, present states plus dynamical laws are the necessary and sufficient conditions for determining the successor state, and so on. The Newtonian paradigm relates a given state to past, present and future states by means of dynamical laws that specify the forces acting on that state. It is this paradigm which informs the model of change adopted by the Neogrammarians. In the Newtonian paradigm, the notion of cause is closely tied to that of force and, hence, of mass. In the nineteenth century, Newton's dynamics were re-stated as conservation principles. His laws of mechanics were shown to be the necessary consequences of systems operating under the conservational invariants of mass, momentum and energy. Notwithstanding these developments, the language of forces remained predominant in this paradigm.

In the thermodynamic–statistical coupling, however, equilibrium states are defined in terms of geometric properties that are created by the dissipation of energy. The dissipative geometries emerge as a result of the constant dialectic between global thermodynamic criteria and locally defined (statistical–mechanical) or fluctuational criteria. A synchronic state of a language system exhibits equilibrium (stability) in the face of small-scale perturbations in the speech practices of *parole*. Crucially, this stability is linked to the absorptive capacity of the system's microlevel processes: that is, to the system's dissipative ability. This is why Saussure observes that 'all innovations in *parole* do not have the same success' (*CLG*: 138). So long as the innovations are confined to just a few individuals there is no need to account for them. Thus, the individual innovations that are not incorporated in the language system do, nevertheless, serve an important dissipative function. That is, they absorb and preserve a reserve flexibility which ensures that the system does not rigidify.

Prigogine and colleagues have called systems whose organizational constraints are dissipated in this way *dissipative structures*. The microlevel practices in *parole* may serve either to promote change or to dissipate and absorb it in order to neutralize it. Saussure's observations suggest that *langue*, as a subclass of social-semiological system, is dissipative in precisely this sense. However, such systems have characteristics that make them more complex than the atomisms and force-dominated interactions of simple, mechanical systems. In both biological and social-semiological systems, the various systemic levels of organization are interrelated by cross-couplings of informational flows and interactions, rather than force-dominated ones, as in the Newtonian paradigm.

11 CONCLUSION

Saussure's perspective on change was that of the system (*langue*). This is the evolutionary perspective of the *system*: the system evolves through processes of linguistic innovation in *parole*. This is the *instance* perspective. In time, these alter the distributional probabilities of the system itself. One of Saussure's great merits, in developing this perspective, was to show that change is not confined to the sound system of a given language. Most centrally, it extends to the grammatical systems of the language. Saussure acknowledges the central role that *parole* plays in this process. He is aware that the system changes in and through its patterns of use by speakers in specific contexts. It is these patterns of use of the system's potential which act back on the system and, in time, change it.

Saussure's re-formulation of the relationship between synchrony and diachrony is a pioneering attempt to answer the crucial question as to how instability leads to the breaking of spatio-temporal symmetry in cultural systems (Prigogine and Stengers 1985: 171). In the nineteenth century, Darwin's theory of biological evolution began to provide a conceptual framework for theorizing evolutionary change in both biological and cultural systems. Darwin showed that spontaneous fluctuations in organic forms can lead to irreversible biological evolution through selection. The 'arrow of time' of the second law of thermodynamics was introduced into scientific conceptions of the natural order. Biological evolution leads to self-organization and increasing complexity (Prigogine and Stengers 1985: 128).

These nineteenth-century developments contrasted with the Newtonian cosmology of an eternal and harmonious natural order, disjoined from the social order. The laws of nature were seen as constant and eternal. Change was reversible. However, the formulation of the thermodynamic and evolutionary perspectives in the physical and life sciences in the nineteenth century brought in a radical change of perspective. There were important precursors of these developments. These extend right back to the ancient world and include figures such as Heraclitus and Aristotle, as distinct from Plato, Democritus and Parmenides.

Saussure's social-semiological theory participates in this epistemological shift. Biological and social evolution presuppose neither a definite set of interacting units nor definite and reversible transformations of these. Synchrony is changed by diachronic process. Innovations in the practices of *parole* may in time come to ramify across many different speakers. In time these may become part of the processes internal to the system. If the new practices get a hold on the system, then they have the possibility of altering its previous mode of functioning and, therefore, of shifting the entire system to a new mode of functioning (Prigogine and Stengers 1985: 190).

If, in Chapters 3 and 4 I have focused on *langue*, rather than *parole*, I have also shown the impossibility of discussing the two concepts separately. Chapters 5 and 6 shift the focus to *parole*. However, the theoretical interdependence of the two concepts in explaining both the system and the instance perspectives on language remains central.

Part III

Langue and *parole*:
re-articulating the links

Chapter 5

Parole and the individual

1 AN ALTERNATIVE TO THE INDIVIDUAL-CENTRED INTERPRETATION OF *PAROLE*

What is the status of the individual in Saussure's theory? How does the individual relate to *langue*? And to *parole*? A number of commentators suggest that, for Saussure, the individual and the social are opposed to each other: that is, these commentators assume the relationship between the two to be a dichotomous one. Holdcroft (1991: 20–1), for example, distinguishes *langue* and *parole* in terms of the following set of contrasts:

Langue	*Parole*
social	individual
essential	contingent
no active individual role	active role
not designed	designed
conventional	not conventional
furnishes a homogeneous subject matter for a branch of social psychology	furnishes a heterogeneous subject matter studied by different disciplines

Parole is the realization of *langue* through the exercise of the individual's language faculty. Saussure's use of the term 'realization' in this sense refers to the *instantiation* of the system of *langue* in acts of *parole*. To some extent, no doubt, the choices made by the editors of *CLG* may favour the dichotomous reading. However, it is in the *Notes* to the second course that Saussure's conception of this relationship emerges with greater clarity (Saussure 1957). It is worth paying careful attention to the following quotation from the *Notes*. Speaking of the 'correspondence' between a vocal sound (*un son vocal*) and a sense (*un sens*) in the sign, Saussure observes:

> This correspondence is borne out at each stage of linguistics, to such an extent that one cannot say what a form is without considering at the same time the sound and the sense.

A, complex acoustico-vocal   complex mental and physiological
unit   unit

But in this case it is the language system [*la langue*] seen in ourselves, if we observe an individual. The domain [*sphère*] of this complex unity must be found in at least two individuals; hence, third complex unit

constituted by a minimum of two individuals.

The passage from the mouth of A to the ear of B, and vice versa, is entirely by means of the language system, which implicates each time the passage through the mind of the speaking subjects. In order to make use of this dually complex unit, at least two individuals are required; to one alone, the language system is of no use at all. The language system is made for communicating with one's fellows. Lastly, it is only by means of social life that the language system receives its consecration. In the language system, there is always a dual aspect which corresponds to it: it is:

social
———
individual

If one considers then the domain in which the language system lives, there will always be the individual language system [*la langue indivi-duelle*] and the social language system [*la langue sociale*]. Forms, grammar only exist socially, but changes come from the individual.

(Saussure 1957: 8–9)

In this passage, Saussure provides us with an alternative to the dichotomous reading of the distinction between *langue* and *parole*. The social and the individual are not opposed to each other. Saussure does not simply speak of two or more individuals, atomistically defined, who happen to come together and interact. Instead, he refers to a 'complex unit' which is not reducible to the individuals who participate in it. The constitutive basis of this 'complex unity' is the language system (*la langue*). In this way, Saussure shows that this 'complex unit' is not based on contingent, situational factors, but on systemic ones. The basic unit of analysis is not the individual speaking subject *per se*, but some higher-order unit. Saussure's description of the kinds of things that might be included is highly schematic. It is suggestive rather than specific about these possibilities. In my view, the higher-order 'complex unit' to which Saussure refers is a way of talking about the structured nature of the social activity types in which individuals jointly participate in the making and negotiating of social meanings (Chapter 3, sections 6–8).

This interpretation seems to be confirmed when Saussure then draws attention to the simultaneously social and individual dimensions of *langue*. This does not mean that Saussure has abandoned the individual. More correctly, I think the above passage reveals an attempt to formulate an alternative to the opposition between the social and the individual. The radical nature of this move cannot be underestimated. Unfortunately, neither the editors of *CLG* nor many subsequent commentators have heeded the theoretical implications of Saussure's proposals. Thus, the distinction between the social and individual dimensions of analysis has been read in terms of the ideologically dominant assumption in social theory that (1) the fundamental unit of analysis is the individual *per se* and (2) the individual is opposed to the social. Saussure attempts to give voice to an alternative theory: both the individual's relationship with the language system and with other individuals is always and necessarily mediated by higher-order units and relations that are not reducible to the individuals who participate in these (Chapter 3, section 8). As I showed in Chapter 3, it is some co-articulated ensemble of these that forms the basis of the global organization of *langue*$_3$ as a social-semiological system.

Further support for my interpretation may be found in Saussure's definition of *parole* in the following page of the *Notes*:

> *Parole* designates the act of the individual in realizing his [language] faculty by means of the social convention, which is the language system [*la langue*]. In *parole*, there is an idea of realization of that which is permitted by social convention.
>
> (Saussure 1957: 10)

Now, Holdcroft (1991: 24) has difficulty in accounting for 'what is left of *langage* when *langue* is ... subtracted from it' in *CLG*. But the real difficulty lies in Holdcroft's assumption that the individual is the pre-eminent unit of analysis. Again, the *Notes* are clearer on this issue, as the passage I have just quoted demonstrates. I shall now discuss this passage.

Saussure makes it very clear in the above passage that the act of realization in *parole* occurs 'by means of the social convention'. The significance of this 'by means of' appears to have eluded both Culler (1976: 30) and Holdcroft (1991). The individual does not *directly* use or access *langue* (Chapter 3, section 8). Acts of *parole* are contextualized in and through the systemic resources of *langue*. In Chapter 3, I argued that Saussure's notions of the 'social mass' and the 'social body' are the typical systems of relations and practices which mediate this link. Saussure's theoretical discourse represents an attempt to break with the individual as the fundamental unit in social analysis.

Generally speaking, this last point has been seriously misunderstood. Two consequences follow from this. One is the dichotomous reading of the distinction between *langue* and *parole* that I discussed above. The other is the criticism that Saussure failed to develop a linguistics of *parole* which would complement his privileging of the 'internal' linguistics of *langue*. Those who level this criticism at Saussure have, in my view, missed the more essential point about *parole*. I shall discuss this shortly. In projecting the opposition of the individual and the social onto the Saussurean discourse, they have failed to heed Saussure's attempt to give voice to an alternative way of theorizing this relation. Holdcroft is a case in point:

> Since *parole* is on this account such a rag-bag, corresponding to no natural category, the description of it as heterogeneous is, as I said, hardly surprising. However, the proper response to this is surely that what is called for is not concentration on the allegedly well-defined object *langue* to the exclusion of everything else, but an attempt to distinguish well-defined areas within this heterogeneous domain.
>
> (Holdcroft 1991: 32)

In section 2 below, I shall argue that both *langue* and *parole* do represent such an attempt to distinguish well-defined areas within the heterogeneous domain of *langage*. Holdcroft's critique rests on the assumption that *parole* designates some notion of individual-centred linguistic production, whether this is sentence-, text- or discourse-based. Consequently, he argues that Saussure fails to deal with the 'heterogeneity' and the variability which such a notion entails. In turn, this leads to the assumption that a homogeneous, coercively social *langue* is opposed to a heterogeneous, individual-centred *parole*. Thus, Saussure, according to Holdcroft, fails to deal with language in its contexts-of-use. Saussure does not assume a 'completely homogeneous speech-community' after the fashion of Chomsky (1965: 3) (see below).

Now, it is certainly true that Saussure does not explicitly theorize this issue. However, the fact that Saussure's theory can do so is not disputed in the present study. At this stage, I should like to examine the assumption made by Holdcroft and others that *langue* is homogeneous and invariable, whereas *parole* is heterogeneous and variable. In this reading, individual-centred linguistic productions are necessarily heterogeneous. However, this reading fails to account for a number of important aspects of Saussure's position.

The first of these relates to the notion of a 'complex unit' discussed above. This shows that linguistic productions are both jointly produced and socially constrained by higher-order systemic factors. This does not, in principle, exclude heterogeneity and variation; rather, these, too, are both socially constrained and motivated. *Parole* does not equate with the individual in any simple way; rather, *parole* refers to specific linguistic productions in a given time and place. The problem Saussure addresses is not how the linguist accounts for specific linguistic productions *per se*; rather, he is concerned with the ways in which a given linguistic production is related to the typical higher-order formations in *langue* in and through which it obtains its meaning (Chapter 3, sections 6–8).

In opposing a purportedly 'homogeneous' *langue* to a 'heterogeneous' *parole*, Holdcroft fails to account for the following aspects of the Saussurean discourse. First, *langue* is not monolithic and homogeneous; it is, on the contrary, comprised of internal subsystems (dialects, subdialects and so on). Saussure's term for this is *idiosynchronic* (Chapter 4, section 4). That is, the system of potential meanings is differentially distributed over the various subsystems of the language. Second, *langue* does not cause or determine instances of *parole*; rather, it is a systemic resource which social agents draw on in the joint social construction of linguistic, and other semiotic, activities. Third, specific linguistic productions are never random and contingent; rather, they are socially organized and structured in determinate ways. All three of these points are dealt with in Saussure's *langue*$_3$, which I discussed in Chapter 3.

Holdcroft is wrong, in my view, to project an individual-centred view of linguistic production onto the notion of *parole*. This assumes that an unproblematic 'individual' is the source and ground of all social phenomena. In turn, the social is dichotomously opposed to the individual. Saussure, on the other hand, makes it clear that *both* the social and the individual belong to *langue*. However, the moment that the social and the individual dimensions are seen as opposed to each other, this important point eludes the analyst. Consequently, the individual is taken to be the fundamental unit of analysis. Society, in this view, is an epiphenomenon which results from the individual's use of the system to interact with others. That is, society is no more than a mere aggregrate of the individuals who comprise it. The individual is taken to be more real because he or she is grounded in the materiality of the individual *qua* biological organism. In this way, the socially constituted positions which the individual may occupy in jointly constructed social activities and relations is conflated with the individual as biological organism (Lemke 1988: 2).

2 SOCIAL AND NON-SOCIAL DIMENSIONS OF THE INDIVIDUAL

Once it is understood that Saussure does not oppose the social to the individual, it then becomes easier to distinguish the social and the non-social dimensions of the individual, the particular place these are assigned in his overall conceptual framework and the interrelations between these. I shall now endeavour to reconstruct the relationship among these various components. These may be summarized as follows:

1   *Langue* is a social-semiological system of great complexity and diversity. It provides the members of a given community with the meaning-making resources for interacting with each other in socially determinate ways.

2   The 'social body' deploys these resources in regular and typical patterns of linguistic and other social-semiological actions in a given community. A community, so defined, is not comprised of individuals *per se*. Instead, it is a system of higher-order 'complex units' of various kinds. In Saussure's description, these are minimally defined signifying acts, or patterns of interaction. They always involve at least two individuals. They suggest, in an admittedly undeveloped way, the *typical* patterns of jointly constructed social action – the social activity types, the discourse genres and so on – of some community (section 1).

3   The individual's language faculty (*la faculté du langage*) is, dually, social and biological. It is social in so far as it designates the individual's potential to interact with others who are linked by the same language system. However, this potential is vacuous, as Saussure points out (1957: 9), if the individual is isolated from the social. The individual's language faculty is also *biological* in the sense that the individual is endowed with neuroanatomical and neurophysiological capabilities (e.g., the brain, the speech organs and so on) which predispose him or her to activate this potential in interaction with others.

4   *Parole* designates particular occasions of language-in-use. These are uttered – Saussure's term is 'externalized' or 'executed' – by particular individuals in particular times and places. However, this does not reduce to an individual-centred model of linguistic production. Execution is not the same as production. The former is individual; the latter is social. That which is 'realized' (instantiated) in *parole* can only occur, as Saussure points out, 'by means of the social convention' of *langue* (see above).

It is quite misleading to claim, as does Holdcroft, that *parole* is no more than a 'rag-bag' of heterogeneous elements or leftovers from the 'individual' side of linguistic execution, which the linguist is obliged to discard. Saussure (*CLG*: 37) makes it very clear that *langue* and *parole* are interdependent theoretical concepts: it is only through observing acts of *parole* that the system can be analytically re-constructed. Holdcroft's argument rests on the presumed opposition between the commonsense notion of a unique biographical individual and a social system which remains external to the individual, so defined. This is not Saussure's position. The relevant question is not whether purportedly individual-centred acts of *parole* are opposed to the social or not. Rather, it is how to relate particular acts of *parole*, which are 'executed' by specific biographical individuals in some concrete historical time and place, to the regular and typical systems of relations and practices in *langue₃*.

Saussure, as I pointed out above, draws attention to the dually social and individual nature of *langue*. In this way, two distinct perspectives on the individual emerge in Saussure's conceptual framework. This distinction is less evident in *CLG*. It emerges with greater clarity in Engler's critical edition (1967), in Godel's *Sources manuscrites* (1957) and the *Notes* (Saussure 1957). I shall now explain what I believe the basis of this distinction is. This has important implications for social-semiological theory.

From the point of view of *langue*, the individual is a social type, rather than a unique biographical individual. In this perspective, the analyst's interest lies in establishing what is common to a particular participant role or category of speaking subject across its many different occasion-specific performances by different historical–biographical individuals. For example, what common features characterize the socially defined participant roles of 'teacher' and 'student' in classroom interaction, or of 'mother' and 'child' in, say, white middle-class Anglo-Saxon culture, in spite of many individual differences from one performance to another, and in one individual embodiment of the social type to another? A *langue*-based theory of the individual looks for features which are *criterial* for the performance of the given participant role, defined as a social type (Lemke 1988: 8).

What, then, does a *parole*-based perspective on the individual look like? This perspective is concerned with those features which are *non-criterial* for the definition of the individual as a social type. The focus is on specific features of particular acts of *parole*, or linguistic tokens (instantiations), which are performed – or 'executed', to use Saussure's term – by specific biographical individuals on particular occasions. The biographical individual is the material embodiment of the social type. He or she may enact or perform the role in ways which are non-criterial for the definition of the social type, but which are, however, criterial for the identification of that particular individual *qua* historical–biographical individual.

3 THE THEORETICAL SCOPE OF *PAROLE*

Langue and *parole* are both analytical constructs. They are analytical approximations of different facets of the same overall phenomenon. It is simply not correct to claim that *langue* is a well-defined theoretical object, whereas *parole* fails to correspond to any 'natural category' (cf. Holdcroft 1991: 32). *Parole* is not a 'natural category'. It does not reduce to the observable 'raw data', empirically defined, which the linguist gathers and analyses in order to establish the language system (Chapter 2, section 8). This is not the relationship which Saussure proposes between the two terms. Saussure's point is that both *langue* and *parole* are the result of a metatheoretical decision to split the phenomenon of language, in all of its heterogeneity

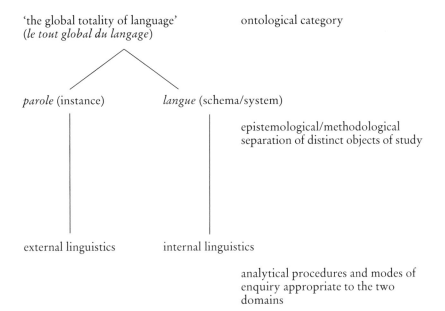

Figure 5.1 Co-articulated theoretical relations between *langue* and *parole* in relation to *langage*

and diversity, into two principal domains of enquiry. Therefore, it is an error to project onto Saussure's methodological separation of these two domains of enquiry an ontological distinction between, say, society and individual, or between 'homogeneous' and 'heterogeneous'. Neither *langue* nor *parole* is ontologically given as an *a priori* category; rather, they are analytically derived, *a posteriori*, by the linguist. That is, the linguist constructs a meaningful set of theoretical categories for talking about and imposing order on what Saussure (*CLG*: 38) refers to as 'the global totality of language [which] is unknowable, because it is not homogeneous, whereas the proposed distinction [between *langue* and *parole*] and the subordination [of *parole* to *langue*] explain everything'. Saussure's argument may be schematized as in Figure 5.1.

Langue, I have argued, focuses on what is common to or shared by many different material instantiations of the same semiotic type. It is also concerned with specifying the overall systemic parameters, or constraints, in relation to which both stability and change are defined. *Parole*, by contrast, is concerned with what is unique, non-criterial and specific to the (always social) performances of embodied biographical individuals. Saussure suggests a number of ways in which a linguistics of *parole* may be constructed. These are as follows:

1   In distinguishing 'what is social from what is individual' (*CLG*: 30), Saussure alludes to the distinction I have already referred to between the individual as abstract social type and the embodied biographical individual's participation in a given act of *parole*.

2   Saussure also makes a second distinction between 'what is essential and what is accessory and more or less accidental' (*CLG*: 30). This distinction corresponds to the one I have already made between those features which are criterial for the definition of a given social type, independently of any given semiotic performance, and those features which are non-criterial for the definition of the type.

3   *Parole* is the individual's realization or manifestation (instantiation) of linguistic tokens by means of his or her language faculty *in and through* the social conventions of *langue*.

4   *Parole* is defined in teleological terms as 'an individual act of will and intelligence' (*CLG*: 30). It is the means whereby 'the speaking subject uses the code of language to express his personal thoughts' (*CLG*: 31). In this way, Saussure is careful to locate means–end or teleological explanations of language use in *parole*, rather than in *langue*. The intentions, goals and purposes of individual social agents are excluded from the explanation of the language system. This may echo Durkheim's claim that the sheer diversity of human wills would mitigate the possibility of a science of society which is based on collective structures and relations. However, Saussure's location of specifically teleological explanations in *parole* is also important in another way. He opposes his theory of *langue* as a system of contextualizing relations to those non-semiotic and unifunctional conceptions of context which reduce social-semiological structures and relations to some notion of an individual-centred and largely asocial cognitive competence (Silverstein 1992: 57). Saussure does not develop all of the implications of this argument; however, the main thrust of his argument goes in this direction. *Langue* is a system of contextualizing relations (Chapter 7, section 2). Acts of *parole* are always contextualized in and through the systems of contextualizing relations in *langue*. This contrasts markedly with the overwhelming tendency in recent decades towards individual-centred interpretations of linguistic performance. In this way, speech act theory, linguistic pragmatics, cognitive science and individual-centred conceptions of discourse analysis have all tended to define context in largely psychological and teleological, rather than in systemic and social-semiological, terms.

5   *Parole* is the domain of 'freedom of combination' (*CLG*: 38). Historically unique social–biographical individuals necessarily draw upon a more or less stable system of social-semiological types whenever they innovate some novel variant of the system of types. These innovations are not predictable in terms of the regular patterns of the already

available types (Chapter 4, section 9).

6   *Parole* also designates the psychophysical and biological processes which are involved in the individual's execution and reception of speech sounds (*CLG*: 36). By extension, this may also include the execution and reception of visual signs (e.g., writing, sign language). Saussure refers to these as 'the psycho-physical mechanisms which allow [the speaking subject] to externalize these combinations' (*CLG*: 31). Saussure excludes these mechanisms from the social-semiological domain of *langue* because they belong to a level of explanation which pertains to the neuroanatomical capabilities of the individual *qua* biological organism. Saussure acknowledges the biological basis of the language faculty when he, *contra* Whitney, refers to both the natural (not social) basis of the organs of speech, as well as to Paul Broca's 'discovery of the localization of the faculty of speech in the third frontal convolution of the left hemisphere of the brain' (*CLG*: 26). The localization of the language faculty in a specific part of the brain is nowadays taken less seriously in the neurosciences (Thibault, forthcoming). This does not alter the more fundamental point that Saussure is making. That is, the biological individual who is endowed with specific neuroanatomical capabilities and the historical–biographical individual who participates in acts of *parole* are discontinuous with respect to each other. They belong to different, though interrelated, ontological domains of theoretical discourse and the one cannot be reduced to the other.

7   *Langue* is materially embodied in acts of *parole*. That is, *langue* is distributed over the 'ensemble of individuals' who constitute a particular social group. Saussure expresses this point as follows: '[*Langue*] is a treasure which is deposited through the practices of *parole* in the subjects belonging to the same community, [it is] a grammatical system which exists virtually in each brain, or more exactly in the brains of an ensemble of individuals; for the language system [*langue*] is not complete in anyone, it only exists perfectly in the mass' (*CLG*: 30).

In saying that *langue* has an individual dimension, this does not mean that it reduces to the individual *per se*. This would amount to saying that *langue* and *parole* are indistinguishable. The perspective which Saussure adopts here is not that of the unique biographical individual, but of the individual as social type. Saussure shifts the emphasis from the individual to the social 'ensemble of individuals' in order to capture this point (Chapter 3, section 8). If *langue* were simply distributed among unique historical–biographical individuals, then social and individual facts would not be different in kind. Saussure avoids the implications of such a hypothesis. It is one thing to claim that a given speech community is a structured system of social relations, positions and practices over which a shared *langue* is distributed; it is quite another to say that it is a collection of individuals *per se* who have a common grammatical system in their brains. Saussure makes it clear that he does not intend this second, reductionist hypothesis when he emphasizes that it is the structure of the group which is the basis for talking about the language system. *Langue*, he argues, is not complete in any individual and cannot, therefore, be theorized on the basis of the individual *per se*. For this reason, *langue* and *parole* cannot be equated with Chomsky's (1965: 3–4) individual-centred distinction between an asocial linguistic competence and performance.

Saussure distinguishes between the 'actual' and 'virtual' dimensions of *langue*. *Langue* is 'actual' when it is instantiated in and through the practices of *parole*. The former is always immanent in the latter. *Langue* also has a 'virtual' dimension. From the point of view of the language system, the social-semiological conventions of *langue* are not actually deployed by any given individual all the time. However, this does not mean that *langue* ceases to exist whenever any given individual ceases to use it. The point is that the social-semiological conventions and resources of *langue* are distributed across some socially defined 'ensemble of individuals', irrespective of whether a given individual in that 'ensemble' uses them or not at any given moment. These conventions and resources endure in time precisely because they are distributed not across individuals *per se*, but across some transindividual 'ensemble of individuals'. In this sense, *langue* is *virtual* because it exists as a set of capacities, dispositions and expectations which are only discontinuously realized by any given individual when he or she engages in jointly constructed acts of *parole*. The ontological reality of *langue* as systemic resource must be understood in this sense.

Saussure provides us with a series of interrelated theoretical constructs, rather than a simple dichotomy. First, there is a system (*langue*) of social-semiological types and the relationships among these. Second, there is a theoretical discourse which relates this system to its instantiations in what Saussure calls 'the practices of *parole*'. That is, acts of *parole* are always mediated by the system of contextualizing relations in *langue* (see above). Third, the notion of an 'ensemble of individuals' does not refer to a mere aggregate of individuals; rather, this 'ensemble' is based on the structured relations among the 'practices of *parole*' in which individuals participate, rather than the mere sum of the individuals who comprise the social ensemble. *Langue* exists virtually in the brains of individuals seen as social types, rather than as unique biographical individuals.

4 *PAROLE* AND DISCOURSE: AN IMPORTANT DISTINCTION

Parole does not refer to actual speech *per se*. Saussure refers to actual speech with quite another term, that is, *discourse* (*discours*) (*CLG*: 148; 170). Speaking of the analytical problems the linguist encounters in delimiting units in the spoken chain, Saussure observes:

Doubtless, speaking subjects do not know about these difficulties; everything which is significant to some degree appears to them as a concrete element, and they distinguish it without fail in discourse [*le discours*]. But it is one thing to be aware of this rapid and subtle play of units, and another to account for them in a methodical analysis.

(*CLG*: 148)

Discourse refers to actual speech from the point of view of the users of the language. *Parole*, on the other hand, is a theoretical construct of the linguist. It is the re-constructed object on which the linguist performs a 'methodical analysis'. How are *parole* and discourse distinguished in Saussure's framework? Discourse is the real-time and frequently imperceptible unfolding of 'concrete elements' from the point of view of the speakers and listeners who are engaged in conversation together. Both *langue* and *parole* are theoretical projections onto this concrete and lived reality: that is, they are two different perspectives from the point of view of the theorist, rather than that of the language user. Having distinguished between syntagmatic and associative relations in *langue*, Saussure introduces a second perspective, as follows:

in discourse [*discours*], words contract among themselves, in virtue of their enchainment, relationships founded on the linear character of the language system [*le caractère linéaire de la langue*], which rules out the possibility of pronouncing two elements at the same time. This arranges them one after the other on the chain of speech [*la chaîne de la parole*].

(*CLG*: 170)

This passage repays very careful consideration. In it Saussure explains the theoretical relations among three clearly distinguished terms. These are (1) discourse (*le discours*); (2) the linear character of *langue* (*le caractère linéaire de la langue*); and (3) the chain of *parole* (*la chaîne de la parole*). Saussure points out that the concrete 'enchaining' of words in discourse is based on the linear character of *langue*, not *parole*. In other words, linearity is not the exclusive province of either discourse or *parole*. I take this to mean that the principle of the linearity of the signifier (*CLG*: 103) is an intrinsic design feature of the language system itself. The typical syntagmatic patterns in *langue* specify the principles of linear combination from the system point of view (Chapter 11, sections 1–2). In this sense, it is a *virtual* and non-temporal principle of linear construction. When this principle works on the concrete enchaining of elements in discourse, it gives rise to a theoretical model of the actual linear and temporal character of real-time discourse. This model is what Saussure intends by his term *parole*. The 'chain of *parole*' is a method for analytically re-constructing the syntagmatic principles of combination which operate on concrete discursive events. These principles are not normally fully available to the conscious awareness of the participants in real-time discursive events. *Parole* is the analytical principle whereby the principles of syntagmatic combination which are projected from *langue*, and which operate on the real-time unfolding of discourse, are, analytically speaking, made explicit. It is in this sense that value is assigned to units on the syntagmatic dimension of contextualization. The syntagm specifies the respective values of the terms which are contrasted with each other by virtue of their being contextualized by a given combination, or enchainment, of units which is recognized or permitted by the *langue*-based system of types.

To sum up: Saussure's term *discourse* indicates the real-time 'enchainment' of concrete elements. It is the interaction time of the participants who take part in some discursive event. This should not be confused with *parole*. *Parole* is an analytical construct. It represents the projection onto discourse of the analytical criteria of linearity and temporality. The temporal linearity of *parole*, in turn, constitutes the basis of the constructional and non-temporal linearity of syntagmatic relations (as types) in *langue*. This constructional principle is that of the functional values which are assigned to the terms that are related to each other on the syntagmatic dimension of contextualization (*CLG*: 170–1; see above). Syntagmatic values are 'effective' from the point of view of *langue* because they occur outside of space–time. In *parole*, the syntagmatic values which are projected onto a given combination of elements may be said to have been 'effected'. The relations among the three terms *discourse*, *parole* and *langue* are presented in Figure 5.2.

5 *PAROLE* IS THE 'SEED' OF CHANGE IN THE LANGUAGE SYSTEM

The starting point for change in the language system, Saussure argues, is in the speech practices of *parole* (Chapter 4, section 9). *Langue* does not change of its own accord. In other words, change is not instigated by the system of social-semiological types. Logically, it cannot be, for the typical systems of social-semiological relations and practices are analytical abstractions. These have no concrete 'effectivity'. They rightly belong to *langue*, not to *parole*.

Is there a contradiction in Saussure's claim that system change starts in *parole*? The answer to this question must be a very definite 'no'. Social types do not and cannot bring about change on account of their analytical status as theoretical abstractions. Saussure locates the 'seed' of change in *parole* because it is only through the speech practices of specific, historical–biographical individuals that innovations in language use occur. A social type is an analytical abstraction in the sense that it is derived by comparing the features which many specific enactments are said to have in common according to some specifiable criterion. A social type corresponds to what Saussure calls 'a fact of the language system' (*un fait de langue*). Such facts designate an abstract class of social-semiological relations and practices which have become institutionalized in the social life of some community. But the practices of individuals are not simply defined, in a top-down

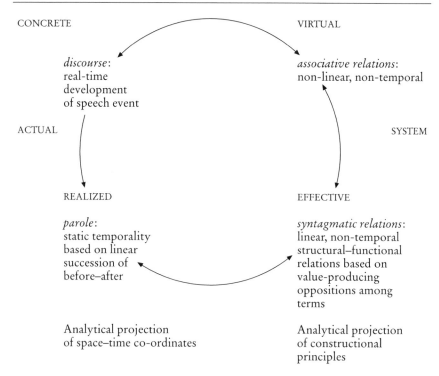

CONCRETE   VIRTUAL

discourse: *associative relations*:
real-time   non-linear, non-temporal
development
of speech event

ACTUAL   SYSTEM

REALIZED   EFFECTIVE

parole: *syntagmatic relations*:
static temporality   linear, non-temporal
based on linear   structural–functional
succession of   relations based on
before–after   value-producing
                                      oppositions among
                                      terms

Analytical projection   Analytical projection
of space–time co-ordinates   of constructional
                                      principles

Figure 5.2 Analytical relations among discourse, *parole* and *langue*

fashion, by an abstract class or type. In other words, individuals do not simply replicate in a mechanical way the abstract institutionalized fact. That they *may* do, on occasions, is not an issue here. The point is that individuals are historically unique intersections of specific social practices.

The individual, so defined, in the discourse of socio-evolution is the ontological equivalent of the gene in the discourse of bio-evolution. To avoid misunderstanding on this point, I should point out straightaway that the suggestion that the former can be equated with the latter, as in some contemporary versions of socio-biology, is a total nonsense. Saussure's evolutionary model of *langue* scrupulously avoids this reductionism. For Saussure, language change 'is launched in the first instance by a certain number of individuals before entering into usage' (*CLG*: 138). *Parole* is, then, what is specific to the individual's speech practices on historically unique occasions of discourse. In Saussure's terms, this is what 'a fact of speech' (*un fait de parole*) means. However, this should not be understood in an individualistic sense. The specific is not opposed to the typical; rather, the former *instantiates* the latter.

Innovation, in Saussure's view, is always initiated by individuals because only individuals can re-articulate the typical patterns in novel ways. Saussure also points out that there is always some group basis to the processes of innovation. Innovation requires 'a certain number of individuals': that is, innovation, if it is to become consolidated, cannot remain the exclusive province of a single individual. Only if the innovation spreads among a sufficiently large number of individuals can it enter into the system of types as a new social-semiological category. In this way, the innovation, if successful, will, in time, become a conventional linguistic, or other social-semiological, practice in some community, or in some subgroup of that community.

Saussure does not, as I pointed out above, locate change in the individual *per se*. The lone individual can, of course, innovate in ways that do not conform to the social type. But unless that innovation is taken up by others in their collective speech practices, it will not become 'socialized' by at least some subgroup in a given community. Saussure recognizes that individuals belong to social groups – to some internally structured 'ensemble of individuals'. They do not exist as isolated social atoms. Such an 'ensemble' may consist of a very small number of individuals, or a very large number. The point is that the members of an ensemble are internally related to each other, or become so, through the taking up of an innovative speech practice which, in time, may come to define the 'ensemble' itself as a recognizeable social institution.

One illustration of Saussure's basic argument is his comparison of the modern and Old German forms of the past tense. In the older form of the language, there was a stable systemic opposition between *ich was* ('I was') and *wir waren* ('we were'). In evolutionary parlance, there is a 'lineage' relationship between these two successor states of the system. Given this, Saussure poses the further question as to which factors 'influenced' or induced a certain number of individuals, in the first instance, to adapt their language practices to the environment so as to select the new form. The explanation he gives is based on the creation of *war* by analogy with *waren*. Thus, *waren* in the old system constitutes a systemic environment in which the potential analogy with the not-yet-existent form *war* already exists.

This lineage relationship is represented in Figure 5.3. The two successor

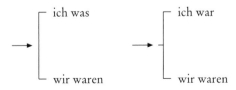

Figure 5.3 Lineage relationship between Old and modern German forms of the past tense

states shown in this figure represent two very tiny slices of two different *états de langue*. Ontologically speaking, it is not clear what status Saussure gives to this. Do the two 'states' refer to a gradual process of continual change whereby the initially subcriterial innovation *ich war* is, in time, accepted as criterial? Or, is there a sudden quantum leap such that the prior *état de langue* is re-contextualized by the successor state? Ontologically, *langue* has a dual status in Saussure's theory. It exists virtually in the brains of the individuals whose overlapping characteristics link them together as members of some larger-scale social ensemble. It is also a temporally enduring language system (*CLG*: 142). This dual status of *langue* means: (1) it is a virtual social-semiological resource; this further entails that these resources are structurally isomorphic for the individuals in a given speech community (Harré 1979: 372); and (2) it is an actual, transindividual social-semiological system. The idealized *état de langue* resembles Sartre's notion of 'the static temporal' (1969: 130). In the static temporal, as Sartre explains, the 'notion of before and after can be considered in a strictly ordinal arrangement independent of change proper'. It is time defined as 'a fixed order for a determined multiplicity' (*ibid.*). *Langue*, from this point of view, is a form of spatial contiguity in time: 'In practice, a state of the language system [*un état de langue*] is not a point, but a temporal space' (*CLG*: 142).

In this passage, Saussure clearly draws attention to the temporal dimension of *langue*. This is the diachronic perspective discussed in Chapter 4. Saussure recognizes that *langue*, too, changes over time. But what distinguishes *langue* from *parole* here is the time-scale which is involved. *Parole*, I have argued, is an analytical re-construction of the actual speech practices which individuals engage in. It refers to the real-time instantiation of *langue* in discourse. In showing that *parole* is the 'seed' of change in *langue*, Saussure achieves two major theoretical insights. First, he demonstrates the irreducibility of *parole* to *langue*: that is, the real-time unfolding of some discourse event does not simply recapitulate the very different time-scale that is involved in evolutionary change in *langue*.

By the same token – and this is a crucial point – a given discourse event always represents the point of contact between the system and its material and social environments. Thus, innovation in *parole* may take root or not in a community. This depends on whether or not the innovation is selected by a sufficiently large number of socially related individuals on the basis of its adaptiveness to the social-semiological and material environments in which it arises.

Second, and consequent upon the first point, *langue* and *parole* do not designate two distinct phenomena. As far as Saussure is concerned, there is a single overall phenomenon, 'the global totality of language' (section 3). Both *langue* and *parole* are complementary analytical perspectives on this one overall phenomenon. It is the complementarity of the two viewpoints which is important. It is simply wrong to suggest, as Holdcroft does (1991:

31–2), that *parole* is ill defined and poorly delimited. *Parole* is not 'the facts that are left when those belonging to *langue* are substracted from those belonging to *langage*' (Holdcroft 1991: 32). Saussure shows, on the contrary, that *langue* and *parole* represent two necessary and complementary perspectives on a single overall phenomenon. The question of change serves to underscore the deeper unity which underlies Saussure's distinction.

Langue represents the system perspective; *parole*, on the other hand, represents the instance perspective. For this reason, Saussure includes in *parole* a range of material phenomena such as phonation or articulation, the physiology of the speech organs and so on. Such phenomena have no place in an abstract *langue*-based system of social-semiological types. Nevertheless, they always play a very real and constitutive part in any discourse event which is enacted by some historically unique social–biographical individual. They are part of the material environment in and through which the language system participates in exchanges of matter, energy and information with its environments, including the material bodies of the participants in discursive interaction (Thibault, forthcoming).

Both *langue* and *parole* are necessary perspectives for explaining language change. Change in *langue* is defined as a chronological succession of events (*CLG*: 202). Events refer to different, successive developments in the overall temporal system of social types. This exemplifies the lineage principle in socio-evolution. Each successive development represents a particular state in the evolution of a lineage. The lineage consists of a succession of social-semiological types as the system evolves in time. To form a lineage, there must be (1) some criterion of causal relations among the successive members of the lineage; and (2) some criterion of structural continuity such that the members of the lineage are similar to each other according to some functionally defined principle of co-classification (Harré 1979: 370). Saussure's discussion of phonetic change is a good case in point:

> phonetic phenomena, far from being always absolute, are more often tied to determinate conditions: in other words, it is not the phonological type which changes, but the phoneme as it [actually] appears in certain conditions which surround it, stress, etc.
>
> (*CLG*: 199)

Saussure raises the question of lineage just a few pages later (*CLG*: 202; quoted above). From the perspective of *langue*, change is manifested retroactively as a chronological succession of changing linguistic states. A given lineage is indicated by the successive mutations in specific social types. At any given state, innovative practices in *parole* may select certain features (phonic terms) of the sound in question, now seen as a material instance. Such features, which were previously sub- or non-criterial for the definition of the prevailing sound type, may become criterial for the new type which results. That is, the innovative practices in *parole* selectively adapt such features in relation to specific conditions in the material and/or social-semiological environment(s) of the sound in question. The phonological type *qua* type does not, and cannot, change in and of itself. The type as such has schematic, not specific, content only. The point is that changing speech practices in *parole* create the conditions whereby some previously non-salient material difference in, for example, the articulation of the sound becomes relevant to the definition of the type, and it does so in ways which alter the type and its functional value in the system.

6 SAUSSURE'S ANTI-REDUCTIONIST THESIS

The distinction between *langue* and *parole*, and the ontological hiatus between society and individual which this distinction presupposes, serve to avoid any kind of unilinear reduction of the one to the other. In making this distinction, Saussure avoids a number of reductionisms. These are as follows:

1   The teleonomic, or dynamic, open, adaptive and goal-seeking character of *langue* is not reduced to the teleology of individual psychological states (goals, intentions and purposes) in *parole*.
2   The social-semiological order is not reduced to the biological processes of the individual organism.
3   Systemic change in *langue* is not reduced to individual innovation in *parole*.
4   The social individual as type is not reduced to the unique historical–biographical individual.

In this chapter I have sought to clarify the individual and social dimensions of both *langue* and *parole*, and their interrelations. With these considerations in mind, I shall examine in the next chapter the place of the individual in the speech circuit.

Chapter 6

The speech circuit

Cross-coupling the individual with the system

1 THE SPEECH CIRCUIT AND THE CODE MODEL OF COMMUNICATION

The previous chapter opened with a number of questions concerning the status of the individual in Saussure's theory. These questions remain central in the present chapter. In this chapter, I shall propose a reading of Saussure's notion of the speech circuit (*le circuit de la parole*) which differs in significant ways from the standard reading. Typically, Saussure's model has been assimilated to the code model of communication. In my view, Saussure's conception does not correspond to this model. Before seeing why, I shall examine the code model of communication with reference to Roy Harris' (1987) discussion of the speech circuit and the specific characterization of the code model which Sperber and Wilson (1986), incorrectly, in my view, ascribe to Saussure.

The notion of code may be defined as the shared rules of interpretation which enable a Sender (S) and Receiver (R) successfully to encode and decode messages which are transmitted from S to R (Thibault, in press b). In this way, thoughts, ideas, etc. are said to be 'communicated' in the process of transmission. In my reading of Saussure, the language system is not a code in this sense; rather, it is a meaning-making resource (Chapter 3). Meanings, in this second view, are *not* 'transmitted' and, hence, 'communicated' by S to R; rather, they are jointly made or constructed by the ways in which interactants co-deploy the available social-semiological resources on a given social occasion of discourse. This is a significant difference. A central thesis of this book is that Saussure's theory belongs to the second view. However, it is the notion of code which is at issue here.

According to proponents of the code view, communication may be modelled as follows: the Sender of a message has an idea, thought or piece of information in his or her mind. S wishes to transmit this to someone. S encodes this in a suitable medium of expression, as a message. S transmits the message to the Receiver. R perceives the message and seeks to extract (decode) S's thought from the message. R does this by making an intelligent guess as to S's thoughts or intentions. In so far as R guesses correctly, R has decoded the message which S transmitted. S and R have successfully communicated.

The salient features of this model are that there are two 'minds', respectively housed in S and R, which are separate from each other. The two minds 'think' thoughts. The material means of expression is the medium in which S's thoughts are encoded for transmission to R. The medium, then, exercises no shaping influence on the 'thoughts' so transmitted. The medium of expression is a neutral vehicle for packaging and conveying the non-semiotic thoughts of S. For the communication to succeed, S and R must share a common code. R applies the code to the message so as to make correct interpretations concerning the thoughts which S wishes to communicate.

This model was influential in the development of semiotics in the 1960s and 1970s. It derives from the first generation of research in information theory (Shannon and Weaver 1949) and cybernetics (Ashby 1956). The code is a context-free set of rules for the encoding, transmission and decoding of information. The theory sought to define information transmission in quantitative and statistical terms, using the closed system and mechanistic cybernetic models of the time.

Thus, Sperber and Wilson claim that Saussure's semiological approach is 'a generalisation of the code model of communication to all forms of communication' (1986: 6–7). I should point out that Sperber and Wilson are critics of the code model. Nevertheless, I consider their characterization of Saussure's 'semiological approach' as an example of the code model to be incorrect. In a similar vein, Roy Harris argues that Saussure's model of the speech circuit 'takes over' the following premises from John Locke's translation theory of understanding:

> The term 'translation theory' refers to the fact that, according to the theory in question, when language is the vehicle of communication understanding requires a double process of 'translation': a speaker's thoughts are first translated into sounds, and then the sounds uttered are translated back again into thoughts by the hearer. This is clearly the basic idea behind Saussure's account of what happens when A and B engage in discourse. A and B are each responsible for the translation required in their respective sections of the circuit. A cannot translate on behalf of B, nor B on behalf of A: this is the essence of *la parole*. It is conceived by Saussure as an individual enterprise, as distinct from the social or collective enterprise which constitutes *la langue*. If for any reason either A or B fails in this individual responsibility, or the process of double translation is otherwise prevented, the speech circuit is broken and the speech act abortive.
>
> (Harris 1987: 205)

The connection which Harris makes with Locke in the paragraph preceding the one quoted above further implies that Saussure's notion of 'association' relates to the psychological theory which was developed by British empiricists such as John Locke, George Berkeley, David Hume and David Hartley in the eighteenth century, and James Mill in the nineteenth century. The basic assumption of the empiricists is that knowledge is formed by the association of ideas with elementary sensory elements in the external world which passively register on the mind of the individual. This is the basis, for instance, of Locke's theory of phenomenal elementarism.

Sperber and Wilson reach a very similar conclusion in their discussion of the code model:

> A *code* ... is a system which pairs messages with signals, enabling two information-processing devices (organisms or machines) to communicate. A *message* is a representation internal to the communicating devices. A *signal* is a modification of the external environment which can be produced by one device and recognised by the other. A simple code, such as the Morse code, may consist of a straightforward list of message–signal pairs. A more complex code, such as English, may consist of a system of symbols and rules generating such pairs.
>
> (Sperber and Wilson 1986: 3–4)

Proponents of the code model assume that communication is describable in terms of a mechanistic model of causation. That is, communication comprises a number of discrete stages, viz. thoughts in the mind of the speaker, thought transmission and thought reception by the listener. Each stage causes or 'triggers' the succeeding stage. In other words, it is a logic of unilinear or efficient causality: the cause precedes the effect. Acoustic signals function as immediate stimuli that bring about behavioural responses in the listener.

2 RE-THINKING THE SPEECH CIRCUIT: AN ALTERNATIVE TO THE CODE MODEL

Saussure's conception of the speech circuit differs significantly from explanations in modern behavioural and cognitive psychology in several important ways. Saussure, in spite of widespread belief to the contrary, does not propose a conduit model of the 'thoughts', 'concepts', 'ideas' and so on which are 'transmitted' from a sender to a receiver whenever these engage in linguistic communication. He is entirely explicit on this point (see quotation below). Saussure does not have a theory of 'communication' in the way that Harris, for example, defines this term. Saussure does not say that a speaker encodes his or her thoughts in some suitable medium or channel and then 'communicates' or transmits these to the listener. Nor does Saussure say that the listener, on receiving the message so conveyed, first perceives an auditory signal and then proceeds to decode this in order to retrieve the message which

the speaker had encoded in this signal. Here is the first part of Saussure's
description of the speech circuit:

> In order to find in the whole of language [*langage*] the domain which
> corresponds to the language system [*langue*], it is necessary to place
> before one the individual act which allows the speech circuit [*le circuit de
> la parole*] to be reconstituted. This act supposes at least two individuals;
> it is the minimum requirement for the circuit to be complete. Take, then,
> two persons, A and B, who converse with each other:

> The point of departure of the circuit is in the brain of one, for example
> A, where facts of consciousness, which we shall call concepts, are
> associated with representations of linguistic signs or acoustic images
> serving as their expression. Let us suppose that a given concept triggers
> [*déclanche*] in the brain a corresponding acoustic image: it is an entirely
> *psychic* phenomenon, followed in its turn by a *physiological* process: the
> brain transmits to the organs of phonation an impulse correlative to the
> image; then sound waves are propagated from the mouth of A to the ear
> of B: purely *physical* process. Next, the circuit persists in B in the inverse
> order: from the ear to the brain, physiological transmission of the acoustic
> image; in the brain, psychic association of this image with the correspond-
> ing concept. If B speaks in turn, this new act will follow – from his brain
> to that of A – exactly the same course as the first and it will pass through
> the same successive phases, which we represent as follows:

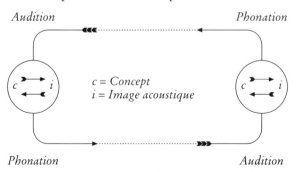

> (*CLG*: 27–8; emphasis in original)

Saussure very carefully points out that the sound waves which are propagated from A's mouth to B's ear in the speech circuit are a 'purely *physical* process' (*CLG*: 28; emphasis in original). The only directionality implied in Saussure's model is, then, the process of energy propagation (not transmission) from A to B. However, I should like to draw particular attention to the fact that, at the very beginning of the above passage, Saussure makes it quite clear that his main interest in the speech circuit has to do with the access it provides the linguist to the study of the language system (*langue*). I shall return to this point.

According to theories of perception in both behavioural and cognitive psychology, sensations of sound are the basis of hearing. The receptor organs in the ear are, according to these theories, stimulated by sound waves, which are taken to be the basis of acoustic perception. Now, the nearest Saussure might appear to get to this line of argument is when he speaks about the physiological dimension of the individual act of audition in the circuit. In behavioural and cognitive theories of acoustic perception, acoustic energy stimulates the relevant nerve cells in the ear. The receptor cells in the ear, in turn, transmit an impulse to the brain. This is the basis of the stimulus–response model of perception. In this strict, physiological reading, it is acoustic energy which stimulates, or brings about, a response in the relevant receptor cells.

Saussure's overall conception of the speech circuit is, however, very different from the stimulus–response model. This fact has been little heeded by Saussure's commentators. In particular, Saussure says that the physiological processes involve the transmission from the brain to the organs of articulation of an impulse which is 'correlative to the [acoustic] image'. He does not say that the acoustic image is itself transmitted; rather, the acoustic image, which is *psychic*, rather than physical, in character, is qualitatively different from the physiological processes involved. It functions to direct or to control the perceptual–motor events of phonation and audition, but is autonomous with respect to these.

Similarly, the important relationship which Saussure postulates between the speech circuit and his view of *langue* as a meaning-making resource has gone unnoticed. I shall discuss this below.

The code model closely resembles the famous reflex arc hypothesis which was developed by structuralist psychologists such as Wilhelm Wundt (1896) in the late nineteenth century. These nineteenth-century predecessors of the code model subscribed to a form of Lockean phenomenal elementarism. In the speech circuit, on the other hand, speaking and listening are parts of a still larger whole which is not reducible to the individual act (phonation or audition) *per se*. Neither phonation nor audition, in Saussure's model, is a function of immediate stimuli. Instead, they are connected to each other as part of a still larger environment in relation to which the individual components of the circuit are defined. Speaking and listening are not predicted on the basis of physical stimuli, but on the basis of the reciprocal and intentional orientation of speaker and listener to each other in the speech circuit.

The salient points may be summarized as follows:

1   Saussure starts with the 'individual act which allows the speech circuit to be reconstructed' (*CLG*: 27). The individual is not a passive recipient of external stimuli which cause his or her behavioural responses. It must be borne in mind here that Saussure's perspective is that of *parole*. Thus, the individual is an active and intentional agent in which no mechanistic theory of causation is assumed (Chapter 5);

2   The individual act of phonation or audition is, however, not sufficient. Saussure points out that the individual act 'supposes two individuals in order to complete the circuit' (*CLG*: 27). In other words, the individual act is orientated to the other in the circuit. Saussure recognizes that speaker and listener *qua* individuals are not the primary units of analysis. Instead, what is primary is the relation which links them in the circuit as part of some still larger whole, or 'complex unity' (Chapter 5, section 1). He gives priority to the dyadic nature of the relationship which links speaker and listener as interdependent participants in the circuit (Chapter 5, section 1);

3   The relations between speaker and listener are not and cannot be defined in terms of the individual's contribution *per se* to the circuit. What is important for Saussure is the relationship between the circuit as a whole and the still higher-order language system which mediates and regulates the relations between the individual participants in the circuit.

3 ACT PSYCHOLOGY AND THE SPEECH CIRCUIT

Saussure's explanation of the speech circuit shares some interesting affinities with the nineteenth-century American psychologist John Dewey's (1896) critique of the so-called 'reflex arc hypothesis' in late nineteenth-century structuralist psychology. Structuralist psychology was a precursor of twentieth-century behaviourism. Dewey was a functionalist and was also influenced by the act psychology of Franz Brentano (1874). He rejected the stimulus–response model of behaviour. For Dewey, the individual is not a passive recipient of external stimuli, but an active participant in perception. Dewey rejected the behavioural elementarism of the structuralist school of psychologists (e.g., Wundt). Behaviour, in Dewey's view, is not a series of discrete elementary reflexes at the molecular level. Instead, it is a co-ordinated and orientated act in relation to its environments. Dewey provides the following critique of the reflex arc hypothesis in his influential paper entitled 'The reflex arc concept in psychology' (1896):

the reflex arc idea, as commonly employed, is defective in that it assumes sensory stimulus and motor response as distinct psychical existences, while in reality they are always inside a coördination; and (secondly) in assuming that the quale of experience which precedes the 'motor' phase and that which succeeds it are two different states, instead of the last being always the first reconstituted, the motor phase coming in only for the sake of such mediation. The result is that the reflex arc idea leaves us with a disjointed psychology, whether viewed from the standpoint of the individual or in the race, or from that of the analysis of the mature consciousness. As to the former, in its failure to see that *the arc of which it talks is virtually a circuit*, a continual reconstitution, it breaks continuity and leaves us nothing but a series of jerks, the origin of each jerk to be sought outside the process of experience itself, in either an external pressure of 'environment', or else in an unaccountable spontaneous variation from within the 'soul' of the 'organism'. As to the latter, failing to see the unity of activity, no matter how much it may prate of unity, it still leaves us with sensation or peripheral stimulus; idea, or central process (the equivalent of attention); and motor response, or act, as three disconnected existences, having to be somehow adjusted to each other, whether through the intervention of an extra-experimental soul, or by mechanical push and pull.

(Dewey 1965 [1896]: 323; my emphasis)

In ways very similar to Dewey, Saussure does not see phonation and audition as comprising a series of discrete, individual and causally related stages (e.g., external stimulus followed by neural activity followed by behavioural response). Dewey talks about a 'circuit' in which the psychic, physiological and physical components are all interrelated as a circular interdependency. He argues that perception is not a question of a physical stimulus causing a motor response, and so on. With reference to the experience of a child's burning him- or herself with a candle, Dewey argues for an alternative view:

we begin not with a sensory stimulus, but with a sensori-motor coördination, the optical–ocular, and that in a certain sense it is the movement which is primary, and the sensation which is secondary, the movement of body, head and eye muscles determining the *quality* of what is experienced. In other words, *the real beginning is with the act of seeing*; it is looking, and not a sensation of light. The sensory quale gives the *value* of the act, just as the movement furnishes its mechanism and control, but both sensation and movement lie inside, not outside the act.

(Dewey 1965 [1896]: 322; my emphasis)

Dewey emphasizes the way in which individual *activity* produces a co-ordinated response to the stimulation. In turn, this response affects the *quality* of the perceptual experience itself. Dewey's notion of the 'circuit', which he proposes as an alternative to the reflex arc hypothesis, is remarkably similar to Saussure's model of the speech circuit. For Dewey, perception is not reducible to purely quantitative (physical and physio-logical) terms. Perception, in Dewey's view, is qualitative: it depends on the intentional orientation of the individual to that which is perceived.

Furthermore, experience is not reducible to one-off environmental contingencies, or 'jerks', but is internal to the circuit and its functioning. Experience in turn feeds back into and helps to determine the quality of the act of perception. Perception is not externally imposed on the individual; it is the result of the experience which the individual accumulates in and through his or her participation in the circuit. With these observations in mind, I shall now turn my attention to Saussure's account.

Saussure's account, like Dewey's, is *functional* in character. Having established the constituent parts of the speech circuit, Saussure then proceeds to consider the way these function in the circuit as a whole. His starting point is the brain of one of the two individuals in the circuit. Specifically, Saussure refers to 'the facts of consciousness' (*les faits de conscience*) which are in the individual's brain (*CLG*: 28). These are, Saussure claims, the concepts which are 'associated with representations of linguistic signs or acoustic images serving as their expression' (*CLG*: 28). It is important to establish at the outset that Saussure's notion of consciousness entails a rejection of the empiricist theory of association in psychology. According to the empiricist theory, the mind consists of elementary ideas that are simply correlated with their associated causes (sensations) in the external world. Saussure does not intend 'association' in this empiricist sense. Locke's view, which Harris draws on in his description of the speech circuit, is, on the other hand, empiricist in this sense (section 1). Elementary associations between 'sensa-tion' and 'idea' are reduced to the level of naturalistically defined individual habits by the empiricists.

There are two good reasons for arguing against this interpretation of the speech circuit. First, Saussure, unlike the empiricists, does not reduce systemic regularities in social-semiological relations and processes to a more naturalistic level of individual, and hence non-social, habits. The circuit is dyadic (transindividual) and connected to a higher-order social-semiological system which regulates the transactions in the circuit.

Second, Saussure regards association as a fact of *consciousness*, rather than the passive reception of external stimuli. In so doing, Saussure locates himself in the tradition of act psychology which was founded by Franz Brentano. Consciousness, according to the act psychologists, is an *activity* of the mind. Brentano stands in a line of thought whose lineage extends back to Aristotle. In Brentano's view, consciousness is a *psychic* activity: that is, the mind is intentionally (psychically) orientated to the objects of consciousness. Thus, 'facts of consciousness' are not passively acquired from the outside by means of external physical sensations. This is an important distinction.

Saussure makes it clear at the very beginning of his discussion that the association of a 'concept' and an 'acoustic image' is an 'entirely psychic phenomenon' (*CLG*: 28). The association of a concept with an acoustic image is, then, a psychic or intentionally directed activity. Signs are not already in the brain. Nor are they simply given from some external source. Rather, they emerge as a result of the acts of consciousness by which the brain selectively orientates to some associations of concept and acoustic image, rather than others in the overall process of jointly construing meanings in the circuit. This process, Saussure argues, is 'an entirely psychic phenomenon' (*CLG*: 28). There is also a physiological and a physical component, but the psychic component which Saussure emphasizes means that the individual's brain is orientated to patterns which have a social-semiological significance. That is, it is orientated to meaning, rather than to physical sensations or physiological activity *per se*.

Saussure (*CLG*: 29) further analyses the speech circuit into its constituent parts. He first distinguishes between that which is 'exterior' and that which is 'interior' to the individual. The exterior part comprises the 'vibrating sounds going from mouth to ear' (*CLG*: 29). Saussure does not actually refer to sound waves here; rather, he refers to the source of the mechanical, vibratory event (the mouth in the process of articulation) and the means of its perception (the ear). He also refers to the means whereby the ear listens to such events, that is, to the 'vibrating sounds'. The point I am making may seem a too subtle one. It is, however, an important one. My point is that Saussure does not say, as might be thought, that the ear listens to or perceives sound waves in the sense understood by acoustic physics; rather, the 'vibrating sounds' provide the ear with *information* relative to the mechanical event of articulation. That is, these sounds provide information that orientates the listener to the speaker. In the ecosocial reality of the speech circuit, this is much more important than the physical reality of sound waves *per se*. Phonation and audition are *complementary* facets of the same overall event, which links A and B in and through the sign relation (Chapter 1, section 7; Chapter 5, section 1).

Saussure's next distinction is that between a 'psychic' and a 'non-psychic' part. The latter includes both internal physiological and external physical facts. This distinction is crucial because the individual act of speaking in the circuit is a relation, and not a thing. It is a signifying act which is functionally orientated to the ecosocial environment of the circuit as a whole. This explains why the psychic cannot be reduced to the non-psychic. These two 'parts' have a distinct ontological status: 'psychic' refers to semiological functions, values and *relations*; 'non-psychic' to physiological and physical *things*. The latter constitute the physical–material substrate of the former. The former are always cross-coupled with the latter in *parole*, but the one is not reducible to the other.

In the next stage of his description, Saussure assigns to the circuit both an 'active' and a 'passive' part:

everything is active that goes from the association centre of one of the subjects to the ear of the other subject, and passive everything that goes from the ear of the latter to his association centre.

(*CLG*: 29)

Saussure's conception of the individual's role in the circuit is activity-centred. This activity is directed to the other (the listener), rather than to internal subjective states or mental experience. There has been some misunderstanding of the term 'passive' in this discussion. Tullio de Mauro points out in the commentary to his critical edition of *CLG* that, on the basis of modern research, 'audition is very far from being considered a mere receptive mechanism, an inert registration' (Saussure 1994 [1967]: 385, n. 61). But Saussure's point is that it is what 'goes from the ear to the association centre' in the brain of the subject that is passive. That is, the passive component refers to a purely *physiological* process which is internal to the individual. It does not refer to the psychic and, hence, active and intentional orientation of the individual (speaker or listener) to the other. The terms 'active' and 'passive' designate two poles of attention or awareness with respect to a single overall phenomenon, that is, the 'complex unity', seen as a jointly constructed signifying act in the speech circuit.

In the first case, the orientation is 'outwards' to the other; in the second, the orientation is 'inwards' to the self. These are two distinct, though related, intentional objects. Saussure sees both as constitutive parts in a circular and continuous process of selective attention. The two poles of awareness – the 'active' and the 'passive' – designate different states of distinct subsystems in a still larger ecosocial environment. Saussure makes it clear that the two poles are not separable; they are interdependent. This view contrasts with the dominant view in nineteenth century psychology and physiology. According to the dominant theories (e.g., the structuralist psychology of Wundt), an external sensory input is processed internally. The perceptual organ transmits via a neural channel a sensory input to the brain. This view is a purely passive, unidirectional (from outside to inside) and causal one. In the brain, neural sensations are 'associated' with ideas by central neural activities.

Saussure's psychic conception does not conform to this model. By definition, it is a functional conception in which activity is directed to the environment, as defined by the circuit. There is a continuous feedback loop between the 'active' and 'passive' poles of attention. Saussure further explains 'active' and 'passive' as follows: 'In the psychic part localized in the brain, one may call executive all that which is active (c → i) and receptive all that which is passive (i → c)' (*CLG*: 29). Again, the key word here is *psychic*. The circuit is a macroscopic ecosocial environment which synchronizes the activities, both internal and external, of the participants in the circuit. The circuit as a whole regulates these activities. Individuals *per se* do not.

Another significant absence in Saussure's model is any sort of internal regulatory mechanism, as in the homunculus view of the 'inner' mind which controls and directs the individual. 'Executive' and 'receptive', as particular states of awareness or readiness, pertain to different parts of the circuit as a whole. What matters is their reciprocal orientation to each other. It is this which gets the circuit going, rather than some prior prescriptive state or 'inner' programme which controls the individual.

I have indicated that the overall stability and functioning of the speech circuit is regulated by the higher-order social-semiological system of *langue*. Saussure concludes that part of his discussion which is concerned with the constituent parts of the circuit with these words:

> It is necessary to add a faculty of association and coordination, which is manifested as soon as it is no longer a question of isolated signs; it is this faculty which plays the main role in the organization of the language system (see pp. 170ff.).
>
> But in order to understand this role, it is necessary to leave the individual act, which is only the embryo of language [*langage*], and tackle the social fact.
>
> (*CLG*: 29)

Linguistically, the nominalizations *association* and *co-ordination* in this passage are transformed verb processes. They imply, in each case, some sort of agency which is responsible for the activities of 'associating' and 'co-ordinating'. However, this is not located in the brain *per se*. The crucial factor in Saussure's view is the role played by the language system. *Langue* is a transindividual social-semiological system (Chapter 3). It is not a matter of external sensations or sensory inputs being 'associated' with ideas by internal neural activity. The cross-coupling of individual language activity and the higher-order system of *langue* in the speech circuit means that acoustic image and concept become contexts for each other's reciprocal interpretation. It is at this intersection that the agency of the processes of 'association' and 'co-ordination' is located. The psychic conception of the sign means that the association of concept and acoustic image is 'co-ordinated', rather than contingent, because of the *systemic* basis of signs. No association between concept and acoustic image can take place in the absence of a socially shared system of semiological values. That is why Saussure shifts the explanatory basis away from his starting point – the individual act – to the 'social fact' of *langue*.

4 THE PSYCHIC BASIS OF THE CIRCUIT: MEANING, NOT MATTER

The psychic basis of this process is consistent with Saussure's emphasis on the active nature of *parole*, which is the product of individual 'will' and 'intelligence' (Chapter 5). In the speech circuit, the individual does not simply interact with another individual in a circuit which organizes the relations between them. The individual is *actively* orientated to the other and to the circuit as a whole by what these relations *mean* for the individual. What these relations mean depends in turn on how the circuit is connected to the higher-order social-semiological system of *langue*.

Saussure argues that the starting point in his description of the speech circuit – the individual act – is no more than 'the embryo of language' (*CLG*: 29). *Parole*, as distinct from the individual *per se*, is not localizable at any given point or moment in the speech circuit. It depends on the entire circuit for its definition. Nor is an act of *parole* something which simply takes place 'between' two individuals. As Saussure's discussion makes clear, it also occurs 'inside' the individuals as psychic activity in their brains. *Parole*, in other words, cuts across the dichotomy between 'inner' and 'outer'. It refers equally to both dimensions of the individual's linguistic activity in the circuit.

Consciousness is, then, a psychic, or intentional, activity for Saussure. It is always directed to some 'object' of consciousness. This echoes Brentano's view: consciousness, according to Brentano, is always *about* something. This point of view was also shared by Dewey, who stands in the same tradition of act psychology as was initiated by Brentano. In Saussure's account, the association of a concept with an acoustic image is an act of consciousness. For this reason, it is psychic in character. At the same time, this act of consciousness and the sign which is its 'object' are not entirely distinguishable. Higher-order consciousness depends on social meaning-making. The sign which results is a psychic phenomenon which is in turn orientated to the other in the speech circuit. The psychic character of the sign in the speech circuit means that phenomenal experience (cf. Dewey's qualia) and consciousness, which are individual, may, however, be shared as jointly constructed signifying acts. The system of *langue* is a social-semiological resource which allows speaker and listener to synchronize individual experience in virtue of the socially shared principles for 'associating' acoustic image to concept (see Edelman 1989: 22 for a remarkably similar view from the point of view of recent developments in the neurosciences).

The psychic act of association between concept and acoustic image in the individual's brain is functionally organized. The sign so organized does not have a structure *sui generis*. In other words, the sign is a psychic act which is correlated to the function it has in the speech circuit. Saussure's use of the word 'correlative' (*corrélative*) to describe this particular stage in the overall process is most revealing. It recalls Aristotle's notion of the 'correlative object' to which an act is psychically orientated. Act psychologists such as Brentano and Dewey developed this notion in terms of the functions that particular psychic acts have in relation to some environment. The intentional orientation of the act to its 'object' means that the latter is the function with which the former 'correlates'.

The next stage that Saussure describes is a 'physiological process: the brain transmits to the organs of phonation an impulse which is correlative to the image' (*CLG*: 28). It is very clear on careful reading that the physiological, for Saussure, does not reduce to a simple transmission of a signal from the brain to the organs of phonation. Such a view would suppose that the signals sent along the sensory nerves from brain to speech organs are processed or interpreted (Gibson 1986 [1979]: 221). But Saussure's notion of an impulse which is 'correlative' to the acoustic image does not refer to the passive output of a sensory nerve; rather, the sign is also psychically (functionally) organized in relation to the act of phonation itself. The act of phonation (articulation) is intentionally organized by the acoustic image as a semiological act which is functionally directed to the other in the circuit.

The final stage is the one Saussure characterizes as 'purely *physical*: sound waves are propagated from the mouth of A to the ear of B' (*CLG*: 28). There is absolutely nothing in what Saussure says that suggests that 'thoughts', 'ideas' or 'information' are transmitted from speaker to listener.

The physical sound waves which are transmitted in speech do register on the receptor organs, but we do not perceive sound waves as such. Speech sounds are much more than physical sound waves and they are not appropriately described at that level of physical reality. When I say that speech sounds constitute a flow of acoustic information, I mean that they specify the information which the speaker–listener in the appropriate ecosocial niche is both biologically equipped and socially trained to extract from the flow of acoustic events. However, this information is not objectively there. In the speech circuit, the informational value of physical speech sounds is also structured and elaborated by both the neurophysiological processes involved in their perception and in their psychic reconstrual as social-semiological values. This is a very different claim from saying that speech sounds are stimuli which the speaker–listener associates with a concept in the brain through the inferring of a pattern from physical sensations (sense data) in the external world.

From the point of view of the listener's reception of the sound waves which are 'propagated' from the speaker, Saussure simply says that the process already described takes place in reverse: 'from the ear to the brain, physiological transmission of the acoustic image; in the brain, psychic association of this image with the corresponding concept' (*CLG*: 28), and so on. Again, Saussure does not use the language of physical stimuli. In other words, he does not say that an acoustic sensation stimulates the receptor cells in the ear. Instead, he refers to the perceptual organ, the ear, in its entirety. Furthermore, the ear is not said to be stimulated by the physical sound waves that are propagated in the air and then converted into neural signals for transmission into the brain. Saussure makes a very different claim, which is, however, absolutely consistent with his previous description of the process of phonation. In the process of audition, it is the *acoustic image* which is transmitted from ear to brain, not neural signals *per se*. This is a critically important distinction. I shall now discuss why.

The difference between the ear, which is a perceptual organ, and the receptor cells of hearing (the hair cells attached to the basilar membrane, the semicircular canals, and the olfactory epithelium) is that the ear is *actively* orientated to the flux of acoustic energy whereas the receptors are merely stimulated by it (Gibson 1986 [1979]: 53). Saussure's description shows that the ear does not convert sound waves into neural signals; rather, the ear is actively and intentionally orientated to extract stimulus invariants from the flow of speech sounds (see also Parret 1994: 22–3). That is, the ear is psychically orientated to the organization of the perceived speech of the other as acoustic images which are then 'associated' with their corresponding concepts in the brain of the listener. In other words, from the respective points of view of both speaker and listener, signs are psychically or functionally orientated to both self and other in the speech circuit.

Saussure is the first to admit that his description is schematic and incomplete. In recognizing this, he adds the following clarificatory observations with respect to specific details which his description omits:

> One could still distinguish: the pure acoustic sensation, the identification of this sensation with the latent acoustic image, the muscular image of phonation, etc. We have taken account of the elements judged to be essential; but our figure allows us to distinguish right away the physical part (sound waves) from the physiological (phonation and audition) and psychic (verbal images and concepts). It is in effect important to observe that the verbal image is not to be confused with the sound itself and that it is psychic in the same way as the concept with which it is associated.
>
> (*CLG*: 28–9)

These additional remarks of Saussure's serve to confirm the interpretation I have given above. The distinction he makes between the 'pure acoustic sensation' and the 'identification of that sensation with the latent acoustic image' relates to the difference between the receptor cells and the ear as a contextualizing organ. The point is this: receptors are stimulated by purely physical sensations, viz. mechanical vibrations in the cochlea fluid cause the basilar membrane to vibrate, and this in turn stimulates the receptor cells (the hair cells). The ear, on the other hand, is a perceptual organ. It is actively orientated to the contextualizing of these patterns of similarity and difference in the stimulus flux as significant (semiotically salient) patterns of difference. The acoustic image functions, psychically speaking, to organize the flux of acoustic energy as information which has potential semiological value.

An analogous process also takes place from the point of view of phonation. In this case, the 'muscular image of phonation' is not the same as the microscopic movements of the muscles in the material processes of articulation; rather, the muscular image intentionally directs and co-ordinates these in the way discussed above. Elsewhere, Saussure uses the term 'motor image' (*l'image motrice des organes*, *CLG*: 63) to refer to this same principle.

Saussure states that physical sound waves travel from 'the mouth of A to the ear of B' (*CLG*: 28). Nowhere in his discussion of the speech circuit does he say that individuals hear these sound waves *qua* mechanical vibrations which are propagated through the medium of air. Saussure's interest is much more focused on the acoustic image than it is on the physical reality of sound waves *per se*. Again, this is an important difference with respect to the code and transmission models. In these models, the air is the channel or medium for the physical transmission of the acoustic signal (Sperber and Wilson 1986: 5). Why, then, does Saussure pay so little attention to this level of reality?

In my view, the answer to this question lies in the self-evident fact that Saussure is not talking about the level of physical reality which is described by the science of physical acoustics. This level of reality refers to the propagation of sound waves through a medium such as air from a mechanical source. Physical acoustics describes sound waves in the language of the low-energy kinetic field. This is the kinetic level of physical interactions described by law-like Newtonian causal descriptions of mechanical events (Chapter 4, section 10). It is concerned with the relations among kinetic observables and properties. These are described in the theoretical language of the mechanical forces which act upon particles in the physical world.

The sign is not a physical entity, however; it has no phenomenal status as such. In the speech circuit, a sign is instantiated as a psychic act. This is the sense of Saussure's terms 'concept' and 'acoustic image', which refer to the instantial dimension of the sign in the speech circuit. The participants in the speech circuit use such signifying acts to organize and co-ordinate their intentional orientations to each other and to semiotically construed substances in their ecosocial environments (Chapter 7, section 4). That is, the sign, in the speech circuit, enacts a joint focusing on the phenomena of experience. By virtue of their being cross-coupled to the same social-semiological system, the participants in the circuit can jointly construe the phenomena of conscious perceptual experience as a socially shareable signified substance. The association of a concept and an acoustic image in the brains of the individuals in the circuit does not mean that 'thoughts' are transmitted from one brain to another. The fact that A and B in the circuit are able to form the same associations in their brains is a consequence of their being cross-coupled to the same higher-order social-semiological system. That is, both A and B share the same meaning system. The sign, as a psychic act, is the dialogic means for co-ordinating this reciprocal focus in a shared semiotic frame of reference.

5 THE NEURO-ANATOMICAL SUBSTRATE: NINETEENTH-CENTURY RESEARCH

Harris claims that 'nothing suggests that Saussure's analysis of oral communication was in any way founded on nineteenth-century advances in the sciences dealing with the actual mechanisms of speech' (1987: 204–5). Similarly, Prampolini asserts that the speech circuit does little to illuminate how language functions, based as it is on 'intuitive notions [which are] not well defined' (1994: 37). These claims are belied by the very terminology Saussure uses. Thus, Saussure's terms *acoustic image, concept* and *muscular* or *motor image* derive from the neuroanatomical researches of Wernicke (1977 [1874]) and Lichtheim (1884). Unlike Paul Broca, whom Saussure does explicitly cite (*CLG*: 26), Wernicke did not confine himself to the description of a particular language disorder, as was the case with the patient whom Broca referred to as 'Tan' in his famous case study (Broca 1965 [1861]). Wernicke conducted research on the neuroanatomical and neurophysiological bases of language disorders. He proposed that 'fibre tracts' joined different parts of the nervous system. According to Wernicke, language is a type of reflex in which the 'auditory images' of words and the 'motor images' of words are associated by fibre tracts. Thus, the child's learning of language depends on his or her linking the auditory images of words with their motor images. Wernicke argued for a reflex association between two cortical centres. This reflex association was, in Wernicke's view, mediated by a specific neural pathway (McCarthy and Warrington 1990: 12).

Lichtheim (1884) proposed a further refinement of Wernicke's model. In addition to 'auditory word images' and 'articulatory images', Lichtheim also proposed the notion of 'concept centres'. These assign concepts to sequences of sounds. This model is schematized in Figure 6.1. The research work of Wernicke and Lichtheim led to the postulation of a number of language centres, located in different parts of the brain. These centres were linked by the fibre tracts mentioned above. The work of these two German researchers meant that by the late nineteenth century there was a detailed account of the neuroanatomical and neurophysiological bases of the language faculty in the

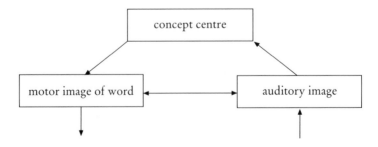

Figure 6.1 Lichtheim's (1884) model, showing transcortical fibre tract connections

individual, its links to specific language disorders, and specific domains of language processing (speaking, speech comprehension, writing, reading, spelling).

The function of the 'motor image' in phonation and of the 'acoustic image' in audition is to extract a schematization from the rich detail of the microscopic physical processes involved. That is, a macroscopic motor image or acoustic image co-ordinates and orientates the speaker–listener's perceptions of the acoustic flux. According to Wernicke, both the motor image and the acoustic image are 'memory images' which are 'deposited' in the cortex on the basis of 'countless sensory impressions' (1977 [1874]: 193). In this way, the speaker–listener builds up in memory a stock of global percepts which serve as an *a priori* principle for classifying a given set of features in the acoustic flux as instantiations of a given phonological category. At the psychoperceptual level, the acoustic image controls the perception of the acoustic flux as instantiations of distinct phonological categories. In Wernicke's own words, the acoustic image is responsible for the *'unconscious monitoring of the imagery of the spoken word'* (Wernicke 1977 [1874]: 107; emphasis in original). In Wernicke's account, the acoustic image functions to 'activate' the word: that is, the speaker–listener's ability to produce and comprehend speech sounds. In various types of speech disorder, the concept itself may remain intact, yet the speaker–listener's ability to produce or comprehend speech sounds is lost on account of the destruction of the association fibres connecting acoustic imagery to, say, touch and tactual imagery, which are 'intrinsic components' of the concept (Wernicke 1977: [1874]: 107; McCarthy and Warrington 1990: 146–50).

6 THE ECOSOCIAL BASIS OF THE SPEECH CIRCUIT

Saussure's model of the speech circuit focuses, then, on the psychic, rather than the physical, level of reality. It anticipates in important ways the directions taken in the late James J. Gibson's ecological theory of perception, as well as recent theoretical developments concerning the *ecosocial* basis of meaning-making (Lemke 1993). In this section, I shall assume that the speech circuit is a precursor model of these developments. My claim rests, in the first instance, on the dually psychic and social-semiological bases of Saussure's account.

Gibson (1986 [1979]) developed a theory of ecological optics to describe the structured patternings of light fields at the ecological level of interactions between organism and environment. Gibson argued that organisms do not perceive light *per se*; they do not perceive the quantum level of wave/particle emission and absorption. Instead, they perceive structured patterns of information in this. The organism is actively orientated to obtain information about its environment from the patterned variants and invariants which are structured in light. Gibson also focused his argument on all of the five senses, though most of his research career was dedicated to the development of his ecological optics.

The difference between the ecological level of interactions between organism and environment and the one described by, say, physical optics (or acoustics) is one of scale. The ecological level is a qualitatively different scale of reality from the quantum level studied by physical optics or acoustics. The former is the level of reality in which organisms live, move and interact with their environment, including other organisms. The latter is the world of atomic particles which physicists study.

The speech circuit represents, in my view, Saussure's attempt to model this ecological level of description. Of course, Saussure's verbal and graphic representations of the speech circuit are highly schematic (section 2). They are a high-level generalization from actual instances of spoken linguistic interaction. For this reason, the speech circuit does not include the rich detail that a description of some actual social occasion might be expected to include. Nor is Saussure specific about the differences among the various types or genres of spoken discourse which may be found in a given community. However, these limitations do not invalidate the main purpose of Saussure's model. Its importance lies at a much more general level of explanation, which may be said to underlie all occasions of spoken interaction (section 7 below).

First a few observations concerning the level of physical kinetics that I mentioned in section 4. This refers to a level of interaction whose kinetics are said to be microscopic with respect to the macroscopic ecological level. The kinetic energy of these interactions is too low relative to the ecological level. The physical level is the substrate of the ecological level. However, the latter is not reducible to the former. That is, the information on the ecological level of the speech circuit is not reducible to the kinetic level, though the former requires the latter for its definition. At the mechanical level, the play of the speech organs in phonation and the receptors in audition generate and/or receive kinetic events (vibrations propagated through a medium from a mechanical source).

This alternative ecological level of description shows, however, that the cross-coupling of organisms (i.e., speaker and listener) to their environments does not occur uniquely on the kinetic level of mechanical forces. Importantly, there are also informational and perceptual cross-couplings which orientate the organism in relation to the environment, including that of other social beings. These informational cross-couplings occur on the basis of a low-energy field such as sound waves. This is the kinetic level. It is lawfully structured by the high-energy material environment of surfaces, objects and the medium (Gibson 1986 [1979]: 7–15), along with the organism's movements in this. Consequently, the macroscopic patternings and flows of information in the acoustic field correspond to properties and events of the material environment, including the internal states of speaker and listener as embodied participants in the interaction. Such events include the act of phonation and what this tells listeners about the bodily and other states of the speaker.

I have benefited enormously from reading James J. Gibson's remarkable book, *The Ecological Approach to Visual Perception* (1986 [1979]), in my own efforts to sort out this relationship. According to Gibson, 'A stimulus in this strict [i.e., physiological] meaning carries no information about its source in the world; that is, it does not specify its source. Only stimulation that comes in a structured array and that changes over time specifies its external source' (1986 [1979]: 56). Gibson's point is that perception 'is not a response to a stimulus but an act of information pick up' (1986 [1979]: 56–7). Sound waves stimulate the receptor organs in the ear and are transformed into nerve impulses which are then transmitted to the brain. Nevertheless, this does not explain, for Gibson, the fact that 'stimulus information' cannot be so transmitted for it is something which has to be 'isolated and extracted from the ambient energy' (1986 [1979]: 57). To explain this, Gibson proposes the notion of an 'ambient optic array at a point of observation': 'To be an *array* means to have an arrangement, and to be *ambient at a point* means to surround a position in the environment that could be occupied by an observer' (1986 [1979]: 65).

The key theoretical concept in Gibson's account is that of *affordance*. The affordances of the environment are, for Gibson, 'what it *offers* the animal, what it *provides* or *furnishes*, either for good or ill' (1986 [1979]: 127). The concept of an affordance is always a relative concept. It cannot be measured in the 'absolute' terms of physics or mathematics; rather, it is relative both to the organism and to the ecosocial niche in which it lives. Some examples of affordances are the following: the different substances of the environment can variously afford nutrition and manufacture; the different objects in the environment afford various possibilities of manipulation; other social beings afford the various possibilities of social interaction; the different media (e.g., air, water) afford various possibilities of energy transmission and, hence, of optical and acoustical information (Gibson 1986 [1979]: 128).

What kind of information do the sounds of speech afford? How is this information 'extracted' from the ambient aural array? Speech sound is a continuous flow; it is not comprised of discrete units which form the input stimuli to the receptor organs (the eardrum). There are, as Gibson points out, episodes in the flow of stimulus energy, 'but these are nested within one another and cannot be cut up into elementary units. Stimulation is not momentary' (1986 [1979]: 58).

According to the generally accepted theory of perception, the ear forms a psychological image of the sound waves which stimulate the receptor organ. That is, it infers a pattern from the sense data which stimulate the receptors. Perception comes after sensation: physical sensations are 'processed' or 'decoded' by the receptors as an inferred pattern. There is, according to this line of reasoning, a correspondence between the sound waves which register on the ear drum and the 'acoustic image' which registers on the brain. Saussure is not specific about the neurophysiological processes in his model. Yet it is clear in his description that the acoustic image is autonomous with respect to the processes of perception and articulation for the reasons given above. The storing of acoustic imagery in the brain in the way described by Wernicke means that the perceptual categorization of the acoustic flux is prior to physical stimulation. Acoustic images are *a priori* psychoperceptual categories. They can function independently of the motor activities of articulation and of the perception of auditory events in the acoustic flux, as in so called 'inner' speech (Langacker 1987: 113–14).

There is a still more sophisticated version of this sensation-based theory of perception. This says, in effect, that an acoustic image is transmitted as a coded signal along the receptor nerves to the brain. Gibson (1986 [1979]: 61) points out that this implies a code model of message transmission: the signals transmitted along the nerve fibres are in code and they have to be decoded. Thus, the receptor organ (eye, ear, skin and so on) sends, the nerve fibres transmit and the brain receives. Such theories embody a version of the mind–body dualism. Gibson has reformulated the whole question as follows:

> It is not necessary to assume that *anything whatever* is transmitted along the optic nerve in the activity of perception. We need not believe that *either* an inverted picture or a set of messages is delivered to the brain. We can think of vision as a perceptual system, the brain being simply part of the system. The eye is also part of the system, since retinal inputs lead to ocular adjustments and then to altered retinal inputs, and so on. The process is circular, not a one-way transmission. The eye–head–brain–body system registers the invariants in the structure of ambient light. The eye is not a camera that forms and delivers an image, nor is the retina simply a keyboard that can be struck by fingers of light.
>
> (Gibson 1986 [1979]: 61)

I believe that something analogous is true of acoustic perception. Saussure's account of the speech circuit contains the necessary elements of such an alternative account. By analogy with Gibson's notion of the *ambient optic array*, I propose the concept of the *ambient acoustic array*. The essential point here is that Saussure does not speak the theoretical language of a speaker who sends a message, this message is transmitted along some physical medium, and is then received by a listener, who decodes the message. In Saussure's account, the psychic function of the acoustic image is to enable the body–brain complex as a whole to adjust to and respond to the information in the ambient acoustic array in semiotically appropriate ways.

The acoustic image enables the speaker–listener to construe informational variants and invariants in the acoustic flux as phonic substance. The psychic character of the acoustic image presupposes (1) the *a priori* perceptual categorization of speech sounds as instantiations of this or that phonological type-category; (2) an intentional and selective focusing on speech sounds as affording possibilities of interaction with social others; and (3) the 'associating' of these with higher-order conceptual categories. Acoustic energy already constitutes what Gibson calls 'ambient stimulus information' (1986 [1979]: 63). It is a structured array of information in relation to its ecosocial environments. The sound waves propagated by a speaker do not 'contain' a message, which the receiver must then 'decode'; rather, this structured array of information 'specifies', as Gibson (*ibid.*) puts it, the world for those who are equipped to pick up the structured information which it provides about the environment.

This implies the complementary existence in the same ecosocial environment of other social beings who are equipped to do so. The equipment for doing so is provided by what Saussure calls 'a faculty of association and coordination' (*CLG*: 29), which associates concept and acoustic image in the brain of the individual. It is this faculty 'which plays the biggest role in the organization of language as system' (*CLG*: 29). Saussure focuses on the 'social phenomenon' of the language system which makes possible such psychic faculties of 'association and coordination', rather than the individual linguistic act:

> in order to understand this role [of the language system], it is necessary to leave behind the individual act, which is no more than the embryo of language, and to tackle the social fact.
>
> (*CLG*: 29)

Saussure undertakes a decisive and radical theoretical step with these words. It is only through the resources of the system of *langue* that the individual can construe the categorical distinctions in the acoustic flux as phonic substance:

> Among all the individuals linked in this way by the language faculty, a sort of mean will be established: all will reproduce, – doubtless not exactly, but approximately – the same signs linked to the same concepts.
>
> (*CLG*: 29)

Phonation and audition are really complementary facets of a single more global event (Chapter 1, section 7). The speaker does not simply propagate physical sound waves from a mechanical source (the mouth). The listener does not simply pick up the structured information in speech sounds by chance. The fact that they go together in this way is an *ecosocial* fact. Speech sounds are topologically organized and categorically construed as instantiations of the phonological categories of a given language system. It is not an undifferentiated mass of sound. It is, as I pointed out earlier, a flow of ecological events (Gibson 1986 [1979]: 101–2). Speech sounds display morphological properties: that is, they have higher-order functional patterns (informational variants and invariants) relative to some ecosocial environment. The flow of speech sounds *qua* ecosocial event has a saccadic (stepping) and rhythmic quality. Speech, like other intentional acts, surges in 'self-generative impulses' (Trevarthen 1978: 129). For this reason, it constitutes ecosocial information which other suitably equipped social beings in the relevant environment can recognize as intentional. It is information which affords a dialogically co-ordinated response on the part of other social beings. Gibson calls this relation of complementarity, or correspondence, 'disturbance of structure' (1986 [1979]: 107):

> events in the world should not be confused with the information in the light corresponding to them. Just as there are no material objects in an array but only the invariants to specify objects, so there are no material events in an array but only the information to specify events. No object in the world is literally replicated in ambient light by a copy or simulacrum.
>
> (Gibson 1986 [1979]: 102)

Gibson has argued that his 'theory of information pick up requires that the visual system be able to detect both persistence and change' (1986 [1979]: 246–7). This same basic principle also applies in the case of the non-visual perceptual systems. The perceiving of persistence and change in the acoustic information which the sounds of speech afford to suitably situated social beings may take various forms. I outlined these in the previous section. The central point is that the speaker–listener distinguishes persistent features of the array from the flux of change. Speech sounds constitute an ecosocial event. The speaker–listener learns to distinguish regular patterns of stable features in given occurrences of such events. In Gibson's terms, 'The perceiver extracts the invariants of structure from the flux of stimulation while still noticing the flux' (1986 [1979]: 247). The speaker–listener tunes into the regularities in the acoustic information which is made available, as well as into the relations of sameness and difference which can be construed from one such event to another. This is not something which we do on the basis of a pre-wired or innate knowledge of the world. Instead, we are trained to recognize persistence and change and sameness and difference in and through specific social practices. The linguistic system affords its users the semiotic resources for doing so.

Further, this flow of events is not transmitted by a speaker to a listener in a linear, unidirectional way. The ambient acoustic array is 'ambient at a point' Gibson (1986 [1979]: 65). Sound waves do not travel in a straight line from point A to B; rather, they are *ambient*. They spread throughout some ecosocial space and surround (environ) the objects and social beings in it. Such a space is not reducible to physical space. The flow of speech sound surrounds a position in this ecosocial space that could (potentially) be occupied by an embodied social being.

Such a position also implies what Gibson (1986 [1979]: 65) calls a 'point of observation'. Speaker and listener are not simply physical objects who emit and receive sound waves in an abstract physical space, as in the code model; rather, they are located at positions in an ecosocial space of actual and potential points of observation and points of action. Such a space is more than just a medium for the physical transmission of sound waves. It implies a structured array of such social places and positions. This always occurs in ecosocial, rather than reductively physical, space–time.

Saussure's model of the speech circuit can be thought of as a mouth–brain–body–environment–ear complex. It is a circular chain of ecosocial interdependencies. Change or disturbance in the array does not simply register on the nerve cells of some listener's receptor organs as physical sensations. Instead, it impacts upon the consciousness of an embodied social being. Such a being, as I argued above, is equipped not only neurophysiologically, but also semiotically, to construe the array in meaningful ways. This process is an ecosocial event in the relevant ecosocial environment.

A vibratory mechanical event (phonation) in the ecosocial environment impacts upon both the ambient acoustic array and, hence, on the embodied consciousness of a dialogically orientated listener. It is neither an objectified, physical event in the world nor a subjective act of perception in the mind of the individual. It is, strictly speaking, neither objective nor subjective, neither 'physical' nor 'psychological'. Instead, it is 'psychic' and social-semiological. In 'leaving behind the individual act' to 'tackle the social fact' (see above) Saussure makes a decisive break with mind–body dualism.

It is the 'social reality' (*CLG*: 29) of the language system that enables the affordances of the ecosocial environment, including speech sounds, to be specified. The psychic character of the signifying act is crucial to this: acoustic images 'face' two ways: to the ambient acoustic array in the environment of the sound event and to the speaker–listener. It construes the acoustic flux as semiotically significant phonic substance at the same time as it dialogically orientates the self to the other. The language system affords both of these possibilities, simultaneously.

7 SEMIOLOGICAL VALUES AS NON-HOLONOMIC CONSTRAINTS

The speech circuit is an entire *psychoperceptual system*. As Gibson (1986 [1979]: 244) explains, a perceptual system is not the 'passive inputs of a sensory nerve'; it is the entire activity of seeing, hearing, listening, touching, tasting and so on. Whenever a perceptual system is globally adjusted to its environments, a sensory receptor connects local stimuli at a sensory surface to a projection centre in the brain (Gibson (1986 [1979]: 245). The perceptual *system* described by Saussure is not restricted to the sensory receptors which fire when stimulated by what Saussure calls 'pure acoustic sensation' in the physical sense. A perceptual system is an intentional system. This is the reason for Saussure's insistence on the *psychic* character of acts of speaking and listening. These are not reducible to the non-psychic (physiological and physical) processes that support them.

When Saussure (*CLG*: 64) points out the impossibility of 'photographing' the microscopic detail of the articulatory movements which take place in phonation he is making a claim about much more than the merely practical difficulties of such an enterprise. The photographing of these microlevel physical processes would tell us nothing about the psychic character of the motor image and the acoustic image. In the language of modern physics, acoustic image and motor image are constraints of the *non-holonomic* sort.

The acoustic image is said to be non-holonomic because it directs and constrains the lower-level articulatory and perceptual processes from which it emerges. These lower-level processes are not explicable in physical or physiological (kinetic) terms alone because, and in addition to the kinetic substrate, they have *semiological value*. This means that they are intentional. That is, the organization of the lower-level (physical and physiological) processes is orientated to a semiological value which functions as a field boundary condition of the non-holonomic sort. Saussure does not use the term non-holonomic. Nevertheless, he understands that semiological values emerge from, act back on and constrain biophysical systems such as articulation. Semiological values constitute boundary conditions which direct and orientate the lower-level biophysical processes of articulation. The latter are thus phonologically motivated. The emergence of these two distinct levels implies the ontological stratification of the social-semiological with respect to the biophysical (section 9 below; see also Chapter 1, section 7; Chapter 13, sections 11–14).

Properly speaking, the emergence of organized macroscopic simplicity from lower-level microscopic complexity is not causal but *realizational*. The constraints are two-way and stratified. Strictly speaking, a causal relation would mean, for example, that in phonation a given articulatory movement x causes sound y. More accurately, the articulatory movement signifies, or semiotically construes, a given acoustic image for both speaker and listener. The two-way nature of the stratification means that the reverse is also the case: the acoustic image is signified, or semiotically construed, by the articulatory movement. Langacker (1987: 112) similarly points out that motor image and acoustic image are autonomous with respect to the physical event of articulation (phonation) or reception (audition). From the point of view of articulation, it is more accurate to say that phonation (articulation) signifies and is signified by the signification of the acoustic image in the information which is structured in the acoustic flux. This information corresponds to the patterned variants and invariants which the organism actively extracts from the flux of acoustic energy. I have already referred to this as the *ambient acoustic array* (section 6). Non-holonomic constraints are not based on the principle of physical cause and effect.

Stratification in semiotic systems is based on the very different principle of 'metaredundancy' (Lemke 1984b: 64; Thibault 1991: Ch. 4; Halliday 1992: 23–5). When Saussure says that there is a two-way and reciprocal relationship between signifier and signified, this means that there is a metaredundancy relation between these two strata (Chapter 9, sections 1 and 5): that is, if signifier x occurs then we can predict to a high degree of probability its co-occurrence with signified y. The reciprocal nature of this relation also means it is fully reversible: x signifies y, and y is signified by x. This same principle applies at all levels of the sign relation, including that between the material act of articulation and the phonological category which this is construed as signifying. In other words, articulation does not physically cause a given phoneme. It makes no sense to say so because articulation and phoneme are two distinct levels of abstraction in an interstratal relation of symbolic construal. Articulation is a physical process; a phoneme, on the other hand, is a phonological category or value deriving from its position relative to other such values in a given phonological system.

Let us consider the phoneme /d/ from this point of view. The relationship between articulatory act and phoneme is as follows. The phonic terms [+voice; +apical; +obstruent] which configure in the act of articulation symbolically construe the phoneme category /d/ (Chapter 3, section 3). However, there are 'not two separate dyadic relationships' (Halliday 1992: 24) involved in this process. That is, a given phonic term, say, [+voice], which indicates a vibration of the vocal cords in the physical process of articulation, does not directly 'cause' a particular phoneme. Instead, these two distinct levels are related by a very different, non-physicalist principle. This is what Lemke calls a 'metaredundancy' relation (Chapter 9, section 1). This means that the phonic terms that configure in the act of articulation redound not with the phoneme *per se*, but with the redundancy of this with some submorphemic or morphemic conceptual distinction on the higher-order stratum of the signified, as shown in Figure 6.2. The signified is, therefore, the higher-order contextualizing principle which re-construes and constrains

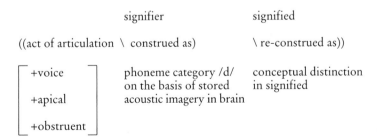

Figure 6.2 Metaredundancy relation between articulatory act, phoneme category and concept

the lower-level redundancy relation between phoneme and articulatory event. This illustrates the emergence of semiological value from the material–kinetic (articulatory) processes of the body. Articulation does not physically 'cause' a phoneme such as /d/ to occur. The acoustic image is not a property of the physical processes of articulation; rather, it is a constraint of the non-holonomic sort. It reconstrues the lower-level, kinetic processes of articulation as semiological values. There is, then, no direct, unmediated (non-semiotic) link of a causal nature between the kinetic processes of articulation and the acoustic image. 'Psychic' does not equate with physical cause and effect.

Where do non-holonomic constraints come from? Do they already exist in the brain of each individual? As I pointed out earlier, the acoustic image is one level or stratum of organization in the sign relation. If Saussure's model really were a code and transmission one, then it would amount to a description of two separate brains interacting by means of passively acquired external stimuli. In such a view, the brain 'directs' or controls the physiological (perceptual–motor) processes of phonation and audition on the basis of externally acquired and physically based associations between concepts and acoustic images. But that is not what Saussure actually says. If this were so, then the basis for the individual's interaction with the circuit would be no more than the physical one of the sound waves which are propagated from speaker to listener. This is a consequence of assuming that the code is no more than a device for pairing or associating acoustic signals with thoughts (section 1 above). That is, it would be a mechanical model of physical causation, based on the behaviourists' model of stimulus and response.

Saussure's alternative solution lies in the fact that the acoustic image is a schematic category of sound. It belongs to the language system, rather than to physical reality *per se*. The individuals in the speech circuit are cross-coupled to a higher-order social-semiological system (*langue*) which provides them with categorical criteria for orientating to the flux of acoustic information in the ambient acoustic array. That is, the phonological categories that belong to a given language system provide the participants in the speech circuit with the resources for selectively orientating to speech sounds so as to be able both to recognize and produce phonologically salient patterns. These abilities are not intrinsic to the brains of the individuals. Nor do they derive from the mechanical association of physical stimuli to thoughts in the empiricist sense. Rather, they derive from the individual's belonging to and participating in the practices of a given language system:

> It is by the functioning of the receptive and coordinative faculties that imprints which happen to be perceptibly the same for everyone are formed in speaking subjects. How must this social product be represented so that the language system appears perfectly disengaged from the rest? If we could embrace the sum of the verbal images stored in all these

individuals, we would make contact with the social bond which constitutes the language system [*langue*]. It is a treasure *deposited by the practices of* parole in all of the subjects belonging to a single community, a grammatical system existing virtually in each brain, or more exactly in the brains of an ensemble of individuals; for the language system is not complete in any one, it only exists perfectly in the mass.

(CLG: 30; my emphasis)

It is worth while pausing to examine more carefully some of Saussure's specific formulations in this passage. He points out that it is through the 'receptive and coordinative faculties' of speaking subjects that the latter all come to share, more or less, the same signs when they speak to each other. But this 'social product' is said to be 'disengaged' (*dégagé*) from these faculties. Why does Saussure propose to separate the one from the other in this way? The answer to this is discussed in the next section.

8 EMBODYING THE SYSTEM

The problem Saussures poses in the above quotation concerns how to represent, theoretically speaking, the social product of *langue* in such a way that it does not reduce to and, therefore, conflate with the individual's faculties of reception and co-ordination. These faculties have their basis in the individual's psychophysical make-up. They correspond to the physiological (perceptual–motor) abilities and skills of the individual. But Saussure's point is that in 'disengaging' the language system from these, it is necessary to distinguish the higher-order system of social-semiological relations and practices from the individual's biological faculties. It is through the individual's participation in the practices of *parole* that the language system is learned. These include the practices which enable individuals to distinguish salient differences in the flow of acoustic information in the ambient acoustic array. In so doing, they learn to construe these as instantiations of the phonological categories belonging to a particular language system. Saussure's point is that the speech circuit does not only cross-couple the individuals who interact with each other. The speech circuit is also the 'complex unit' discussed in Chapter 5 which cross-couples the individuals with the higher-order social-semiological system of *langue*.

These socially shared and distributed meaning-making resources and their typical patterns of use are, Saussure says, 'imprinted' in individual speaking subjects by virtue of their participation in the practices of *parole*. The individual's participation in the practices of *parole* is the point of intersection between the individual as biological organism and the higher-order system of *langue*. This is so because *parole* is the cross-coupling of both the physical–material and the social-semiological; the individual as biological organism and the language system in concrete acts of meaning-making. The history of the individual's participation in this socially shared system means that individuals literally *embody* the system which links them to other individuals. In other words, and as a careful examination of Saussure's diagram of the speech circuit will show, both concept and acoustic image already exist as socially significant patterns in the brains of the individuals who belong to a given social group. That is, neither concept nor acoustic image is actually 'transmitted' from speaker to listener. They do not have to be because the social-semiological resources for interacting with others on any given occasion – that is, whenever the circuit is activated – have already been learned ('imprinted' and, hence, embodied) though prior social interaction. Signs are not, then, innate or pre-given categories in the brains of individuals. They are socially learned. They provide individuals with the means for mutually orientating to other physical bodies (organisms), to flows of acoustic and other forms of energy in the ambient flux, to material objects and so on, in the circuit on the basis of the stable and socially shareable semiotic values which these have from one occasion to another.

Individuals co-ordinate their orientations to each other by virtue of a shared meaning system. The alternative would be for the individual *qua* biophysical entity to be controlled exclusively by the workings of mechanical necessity on account of his or her material, rather than informational and semiotic, cross-couplings with an environment defined in terms of mechanical forces operating on particles in Newtonian space–time. However, the emergent psychic properties of the circuit as a whole implicate that speaking subjects and their activities (e.g., phonation and audition) are directed and constrained by semiological values, rather than by the law-like operation of physical (holonomic) constraints in Newtonian space–time.

9 THE ONTOLOGICAL STRATIFICATION OF THE SIGN: LINKING THE CIRCUIT TO THE SYSTEM

Saussure's discussion of the speech circuit is also the first occasion in *CLG* in which the terminology of the sign is introduced. In this case, he uses the terminology of *acoustic image* and *concept* to designate the two strata of the linguistic sign. This terminology is later replaced by that of *signifier* and *signified* to mark the shift to the system perspective (Chapter 9). Saussure's preference for the terms acoustic image and concept in his discussion of the speech circuit captures the dually biophysical and psychic nature of the material and semiotic processes that are cross-coupled in acts of *parole*.

In the light of this, I shall now consider the question of the *ontological stratification* of the sign (see also section 7 and references therein). This provides an alternative explanation to that of psychophysical dualism. The starting point for such an explanation is the re-assessment which Saussure provides of speech as a flow of acoustic information in some ecosocial environment, rather than the physical transmission of sound waves from A to B *per se*. Gibson (1986 [1979]: 141) points out that the information which specifies an affordance 'points two ways, to the environment and to the observer':

> this does not in the least imply separate realms of consciousness and matter, psychophysical dualism. It says only that the information to specify the utilities of the environment is accompanied by the information to specify the observer himself, his body, legs, hands, and mouth.
>
> (Gibson 1986 [1979]: 141)

This means that the ontological stratification of the sign need no longer be explained in terms of psychophysical dualism. Matter need no longer be opposed to consciousness. Instead, the flow of acoustic information is ontologically stratified into a number of different levels, or strata, of meaning which are available to the inhabitants of some ecosocial environment. A first approximation of the different strata which are construable in the acoustic flux of speech sounds now follows:

1   information about the speaker's own body, for example, the position of the organs of speech relative to the production of specific speech sounds in phonation; the saccadic and rhythmic qualities of speech, which indicate the presence of an embodied subjectivity;
2   information about the variants and invariants in sound in the ambient acoustic array which are categorically construed as making a difference in a given language system;
3   information about how to relate the flow of acoustic information to the concepts which interpret the environment of speaker and listener in and through relevant social-semiological practices;
4   information about the listener/observer's own embodied position in the ecosocial environment in the processes of audition.

The dynamics of the speech circuit depend on the interdependencies that relate the various components of the speech circuit to each other. Saussure identifies three types of processes and relations which are responsible for the self-organization of the circuit as an ecosocial system. These are the physical, the physiological and the psychic. The overall dynamics of the circuit depend on the circular interdependencies that connect elements at each of these three levels. Most importantly, the psychic level means that the circuit is not just based on flows of matter and energy on the biophysical level. It also depends on the social meanings that these have for the participants in the circuit. Psychic refers to constraints of the non-holonomic sort. These constrain and entrain the lower-level physical and physiological processes in intentionally directed ways.

For Saussure, the sign is a 'complex unity' which links speaker and listener (Chapter 5, section 1). He also points out that 'the domain of this complex unity must be found in at least two individuals' (Saussure 1957: 8). That is, the domain of the sign-in-use is the speech circuit. The speech circuit is an ecosocial environment in which more than just acoustic images are linked to concepts in the sign relation. The sign is also the means whereby the two individuals who interact are linked to each other. This explains the bi-directionality of the arrows in the figures Saussure proposes in his description of the circuit (section 2 above). In phonation, the direction is concept → acoustic image; in audition it is acoustic image → concept (*CLG*: 29). In each direction, there is an orientation to the other, either as addressee or as addresser.

In this way, it can be seen that the acoustic image specifies the body of the speaker in relation both to the listener, as well as to the circuit as a whole. By the same token, the concept construes the physical–material environment, including that of 'inner' psychophysiological states and processes, as socially shareable meanings in relation to both speaker and listener. The complementarity of acoustic image and concept in the sign specifies both the meanings the environment has for the speaker–listener and their embodied relations to it. The two are not separable.

The dual nature of this 'complex unity' means that the sign enacts both (1) a system of social meanings when a concept and an acoustic image are psychically associated in the process of construing some phenomenon of experience as a socially shared signifying act, and (2) socially significant transactions which dialogically co-ordinate the individuals in the circuit in relation to each other. In this way, the sign is more appropriately seen as a *signifying act* in which social meaning and psychic activity are integrated.

Part IV

Linguistic value

Chapter 7

Linguistic value and how language construes the world

The schemata of the pure concepts of understanding are thus the true and sole conditions under which these concepts obtain relations to objects and so possess *significance*.

(Immanuel Kant 1970 [1781]: 186)

1 THE NON-NATURALISTIC BASIS OF LINGUISTIC VALUE

Saussure makes two references to the theory of political economy in connection with the notion of linguistic value. The first of these is in connection with his methodological decision to distinguish 'static linguistics' from 'evolutionary linguistics' (Chapter 4, section 1). He argues that this choice is imposed on any science which, like the economic sciences and linguistics, is concerned with the question of value:

> In linguistics, as in political science, one has before one the notion of *value*; in the two sciences, there is a *system of equivalence between different orders of things*: in one between work and wages, in the other, a signified and a signifier.
>
> (*CLG*: 115)

Language categories are not organized on the basis of a direct, unmediated link with natural kinds in the physical world. If the meanings of linguistic terms really were based on some sort of direct and naturalistic connection with real-world events, objects and so on, then, and in so far as physical reality is itself in a constant state of change and flux, there would be no historically stable basis for categorizing the phenomena of our experience. For this reason, categorization cannot be done on the basis of naturalistic criteria which inhere in the phenomena themselves.

In his second reference to economic value (*CLG*: 116), Saussure illustrates this problem with respect to the relation between a plot of land and its worth. In this case, the naturalistic (non-semiotic) nature of the connection is unable to provide any principle which would indicate how linguistic values are used to categorize the phenomena of experience in historically and culturally stable ways. Saussure points to the difficulty of keeping track of a certain value through time when, at every moment, the 'system of contemporary values' would need constantly to alter in order to assign the appropriate value to some object at any given moment in time. The value which is naturalistically assigned to the object, on the one hand, and the system which this depends on, on the other, would have no stability and continuity in time. In such a state of affairs, language would be hard pressed to confer any order on the phenomena of experience. The connection between the two would be a contingent and *ad hoc* one: values would constantly have to be invented to cope with moment-to-moment changes in phenomena. Clearly, the language system does not work on this basis. If it did, then the users of the system would be required to invent a new category in order to deal with every new occurrence of some phenomenon. Such a 'system' would prove to be both highly inefficient and essentially unworkable. That is, there would be no intrinsic principles of linguistic organization which would allow speaking subjects to classify the diverse and varied phenomena of perceptual experience on the basis of more general and shareable categories.

2 VALUE: THE CONTEXTUALIZING PRINCIPLE UNDERLYING LINGUISTIC SIGNS

Saussure appeals to *intrinsic* systemic, rather than extrinsic, criteria for defining linguistic units and their functions. This appeal rests on the concept of linguistic value. Value represents Saussure's attempt to show that language is not simply a transparent medium or vehicle for the coding and transmission of meanings which are external to it. Instead, the value-producing relations which are internal to the organization of language are themselves the means through which meanings are constructed in relation to what lies 'outside' language. Rather than starting with the question as to how language names or refers to extralinguistic reality, Saussure starts with a very different question: how do the value-producing relations which belong to the internal organization of the language system enable language users to construct and construe meaningful relations between language form and the world? Further, this occurs in regular and predictable ways in spite of the innumerable material and situational differences which characterize the phenomena of experience in the world.

Value means that language and all other social-semiological systems are organized on the basis of the relations among the terms internal to the system itself (Chapter 3, section 3). Thus, 'making love' contrasts with 'giving a lecture' in a cultural system where these two activities are distinguished in a regular and systematic way. Likewise, part of the meaning of 'snake' derives from its contrasting with 'lizard' in a system where these terms are systematically contrasted. There is, then, no need to postulate a separate and pre-existing world of snakes and lizards, and which these words simply name or label, or of some language-independent realm of 'concepts' or 'ideas' of snakes and lizards. That is, the meaning-making potential of language is inherent in its own intrinsic design principles, including its taxonomic principles of classification, rather than in properties of the external world. Value is a system of contextualizing relations for construing and categorizing the phenomena of experience in the world.

For this reason, value is distinguished from another important concept in Saussure's conceptual framework, viz. the notion of *signification* (Chapter 10). Value is concerned with discovering those 'factors' which a given linguistic unit maintains constant from any given occasion of use to another. Such factors cannot, for Saussure, be based on criteria of use, which Saussure more closely associates with signification. However, this does not mean that value and signification are two different kinds of meaning (cf. Culler 1976: 32–3); rather, they are two perspectives on the way in which meaning is made. A sign does not randomly change its meaning every time it is used; rather, its value-producing potential for making meaning in specific acts of *parole* is renewed in ways which allow the same structurally stable form to be approximately replicated on many different (material and psychological) occasions of use (see Chapter 13, section 4 for the notion of *synchronic identity*). Saussure seeks to discover the principle of internal organization which makes this possible. Value is, then, a meaning-making potential which is expressed in the relations of difference which hold among all the terms in the language system, abstracted from specific occasions of use (Chapter 3, section 3).

3 ARBITRARINESS AND THE CATEGORICAL BASIS OF LANGUAGE FORM

A second reason as to why the semiotic relation between language and what exists outside it has no naturalistic basis takes us back to the principle of arbitrariness. *Langue*$_1$ is a system of categorical terms that speaking subjects deploy to construe human experience in culturally specific ways. The system of linguistic categories shapes and guides the perceptions, actions and interactions of speaking subjects in largely unconscious ways. The categories internal to *langue* do not 'reflect' or 'correspond to' pre-given natural kinds in the external world. Instead, we use the categories of the language system to construe order, pattern and meaning in the phenomena of experience. The categories that belong to a given *langue* constitute a finite, though adaptable, dynamic and historically changing systemic resource for doing so.

In order to function, the language system must necessarily reduce and simplify the constantly changing phenomena in the ambient flux to a more manageable set of such categories that are internal to a specific language system. These are functionally organized in ways that 'reflect' not the 'real world' *per se*, but the principles in and through which the members of a given culture construe meaning and pattern in the phenomena of experience and organize their responses to these. The basis of the categories is social-semiological, rather than naturalistic. A given categorical distinction is defined by its value in the system of differences to which it belongs.

Arbitrariness designates the fact that the categories belonging to the system are functionally organized on the basis of relations of similarity and difference among the categorical terms that constitute the system. Speaking subjects construe phenomena of experience as conforming, in varying degrees, to this or that category on the basis of these criteria. Thus, two or more events, entities, things, etc. in the material–phenomenal world may be construed as conforming to the criteria of a given category, even though any given material occurrence may differ in other respects which are not relevant to the category in question. A given category *selectively* construes what is salient or relevant about some phenomenon for the social purposes to hand. By the same token, non-salient or otherwise insignificant material and other features of the phenomenon are ignored or backgrounded. This follows from the fact that the selection of a given semiotic category, rather than some other, in a given system functions to orientate interactants in some ways rather than others to the phenomena of experience.

4 THE LINGUISTIC CONSTRUAL OF THOUGHT AND SOUND AS THOUGHT-SUBSTANCE AND PHONIC SUBSTANCE

The problem with which Saussure opens the chapter on linguistic value concerns the way in which the system of *langue* confers form, pattern and meaning on the otherwise 'amorphous and indistinct mass' which is 'our thought':

> Psychologically, when abstracted from its expression in words, our thought [*pensée*] is no more than an amorphous and indistinct mass. Philosophers and linguists have always agreed in recognizing that, without the help of signs, we would be unable to distinguish two ideas in a clear and constant way. Taken in itself, thought is like a nebula in which nothing is necessarily delimited. There are no pre-established ideas, and nothing is distinct before the appearance of the language system [*la langue*].
>
> Faced with this fluctuating realm, do sounds in themselves afford entities circumscribed in advance? Phonic substance is neither more fixed nor more rigid; it is not a mould whose forms thought must necessarily fit, but a plastic material which is in turn divided into distinct parts in order to provide the signifiers of which thought has need. We can therefore represent the linguistic fact in its entirety – that is to say, the

language system – as a series of contiguous subdivisions simultaneously patterned on the undefined plane of inchoate ideas (A) and on the no less indeterminate plane of sounds (B). This may be represented very approximately by the schema:

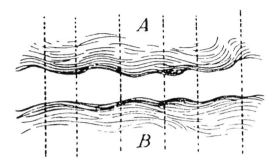

The characteristic role of the language system vis-a-vis thought is not to create a material phonic means for the expression of ideas, but to serve as the intermediary between thought and sound [*son*], so that their union necessarily brings about reciprocal delimitations of units. Thought, chaotic by nature, is forced to become precise in the process of being decomposed. There is therefore neither the materialization of thoughts nor the spiritualization of sounds, but it is a question of the in some ways mysterious fact that 'thought–sound' implicates divisions, and that the language system elaborates its units in being constituted between two amorphous masses.

(*CLG*: 155–6)

The distinction Saussure makes between 'thought' (*pensée*) and the language system (*langue*) represents a major attempt to explain how the variety and complexity of 'thought' is reduced to a smaller and, hence, more manageable set of categories that are internal to the language system. 'Thought' has form and meaning only in and through a system of social-semiological values which delimit this otherwise 'amorphous and indistinct mass'. Nevertheless, there has been a good deal of confusion concerning just what Saussure means by this term. In the remainder of this section, I shall attempt to provide an answer to this question.

In some respects, the problem which Saussure confronts is reminiscent of the one Kant grappled with in trying to theorize what he called 'a *necessary agreement* of experience with the concepts of its objects' (Kant 1970 [1781]: 174). Kant envisaged two possible ways of resolving this problem: 'either experience makes these concepts possible or these concepts make experience possible' (*ibid.*). Kant came down on the side of the second of these: 'the categories contain, on the side of the understanding, the grounds of the possibility of all experience in general' (*ibid.*). For Kant, the mind produces representations on the basis of *a priori* categories which are already given to the knowing subject by the faculty of pure reason. Pure reason, in Kant's theory, is concerned only with the 'form under which something is intuited; the pure concept [is] only the form of the thought of an object in general' (1970 [1781]: 92). Pure reason, which Kant distinguishes from 'empirical reason', has nothing to do with material and bodily sensations.

Now, the priority which Saussure assigns to the social-semiological system of pure values, while influenced by Kant's theory of schematic categories, represents an important shift in emphasis with respect to Kant's position. Whereas Kant takes the faculty of pure reason to be a subjective faculty in the mind of the individual, Saussure clearly relocates the categories in the system of *langue*: that is, in a historically and socially made system of linguistic values. Nevertheless, both Kant and Saussure share the notion of pure form which operates on and gives categorical shape to the phenomena of experience.

What, then, does Saussure's term 'thought' refer to? It would be too easy for the modern reader to interpret Saussure's use of this term with reference to more recent notions of 'cognitive processing', as in cognitive science. Saussure does not actually say where 'thought' is located. Is it in the mind of the individual? In the social system? In the external world? Thought is an ambiguous notion in Saussure's discussion. Nevertheless, this very ambiguity can be put to good use in attempting to understand the relationship between language form and the world.

The paragraph quoted above reveals Saussure's attempt to come to grips with the relationship between the language system *qua* system of pure values and what lies outside this. Why, then, does Saussure use the term 'thought', instead of talking about the world or extralinguistic reality? This is a crucial question and it is important to be clear about this from the outset. In particular, our understanding of the principle of arbitrariness depends on a clear understanding of this relationship.

The problem is illustrated, for example, by Eleanor Rosch's discussion of the role of prototypes in the classification of real-world objects. According to Rosch, 'a view of categories as initially arbitrary would be reasonable only if the world were entirely unstructured' (1977: 212). Saussure does not talk about the 'world' as such. This has led many readers of Saussure to assume that his theory is incapable of making the connection between the system of pure values in *langue* and the 'real world' (Lee 1985: 113). However, Saussure does not say that the world is unstructured. On the contrary, his description of thought as a 'nebula of which nothing is necessarily delimited' is worth examining in some detail in order to clarify this problem.

The psychological (not psychic) realm to which Saussure refers is analogous to Kant's noumenon. That is, it is an undifferentiated realm which lacks the 'unity of intuition in space and time', as Kant (1970: [1781]: 258) would say, on account of its not being connected to the *a priori* categories of pure understanding which confer on it a meaning. In Kant's view, these categories are 'pure schema of possible experience' (*ibid.*). They have no basis in empirical experience. Saussure's term 'psychological' designates a subjective realm of undifferentiated sensations that have not been connected to the categories of the language system. In other words, 'psychological' refers to undifferentiated noumena which are not the focus of intentionally directed psychic acts in *parole*. They are not, therefore, cross-coupled with the categories of some higher-order social-semiological system.

For these two reasons, (noumenal) thought is an 'amorphous and indistinct mass'. However, Saussure differs from Kant as to the location of the schemata which make the process of categorization possible. Whereas for Kant the schemata are 'constitutive *a priori* in pure understanding' (1970: [1789]: 258), and not therefore derived from empirical experience, in Saussure they are derived from the practices of *parole* and 'imprinted' in the brains of individuals (Chapter 5, section 3).

A number of points follow from the arguments in the preceding paragraphs. Saussure, like Kant, is concerned with the relationship between a system of pure forms and 'thought'. Such a system presupposes that there is no contact with the phenomenal world of material and sensual experience. Had Saussure talked about the 'world', he would have been obliged to deal with the domain of 'empirical concepts', to use the Kantian terminology. Instead, Saussure's focus is on the historically and socially made categories that are internal to the language system. These are *a priori* in the sense that the individual is assimilated into a given social-semiological system and its categories irrespective of criteria of individual 'will' and 'intelligence' in *parole*. The principle of arbitrariness is centrally concerned with this fact. *Langue*, seen as a system of pure values, refers to the intrinsic organization of language form. Saussure makes a further important theoretical point when he proposes that language form is interposed between 'thought' and 'sound', respectively.

What does Saussure mean by the terms 'thought' and 'sound'? The key to understanding the meaning of 'thought', in particular, lies in Saussure's use of the qualifying adverbial 'psychologically' at the beginning of the above quotation. That is, 'thought' is here defined in *non*-psychic terms as belonging to a pre-semiotic and subjective psychological realm. This is so in two ways: in this 'psychological', rather than psychic, definition, 'thought' is (1) non-intentional in the sense that it is not directed to a specific object in any clear way, and (2) purely private and subjective rather than social-semiological because it is not cross-coupled with language or some other social-semiological resource system. It should be clarified here that (2) does not refer to 'inner' acts of *parole* which are not revealed in the public domain. This is something very different, and it is not at issue here. The crucial distinction here is that between the non-intentional meaning of 'psychological', on the one hand, and the 'psychic' and, hence, intentional character of acts of consciousness, on the other (Chapter 6, section 4).

It is the system of differences internal to language form which shapes and construes 'thought', and in ways which are specific to a given language system. To paraphrase Kant, language form is the form of the thought of an object in general (section 4). Language, to adopt the term proposed by Reddy (1979), is not a 'conduit' through which pre-existing extralinguistic concepts or meanings are simply 'moulded' into linguistic shape. Saussure makes precisely this point in the quotation above. Rather, the value-producing differences in language form provide the means for construing meaningful relationships between the internal organization of language and what lies outside it. Thus, 'thought' designates the semiotically unformed perceptual flux which has, however, the potential to be construed as a semiotically formed signified substance in and through the categories of the language system. For this reason, thought is *pre*-semiotic. 'Pre-semiotic' implies, however, that thought has the potential to be construed semiotically.

It is not, then, a question of the linguistic sign simply 'standing for' the 'thing' which lies outside it in the 'real' world. Derossi (1976: 53) makes the point that this 'thing' is not in itself thinkable. It is only 'thinkable' in so far as it is categorized, or able to be categorized, in and through the categorical distinctions which are internal to language form. These are the categorical resources for semiotically construing perceptual experience in socially salient ways.

I may observe, for example, a given material event, which I shall gloss here as 'Mary's shaking hand'. Simplifying matters somewhat, I can either say *Mary shook her hand*, or *Mary's hand shook*. Now, the observed event is a material event which impinges on my consciousness as a given phenomenon of experience in the perceptual flux. I can interpret this event as a given category of experience by choosing either of the two clauses given here. Each of these two clauses signifies a given experiential semantic structure. In the first clause, this may be expressed as [ACTOR + PROCESS: MATERIAL + GOAL]; in the second as [MEDIUM + PROCESS: MATERIAL] (Halliday 1994: 161–75). The selection of one of these rather than the other implies a different categorical semantic construal of the 'same' material event. The two semantic structures are made possible by the value-producing differences which are intrinsic to the experiential grammar of the English clause. They are not natural kinds which inhere in the event itself. The basic distinction is that between the presence of two participants, *Mary* (Actor) and *her hand* (Goal), in the first clause, and the presence of just one participant, *Mary's hand* (Medium), in the second. If I select the first type of structure, I construe the material event as an intentional, goal-directed action on the part of the semantic Actor, *Mary*. That is, *Mary* intentionally did something with her hand. In the second clause, things are different. There is no suggestion in the semantics of this clause of an intentional, goal-directed action on the part of some Actor. In this case, a process was brought about, or instigated, by some causal agency which is not, in this case, grammaticalized. This is, of course, an invented example, but it may be the case that Mary's hand shook on account of some purely involuntary, internal cause over which she has no conscious control.

5 LANGUAGE DOES NOT REPRESENT PRE-ESTABLISHED IDEAS

Saussure's view of the relationship between thought and *langue* is a non-representational one. *Langue* does not exist in order to represent thought. In any case, that which is 'amorphous and indistinct' cannot simply be represented since this would require the existence in thought of distinctive and pre-established entities which language simply re-presents or duplicates. Saussure is absolutely clear on this issue. He says: 'There are no pre-established ideas, and nothing is distinct before the appearance of the language system' (*CLG*: 155). He also points out: 'If words were charged with representing concepts given in advance, they would each have, from one language system to the next, exact correspondences in sense [*sens*]; yet this is not so' (*CLG*: 161). Saussure goes on to illustrate this second point with some lexical differences between German and French and some grammatical differences between the Hebrew and Proto-Germanic verb forms. Saussure challenges the assumption that language is organized on the basis of universal principles that are extrinsic to language form. The very view which Saussure challenges here is predominant in much of modern-day linguistics and cognitive science. That is, Saussure rejects the assumption that the categories of the world are pre-specified, and that the organism is pre-programmed to respond to these (Edelman 1989: 267). Semiotically, the individual selectively attends to an open-ended environment and further elaborates this through the available social-semiological resource systems. Thought is Saussure's term for describing a world which is neither pre-specified nor closed.

Given these two claims, why, then, does Saussure insist on the distinction between thought and the language system? I shall now try to answer this question in four closely related stages, as follows.

1 *Langue* does not re-present and transmit pre-established ideas. Instead, it acts upon, intervenes in and elaborates thought as signified substance. In this view, the language system provides the categorical resources whereby speaking subjects may orientate to the richness and density of the perceptual experience in their ecosocial environments. Such experience is always richer than the categorical distinctions made by the system of values in a given language system. The richness of this experience affords its semiotic re-construal and re-elaboration in a variety of possible ways.
2 The ambiguity in Saussure's definition of thought enables the insight that higher-order consciousness is not a uniquely private and subjective

affair which is confined to the individual. The system of *langue* is a social resource which enables acts of consciousness to be jointly and dialogically focused on, elaborated and shared in *parole* (Chapter 6, section 4). Instead of re-presenting or 'reflecting' pre-established ideas, *langue* is the means whereby ideas are produced in the process of bringing them to consciousness.

3   'Ideas' emerge on the basis of the value-producing differences that are internal to language form. The fact that there are no 'pre-established ideas' suggests that 'thought' and 'ideas' refer to two theoretically distinct, though related, notions in Saussure (Chapter 13, section 15). 'Ideas' refer, in my view, to the conceptual forming of thought as a semiotic thought-substance (signified substance). Ideas, in the sense that Saussure uses this term, can only be 'established' on the basis of semiological processes. Therefore, they are distinct from thought. They are its semiotic elaboration. To paraphrase Kant (1970 [1781]: 260), an 'idea' is a thought 'made sensible' in relation to a conceptual sense, or a signification, in a given sign relation. From the 'psychological' point of view, thought, in Saussure's definition, is pre-semiotic; ideas are both psychic and semiotic (Chapter 13, section 15).

4   It does not make sense to talk of a single category in isolation from the system which gave rise to it in the first place. Minimally speaking, a given category is established on the basis of its systemic contrasts with at least one other term in some associative group. For example, the conceptual terms, or categories, [SINGULAR] and [PLURAL] in English do not exist *sui generis*. Nor do they exist on the basis of a direct, unmediated link with the world. Rather, they are systematic distinctions which the English language makes in order to interpret in linguistically relevant and culturally stable ways the phenomena of experience (Chapter 3, section 3).

'Thought' refers to the richness and diversity of the phenomena of our perceptual experience. All perceptual experience is based on the individual's active orientation to and interaction with his or her ecosocial environment (Chapter 6, section 6). 'Thought' refers to the macroscopic phenomena which are picked up by the individual's perceptual systems. However, the individual's capacity to respond to the richness and diversity of the perceptual flux, so defined, is constrained both by inbuilt biological criteria (Chapter 6, section 4) and by the system of social-semiological values. Saussure's 'thought' refers to the phenomena of perceptual experience *'before'* the intervention of social semiosis. His notion closely resembles a number of related ones. These include Kant's noumenon, Hjelmslev's content-purport (1969 [1943]: 57), Gibson's (1986 [1979]) ambient array of perceptual information, Peng's (1994: 124) proto-meaning and Edelman's (1989) unlabelled world. All of these refer to the notion of a pre-semiotic realm before the intervention of the categorical resources of *langue*. The principle of arbitrariness is crucial in this sense:

> Not only are the two domains which are linked by the linguistic fact inchoate and amorphous, but the choice which assigns each acoustic segment to each idea is perfectly arbitrary. If this were not the case, the notion of value would lose something of its character, since it would contain an element imposed from outside. But in fact values remain entirely relative, and that is why the link between idea and sound is radically arbitrary.
>
> (*CLG*: 157)

Saussure emphasizes that sound is not 'a material phonic means for the expression of ideas' (*CLG*: 156). Such a notion would presuppose the existence of pre-established ideas from outside the system of *langue*, and which are simply in need of a material means of expression. Again, this would entail a naturalistic conception of pre-semiotic ideas that originate outside semiosis.

6 SCHEMATICITY, INSTANTIATION AND THE RELATIVITY OF VALUES

Values are 'entirely relative' and for this reason the link between sound and idea is 'radically arbitrary' (Chapter 12, section 1). The fact that sounds are not simply the material carriers of pre-established ideas means that the language system is based on internal principles of functional differentiation which are driven by the continuous linguistic work of individuals to adjust the system to the world. The 'relative' and 'arbitrary' character of the system of values means that it is a system of contextualizing relations which endures in historical time and which exists independently of individual intention and consciousness. By the same token, it is the means whereby individual intention and consciousness emerge in acts of *parole*.

The 'relativity' of values thus refers to their inherently contextual character. Categories are not immutable natural kinds of the sort suggested by Rosch's empirical realism (Thibault 1986). Categories can be altered by the differential weighting of terms according to specific contextual and systemic factors. This leads in time to further enrichment of the category, both individually and socially.

> The arbitrariness of the sign allows us better to understand why the social fact alone can create a linguistic system. The collectivity is necessary in order to establish values whose only *raison d'être* is in usage and in general agreement; the individual alone is incapable of determining one.
>
> (*CLG*: 157)

The system of values in *langue* enshrines the collective concerns and orientations to meaning that are shared, usually unconsciously, by the members of a given culture (Ellis 1993: 34). In particular, the grammatical categories of the language constitute a theory, or, more accurately, a complementary plurality of theories about the ways in which the members of the community construct and orientate to their social reality (Halliday 1993). The distinction I discussed above between the transitive and ergative construals of Mary's shaking hand is a case in point. The systemic basis of value is the means whereby such theories are elaborated:

> Moreover, the idea of value, so determined, shows us that it is a great illusion to consider a term as simply the union of a certain sound with a certain concept. To define it in this way would be to isolate it from the system of which it is a part; it would be to think that one can start from the terms and construct the system by adding them up, whereas on the contrary it is necessary to start from the whole in order to obtain by analysis the elements that it contains.
>
> (*CLG*: 157)

Saussure focuses on a key theoretical distinction here, viz. that between the terms and the system that gives rise to these (Chapter 3, section 3). With respect to the terms, the system is the superordinate notion. It is a mistake to think that one can start with the terms and then derive the system by a simple process of aggregration of the former. What, then, is the relationship between the system and the terms that comprise this?

The answer to this question requires a partial re-orientation in the way we look at the sign. Typically, Saussure's conception of the sign has been exclusively discussed in terms of the *inter*stratal relation of symbolic construal which links signifier to signified, or sound to idea (Chapter 9, section 1). Insufficient attention has been paid to Saussure's discussion of a no less important dimension of the sign. The relationship between the system and the terms in the system is, following Kant, one of *schematicity*. The system is the more superordinate or schematic notion and the terms are more specific in relation to the system. That is, the system is at a higher order of both generality and abstraction with respect to the terms that comprise it. The linguistic notion of *instantiation* best captures what is involved here. The linguist who has, perhaps, most extended recent thinking in this area is the American Ronald Langacker. Langacker defines schematicity, which derives ultimately from Kant's theory of the schema of pure reason, as follows:

> Schematicity can be equated with the relation between a superordinate node and a subordinate node in a taxonomic hierarchy; the concept [TREE], for instance, is schematic with respect to the concept [OAK]: [[TREE] → [OAK]]. In such relationships I call the superordinate structure a **schema**, and the subordinate structure an **elaboration** or **instantiation** of the schema. The conceptual import of this relationship, I suggest, is that an

instantiation is fully compatible with the specifications of the schema, but is characterized in finer detail. . . . The schema [TREE], for example, defines a category that is instantiated by a variety of more specific concepts, all of them compatible with its specifications ([OAK], [MAPLE], [ELM], and so on). These instantiations elaborate the schema in different ways along various parameters to yield more precisely articulated notions.

(Langacker 1987: 68)

The linguistic system is comprised of a very large number of ordered hierarchies of categories (cf. terms). These hierarchies are characterized by a scale of generality (superordinate) and a scale of specificity (subordinate). Categories at the highest levels are both more general and more abstract and have correspondingly fewer semantic specifications. Categories at the lower levels have more detailed, or more delicate, semantic specifications. In Langacker's example, the superordinate category [TREE] is schematic to the subordinate category [ELM] in this sense.

Exactly the same principle holds for grammatical categories. In English grammar the superordinate term [DEICTIC] is schematic to very many, much more finely specified categories. These include, for instance, [SPECIFIC; DETERMINATIVE; DEMONSTRATIVE] and [SPECIFIC; DETERMINATIVE; POSSESSIVE]. Without going into any further detail here, we can say that the first category is schematic to instances such as *this, that, these, those* and *the*, all of which may be further specified by even finer categorical distinctions. The second category is schematic to instances such as *my, your, our, his, her, its, theirs* and so on. Again, all of these may be further subcategorized. In the two cases, the two sets of more specific instantiations more finely specify the superordinate, or schematic, category [DEICTIC].

Importantly, instantiation is a unidirectional relation (Davidse 1992: 101): the Schema–Instance relation cannot be reversed. Thus, [TREE] is schematic to [ELM], but [ELM] is not schematic to [TREE]. The same also applies to grammatical categories. Instantiation, unlike the relation of symbolic construal which refers to the two-way and reciprocal link between signifier and signified (Chapter 9, section 1), is a one-way and non-reversible relationship. This is the reason why, as Saussure points out, one cannot 'start with the terms and construct the system'. The relationship between the system and the terms that constitute it is one of instantiation: that is, the terms instantiate the system, whereas the reverse is not so. Therefore, the system of pure values is schematic to the terms, but their instantiations in lexicogrammatical form are not schematic to the system that gives rise to them.

Instantiation is no less important to our understanding of the workings of the system of pure values in relation to the signs that this produces than is the more generally recognized two-way relationship of symbolic construal which links signifier to signified in the sign. The semiotic notions of instantiation and symbolic construal will be discussed more fully in Chapter

13 (see also Chapter 8, sections 2 and 3), but some preliminary discussion is required here on account of the close connection between instantiation and the linguistic categorization of the phenomena of experience. As we shall see, the linguistic relationship between the system of pure values and the phenomena of experience which are so categorized is one of instantiation.

Saussure's discussion shows that the sign results from two kinds of semiotic relations, viz. interstratal symbolic construal and intrastratal instantiation. That is, the signs that arise from the system of pure values may be seen as CONSTRUAL–INSTANTIATION complexes. Without this dual perspective, it would be impossible to relate the social-semiological potential of the system of pure values to concrete acts of *parole*.

In the concluding paragraph of the section of *CLG* under discussion here, Saussure makes an important observation on the methodological procedures that the linguist is required to adopt in order to re-construct analytically the system of pure values:

> Not being able to grasp directly the concrete entities or the units of *langue*, we will work on words [*mots*]. These, without covering exactly the definition of the linguistic unit (see p. 147), at least give an approximate idea of it, which has the advantage of being concrete; we will therefore consider them as specimens equivalent to the actual terms [*termes réels*] of a synchronic system, and the principles elicited with regard to words will be valid for entities in general.
>
> (*CLG*: 158)

The problem addressed in this passage concerns the means of access, analytically speaking, to the more schematic or higher-order terms in the system of pure values. In keeping with Kant's notion of pure reason, these have neither form nor phenomenal status. For this reason, they are not directly accessible to the linguist. Only lexicogrammatical form (words, etc.) is so accessible. Terms, rather than words, are the constitutive basis of the system (Chapter 3, section 3). However, the linguist must analytically re-construct the system, and therefore the terms that constitute it, on the basis of observed lexicogrammatical patterns. These *instantiate* the higher-order terms of the system. They are the modes of deployment of the terms in the system. Terms do not occur singularly. For this reason, Saussure says that the linguist must work on the words (lexicogrammatical forms), which are instantiations of the higher-order terms, in order to gain access to the latter. The linguist must look 'behind' the forms to re-construct the system of pure values and the terms that comprise this.

Roy Harris, in his translation of *CLG*, translates the critically important phrase *termes réels* in the above quotation as 'actual signs' (Saussure 1983: 112). In so doing, Harris destroys the main point of Saussure's argument here. Words are synonymous with signs, not terms, in *CLG*. They are not on the same level of schematicity with respect to the higher-order terms. In translating Saussure's *termes réels* in this way, Harris ignores the important logical and terminological distinction which Saussure makes between these two different levels of schematicity. In the synchronic system of pure values, or *langue*$_1$, both conceptual and phonic terms belong to the two orders of difference that constitute the system. Words and signs, on the other hand, result from the combining of the two orders of difference in order to instantiate specific combinations of terms in *langue*$_2$. In effect, Harris puts Saussure's distinction between terms, on the one hand, and signs or words, on the other, on the same level of abstraction. In the process, he loses sight of the non-reversible schematicity relation between these two distinct levels of, respectively, the systemic and the instantial.

To illustrate the principle at issue here I shall now analyse a concrete example. Compare clauses (1a) and (1b) and (2a) and (2b) below.

(1) a. John pricked the balloon
     b. John pricked
(2) a. A pin burst the balloon
     b. The balloon burst

Clauses (1a) and (1b) are concerned with the extension of the Actor's intentionality. The relevant question concerns whether this extends to a second semantic participant, the Goal, or not. For this reason, these clauses are assignable to the transitive system in the experiential grammar of English. Clauses (2a) and (2b) show a different tendency. The focus is no longer on the intentional Actor, but on the semantic Medium through which some process takes place. Intentionality is not relevant in the semantics of these clauses. These belong to the ergative system in the experiential grammar of English. The Medium-centredness of ergative processes is concerned, instead, with a 'change of state' (Davidse 1991: 61). Here, the relevant question is whether this change of state was instigated by some specified 'external' agency, as in (2a), or whether it was self-instigated, as in (2b). In (2b), the source of the change of state which occurs in the Medium is not grammaticalized. In both the transitive and ergative types, there is, then, a basic distinction between clauses which have one semantic participant ((1b) and (2b)), and those which have two ((1a) and (2a)). The two sets of distinctions between (1) transitive and ergative and (2) one-participant and two-participant clauses allow the following semantic features, or conceptual terms, to be applied to the lexicalized participants in each of the four clauses. The four clauses and the feature analysis of the conceptual terms that configure in their respective participants are set out as follows:

(1) a. [CLAUSE: EFFECTIVE: TRANSITIVE]

    John   pricked   the balloon
    [+ACTOR: [+GOAL:
    +INTENTIONALITY: −INTENTIONALITY:

+GOAL-DIRECTED]   +RECIPIENT]
b. [CLAUSE: MIDDLE: INTRANSITIVE]
John   pricked
[+ACTOR:
+INTENTIONALITY:
+GOAL-DIRECTED:
(Goal implied)]

(2) a. [CLAUSE: EFFECTIVE: ERGATIVE: INSTIGATION OF RESULTANT STATE]
A pin   burst   the balloon
[+INSTIGATOR: [−SELF-INSTIGATING:
+EXTERNALLY INSTIGATIVE: +RESULTANT STATE:
−VOLITIVE]   −VOLITIVE]
b. [CLAUSE: MIDDLE: ERGATIVE]
The balloon   burst
[+SELF-INSTIGATING:
+EXTERNALLY INSTIGATIVE:
−VOLITIVE]

The analysis above is a concrete illustration of Saussure's insight that a given syntagm is the result of 'various associative groups, at whose intersection appears the syntagm' (*CLG*: 179; Chapter 11). In the analysis, I have concentrated on the conceptual terms (semantic features) that configure to produce the various clause-level participants in their respective syntagms. Each of these participants has a lexical realization, viz. *John, the balloon, the pin* which instantiates the more schematic terms which configure in the lexicalized participant. Thus, a given configuration of terms specifies the functional value of the participants in their respective clause-level configurations.

This brief description is a very drastic simplification of a very complex area in the grammar and semantics of English. My point is to show, as was the case with the earlier example of 'Mary's hand shaking', that these are value-producing distinctions which are intrinsic to the internal design of the grammar. If language really did simply refer to a set of universal and unchanging concepts, fixed in advance, then we would need a new term every time a concept occurred. Otherwise the fact that the same term can be repeatedly used to construe different material instances of a given phenomenon as belonging to the same category has to be explained (see also Derossi 1976: 55).

The basic principle which unites the terms as an associative group is the way in which value-producing similarities and differences are distributed across the associative groups in which the terms belong (Chapter 3, section 3). For example, the distinction between [EFFECTIVE] and [MIDDLE], which refers to two-participant and one-participant material process clauses, respectively, serves to co-classify more specific (more delicate) terms as

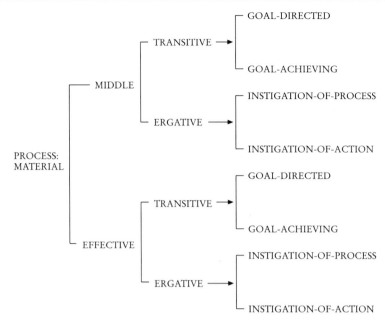

Figure 7.1 Associative group; Middle and Effective clause types in English; process type: material (adapted from Davidse 1991: 17)

belonging to the same associative group, or subsystem. Let us take the case of [EFFECTIVE] by way of an illustrative example. The associative group which subclassifies clauses belonging to this category in terms of still more specific distinctions is presented in Figure 7.1. This figure shows that whenever a speaking subject selects a clause with the schematic terms [MIDDLE] or [EFFECTIVE], then he or she must select either [TRANSITIVE] or [ERGATIVE]. These two terms are, in turn, schematic to still more specific selections. Thus, the choice between, say, [GOAL-DIRECTED] and [GOAL-ACHIEVING] is only available if the more schematic term [TRANSITIVE] is selected. Each of the most specific selections on the far right in Figure 7.1 is instantiated as a given configuration of terms. These configure to produce a particular type of more specific option in the associative group of effective clauses in English. The terms that configure to produce these possibilities, along with sample lexicogrammatical instantiations, are listed below:

[MIDDLE: TRANSITIVE: GOAL-DIRECTED]:
Actor (intentional)^Process – *John kicked*
[MIDDLE: TRANSITIVE: GOAL-ACHIEVING]:
Actor (non-intentional)^Process – *The spacecraft landed*; *Lightning struck.*
[MIDDLE: ERGATIVE: INSTIGATION-OF-PROCESS; SELF-INSTIGATING OR EXTERNALLY INSTIGATED]:

Medium^Process – *The balloon burst*; *The gun fired*; *The building shook*; *The stock exchange crashed*; *Shares slumped.*
[MIDDLE: ERGATIVE: INSTIGATION-OF-ACTION; SUPERVENING AGENCY IMPLIED]:
Medium^Process – *The class hurried*; *The dog is walking.*
[EFFECTIVE: TRANSITIVE: GOAL-DIRECTED]:
Actor (intentional)^Process^Goal – *John kicked the balloon.*
[EFFECTIVE: TRANSITIVE: GOAL-ACHIEVING]:
Actor (non-intentional)^Process^Goal – *The rock hit Mary*; *The bullet hit the soldier.*
[EFFECTIVE: ERGATIVE: INSTIGATION-OF-PROCESS]
Instigator/Agent^Process^Medium – *The dog broke the glass.*
[EFFECTIVE: ERGATIVE: INSTIGATION-OF-ACTION; SUPERVENING AGENCY]:
Instigator/Agent^Process^Actor – *John walked the dog*; *The teacher hurried the class.*

7 LANGUAGE FORM RECURSIVELY OPERATES ON THE REAL

Saussure's argument concerning the relations between thought and sound can be set up as a series of proportionalities, as shown below. Thus, 'thought–sound' is to 'language form' as sound is to the signifier, as thought is to the signified, as the sign is to the value-producing distinctions which are construed in and through the sign relation. Sound is not simply a vehicle or carrier of thought. The relevant proportionalities are set out as follows:

thought–sound : language form ::
sound : signifier ::
thought : signified ::
SIGN : VALUE-PRODUCING/CONSTRUING DIFFERENCES IN EXTERNAL REALITY

Saussure suggests that the 'correlation' between thought and sound is analogous to air being in contact with water (*CLG*: 156). This pedagogical example should not be taken to imply a physicalist reductionism in his conception of the sign. Saussure's constant emphasis on the psychic basis of the sign avoids this reading. The comparison is a purely externally derived one of *analogy*. Saussure's example, derived as it is from inorganic nature, shows how water responds to differences in the atmospheric pressure of the air, which the water transforms into meaningful distinctions in the form of waves. What Saussure does not include in his analogy is the role of the interpreter who construes this difference as meaningful. It is the role of his conception of the sign as 'psychic' which does just that.

The interfacing of water with air in Saussure's analogy serves to demonstrate that it is not strictly correct to say the one is external to the other. Instead, the changes in the atmospheric pressure of the air bring about meaningful changes in the water. This occurs on the basis of the meaningful relationship which is construed *between* the two phenomena. They are not quite distinct phenomena in any case. Saussure's point is that by virtue of the contact between them they belong to the same more global system of relations. It is the same with the thought–sound relationship which Saussure speaks about here. Thought does not operate directly on sound, but on the phonic distinctions that are construed on the stratum of the signifier. Language form, interfaced between thought and sound, performs the same function in relation to these two levels of pre-semiotic reality.

Thought, said to be 'chaotic in nature', is 'made precise by this process of segmentation'. It is a pre-semiotic realm of purely analogue differences which have not been digitalized as categorical distinctions by the intervention of language form. Like the interfacing of water with air, it is not, however, the case that thought is simply 'external' to language form. As we shall see below, the latter is not directly dependent on the former. What is important to emphasize here is that the 'process of segmentation' of the pre-semiotic and undifferentiated 'chaos' of thought means that the two interface with each other as part of a still wider system of contextualizing relations and values.

Saussure carefully points out that there is no direct re-construal, or re-contextualization, of 'thoughts into sounds', or of 'sounds into ideas'. In both of these pairs, the one does not operate directly on the other. In between the two planes of pre-semiotic thought and sound there evolves the interface of language form – the sign. This is no longer directly dependent on either pre-semiotic sound or thought. This level of semiotic organization – language form, or the sign – now evolves an internal structure of its own, no longer directly tied to the material, and in ways which enable its meaning-making potential to expand and adapt to changing social–historical and material needs and circumstances (Halliday 1992: 22–3).

Let us pause for a moment to take further stock of the earlier points I made in connection with the admittedly invented example of 'Mary's shaking hand'. I said we have the perception of a material event and a linguistic construal of this. The latter is made possible by the value-producing distinctions in the grammatical systems of the language. Language does not mirror, reflect or re-present the world. At the same time, the materiality of the perceived event is not being denied. In Saussure's terms, the perceived event occurs in the domain of thought: that is, in the flux of perceptual experience. My act of construing this with one or the other of the grammatical possibilities discussed above selectively attends to and focuses on some aspects and dimensions of this event rather than others in the ambient flux. The psychic act of consciously focusing on the material event by discursive means entails the cross-coupling of this material event with semiotic form. The cross-coupling of the two produces a semiotically formed substance (see also the notion of 'substance-effect' in Godzich 1984). In other words, the event is assimilated to the categories of a social-semiological system and for this reason it may be the joint focus of conscious attention in discursive interaction.

These language-internal resources are value-producing, as shown, for example, by the system of options in Figure 7.1. What does this mean? My point is that the value-producing distinctions which are intrinsic to the design of the grammar confer semiotic value on material entities, events and processes, and so on. That is, they selectively contextualize these in socially significant ways. These language-internal resources enable the users of the language to establish that which is relevant and significant from among the countless possibilities in the pre-semiotic material event. We use language to make what is semiotically relevant *emerge* out of the perceptual flux. This is the realm Saussure identified as pre-semiotic 'thought'. Thought always has the potential to be selectively attended to and made semiotically salient in this way.

In the final analysis, Saussure uses the term 'thought' because the material world which is construed by some signifying act and the sign in and through which this takes place are *not* totally separable phenomena. They are different 'moments' in one overall process. 'Thought' refers to that which is *potentially* significant. It is that which is able to be 'thought' in and through the value-producing distinctions in *langue*. It is not non-semiotic; rather, it is a *pre*-semiotic potential which can be selected, acted on and intervened in by the value-producing distinctions in linguistic form in the social processes of meaning-making. A simple re-alignment of the basic principles involved shows that Saussure's conception of the sign, far from corresponding to the oversimplified biplanar definition with which it is usually saddled, is in actual fact triadic, as shown in Figure 7.2.

The value-producing distinctions in *langue* themselves constitute the premises for acting on and interacting with what lies 'outside' linguistic form. The value-producing resources of the grammar embody two principles which are only apparently in contradiction with each other. On the one hand, the system of pure values is a rich and highly complex, though by no means

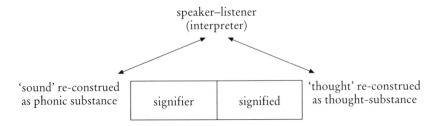

Figure 7.2 Triadic nature of Saussurean view of semiosis, showing semiotically mediated relation of the speaker–listener to the analogue flux of 'sound' and 'thought'

infinite, set of meaning-making resources. This means that a given language system functions as a precise and subtle instrument in specific contexts. It is able to circumscribe and delimit this reality so as to make it a specific object of human knowledge and action. On the other hand, this embodies an understanding of the otherness and the independence of this material reality from the specifically linguistic instrument. This reality is not simply given; rather, it emerges in and through the value-producing resources which the users of a language deploy to construe it, act on it and intervene in it.

The relationship between language form, on the one hand, and thought and sound, on the other, is a permeable and open one between the language system and its environments. Saussure's term 'thought' does not refer to a phenomenon which is already segmented and delimited by linguistic form. Language form is that which *forms* substance. In other words, it is the action of form on both thought and sound which enables semiotically formed thought-substance and phonic substance progressively to emerge from the apparent flux of pre-semiotic perceptual and sensory-motor experience (for a contrasting view see Petitot-Cocorda 1990 [1985]: 238).

Saussure recognizes, as Derossi (1976: 53) points out, that the 'thing' outside language is not in itself 'thinkable'. On the one hand, the system of *langue*, in order that it may be accorded its specificity and independence, must have a limit, or a border which separates and distinguishes it from its material environments. On the other hand, the permeable, dynamic and open nature of the relationship between the language system and its material environments means that there is considerable uncertainty and, precisely, ambivalence as to where to draw the line, so to speak, between the two. The value-producing distinctions internal to linguistic form, in their interactions with their environment, constitute, in the final analysis, not two separate domains, but a single, more global system of relations. I would suggest this is the direction in which Saussure's conception of social meaning-making was moving.

Instead of pre-established ideas which are re-presented by language, there is a progressive *synchronic convergence* of the value-producing distinctions internal to language form and the outside reality which the speaker uses the language system to intervene in and construe. The external world of thought and sound is not, in Saussure's reckoning, a complex of pre-given data just waiting to be interpreted or represented by their being segmented into ever smaller units. Saussure's metaphor of the 'nebula' refers to the process whereby, from an indeterminate background in the perceptual flux, specific features are progressively made to emerge, rather like the progressive bringing into focus of a distant galaxy by means of a telescope. It is the categorical attribution to these of semiotic value which makes them relevant in some specific context, or socially stabilized context type. This results from the processes of categorization of the phenomena of the world by a continual and progressive convergence of these with the internal organization of language and other semiotic resource systems. The boundary between the two is neither fixed nor absolute. There is a constant dialectical exchange between the internal organization of the language system and its material environments.

The border or the point of contact between language system and environment is represented by *parole*. *Parole* is the interface between language form and its material–phenomenal environments. In this sense, *parole* 'faces two ways' in the process of cross-coupling the individual body–brain complex with the higher-order social semiological system. It does so by (1) selectively transducing the ambient flux of matter–energy which surrounds the organism (cf. Saussure's thought) into semiotic categories, and (2) selectively projecting semiotically relevant information about the organism into its ecosocial context (cf. Saussure's sound). The language system is a stratified system which exists both 'inside' and 'outside' the individual. Instead of processing sensory data, or input, from the world as information (output) in the brain, the recursive nature of Saussure's stratified model of semiosis means that the system generates order and pattern in the process of semiotically re-construing the external disorder of thought and sound. It does so in ways which recursively and dialogically connect self to non-self in and through the resources of the higher-order social-semiological system of values in *langue*.

We can go one step further with Saussure's formulation of the relationship between language and what lies outside it. The value-producing systems of the language are extensions and further elaborations of our human sensory apparatus. Here I am, somewhat indirectly, following some suggestions made by Harré (1990: 301) in his discussion of Gibson's psychology of perception. Language does not represent or reveal a fixed, universal order of nature which is already there, present to our senses. In acting on and intervening in the world, it is capable of enlarging or diminishing what Harré, drawing on J. von Uexküll's notion, designates as the human *Umwelt*. Language is a resource for construing, acting on and intervening in the material world. In so doing, we adapt and modify it in socially and culturally specific ways in a given ecosocial environment.

Gibson, through Harré's mediation, explains that the phenomena we observe in the *Umwelt* through our perceptual systems are 'properties of the Umwelt but affordances of the "total" world'. As 'affordances', they are 'material dispositions relative to human activities and practices.... A paved patio affords walking and a particle accelerator affords the photographing of tracks' (Harré 1990: 301). Thought and sound are affordances in this sense. What do they afford? Above all, they afford the possibility of their construal as semiotically formed substance. In this way, they become relevant properties of the ecosocial environment in which we live.

8 LINGUISTIC VALUE AND QUANTUM MECHANICS

The year Saussure died, 1913, the Danish physicist Niels Bohr made important progress in the development of the theory known as quantum mechanics. I do not wish to suggest Saussure was in any way directly influenced by these developments. Certainly, I have no evidence of this. However, there are parallels which seem less than merely accidental in the overall historical and cultural context. Both Fredric Jameson (1972: 14) and Edward Small (1987: 457) have also suggested a possible influence along these lines. Saussure's claim that 'words do not have the job of representing concepts fixed in advance' is strikingly similar to the claims made by the then newly emergent theory of quantum mechanics in physics. Saussure recognized that language is not just a function of what lies outside it *per se*. Linguistic form is like an operator which operates on 'outside' reality. 'To each operator', as Prigogine and Stengers (1985: 221) explain in their discussion of quantum mechanics, 'there thus corresponds an ensemble, a "reservoir" of numerical values' (cf. terms). Saussure's rejection of 'concepts fixed in advance' is parallel to the place given to operators in quantum mechanics, rather than physical quantities, as in classical physics. The point is that just as quantum mechanics distinguished the concept of physical quantity from its numerical values, as represented by the eigenvalues of the operator, Saussure understands that the material world is construed and made socially relevant by value-producing terms defined by the purely differential relations among them (cf. operators). What is so construed in the 'outer' world will be identified with some contextual weighting of the values which are intrinsic to language form. I am not, in saying this, arguing for a reductively mathematical formalization of language. Instead, I wish to draw attention to the overall epistemological and ontological convergence between Saussure's theory of value and these important developments in quantum mechanics.

Like quantum mechanics, the concept of linguistic value means that we cannot speak with absolute certainty about a fixed and universal extra-linguistic order of things. Commenting on Bohr's reaction to Planck's constant, Prigogine and Stengers observe:

It is only to the quantum phenomenon as a whole, including the measurement interaction, that we can ascribe numerical values. All description thus implies a choice of the measurement device, a choice of the question asked. In this sense, the answer, the result of the measurement, does not give us access to a given reality. We have to decide which measurement we are going to perform and which question our experiments will ask the system. Thus there is an irreducible multiplicity of representations for a system, each connected with a determined set of operators.

This implies a departure from the classical notion of objectivity, since in the classical view the only 'objective' description is the complete description of *the system as it is*, independent of the choice of how it is observed.

(Prigogine and Stengers 1985: 224–5; emphasis in original)

Thus, the ambivalence I spoke of earlier in relation to the notion of 'thought' may be explained in terms of the fact that Saussure was struggling, against the scientific and terminological limitations of his time, to give voice to a non-objectivist and non-universalist account of the foundational principles of human meaning-making (Chapter 1, section 5). In such an account, 'thought' is neither a set of extralinguistic 'concepts fixed in advance' nor is it simply inherent in linguistic form; rather, it is on this 'thought phenomenon' as a whole, itself the product of the interaction between material affordances in the human *Umwelt* and the semiotic resources for construing these and acting on them, that values are conferred in and through the work that is invested in the making of meanings. It is to the question of linguistic work in relation to the economic dimension of linguistic value that I shall turn in the following chapter.

Chapter 8

Linguistic and economic value

A homology

1 LINGUISTIC VALUE AND THE MARGINALIST SCHOOL OF POLITICAL ECONOMY: A MISLEADING ANALOGY

In his comparison of the methodological viewpoints shared by economics and linguistics (Chapter 7, section 1), Saussure draws attention to the distinction which is made between 'political economy' and 'economic history'. He relates this distinction to that between synchrony and diachrony (*CLG*: 115–16). In order to study these distinctions more effectively, Saussure proposes that the linguist do so along the two axes of 'simultaneity' and 'succession', which correspond to the AB and the CD axes in Saussure's diagram (*CLG*: 115). This is reproduced in Figure 8.1. The axis of simultaneity (AB) 'concerns relations between things which co-exist, relations from which the passage of time is entirely excluded', whereas along the axis of succession (CD) 'one can never consider more than one thing at a time' (*CLG*: 115).

The first axis (AB) considers language as a system of pure values in which

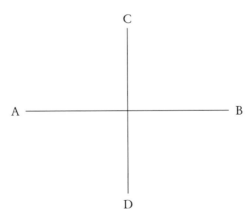

Figure 8.1 Saussure's axes of 'simultaneity' (AB) and 'succession' (CD) (*CLG*: 115)

'the intervention of time is excluded' (*CLG*: 115). *Langue*, from this point of view, comprises the relations of pure difference among the terms in a given synchronic state of the system. There is no reference to the accumulated social work which has produced a given synchronic state of the language system. The second axis (CD) views language from the perspective of its historical evolution. This axis admits of change and variability in time, and this may bring about change in the system itself (Chapter 4).

Saussure cannot allow the analogy with economics to go too far. This would run the danger of importing naturalistic criteria into the explanation of the 'connections' between linguistic and socio-historical processes (Chapter 10, section 3). This obliges Saussure to suppress the dialectic of use-value and exchange-value which is materially embodied in every instance of sign use in *parole*. That is, the jointly constituted linguistic work in and through which a sign token is received as an exchange-value and interpreted as a use-value for some individual or social purpose. This 'suppression' is, of course, a consequence of the methodological decision to privilege the system of pure values, or *langue*. Motivation is not opposed to this perspective. On the contrary, it logically follows from it. The motivated character of the sign comes into view more clearly as soon as one admits the dynamic interaction between the system and the instance perspectives, which is precisely what signification is all about. This possibility is not taken up and systematically developed by Saussure. It will be the focus of attention in Chapter 12 of the present study.

According to the Italian semiotician Augusto Ponzio (1977) Saussure's theory of linguistic value was influenced by the theory of political economy and sociology developed by Vilfredo Pareto and colleagues at the University of Lausanne. Pareto was a leading figure in the marginalist school of political economy which was based at the University of Lausanne during the same period that Saussure taught in Geneva. In the economic theory of the marginalists, value is expressed by a steady-state or equilibrium model: the exchange-value of goods is defined as the pure expression of a system of prices, independently of the social means of their production.

At first sight, there would seem to be a number of points of convergence between Saussure's theory of linguistic value and the political economy of Pareto and colleagues. These include, for example, the distinction that Pareto makes between the 'static' and 'dynamic' perspectives on the social system. Ponzio projects this particular reading onto the notion of *langue*. That is, *langue* is, in Ponzio's view, a 'self-regulating' and 'harmonious' system by analogy with Pareto's economic model. In my view, Ponzio commits the frequently made error of assuming that Saussure's distinction between the synchronic and diachronic perspectives is an ontological, rather than a methodological, one. Saussure, as I pointed out in Chapter 4, understands the fundamental interdependence of the two perspectives. Unlike Pareto, Saussure does not have a reductively physicalist and static conception of the language system. A brief glance at Pareto's own words on the nature of the social system will help to clarify this point:

> 2080. Let us consider the molecules of the social system, in other words, individuals, who are possessed of certain sentiments manifested by residues – which, for the sake of brevity, we shall designate simply as residues. We may say that present in individuals are mixtures of groups of residues that are analogous to the mixtures of chemical compounds found in nature, the groups of residues themselves being analogous to the chemical compounds. We have just examined ... the character of such mixtures and groups, and we found that while some of them appear to be virtually independent, others also are correlated in such a manner that an accentuation in the one is offset by an attenuation in the others, and *vice versa*. Such mixtures and groups, where dependent or independent, are now to be considered among the elements determining the social equilibrium.
>
> 2081. Residues manifest themselves through derivations. These are indications of the forces operating upon the social molecules.
>
> (Pareto 1963 [1935]: 1444)

Saussure's theory of *langue* as a system of pure values is *not* founded on physicalist criteria. Nor is it a static or 'equilibrium' model which does not change unless perturbed by exogenous factors (Chapter 4). Rather, it is a precursor of the theory of dynamic open systems, which depend on continual and adaptive transactions of matter, energy and information between system and environment (Chapter 4, sections 7–10). Saussure's theory is a non-mechanistic and non-causal theory: there is no simple proportionality of cause and effect between signs and the matter–energy processes that they cross-couple with and entrain (Lemke 1993: 251). This follows from the fact that the system of values is not reducible to the matter–energy bearers of the signs that arise from the system.

Saussure's theory of linguistic value remains a pioneering contribution to the theory of organized complexity in the dynamic, open and evolving relations between a social-semiological system and its environments. Pareto's equilibrium theory of social and economic systems, by contrast, is founded on a reductionist and physicalist epistemology of closed systems. This is reflected in the kinds of analogies he often evokes between the study of social and economic systems, on the one hand, and the sciences of physics and biology, on the other.

2 THE HOMOLOGY BETWEEN LINGUISTIC AND MONETARY EXCHANGE

What, then, is the economic basis of Saussure's theory of value? As we shall see in due course, this is pivoted on the principle of arbitrariness. The principle of arbitrariness raises the language system above the workings of natural necessity. The arbitrary and historically evolving character of *langue* forms the basis of a supra-individual conception of human work – one in which humankind, generically conceived, is the bearer of a principle of man's technical domination over nature. The separation of social-semiological systems from natural necessity constitutes the basis of a modernist project of transformation, change and manipulation of the environment. This entails a gnoseological objectification of the world: language is transformed from being a means for the theoretical contemplation of the world to a technical means for intervening in and acting on it. Modernity seeks to replace pre-modern faith and certainty with the categories of Reason and History. In this scenario, Reason entails the arbitrary application of rational procedures and axioms to the global totality of experience under modernity. The modernist project endeavours to bring experience under the control of rational argument and conventional procedures. This implies a historical mission founded on the principles of technique, work and the development of the forces of production. The dissolution of the naturalistic basis of language may be related to the global experience of reality under modernism. In the modernist project, the metaphysical foundations of pre-modernity are called into question. Reality is seen as flux, change, process and radical uncertainty, without secure foundations. Saussure's social-semiological metatheory is a paradigmatic example of the modernist scientific project.

In section 2 of his chapter on linguistic value, Saussure enquires into the crucial distinction between value and signification (Chapter 10, section 2). After discussing the two-way and reciprocal nature of the link between auditory image and concept (*CLG*: 158–9), he makes the following observation:

> Let us take first of all signification as it is usually represented, and as shown on p. 99. It is, as the arrows in the figure indicate, no more than the counterpart of the auditory image. Everything takes place between the auditory image and the concept, within the limits of the word considered as a fixed domain, existing in itself.

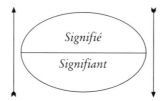

But here is the paradoxical aspect of the matter: on the one hand, the concept appears to us as the counterpart of the auditory image on the interior of the sign, and, on the other, the sign itself, that is, the relationship which links these two elements, is also, accordingly, the counterpart of other signs in the language system.

Since the language system is a system in which all the terms are solidary and in which the value of one is only the result of the simultaneous presence of the others, according to the schema:

how is it that value, so defined, gets confused with signification, that is, with the counterpart of the auditory image?

(CLG: 158–9)

The first relation referred to here is the two-way *inter*stratal relation of symbolic construal which operates between signifier and signified, as indicated by the vertical arrows in Saussure's diagram. The second refers to the *intra*stratal relation of instantiation, which Saussure revealingly illustrates by means of the horizontal lines linking each sign to its counterparts. Saussure's response to the question he poses takes the form of his well-known comparison between linguistic and monetary forms of exchange:

To answer this question, we shall note first of all that even outside of the language system, all values seem to be governed by this paradoxical principle. They are always constituted:

1   by something *different* which is liable to be *exchanged* with the thing whose value is to be determined;
2   by *similar* things that can be *compared* with the thing whose value is in question.

These two factors are necessary for the existence of a value. Thus, in order to determine what a five franc coin is worth, one must know: 1. that it can be exchanged with a determinate quantity of a different thing, for example, bread; 2. that it can be compared with a similar value in the same system, for example, a one franc coin, or with the currency of another system (a dollar, etc.). Likewise, a word can be exchanged with something different: an idea; moreover, it can be compared with something having the same nature: another word. Its value is not then established as long as one confines oneself to noting that it can be 'exchanged' with this or that concept, that is to say with this or that signification; it must also be compared with similar values, with the other words which are opposed to it. Its content is really only determined by the competition [*le concours*] with that which exists outside of it. Being part of a system, it is endowed not only with a signification, but also and above all with a value, and that is something altogether different.

(CLG: 159–60)

Saussure presents us with a deceptively simple comparision between two different artefacts: money and signs. However, the basis of his comparison goes deeper than one of simple analogy between two essentially different phenomena. A relation of analogy would presume that the two phenomena are only provisionally related by some 'immediate external similarity', to borrow the Italian semiotician, the late Ferruccio Rossi-Landi's, insightful expression (1977: 74–5). Saussure's analysis arrests the two phenomena he examines at the particular stage in which their full-fledged status becomes evident, that is, in the linguistic and the economic marketplaces. However, the basis of his comparison does not stop there. Instead, it reveals something essential to both phenomena, and which unites them in a relationship of *internal* similarity at a stage prior to their arrested status as, respectively, money and signs in the marketplace of economic and linguistic transactions. This is the kind of relationship which Rossi-Landi has identified as a relation of *homology* (1977: 74). A homological relationship is, to use Rossi-Landi's own words, the revealing of 'the same essence in different fields' (1977: 74). In the case of both money and language, this essence is the social mode of economic production – the social work – which produces both linguistic and monetary tokens and the social relations which are implicated in and reproduced by this.

Saussure's homology between money and signs refers to the emergence of discrete, discontinuous sign units from the non-discrete analogue continuum of pure difference in thought and sound (Chapter 7, section 4; Chapter 10, section 1). It refers, in other words, to the emergence of 'society' from 'nature' through the social work which is expended in the making of signs. This depends on the dialectic of similarity and difference which Saussure describes in the above quotation. Both of the 'factors' that Saussure refers to are necessary for the emergence of a value. In saying this, Saussure draws attention to two most fundamental aspects of the sign, viz. the notions of interstratal symbolic construal and intrastratal instantiation. It is the dialectic between these two factors which constitutes the systemic value of a given sign. I shall now examine these two factors. As we shall see below, they have to do with the dialectic between use-value and exchange-value, which is intrinsic to all sign production.

3 LINGUISTIC USE-VALUE AND EXCHANGE-VALUE

The two orders of difference which combine in the making of signs consist of terms rather than full-fledged signs. Terms belong to the non-discrete analogue continuum of pure values (Chapter 3, section 3). The first of the two factors identified by Saussure refers to the linguistic work whereby a sign is produced by the cross-coupling of phonic and conceptual terms from the two orders of difference. Terms in the conceptual order of differences are exchanged with terms in the phonic order. The linguistic work which is enacted in and through this process of exchange gives rise to the emergence of an interstratal relation of *symbolic construal* between a signifier and a signified. The 'something different' in this case is the conceptual order of difference with respect to the phonic order, or vice versa. The two orders of difference are 'different' in the specific sense that the conceptual level is of a higher order of symbolic abstraction than is the phonic order (Chapter 6, section 7). Rossi-Landi (1977: 159–61) points out that the exchange of a signified by means of a signifier entails the satisfying of a social need. The signified which arises in the exchange of a signified for a signifier has an elementary use-value. That is, it has a meaning-making potential: it is a potentially usable sign type in a given social system for some purpose.

Saussure also points out that a sign cannot be isolated from the system to which it belongs. This brings us to the second of the two factors which Saussure identifies. A given sign may be *compared* with other signs from the same language system, or from some other system. Comparison is a fundamental activity in distinguishing different categories of terms. It depends on the kinds of ordered hierarchies, ranging from most schematic to most specific, that I discussed in Chapter 7, section 6. Comparison, Saussure points out, takes place on the basis of criteria of similarity and equivalence between, say, a superordinate category and its instantiations. The act of comparing is based on the principle of intrastratal instantiation, or schematicity. Unlike the two-way interstratal relation of symbolic construal, the relation of instantiation which is implicated in the act of comparison is unidirectional and non-reversible. I can compare the subordinate term [COMMON BLUE TONGUE] to the superordinate term [LIZARD], but I cannot compare the superordinate, or schematic, category to the subordinate category, or to specific instantiations. Comparison is always made on the basis of the higher-order (more schematic) similarities which two or more items are seen as having in common in relation to specifiable schematic criteria.

In the case of Saussure's second factor, the value of 'that which is in question' acts as a constant relative to which 'similar things' can be compared. The constant is the more schematic term in some hierarchy of terms. Thus, [COMMON BLUE TONGUE] and [BEARDED DRAGON], which terms designate two species of lizard found in Australia, may be compared on the basis of the more schematic category [LIZARD]. Hjelmslev, in his essay 'Langue et parole' (1942), sums this point up as follows:

> it is the form which constitutes the value and the constant, and it is substance which identifies the variables, to which are attributed different values depending on circumstances. Thus, a coin and a banknote can change value, in exactly the same way that a sound and a sense can, that is to say, by changing interpretation in relation to different schemas.
>
> (Hjelmslev 1942: 39)

In my example, [LIZARD] is the schematic constant on the basis of which the comparison between the two subordinate terms is made. In this way, [COMMON BLUE TONGUE] and [BEARDED DRAGON] are subordinate terms whose interpretation may vary according to the schema which serves as the basis of the comparison between the two. The superordinate term [LIZARD] is schematic to a very large number of different lexical classifications of the various genera and species of lizard. If I vary the schema, using, say, [SKINK, or SCINCIDAE], which designates a particular genus of smooth-scaled lizard, rather than, say, [DRAGON, or AGAMIDAE], which designates a particular genus of rough- or spiky-scaled lizard, then the basis of the comparison between the two subordinate terms will vary accordingly (Worrell 1963: 34, 65).

A given term has a relatively constant value by virtue of its position in the overall system of relations to which it belongs. Whenever two or more terms are compared, the act of comparison always takes place in relation to a given constant value in the overall system of values. As Hjelmslev points out, this is analogous to the way in which the value of a semiotically formed substance varies relative to the constant value of the schema in relation to which it is instantiated.

Saussure's first 'factor' shows, then, that the value of a given signifier is determined by its being exchanged for something 'different' – a signified – with which it combines. This leads to the emergence of stable semiotic forms, or sign types, in a given sign system. The dialectic of signifier and signified gives rise to stratified semiotic forms. These are the products of the linguistic work of symbolic construal which relates a signifier to a signified. In showing how linguistic forms may also be compared to one another in virtue of the stable criteria established by the forms themselves, Saussure's second factor constitutes the dialectic of semiotic form and substance, or of schema and instance. This arises by virtue of a given form's entering into complex hierarchies of type categories, ranging from most schematic to most specific. On this basis, degrees of generality and specificity may be specified. A given instance in *parole* always embodies this duality of being both a use-value and an exchange-value, simultaneously (Rossi-Landi 1977: 159).

The two principles of interstratal symbolic construal and intrastratal instantiation may be illustrated with reference to the nominal group *common bluetongue*. On the stratum of the signifier, there is a sequence of graphemes which may be specified as the composite graphological structure:

$$<[c + o + m + m + o + n] + [b + l + u + e][t + o + n + g + u + e]>$$

This sequence of graphemes is syntagmatically integrated so as to form the overall visual shape of this composite graphic signifier. In turn, this syntagmatic integration of graphemes symbolically construes a composite conceptual structure on the stratum of the signified. This may be glossed as follows:

[FAMILY: SCINCIDAE; GENUS: TILIQUA; SPECIES: TILIQUA SCINCOIDES SCIN-COIDES]

Thus, the linguistic sign *common bluetongue* is the product of the interstratal relation of symbolic construal between these two strata. The composite graphological structure is exchanged for its signified in this sense. The resulting sign may be represented as in Figure 8.2.

The nominal group *common bluetongue* is also the instantiation of a higher-order schematic category. In this case, the one-way and *intra*stratal relation of instantiation may be represented as in Figure 8.3. A herpetologist would use a more technical system of classification, as in Figure 8.4. Both the commonsense and the technical systems of classification use the same principle, viz. taxonomic hierarchy. This is based on the analysis of the given phenomenon into its categories and subcategories. Superordinate categories are schematic to subordinate categories. Thus, *common bluetongue* is a specific instantiation of the more schematic, or higher-order, category [LIZARD]. In this case, *common bluetongue* is compared to the higher-order schema [LIZARD]. The exchange-value of the sign arises out of the work

signified

[FAMILY: SCINCIDAE; GENUS: TILIQUA; SPECIES: TILIQUA SCINCOIDES SCINCOIDES]

$$<[c + o + m + m + o + n] + [b + l + u + e] [t + o + n + g + u + e]>$$

signifier

Figure 8.2 Composite sign *common bluetongue*, showing interstratal relation of symbolic construal

Schema/form   Instance/substance

[LIZARD] ———————————————➤ [COMMON BLUETONGUE]

Figure 8.3 Intrastratal relation of instantiation; non-technical specification of *common bluetongue*

Figure 8.4 Intrastratal relation of instantiation; technical specification of *common bluetongue*

which is expended so as to relate the given sign to the whole system of relations to which it belongs, or to which it is assigned. This act of comparison reveals what the two have in common according to the common criteria established by the schematic category.

4 THE ONTOLOGICAL PRIORITY OF VALUE

The principal ontological category in Saussure's social-semiological meta-theory is that of value. The values which emanate from the system of differences in *langue* are a system of contextualizing relations (Chapter 7, section 2). Saussure's discussion of the way values are assigned to linguistic and monetary tokens in and through the exchange transactions in which these are made and used shows that signs are more than a simple matching of a concept to an auditory or acoustic image. The exchange transactions are themselves patterned relationships and for this reason signification is never simply a given property of the sign, seen as isolated from the system. Saussure goes further, however. The exchange transactions in and through which use-values and exchange-values are assigned to signs are themselves immanent in a higher-order system of contextualizing relations. These contextualizing relations constitute a system of semiotic values at a higher order than the signs that the system gives rise to. It is the system of contextualizing relations, which is itself comprised of ordered hierarchies of terms, that defines what the signification of any given sign is. Signification is the portion of the total use-value and exchange-value of the system which is expended in the making of a given sign token. In other words, it refers to the way in which the global meaning potential of the system is locally restricted by some higher-order contextualizing relation (Chapter 9, section 2).

Every time a given token is enacted in some exchange transaction it is not simply the case that the token has the same signification for the participants to the transaction; rather, it has the same *value*. Higher-order values are (approximately) replicable from one transaction to another. For this reason, values are generic. Significations, which are subject to factors such as the material and psychological variability of the sign token in some context, are not. They are constantly re-made from one transaction to the next (*CLG*: 152). For this reason, they are specific, or instantial. If signification *per se* were the issue, then this would reduce to a simple matter of imitation, or the association of signifier and signified by contiguity in the empiricist sense. But

Saussure's point is that the process of signification can only take place through the assigning and recognition of values which emanate from a higher-order system of contextualizing relations in *langue* (Chapter 7, section 2). The system is transindividual. The exchange transactions which take place between individuals in *parole* do not simply replicate or imitate some previously established or agreed-upon 'meaning'. Instead, the significations that are jointly construed in these exchange transactions are subsumed by the same metarule of contextualization. This is what the determining of the value of a given sign type entails. Language users do not learn to imitate or replicate meanings or even rules as to their appropriate uses. Instead, they make sense of acts of *parole* by learning the metarules whereby the use-values and exchange-values which emanate from the system are assigned to tokens in the processes of linguistic exchange. Value has ontological priority: it is the structured system of contextualizing values which 'determines' the signification of any given instance.

5 VALUE AND SIGNIFICATION

Saussure discusses how the French word *mouton* 'may have the same *signification* as the English *sheep*; but not have the same value.... The difference in value between *sheep* and *mutton* depends on the fact that the former has beside it a second term *mutton* for the meat, which is not the case for the French word' (*CLG*: 160). The two sets of words in the two languages have different values on account of the work which has been expended so as to insert them into their respective systems of relations. Hence, the value of these terms depends on the specific system of pure values that each belongs to. On the other hand, *mouton* and *sheep* 'may have the same signification' because, as Saussure implicitly recognizes, it is always possible to construe or interpret a term in one language with a term from another language. Signification entails precisely this process of meaning assignment to, or construal of, the spoken chain. This will be more fully explored in Chapter 9, section 5. This process can occur between languages just as much as it can occur within the same language: we can use the system of contextualizing relations, or the system or values, in our own language so as to construe the meanings of linguistic forms in some other language. This is so even when the linguistic values internal to the two systems do not exactly correspond. This necessarily entails the re-evaluation, or re-contextualization, of the two systems in relation to each other (Chapter 2, section 11).

The distinction between value and signification shows that different kinds of linguistic and social work can be expended on the same linguistic form. Thus, the French word *mouton* can be assigned its value in a system of terms to do with the various kinds of prepared and edible meat, for example, *jambon, porc, bifteck, veau* and so on; or it may be assigned another value in a system of terms to do with, say, different kinds of farm animals, such as *cheval, chèvre, cochon, vache* and so on. Which potential dimension of the term's value becomes relevant depends on which systemic and contextual relations are activated in the processes of meaning-making (cf. signification). Value, as we have already seen, is not an inherent property of the term; rather, it is produced in and through the work whereby a term is positioned in a given field of relations – systemic, textual, contextual, intertextual. The value of a given term is only relatively invariant, rather than fixed or universal, with respect to the particular hierarchies of contextualizing relations that it typically enters into in the language system (Chapter 3, section 3).

6 VALUE AND THE SOCIAL WORK OF MAKING SIGNS

Rather than ontologize an aestheticized play of difference in the category of *différance*, as does Derrida (1974/6 [1967]), I would prefer to pursue an alternative line of enquiry. The relevant question now becomes: what is it that unites all modalities of linguistic semiosis (speech, writing and so on) along the entire range of the social work regarding them (Rossi-Landi 1977: 74)? Saussure's claim that *langue* is 'imprinted' in the brains of individuals is not exempt from these same processes. Indeed, this shows that the cognitive resources of individuals are always grounded in and are an appropriation of the social and historical resources of *langue*. The body–brain complex and its extensions are the ground for all of the modalities of linguistic semiosis. This includes the most recent technological developments and extensions of these same modalities. The answer to the above question is simple: value.

The higher-order system of contextualizing relations – the system of values – includes the typical groupings of syntagmatic and associative relations in *langue* (Chapter 11). These integrate the individual body–brain complex into (1) the exchange transactions in which it participates; (2) the ecosocial environment of these transactions; and (3) the social-semiological system as a whole (Chapter 6). The system of values is a system of enabling and constraining conditions on the kinds of meanings that can be made in and through the signifying modalities of the body–brain complex and its technological extensions. There is no ontology of difference as such in Saussure's theory of signification. Language does not reduce to an endless play of self-referring differences.

In rejecting the view of language as nomenclature, Saussure does not go to the other extreme. He does not say that there is nothing outside the endless play of differences in the language system. Saussure does not deny the existence of the material–phenomenal world, as his discussion of thought and sound clearly shows. What he does deny is that language stands in some kind of direct and naturalistic relationship to this. The system of values is a system of contextualizing relations which stands in a productive relationship to thought and sound. That is, the linguistic work which is expressed in the dialectic of use-value and exchange-value in every act of *parole* is a productive appropriation and re-making of thought and sound in and through the meaning-making resources of *langue*.

The language system, seen as a system of pure values, is produced by the totality of the social work which has gone into its production and re-production. The capitalist mode of economic production is the onto-logical foundation of the system of values. In this sense, it assumes the character of a de-anthropomorphized mode of social being. This is work of the undifferentiated kind (Rossi-Landi 1977: 162). It refers to the way in which 'human linguistic labor power' is distributed across all the terms which constitute a particular language system (*ibid.*). For this reason, the concept of social work does not refer to the individual work which goes into the execution of a particular sign on some occasion of use. Undifferentiated work is a kind of averaging out, in Marx's sense, of all of the social work, past and present, which has been performed by a given linguistic community. In this sense, it is an abstraction from 'specific determinations of productive activity' (Rossi-Landi 1977: 52). Value in this sense is a *quantitative*, rather than a qualitative, notion. It is distributional and probabilistic and designates the totality of work which has gone into the social production of a given sign system. Consequently, each term in the system is assigned a portion of the total value which is produced as a result of its position relative to all of the other terms in the entire system. On the basis of the topological distribution of value across all the terms in the system, it is possible to compare one term to another. The terms belong to the analogue continuum of pure difference. The act of comparing one term with another brings the two into a specific sort of relationship. Marx's description of the emergence of exchange-values is relevant here:

> The first step made by an object of utility towards acquiring exchange-value is when it forms a non-use-value for its owner, and that happens when it forms a superfluous portion of some article required for his immediate wants. Objects in themselves are external to man, and consequently alienable to him. In order that this alienation may be reciprocal, it is only necessary for men, by a tacit understanding, to treat each other as private owners of those alienable objects, and by implication as independent individuals.
>
> (Marx 1906 [1867]: 99–100)

Exchange-value emerges when artefacts enter into a specific sort of relation-ship as commodities in a market system. The transformation of artefacts into commodities occurs when, as Marx explains, social agents treat each other as 'independent individuals'. The 'alienable objects' or the commodities in the market emerge as a result of the contact (cf. comparison) among discrete, bounded individuals. Objects and the 'independent individuals' who are the 'private owners of these objects' emerge as a consequence of the digital-ization of the analogue continuum of the social relations characterized by non-capitalist modes of production such as barter, which are based on use-value and relations of dependency among individuals.

In the case of the two factors which Saussure identifies as informing the homology between monetary and linguistic exchange, we may say that (1) every sign is an artefact which serves to fulfil some want or need; (2) every sign is assigned a value as a result of its position in the overall system to which it belongs; and (3) every sign enters into relations with other signs in the same or some other system. Item (1) refers to a sign's use-value; (2) to the value which is assigned to the sign as a result of the undifferentiated work which is averaged out across all of the terms in a given system; and (3) to the exchange-value of the sign as a result of the specific relations it enters into in the ordered hierarchies of terms in the system.

Marx draws attention to the way in which the emergence of private property and 'independent individuals' means that the 'surplus' non-use-value is appropriated by those social agents who control the social means of production and exchange of commodities. The private ownership of the means of production does not allow for an equitable distribution of the value of commodities. Instead, the means of production and the work of social agents are, increasingly, concentrated at certain points (enterprises, etc.) which compete amongst themselves. There is, then, no free and co-operative association of workers who are united in the production of use-values. Instead, the forms of the social relations are themselves increasingly mediated by the processes of competition among opposing enterprises in the market-place. It is in this scenario – that of monopoly capitalism – that exchange-value dominates over use-value. The former functions to deviate the work of individual workers so as to increase the capital of the dominant property-owning classes. This has the further consequence that conflict is, increasingly, under the capitalist mode of production intrinsic to the work process itself.

Saussure refers to the relations of 'opposition' and 'competition' (*concours*) which characterize (3) in particular (*CLG*: 160; section 2 above). He goes on to say:

> In the interior of the same language system, all the words which express neighbouring ideas impose reciprocal limits on each other: synonyms such as *redouter* ('to dread', 'to fear'), *craindre* ('to fear'), *avoir peur* ('to be afraid') only have their particular values through the oppositions among them.
>
> (*CLG*: 160)

The universalization of exchange-value has the effect of replacing the relations of dependence among individuals with that among things. In this way, the social relations among commodities become, indifferently, autonomous and self-regulating and no longer in the control of the individuals themselves. The seeming 'independence' of individuals is, thus, an illusion before the impersonal and self-regulating effects of the mode of economic production itself.

Saussure's use of notions such as 'opposition' and 'competition' among the terms in the system of values is symptomatic of his unconscious assimilation of the dominant ontology of exchange relations under the capitalist mode of social and economic production. The reciprocal, yet competitive, relations among terms digitalizes the unit of exchange as a result of the 'alienation' of both the objects and their 'independent' and 'private' owners from each other. As Marx had pointed out, the emergence of discrete exchange units in this way only comes about through contact with that which is on the 'outside'. At the same time, the 'competitive' and 'conflictual' nature of these exchange relations is also the basis of a fundamental contradiction: in describing the global totality of a given social mode of production, these relations of 'competition' and 'conflict' are also the basis of crisis and potential change. Further, the ontological hiatus between society and individual that I discussed in Chapter 3 shows that individuals have 'will' and 'intelligence'. They have powers of self-reflexivity which are not reducible to the global totality of the social mode of production. This means that they are incompatible with the total commodification of human nature. Commodification does not one-sidedly lead to alienation; it also produces pleasures and desires. In my view, this constitutes a plausible explanation of the liberatory energies which Saussure's work on anagrams seems to have released (Starobinski 1971).

The notion that value is reciprocally averaged out across all of the terms in the system is subtly modified by Saussure's notion of opposition. If a given term were to drop out of the system, Saussure points out that its content 'would go to its competitors' (*CLG*: 160). On other occasions, the inverse may occur: 'there are terms which are enriched through contact with others' (*CLG*: 160).

What we see here is a slide from the correctly differential and analogue conception of the system of pure values to one which projects categories from the dominant mode of economic and social production onto the system. I have pointed out that value represents the averaging out of the total social work which has produced the language system. In other words, the work of very many social agents has led to the social and historical production of a given synchronic state of the language system. The fact that value is defined in this way implies that the category of work is endogenous and intrinsic to the language system and its definition, rather than an extrinsic or exogenous category. This was also Marx's point in the passage I cited earlier. Both the expropriators (the owners of the means of production) and the expropriated are *intrinsic* to the work process. Competition does not only take place among rival competitors in the marketplace, but also between the dominant and the dominated social agents in the work process itself. It is not the case, as is often supposed, that one category of agents (the dominant) are extrinsic to the work process whereas those agents in subordinate roles are intrinsic to it. Both are intrinsic to the work process, seen as self-reproductive of its own forms of social organization and production, its own social hierarchies, and on on.

If, then, work is intrinsic to language as a system of pure values, rather than something which exists only extrinsically in acts of *parole*, then it seems that Saussure has unconsciously projected the categories of the dominant mode of economic production onto the social organization of *langue*. In other words, the law of capitalist competition regulates the modes of social, economic and linguistic production:

> The division of labour within the society brings into contact independent commodity-producers, who acknowledge no other authority but that of competition, of the coercion exerted by the pressure of their mutual interests.
>
> (Marx 1906 [1867]: 391)

The social mode of production hinges on the social mode of work. Work is what human beings do in order to transform nature into products. According to Rossi-Landi (1977: 9), *langue* is 'an organized and stratified totality made up of the sign products of "completed" work': that is, of work which has been done previous to the moment in which sign work is executed in *parole*; and 'a message is a product of new sign work which uses as materials some of the elements of the code' (*ibid*.). Given Rossi-Landi's thesis that there is a relationship of homology between linguistic and economic modes of production of, respectively, signs and utensils, I should like to suggest that it is in work that the social relations of society are made and re-made. Saussure acknowledges on more than one occasion that *langue* is the historical product of social work (e.g., Saussure 1967: 46). In this sense, social reality is the unity of the global totality of the social work in a given society.

Nowhere, however, does he theorize the forms of the social relations implicated in this claim or how these would affect his conception of *langue* as an intrinsically social-semiological system. If *langue* is the product which results from the totality of linguistic work which is performed and of the social relations among individuals (as types) that this implicates, then the category of work cannot be seen, abstractly, as a 'technical' relation among an agent, the means and the object. This amounts to a purely formal schema in so far as an abstract individual, irrespective of social and historical formation, is representative of the category of linguistic work in general. Saussure's model of the speech circuit may be understood in this way. In the first instance, there is a transfer of matter–energy in the form of sound waves which speaker and listener transform into social products (signs) by virtue of the work, psychically defined, which they perform. Yet, all this tells us nothing about the social modes of labour and the social relations which these entail.

The projecting of categories such as 'opposition', 'competition' and 'enrichment' onto the differential relations in the system of pure values represents a concrete working out of the Heideggerian category of Being. Being does not refer to the ontic status of entities 'in' the world; rather, it refers to a global social configuration in which our understanding of these 'entities' and the interrelations among them takes place. It refers, in other words, to the unity of ontology and axiology in social life. Saussure's point of departure for enquiring into the relations between meaning-making and what lies outside this rejects naturalistic criteria. Instead, his reflections on value begin with the split between the domain of meaning and non-meaning, between language form and thought and sound, between Being and Nothing- ness, Order and Chaos. Linguistic value arises from the totality of the linguistic work which has been invested in the unifying of the terms of this polarity.

The significance of Saussure's use of categories such as those referred to above rests on the way in which signs assume the status of commodities in the capitalist mode of social and economic production. The products of human labour, as Marx (1906 [1867]: 81) explains, have a use-value. But when these products assume the form of commodities they are fetishized as 'independent beings' which directly enter into social relations with other commodities. The commodity form itself means that all of the products of human labour are invested with a value which is 'expressed objectively by their products all being equally values' (Marx 1906 [1867]: 82). Marx brilliantly analyses the emergence of commodity forms as follows:

> A commodity is therefore a mysterious thing, simply because in it the social character of men's labour appears to them as an objective character stamped upon the product of that labour; because the relation of the producers to the sum total of their own labour is presented to them as a social relation, existing not between themselves, but between the products of their labour. This is the reason why the products of labour become commodities, social things whose qualities are at the same time perceptible and imperceptible by the senses.
>
> (Marx 1906 [1867]: 83)

Saussure's discussion of the value-producing relations among the terms in *langue* projects the categories of the modes of production of mercantile capitalism (commodity production) onto the language system. It is the status of language forms as commodity forms which conceals, as Marx (1906 [1867]: 87) pointed out, the social character of labour and the social relations among individual producers (speakers, listeners and so on). Thus, it is *as if* language forms themselves enter into social relations of 'opposition' and 'competition' independently of the social labour of the producers and consumers of these forms. To quote Marx again:

> Man's reflections on the forms of social life, and consequently, also, his scientific analysis of these forms, takes a course directly opposite to that

of their actual historical development. He begins, post festum, with the results of the process of development ready to hand before him. The characters that stamp products as commodities, and whose establishment is a necessary preliminary to the circulation of commodities, have already acquired the stability of natural, self-understood forms of social life, before man seeks to decipher, not their historical character, for in his eyes they are immutable, but their meaning.

(Marx 1906 [1867]: 87)

According to Saussure's second 'factor' in the homology between linguistic and monetary tokens, the comparison of one form with another converts the latter into the equivalent of the former (section 2). This is a purely relative process: the former is represented as relative value; the latter functions as the equivalent of the former. Marx (1906 [1867]: 56) had demonstrated this with respect to the following equation: 20 yards of linen = one coat. The point is that two *different* forms are brought into a relation of (relative) *equivalence*. The relative form and the equivalent form, so defined, are 'mutually dependent' but also 'mutually exclusive, antagonistic extremes' (*ibid.*). It makes no sense, as Marx points out, 'to express the value of linen in linen'. What is necessary for the establishment of a value is the positing of an identity/difference relation in the way illustrated by Marx. The nature of a given form is only ever expressed *relatively*, that is, through its comparisons with other forms (cf. commodities and words). Saussure also shows that the thing whose value is in question – that is, whose value is being expressed or the relative form – in the comparison of two forms cannot at the same time assume the equivalent form. Marx has written:

> But the two commodities whose identity of quality is thus assumed, do not play the same part. It is only the value of the linen that is expressed. And how? By its reference to the coat as its equivalent, as something that can be exchanged for it.
>
> (Marx 1906 [1867]: 58)

In making one form the equivalent of the other, we also equate the labour embodied in the one to that in the other (*ibid.*). This is so irrespective of the concrete differences in the labour which is involved in the production of the two commodities. The expression of equivalence between the two commodities works to reduce the two different kinds of labour to 'their common quality of human labour in the abstract' (Marx 1906 [1867]: 59). The result of this process of 'comparison' is that the equivalent form, on being seen as the equal of the relative form, assumes the status of a thing in which 'we see nothing but value, or whose palpable bodily form represents value' (*ibid.*). As the embodiment of a particular value in some 'thing', we see how the equivalent form is the substance (the variable) in which the constant value of a relative form (cf. the schema) is expressed. This illustrates the form–substance dialectic referred to above.

Saussure's discussion of value does not, of course, limit itself to the isolated comparison of terms. Saussure's point is that values emanate from a system (*CLG*: 162), and that it is an error to isolate a term from the system of which it is a constitutive part (*CLG*: 157). The creation of values in the language system is homologous to the emergence of what Marx called the 'general equivalent' in the exchange of commodities:

> a particular kind of commodity acquires the character of general equivalent, because all other commodities make it the material in which they uniformly express their value.
>
> (Marx 1906 [1867]: 79)

The emergence of a general equivalent (i.e., money in the capitalist mode of economic production) means that this form 'gives to the world of commodities a *general social relative form of value*, because, and in so far as, thereby, all commodities, with the exception of one, are excluded from the equivalent form' (Marx 1906 [1867]: 77). The excluded commodity is the one that functions as the general equivalent. The general equivalent is an abstraction which is excluded from the domain of commodities and which functions to regulate the exchanges which take place among them. For Saussure, it is the language system which mediates and regulates all exchanges as the general equivalent of all the terms in the system.

The purely differential and negative character of these relations is governed by the principle of arbitrariness. Arbitrariness is the 'general equivalent' which functions as the regulator of the values of all the terms in the system (Chapter 9, section 2). The sign has a value only when it enters into relations with other signs. Marx shows that precisely the same logic also applies to commodities. Signification, as Saussure points out, could not occur without these relations among values in the system. That is, a given act of signification or sign token cannot be its own equivalent. A given term in the system of pure values, like the commodity, is 'compelled to choose some other commodity for its equivalent' (Marx 1906 [1867]: 65). This is why, as Saussure concludes, it is inexact to say that a word signifies something. The real point is that the use-value of the sign, as expressed in the interstratal relationship of symbolic construal, also becomes the phenomenal form of the exchange-value which is invested in it by virtue of the exchange relations it participates in. But if the use-value of the sign arises from its having the property of a material 'thing', the value which is invested in the sign has no connection with the physical–material properties of the matter–energy bearer which acts as the material support of the sign in *parole*. Signification, as Saussure comments, 'is nothing more than a value which is determined by its relations with other similar values, and without which signification would not exist' (*CLG*: 162). Thus, the value relation which is invested in the sign is abstracted from the material and social relations which produced it.

Marx's discussion of the general equivalent led him to the following genial insight:

> every commodity is a symbol, since, in so far as it is a value, it is only the material envelope of the human labour spent upon it. But if it be declared that the social characters assumed by objects, or the material forms assumed by the social qualities of labour under the regime of a definite mode of production, are mere symbols, it is in the same breath also declared that these characteristics are arbitrary fictions sanctioned by the so-called universal consent of mankind. This suited the mode of explanation in favour during the 18th century. Unable to account for the origin of the puzzling forms assumed by social relations between man and man, people sought to denude them of their strange appearance by ascribing to them a conventional origin.
>
> (Marx 1906 [1867]: 103–4)

The principle of arbitrariness completes the homology between the material production of commodities and the linguistic production of signs. The postulation of principles founded on the 'universal consent of mankind' or 'a conventional origin' of the legislative sort that Saussure criticized in the eighteenth-century philosophical accounts of language and its origins serves to mystify the social mode of production which produces signs and commodities alike. Saussure's solution to this problematic lies in the principle of arbitrariness (Chapter 12). *Langue* is the historical product of the social work expended by individuals in the innumerable acts of *parole* that have gone into the making, maintaining and changing of the language system. In upholding the ontological hiatus between society and individual (Chapter 3, section 5), Saussure correctly understands that teleology and purpose have no constitutive place in *langue* or its explanation (Chapter 4, section 3). The non-imperative, or non-teleological, character of synchronic laws is, however, dialectically related to the teleological or purposeful character of individual acts of *parole*. Individuals have agentive capacities and powers – compare 'will' and 'intelligence' – within the parameters established by *langue* itself. The linguistic work of *parole* is always a teleological positing in the sense defined by Lukács (1980 [1978]). It always takes place in relation to the powers and capacities of individuals to modify both themselves and their ecosocial environment in and through the resources afforded by historically prior linguistic work in *langue*.

The sign is not the same as the material matter–energy bearer which supports it. Whereas the latter is primarily based on matter–energy, the former is based on form, pattern and information. Information does more than co-ordinate matter and energy flows. The sign which emerges from its matter–energy base is, as I showed in my discussion of the speech circuit, more concerned with the organization of a social relationship among interlocutors (Wilden 1980 [1972]: 18). The sign does not signify its matter–energy base. Instead, it signifies the metacommunicative basis on which the social relation between speaker and listener is established in and through the social work of making and re-making signs. The sign which results from this social work will be the focus of discussion in Part V.

Part V

Sign and signification

Chapter 9

The linguistic sign

1 BASIC PRINCIPLES

In Part I, Chapter 1 of *CLG*, Saussure, after making some critical observations on the commonsense view of language as a 'naming' or 'referring' device, provides the following preliminary definition of the linguistic sign:

> We have seen on p. 28 in connection with the speech circuit, that the terms which are implicated in the linguistic sign are both psychic and are united in our brain by the associative link. We must insist on this point.
>
> The linguistic sign unites not a thing and a name, but a concept and an acoustic image. The latter is not the material sound, a purely physical thing, *but the psychic imprint of this sound, the representation which gives us the evidence of our senses; it is sensorial,* and if we happen to call it 'material', it is only in this sense and in opposition to the other term of the association, the concept, usually more abstract.
>
> (*CLG*: 98; my emphasis)

In this first definition, Saussure uses the terminology of 'concept' and 'acoustic image', which derives from his discussion of the speech circuit. On the following page (*CLG*: 99), Saussure replaces this terminology with that of signifier and signified. I shall come back to the reasons for this terminological shift later. In the speech circuit, the sign is relational in two important senses. First, both concept and acoustic image are psychic in character (Chapter 6); they are linked by association in the brains of the individual participants in the speech circuit on this basis. Both Baskin and Harris somewhat misleadingly translate the French word *psychique* with 'psychological' (Chapter 7, section 4). I shall now consider why I consider this choice problematic. It is not without a number of consequences for the arguments I shall present in this section.

Saussure emphasizes the 'psychic' and 'sensorial' aspects of the 'acoustic image'. The 'psychic imprint' of the material sound recalls the Aristotelian notion of the image-forming faculty, which forms the substrate to thought. From the perspective of this faculty, the movement from the physical sound to its psychic–sensorial representation in the acoustic image means that the latter is integrated with our senses. It is the senses which consequently perceive or 'witness' this representation as a true reproduction of the external sound. From the perspective of the 'more abstract' concept, this is only possible, in the Aristotelian view, when an image, which has its basis in the experience of our senses, is sensorially (not physically) present to the psychic faculty. In this way, concept and sensory 'witnessing' (cf. perception) are related through the sensorial image. This line of reasoning, which goes back to Aristotle, remains very influential in some respects to the present day. In so far as a word comprises a sensorial image (sound) which does not refer to or describe an object, idea, etc., it may be said to evoke the *notion* of the object, idea and so on.

Second, Saussure points out that the acoustic image is not the same as 'the material sound'. The acoustic image 'gives us the evidence of our senses' in the sense that I discussed in Chapter 6, section 4. As a global percept it acts as a higher-order constraint on lower-level acoustic or articulatory phenomena.

When Saussure refers to the 'psychic imprint' of the relationship so construed, he is referring to the fact that a meaningful relationship between the two is only possible in the presence of an interpreter who perceives and construes this relationship on the basis of his or her 'senses'. Saussure calls the acoustic image 'the representation which gives us the evidence of our senses': it is a psychic representation of some perceived distinction in the acoustic chain. The point is that speakers and listeners perceive it and intentionally orientate to it as a semiotically salient event. In giving us the evidence of our senses, the acoustic image evidences some potentially salient distinctions, while not drawing attention to others.

Saussure also speaks of an 'opposition' between this level and the more 'abstract' level of the concept. This should not be taken to refer to a binary opposition in the specifically structuralist sense. In a given binary opposition, the two terms in the opposition are postulated as being on the same level of abstraction, logically speaking. This is not the case in Saussure's conception of the relationship between 'concept' and 'acoustic image'. The concept is more 'abstract' than the acoustic image (*CLG*: 98) in the sense that it is not related to bodily processes of articulation and auditory perception in the way that the acoustic image is (Chapter 6, section 7). More precisely, it is a relation of a higher-order of logical typing than the acoustic image. For this reason, the two relata in the sign are two distinct strata. They are two distinct levels of organization in one overall linguistic form. In my view, the fundamental point at issue here is the way in which it is the phonology, in the first instance, which provides the means for mapping conceptual structures onto bodily produced sequences of sounds in the spoken chain. This is central to the stratified nature of semiosis (section 5 below). Saussure's epithet 'abstract' refers, then, to this characteristic of the sign.

Just one paragraph later, after some further discussion of the psychic character of the acoustic image, Saussure makes the following critically important claim:

> The linguistic sign is then a two-sided psychic entity, which can be represented by the figure:

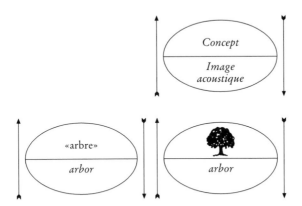

> These two elements are intimately linked and the one calls up the other. Whether we are seeking the sense of the Latin word *arbor* or the word with which Latin designates the concept 'tree', it is clear that only the relationship established by the language system [*la langue*] appears to us to be in conformity with reality, and we put aside whatever else may be imagined.
>
> (*CLG*: 99)

The two strata of the sign are redundant with each other in the sense that, given signifier a, then it is possible to predict to a high degree of probability signified a^1 (Chapter 6, section 7). That is, signifier a 'redounds with' signified a^1, and vice versa (Lemke 1984d: 35–6; Halliday 1992: 24). That is why Saussure says that 'the one calls up the other': the two strata mutually predict each other. The relation between the two strata is a contextual one. These contextualizing relations are symmetrical or two-way. The above formalization is, then, entirely reversible. It is equally valid to say that given signified a^1, then it is possible to predict its co-patterning with signifier a. The sign is organized on the basis of this principle: that is, there is a two-way interstratal relationship of symbolic construal between the two layers of the sign's organization (Chapter 3, section 3; Chapter 10, section 3).

The terminological changes which Saussure proposes are more than a question of consistency. They serve to emphasize that both signifier and signified are internal to language form. Therefore, the signifier is not a form which carries or otherwise designates a meaning which is external to it. This is why it is misleading to say that the sign 'represents' reality (Chapter 7, section 5). The sign is not a picture or a photographic replica of something else in the outside world. This would be a serious misreading of Saussure's argument and, hence, of the nature of the contextualizing relations that are internal to the sign. The point is that the semiological relationship between signifier and signified is the means whereby language users selectively orientate to and give structure to the analogue flux of perceptual phenomena in the outside world. For this reason, the sign is a 'psychic entity' (Chapter 6, section 4); it construes order, pattern and meaning in the flux of perceptual phenomena. Saussure's critique of the view that language is a mere nomenclature emphasizes, then, the dialectical interdependence of the sign and its outside. There is an important homology between this relation and the one that Saussure proposes between linguistic theory and object of study (Chapter 1, section 7). I shall now consider this.

The interdependence of the object of study and the conceptual framework which is used to establish it is also, in Saussure's account, a fundamental characteristic of language form itself. When Saussure critiques the view that language is 'a list of terms corresponding to a list of things' (*CLG*: 97), he observes that this view supposes 'ready made ideas which pre-exist words' (*CLG*: 97). This is a further example of the problem of naturalistic objectivity that I discussed in Chapter 1. However, the difference with respect to that discussion is that Saussure is now talking about a fundamental characteristic of the language system, rather than the relationship between object of study and the metatheoretical conceptual framework for studying it.

In both domains, the epistemological issue is essentially the same. Just like the object of study which the linguist constructs, the extra-linguistic domain is not an objectified reality which is independent of language form. Instead, the categories which are internal to a given language system are themselves incorporated into extralinguistic phenomena in the act of construing and constructing them. This also means that the relationship between the sign and what lies outside it is not a 'standing for' relation; rather, it is a relation of *construal* (Langacker 1987: 128–9; Halliday 1992). In Saussure's example, *arbor* does not 'stand for' the tree in the real world; nor does a signifier 'stand for' a signified. This is the reason why Saussure re-defines the linguistic sign as that which links 'not a thing and a name, but a concept and an acoustic image' (*CLG*: 98).

The difference is fundamental and does not in any way imply that the sign, defined as the internal relationship between a concept and an acoustic image, is divorced from reality. The point is that the conceptual stratum of the sign construes a given extralinguistic object, event, etc. in the perceptual flux by means of the conceptual categories which are intrinsic to a given language system. In other words, the language user deploys a given sign so as to establish a construal relationship between him- or herself and the extra-linguistic phenomenon which he or she is attending to by means of the symbolic, or imaging, resources which are internal to the sign itself. That is, language users use signs not to reflect an already given reality, but to intervene in and to structure reality along the parameters afforded by the internal design features of the sign itself. The sign imposes digital order on the analogue flux of perceptual experience.

I discussed above the intimate and two-way nature of the internal link whereby each of the two strata in the sign 'calls up' the other. What, then, of the notion that this link is arbitrary? Do the two claims contradict each other? Saussure says that the two elements in the sign 'are united in our brain by the associative link' ('*sont unis dans notre cerveau par le lien de l'association*', *CLG*: 98). The agency in this construction is ascribed to 'the associative link' which is, in fact, external to any given sign relation. It acts on any given sign from the outside as a general systemic constraint which produces particular associations of signifiers and signifieds in a given language system. This is a very different kind of relationship from the intimate and internal two-way link discussed above. How, then, may this be explained?

The point is that the overall system of relations, and *not* the relation which is internal to the individual sign *per se*, constitutes the general enabling conditions for the specific relationship that holds between any given signifier and signified in the language system. For Saussure, the former is external to the given sign relation, acting on it from the outside; the latter, on the other hand, is internal to it. I shall discuss the first point in some detail in section 2 below. In sections 4 and 5 I shall further discuss the internal nature of the relation between signifier and signified as one of functional solidarity. There is no contradiction between these two perspectives: it is the system which enables signs to be made, rather than any intrinsic properties of individual signs *per se*.

Immediately after this discussion, Saussure gives us a second definition of the sign. This definition is preceded by some discussion of the need to clarify the terminological issues which are at stake. In particular, Saussure seeks to clarify the terminological ambiguity which the term 'acoustic image' poses. According to Saussure, the term *sign* generally refers in 'current usage', as he puts it, to the acoustic image only. For this reason, he proposes the following terminological change:

> The ambiguity would disappear if the three notions were designated by names which call attention to each other yet are opposed. We propose to keep the word *sign* to designate the whole, and to replace *concept* and *acoustic image* respectively by *signified* and *signifier*; the latter terms have the advantage of marking the opposition which separates them both from each other and from the whole of which they are a part.
>
> (*CLG*: 99)

In effecting this shift, Saussure does much more than clarify a terminological ambiguity. The new terminology which he proposes also entails a shift away from the perspective of the speech circuit to that of the system of *langue*: that is, a shift from the instance to the system perspective on the sign and its theorization. It is only after undertaking this shift that the principle of arbitrariness and its place in Saussure's theory comes into view. In the next section, I shall consider the new perspective which Saussure proposes in the light of this question.

2 ARBITRARINESS AND HIGHER-ORDER CONTEXTUALIZATION

Saussure's initial definition of the principle of arbitrariness and its relationship to the sign is as follows:

> The link unifying signifier and signified is arbitrary or, even more, since we understand by the sign the total result of the association of a signifier with a signified, we can say more simply: *the linguistic sign is arbitrary.*
>
> (*CLG*: 100)

Saussure's arbitrariness principle is generally taken to refer, above all, to the internal link between signifier and signified. This is how the notion emerges in Roy Harris' translation, for instance. Harris translates the first sentence of the passage quoted here as follows: 'The link between signal and signification is arbitrary.' Thus, the preposition 'between' suggests an already-given and internal relationship which is arbitrary. Yet, the French text speaks of 'the link which unites' ('*le lien unissant*', *CLG*: 100). Again, the agency which does the unifying is external, in the way already explained. That is, the link between signifier and signified is the result of systemic factors which are not reducible to any given sign considered in isolation. This point is further evidenced by the reference to the concept of 'associative'. As we have seen, the associative link constitutes a systemic relation which gives rise to the association of the two parts of the sign. It is not a link which originates from inside any given sign. Associative relations and the principles by which they are mapped onto particular syntagms are a property of the language system (Chapter 11).

In his first definition, Saussure does not refer to the notion of arbitrariness. The linking of the principle of arbitrariness to this second definition is accompanied by the critically important terminological shift that I discussed above. It is the general system of relations involved – *langue* – which arbitrarily constitutes the sign relations of that system. On the following page, Saussure asserts:

> the main object will nonetheless be the class of systems founded on the arbitrariness of the sign. In effect, all the received means of expression in a society rest in principle on collective habits [*une habitude collective*] or, and this amounts to the same thing, on convention [*la convention*]. Signs

of politeness, for example, are often endowed with a certain natural expressiveness (one thinks of the Chinese man who greets his emperor by prostrating himself nine times on the ground), are no less fixed by a rule [*une règle*]; it is this rule which obliges them to be used, *not their intrinsic value*.

(*CLG*: 100–1; my emphasis)

First, Saussure gives priority to the system perspective on the sign. In this view, the 'arbitrariness of the sign' is taken to be axiomatic. In saying this, Saussure does not refer to the internal relationship which unifies signifier and signified, but to the *result* of that relationship, that is, the sign taken as a whole. The sign, it must be borne in mind, is always the result of the combining of terms from the two orders of difference (Chapter 3, section 3). He then makes it quite clear that the principle of arbitrariness refers to what he variously calls in the above passage the 'collective habits', 'the convention' or 'the rule'. The principle of arbitrariness refers to the habits, conventions or rules which establish and define the regular and typical combinations or cross-couplings of phonic and conceptual terms in a given language system. These must be held constant – 'approximately' the same, Saussure had said (*CLG*: 29) – for all speakers. 'It is', Saussure says, 'this rule which obliges them to be used, *not their intrinsic value*.' The intrinsic value of the sign derives from the solidary and intimate two-way link between signifier and signified. This is internal to the sign relation (section 4 below). The social rule which obliges all speakers to use, more or less, the same sign relationship in a given situation type is external to the sign itself. It acts on the latter from the outside, in relation to all the other signs in the same system. This relationship is arbitrary in the sense defined here.

Saussure makes it clear that the purpose of the sign is not to name or label things, events and so on which already exist outside it. The two-way and internal relation between signifier and signified is a contextualizing relation. It is this relation which functions in turn to construe what the context of a given sign is. Saussure's point is that the relationship between these two strata of language form is itself meaningful, or, better, *meaning-making*. The internal structure of the sign is, then, a contextualizing relation in the very precise sense that the two strata are two components of the one overall linguistic form. The one symbolically construes the other (Chapter 10, section 3). In other words, there is a redundancy relation between signifier and signified, as I explained in section 1 above (Lemke 1984d: 35).

In the first instance, the contextual nature of this relation arises from the fact that signs are made in and through the cross-coupling of the phonic and conceptual orders of difference. The sign is not a pre-given entity; it is, rather, a patterned relationship between the two layers or strata of its organization, which Saussure calls signifier and signified. If signs were already pre-given, rather than made in this way, then it would be difficult to see how the two orders of difference could be cross-coupled in new ways according to specific contextual contingencies. However, the notion of specific contextual contingencies does not contradict the fact that there are always higher-order redundancy relations that allow language users to construe a given *type* of relation between a given signifier and its signified (Lemke 1984d: 36). For meaning-making to occur, there must be a system of stable and replicable types which the members of a culture can recognize and use from one occasion to another. The principle of arbitrariness provides Saussure with a solution to this question.

Saussure points out that the 'intrinsic value' of the redundancy relation between signifier and signified is not sufficient to explain the ways in which the relationship between, say, signifier a and signified a¹ in the above example is a contextualizing relation. How do we recognize this relation as one which is regularly employed or used by the speakers of a given language? Saussure postulates the principle of arbitrariness in order to show that a given relation between signifier and signified is in turn contextualized by a higher-order system of 'rules', 'habits' or 'conventions' which tell us that a given a/a¹ relation is a sign of a type which corresponds to a regular pattern in some community. It specifies, for example, the social rule or convention as to when the a/a¹ relation is used, and how. In other words, the a/a¹ relation in the sign is contextualized by a still higher-order contextualizing relation which tells us in which context(s) a is related to a¹, and how. If signifier and signified in the a/a¹ relation have an 'intrinsic value' in the sense that they reciprocally contextualize each other, then these higher-order rules or conventions tell us the possible *significations* of a/a¹ in relation to the higher-order contexts in which it is used and interpreted in a given culture. Signification, in this definition, is a productive relationship between a given sign and some higher-order context.

3 ILLUSTRATION OF BASIC PRINCIPLES: THE TRAFFIC LIGHT SYSTEM

I shall now illustrate the principles I have discussed above in connection with a simple sign system, that is, the traffic light system in the state of New South Wales in Australia. I have adapted an early analysis by Fawcett (1982) for this purpose. Figure 9.1 shows that this simple semiotic system distinguishes between the system of rules or conventions which regulate the possible texts of this system – that is, its grammar, or *langue* – and the typical signs which can be made by the users of this simple sign system and the higher-order contexts in which these can be used. The traffic light system displays the two strata of what Fawcett, somewhat misleadingly in my view, calls 'semantics' and 'form'. Fawcett equates these with Saussure's 'concept' and 'acoustic image', respectively. These two levels, Fawcett argues, are related by explicit realization statements which can be specified. Further, each of these two strata is represented in terms of both *langue* and *parole*. Second, both of these levels are representable in terms of associative and syntagmatic relations. However, Fawcett rules out syntagmatic relations in the case of the traffic light system on the grounds that the 'outputs' of the grammar (i.e., in *parole*) may be represented by a single associative feature. However, this contradicts the basic fact that all signs are realized in syntagms which unfold in space and/or time. I do not think that the simple signs of the traffic light system constitute an exception to this basic principle. In the act of instantiation, these signs are supported by a matter–energy base; they also have temporal duration.

Finally, we can see that the semiotic values in the traffic light system are defined relationally, rather than positively, by the differences among the visual terms [GREEN], [AMBER], and [RED] in the visual–optical order of differences. Thus, [GREEN] has the semiotic value it has because it systematically contrasts with [AMBER] and [RED] in this simple system. There is also

System resources		Grammar	Text
Signified	paradigmatic relations	((directive ⎰ go —— ⎱ amber to traffic)) ⎱ stop	[(((directive to traffic)), go] [(((directive to traffic)), prepare to stop] [(((directive to traffic)), stop]
	syntagmatic relations	construal of meaning 'go', etc. by motorist	enactment of appropriate response
Realization/construal rules		((([directive to traffic] r. LIGHT)) [Go] r. GREEN [Prepare to stop] r. AMBER [Stop] r. RED	
Signifier	paradigmatic relations	((LIGHT)) ⎰ GREEN ⎨ AMBER ⎱ RED	((LIGHT)), GREEN ((LIGHT)), AMBER ((LIGHT)), RED
	syntagmatic relations	spatio-temporal occurrence of traffic light in programmed sequence	reception of flashing light by motorist

Key: (( )) = redundant feature; r. = realizes/is realized by

Figure 9.1 A simple traffic light system, showing sign relationships (adapted from Fawcett 1982: 92)

a conceptual order of differences comprising the contrasting conceptual terms [GO], [PREPARE TO STOP] and [STOP].

Fawcett's schema has the benefit of showing that *langue* and *parole*, syntagmatic and associative relations, and acoustic image and concept need to be unified in a 'holistic' model. However, Fawcett's way of doing so illustrates two central though problematic axioms in much of twentieth-century linguistics. Fawcett talks about the 'outputs' of the grammar. This reproduces the speaker, or individual-centred, bias in much of linguistics, without saying anything at all about the semiotic behaviour of the addressees (motorists and pedestrians). By his own definition, such a model must fall short of the explicit aim of modelling the 'socio-psycholinguistic reality' of the users of this sign system.

The traffic light system illustrates three fundamental principles of meaning-making in the Saussurean framework. First, one order of differences construes the other order in the process of cross-coupling the visual and the conceptual terms to create a sign. Thus, [RED] construes the conceptual meaning [STOP]. Likewise, [STOP] construes the visual signifier [RED]. There is a simple redundancy relation between the two terms. This relation is a two-way simultaneity, rather than a linear or causal one (see also Halliday 1992: 24). The result of this cross-coupling is a simple sign which fulfils Saussure's basic definition (section 1 above).

Second, these typical cross-couplings are not, however, fixed. The two orders of difference do not stand in a single determinate relationship to each other. There also exists the possibility of decoupling and recoupling to create new combinatorial possibilities. The result is an expansion of the meaning-making potential of the sign system in question (Halliday 1992: 25). Clearly, the possibilities for doing so in the traffic light system are very limited. However, they are not altogether non-existent, as evidenced by the ways in which a small minority of motorists in Australia have re-construed [AMBER] to mean something like [ACCELERATE TO AVOID THE RED LIGHT], rather than [PREPARE TO STOP]. Similarly, [RED] is re-construed by an irresponsible minority to mean something like [DON'T STOP; KEEP GOING].

Third, a sign such as (GREEN ⅄ GO) requires a higher-order contextualizing relation in order that it may be appropriately interpreted. It is this higher-order contextualizing rule or convention which assigns a sign its signification in relation to a system of interpretative rules or conventions. In the case of the traffic light system, these are the conventions and practices that pertain to the rules of the road, their correct observance, their violation and the system of legal sanctions that pertain to this. In other words, there is a higher-order system of social practices which regulates the interpretation of the signs in this simple semiotic system.

4 THE FUNCTIONAL BASIS OF THE INTERNAL RELATION BETWEEN SIGNIFIER AND SIGNIFIED

'Concept' and 'acoustic image' are not simply stuck together to form the sign. This point can help us to get a little closer to understanding the *functional* basis of the relationship between the two. For this, it is useful to refer to Hjelmslev's important elaboration of the Saussurean conception of the sign in his *Prolegomena to a Theory of Language* (1969 [1943]). For Saussure's terms acoustic image/signifier and concept/signified, Hjelmslev substitutes the terms 'expression' and 'content'. On the relation between these two planes, or strata, of semiosis Hjelmslev writes:

> there is also solidarity between the sign function and its two functives, expression and content. There will never be a sign function without the simultaneous presence of both these functives; and an expression and its content, or a content and its expression, will never appear together without the sign's function also being present between them.
>
> (Hjelmslev 1969 [1943]: 48)

In Hjelmslev's precise terminology, expression and content (signifier and signified), are 'functives', whose mutual 'solidary' relation produces the sign. The linguistic sign is always a function of the interdependent 'functives' of expression and content. It is the internal and functional relationship between the two which produces the sign.

The view I have so far presented corresponds to the 'standard' view of the sign, showing just the two strata illustrated here. However, Saussure's account of the linguistic sign can be reconstructed and further elaborated as a more complex and internally stratified structure than is the case with the basic definition outlined in section 1. I shall develop this issue in section 6 below; but first I shall explore further the implications of the stratified nature of the sign in the processes of making and construing meaning in the phonic sequence.

5 THE SIGN AND THE STRATIFIED NATURE OF SEMIOSIS

As I pointed out in Chapter 2, Saussure constantly emphasizes the methodological aspects of his enterprise. A given linguistic unit, on any given stratum, or even a whole sign relation, is not something which is pre-given before analysis or interpretation takes place. Instead, Saussure points out that 'the linguistic entity is not completely determined until it is *delimited*' (*CLG*: 145). It must be remembered here that Saussure's primary concern is to develop a theory of the internal organization of the language system. However, it would be wrong to read Saussure as saying that language is a system of signs *per se*. Importantly, the language system is not just a system of differences; it is also comprised of syntagmatic and associative groups

(*CLG*: 177). Saussure gives equal priority to both perspectives (Chapter 11). So, the methodological problem of 'delimitation' requires analytical procedures for specifying what the relevant linguistic units are, how these are formed from the 'interdependencies' of syntagmatic and associative groups, and how these relate to each other.

We have already seen that Saussure treats the sign as *internally* comprised of two strata of organization. These are not simply brought together to form a pre-given entity, the sign. Instead, the sign's stratal organization is a result of the operations performed in the making of a signifying act. Again, the problem is a methodological one for Saussure: that is, how do we interpret or construe meaning in the 'amorphous ribbon' of the spoken chain (*CLG*: 145)?

> it is merely a line, a continuous ribbon of sound, along which the ear picks out no adequate or clearly marked divisions. In order to do so, *recourse must be had to meanings* [*significations*]. When we listen to an unknown language, we are not in a position to say how the sounds should be analysed: for the analysis is impossible if one takes into account nothing more than the phonic side of the linguistic event. But *when we know what sense* [*sens*] *and what role* [*rôle*] *to attribute to each segment in the sequence*, then we see those segments separated from one another, and the shapeless ribbon is cut up into pieces. But the analysis involved is in no way a material analysis.
>
> (*CLG*: 145; my emphasis)

The analysis involved is an *interpretative* one. Sense or functional role relations are 'attributed' to the relevant elements in the phonic sequence by the users of the language. Saussure makes it very clear that meanings do not simply exist 'in' the sound sequence in any simple, fixed or pre-given way; rather, the spoken chain is recursively re-construed at successively higher orders of contextualization as an instantiation of (1) the phonological and (2) the conceptual categories of a given language system. In the paragraph which follows the one above, Saussure further comments:

> a language does not present itself to us as a set of signs already delimited, requiring merely to study their meanings and organization. It is an indistinct mass, in which *attention* and *habit* alone enable us to distinguish particular elements.
>
> (*CLG*: 146; my emphasis)

What might Saussure mean by the terms 'attention and habit'? My suggestion is that Saussure is drawing attention to the interpretative (meaning-making) operations and practices that the users of the language selectively deploy in order to construe significance in the phonic (or graphic) sequence. These processes of construal are constrained by social habits and practices which language users draw on in order to attend to and interpret these sequences in regular and non-random ways. Saussure's focus on *langue* leaves him little scope for developing the full implications of this insight. Yet this focus allows him to pose a no less fundamental question: viz. what is it about the *internal* nature of *langue* which makes these interpretative processes possible? Saussure's answer is a major theoretical advance, whose implications continue to be absorbed into linguistic and semiotic theory to this day. In the remaining paragraphs of this section, I shall now consider the further implications of Saussure's proposals.

Saussure does not simply refer to the spoken chain and the 'sense' that is assigned to the elements in this as two entirely separable levels of structure *per se*. Instead, he has emphasized the *process* of interpretation – of making meaning – whereby the first level of analysis – the spoken chain – is interpreted or construed in relation to a second level (the 'sense' or 'role' assigned to a given segment in the sequence). In turn, this is interpreted or construed in relation to the still wider sequence in which it occurs, as the meaning (*signification*) of the whole sequence, and so on. It is this reasoning which is at the heart of Saussure's stratified model of the sign.

Saussure's social-semiological theory of the sign represents the very beginnings of the stratified model of semiosis which was further developed by Hjelmslev and other linguists and semioticians who followed in the structural–functional tradition of linguistic studies. Saussure does not use the terms 'strata' or 'stratification', but the two levels of organization in his concept of the sign may be called appropriately strata, following the terminology proposed by Hjelmslev. This is evident in Saussure's formulation of the methodological issues underlying the problem discussed above:

> A correct delimitation requires that the divisions established in the acoustic chain (αβγ ...) correspond to those in the chain of concepts (α′β′γ′ ...):

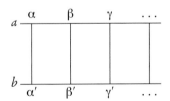

> Take the French *sižlaprã*: can I segment this chain after *l* and take *sižl* as a unit? No: it is enough to consider the concepts to see that this division is false. The segmentation into syllables: *siž-la-prã* is not linguistically *a priori*. The only possible divisions are: 1. *si-ž-la-prã* (*si je la prends*, ['if I take it/her']), and (2) *si-ž-l-aprã* (*si je l'apprends* ['if I learn it']), and they are determined by the sense [*le sens*] that one attaches to these words.

> (*CLG*: 146)

Saussure again emphasizes the interpretative operations whereby we 'attach' sense to the units in the sequence. What Saussure draws attention to are the ways in which the organization of the acoustic chain may or may not match a given unit of sense. The example illustrates that the delimitation of the sound sequence as a unit of sense – a sign – requires the two different strata, each with their own principles of organization, and both indicated in some way in the overall structure of the sign so construed. The stratified view of semiosis also shows, as in Saussure's example, that there is not necessarily any one-to-one fit between the different levels of organization: the same sound sequence, as here, can be meaningfully construed in different possible ways. There is no fixed relation between the two strata. This depends, in turn, on the higher-order context with which the sign redounds (Chapter 2, section 9; section 1 above). Again, we have an illustration of an earlier point: viz. the sign is not pre-given, but is made in and through the interpretative processes whereby units and relations on one stratum are construed and re-construed in relation to units and relations on other strata.

6 TERMINOLOGICAL QUESTIONS: TOWARDS A RE-CONSTRUCTION OF THE SIGN

I should now like to consider some of the apparently puzzling terminological shifts in Saussure's discussion of the sign. Table 9.1 sets out a number of terminological distinctions which form the basis of the discussion in this section. For comparative purposes, I have provided the relevant terms both in the original French and in the two currently available English-language translations of *CLG* by Wade Baskin (1959) and Roy Harris (1983). The first set of terms refers to the distinction between signifier and signified. This is the system perspective. Here, the sign is defined purely in terms of its value in the system of types; it is an abstract sign type, a meaning-making potential, formed out of the combination of the two orders of differences in *langue*$_1$. This relation is a synoptic one: the system of differences is abstracted from specific acts of meaning-making. The link between *signifié* and *signifiant* is viewed purely relationally, rather than dynamically, as an abstract and formal property of the system. From the point of view of *langue*, a sign is a generic type which has a decontextualized 'core' – that is, a formal system – meaning in this sense.

Saussure talks about the second pair in a subtly, yet revealingly, different way. To start with, it is worth while paying careful attention to the fact that Saussure uses the distinction between *concept* and *auditory image* or *acoustic image*, and not the first set of terms, when he tries to explain the difference between *signification* and *valeur*. Speaking of signification, Saussure says that it is a matter of the relation between 'an auditory image and a concept, *within the limits of the word, considered as a fixed domain, existing in itself*' (*CLG*: 159; my emphasis). Here, we are concerned not with abstract sign types, but with actual concrete signs-in-use, or sign tokens, in the speech circuit. These

Table 9.1 Key terms used in talking about the sign; Saussure and his English
translators compared

---

1 The system perspective (*langue*)

signifié	signifiant	(Saussure, p. 158)
signified	signifier	(Baskin, p. 67)
signification	signal	(Harris, p. 67)

2 The instance perspective (*parole*)

concept	image acoustique	(Saussure, p. 99)
concept	sound image	(Baskin, p. 66)
concept	sound pattern	(Harris, p. 67)

**3 Interaction of the system/instance perspectives: delimited units in the linear
sequence**

Saussure:

quel *sens* et quel *rôle* il faut attribuer à chaque partie de la chaîne	entités délimités ou *unités*	(p. 145)

Baskin translation:

the *meaning* and the *function* that must be attributed to each part of the chain	delimited entities or units	(p. 103)

Harris translation:

what *meaning* and what *role* to attribute to each segment in the sequence	delimited entities or units	(p. 102)

**4 The perspective of a restratified signified: the interdependency (solidarity) of form
and function in the grammar**

Saussure:

grammatical dit [synchronique] et *significatif*	La grammaire étudie la langue en tant que système de moyens d'expression.	(p. 185)
formes et fonctions sont solidaires, et il est difficile, pour ne pas dire impossible, de les séparer		(p. 186)

Baskin translation:

Grammatical means [synchronic] and *significant*.	Grammar studies language as a system of means of expression.	(p. 134)
Form and function are interdependent and it is difficult, if not impossible, to separate them.		(p. 135)

Harris translation:

'Grammatical' implies ['synchronic'] and '*meaningful*'.	Grammar studies the language as a system of means of expression.	(p. 133)
Forms and functions are interdependent. It is difficult if not impossible to separate them.		(p. 134)

Table 9.1 continued

---

5 The perspective of signification: Saussure's stratified model of semiosis

Saussure:

significations (p. 145)	syllabes/sons (p. 98)
signification (pp. 158/9)	la chaîne parlée en syllabes (p. 144)
	la chaîne phonique (p. 145)

Baskin translation:

meanings (p. 103)	syllables/sounds (p. 66)
signification (p. 114)	the spoken chain into syllables (p. 103)
	the phonic chain (p. 103)

Harris translation:

meanings (p. 102)	syllables/sounds (p. 66)
	the spoken sequence into syllables (p. 101)
meaning (p. 112)	the spoken sequence (p. 102)

Note: Page references are not exhaustive, but refer to key parts of the French and English texts.

---

are now viewed as material and psychic instantiations of signs, as distinct from the abstract system of types in *langue*. The terminological shift captures the switch in emphasis to the materiality of concrete and intentionally directed uses of signs.

Third, Saussure uses the terms 'sense' and 'role' (*sens* and *rôle*, *CLG*: 145) to talk about the functional value which is attributed to each separate linguistic unit which is 'delimited' in the acoustic chain of speech. These two terms are variously translated by Baskin (1959: 103) as 'meaning' and 'function', and by Harris (1983: 102) as 'meaning' and 'role'. The translation of the French *sens* with the English *meaning* by both Baskin and Harris seems to me unfortunate. In effect, it blurs the distinction Saussure makes here between *sens* and *signification*, given that the latter is sometimes translated by Baskin as 'meaning', and consistently so by Harris (see Table 9.1). If, by the latter term, Saussure is referring to the (global) process of construing meaning in the sequence by an interpreter, as we shall see in the following paragraph, then the former term ('sense') would appear to be restricted to the local functional values of the individual grammatical units which have been delimited in the sequence. These are also referred to as the internal sense relations of grammatical units in some linguistic accounts. This is no overinterpretation on my part, for Saussure makes it absolutely clear that the former term is concerned with the attribution of functional values to the *local* units which are delimited and segmented in the spoken sequence:

> But when we know *what sense and what role must be attributed to each part of the chain*, then we see the parts detach themselves from each other, and the shapeless ribbon is cut up into pieces.
>
> (*CLG*: 145; my emphasis)

There is a fourth set of distinctions which Saussure, if only implicitly, builds into his basic model of the sign. This is where he draws attention to the solidary (*solidaires*, *CLG*: 186) nature of the relationship between grammatical forms and their functions. The solidary relation between grammatical form and function requires that the basic model be re-drawn. Grammatical form and function, as our third set of distinctions already shows, belong on the stratum of the signified, rather than the signifier. The forms are the delimited grammatical units and the functions are the 'sense' or 'role' relations that are attributed to these on the basis of the part they play in the overall whole. This distinction means that the stratum of the signified is itself internally stratified in such a way that grammatical form and function are related in a motivated or solidary way.

What, then, of our fifth set of distinctions? This brings in a new term: *signification*. Saussure, unlike his English-language translators, is careful not to confuse this term with the three preceding sets of distinctions. According to Saussure, grammar is *significatif* (*CLG*: 185). The French adjective may be glossed as 'able to mean' or 'having the potential to mean'. This is what the morphemic suffix -*if* signifies in French adjectives. Given this interpretation, the process noun *signification* designates the actual process of making or construing meaning – of attributing a global significance – to the phonic sequence.

An attentive reading will bear out what I am saying about the careful terminological distinctions Saussure is making here. I have shown that Saussure is careful to distinguish *signification* from *value*. I have also argued in my earlier discussion of the stratification of the sign in section 5 that the 'phonic chain' (*CLG*: 145) can only be delimited and defined in terms of relevant linguistic units on the basis of the meaning(s) (*signification(s)*, *CLG*: 145) that language users attribute to the overall sequence. It is a question of assigning (1) a sense or a functional value to each of the constituent parts (grammatical forms) which are so delimited and (2) a global signification to the whole structure which the constituents referred to in (1) constitute. Saussure comments:

> it is known that the phonic chain is primarily characterized by being linear (see p. 103). Considered in itself, it is no more than a line, a continuous ribbon, in which the ear does not perceive any sufficient and precise division; for this reason it is necessary to appeal to signification.
>
> (*CLG*: 145)

In an interesting paper, Antonelli (1978: 110) draws attention to the reasoning which underlies the distinction between signified and signification in Saussure's theory. In her discussion of this distinction, she carefully echoes the point that Saussure makes in the above passage (1978: 112). However, she then goes on to offer an interpretation of signification which is in some respects different from my own. Antonelli writes:

signification constitutes ... the 'fundamental semantic nucleous' [*sic*] of expressions, that is, it indicates what each single linguistic unit 'means'. It is not the same as *signifié*, because that, as *valeur*, indicates the position of each word in the system of *langue* in relation to the other words.

(Antonelli 1978: 117)

It is context, Antonelli continues, which selects or otherwise determines the relevant signification of the word. This last point is particularly interesting. I shall discuss why shortly.

Rather than say, as does Antonelli, that expressions have a 'semantic nucleus', which is the basis of signification, I would say that signification is the higher-level contextualization or construal of the sign in and through some interpretative practice, convention or rule (section 2). It is the process whereby the interpreter or language user construes or 'attributes', to use Saussure's own turn of phrase, an overall meaning to the entire sequence. Further, we cannot attribute a necessary or given semantic nucleus to the sense or functional roles of each of the units which has been delimited in a given sequence, because these are a product of the functional role each has in the sequence as a whole. This role or sense cannot be separated from its relations to all the other units in the sequence. Functional roles do not pre-exist the phonic sequence, or its 'de-limitation'. After all, a given unit can have quite a different functional role in some other sequence, as Saussure's own analysis shows (Chapter 2, section 9).

Antonelli misses the point, then, when it comes to the relation between signification and phonic sequence. The units which comprise the latter do not have a semantic nucleus in the way Antonelli defines this; rather, the stratified view of semiosis which Saussure begins to articulate shows that signification is the *process* of construing or interpreting a global significance in the phonic sequence (*une suite de sons*, *CLG*: 144; *la chaîne parlée*, *CLG*: 145). In other words, it is the process of constructing a global meaning in and through the functional role relations of the units in the phonic sequence on the basis of the functional values that each separate part contributes to the whole. This is something very different from the notion of a 'semantic nucleus', which is surely contradicted by the notion of value in its capacity as the decontextualized system-meaning of the terms in *langue*₁. If anything can be said to be the 'semantic nucleus' of a sign, it is the value which a term has as a decontextualized formal item in the system.

The teasing apart and the further clarifying of the above sets of distinctions is rich in implications. First, it is clear that Saussure has a much more complex idea of the sign than the simple biplanar relation between a signifier and a signified which is what has generally been attributed to him. Second, Saussure shows a clear awareness of the functional basis of the delimited units which his stratified view of the sign reveals. Third, these units, functionally defined according to their role in the overall sequence, do not have a meaning *per se*. Instead, they are defined in relation to three interrelated perspectives: (a) the 'lower' stratum (the phonic sequence) in relation to which they are delimited; (b) their sense or functional semantic role relations to each other in the overall sequence, that is, on their own stratum, which is that of the linear sequencing of grammatical forms in the signified; and (c) their relations to the overall or global meaning (*signification*) which is attributed to the whole sequence on the stratum 'above' by some still higher-order contextualizing relation. Fourth, the relation of Saussure's stratified model of semiosis to the non-linguistic phenomena of 'thought' and 'sound' now comes more clearly into focus.

I would suggest that it is the stratum Saussure calls *signification* which construes or interprets extralinguistic 'thought-substance' in and through the value-producing distinctions made by the units which are delimited in the grammatical stratum on the level 'below'. Signification is the interface between the internal organization of the signified and pre-semiotic 'thought'. It is by virtue of the cross-coupling of the two that a semiotically formed signified substance emerges (Chapter 7, section 4). It is also, I suggest, a stratum in its own right. Saussure does not develop this point, which means he does not say anything about what kind of organization this stratum may have. The notion of signification moves in the direction of the interface between language form and what lies outside. That is, it suggests the higher-order contextualizing relations which relate a given signifier and signified to pre-semiotic 'thought' and 'sound' (Chapter 7, section 4). Saussure does not develop this point fully (but see Chapter 12, sections 4–5).

The matter discussed above is confused by Culler's assertion that 'philosophers would want to say that what Saussure calls the signification of an utterance involves both meaning and reference' (1976: 33). Indeed, Culler makes the further claim that in Saussure's text there are two kinds of meaning: 'a relational meaning or value, which is based on the linguistic system, and another kind of meaning or signification which involves the use of linguistic elements in actual situations of utterance' (*ibid.*). Saussure makes no such split. Saussure's conception is a unitary one. This means that there is no ontological opposition between the linguistic values internal to the language system and the extralinguistic reality these have the potential to construe. The social uses and determinations of language are undertheorized in *CLG*. Nevertheless, the deeper point that Saussure is making is that such social uses of language are made possible by the very value-producing distinctions in and through which extralinguistic reality and the social are, in fact, constructed and construed. Saussure saw fit to deconstruct the folk-linguistic ideology of reference precisely because the act of 'referring' and the potential of language to perform this function are not external to the linguistic system, as the philosophical tradition which Culler alludes to would have it. There is, in any case, a radical incompatibility between the ontological claims of the two traditions. This is very different, however, from saying that Saussure's linguistic theory is unable to provide its own answers to the question of 'reference'.

An analogous process also occurs at the interface between the linear phonic sequence of signifiers and sound: the signifier – the phonological stratum – construes meaning-making distinctions in the latter as phonic substance. In conclusion, meaning-making takes place at the interface between the signified and 'thought', on the one hand, and at the interface between the signifier and 'sound', on the other (Chapter 7, section 1). It also takes place between the two strata of signifier and signified which are internal to language form. This is so because the internal organization of the linear sequence of signifieds construes what lies outside it on both sides. It faces 'outwards' to the analogue domain of the perceptual flux (Saussure's 'thought') and inwards to the sequence of phonic elements on the stratum of the signifier.

These considerations lead me to re-work Saussure's notion of the sign with the aid of Figure 9.2. A few additional comments are called for with

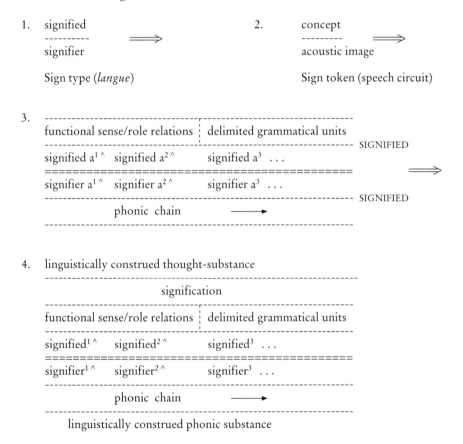

Figure 9.2 Re-constructing Saussure's stratified model of meaning-making

respect to the various stages of the re-construction of the sign I am proposing here. The first stage is concerned with sign types in *langue₂* (Chapter 3, section 5).

At the second stage, we have a material instantiation, or a sign token, in the speech circuit. This is evident in the switch to the more concrete terms 'concept' and 'acoustic image'. Saussure had made this clear by relating this particular distinction to what he calls the 'executive' and 'psychological', as distinct from the psychic, aspects of sign transmission and reception in the speech circuit (Chapter 6). It is in the speech circuit, as Saussure makes plain, that the 'sensorial' and 'psychic' association between concept and acoustic image is made in the active process of making signs. The transition from the first to the second stage in my re-construction of Saussure's theory of the sign does not mean that there are two distinct objects of study. Instead, it is the same object viewed from two different perspectives, that of system and instance, respectively.

With respect to the third stage, it should be borne in mind that Saussure, in the chapter entitled 'Grammar and its subdivisions' (Part II, Chapter 7, p. 133 [p. 185]), makes the important claim that the 'grammatical' is meaningful (*significatif*). The third set of distinctions brings in the principle of linearity, whereby grammatical units are formed and combined in the syntagm (Chapter 11, section 2). In this way, the solidary relation between form and function in the construal of grammatical units and relations is built into the internal structure of the sign (Chapter 13, section 1). This step is entirely plausible on the basis of Saussure's own discussion of grammar, though it was not explicitly undertaken by him. The result is the internal stratification of the signified. That is, the grammatical forms which occur in a given sequence are re-construed as a configuration of functional values in a given sequence.

The fourth stage builds in the notion of signification as a distinct stratum 'above' that of the signified. This highlights the importance of Saussure's claim that the grammar is 'meaningful' (*significatif*). It also demonstrates the absolute consistency and systematicity in Saussure's use of the terms I presented in Table 9.1. I am referring to the theoretical consistency in the use of the same term to designate the stratum I have identified as signification, and the use of the term *significatif* to refer to grammatical units and structures. The explanation for this was given above.

I should like to emphasize that all of the terms that I have used in the re-construction undertaken here are Saussure's. I have added no new terminological innovations of my own. Further, the entirely systematic relationships among these terms is clearly evident in the relevant sections of *CLG*, although the order of exposition chosen by the editors does not always bring this out clearly. For example, Saussure's discussion of grammatical form and function is cut off from the main discussion of the sign. This suggests that these are unrelated issues. On the contrary, they are intrinsically linked to the sign and its workings.

Now, the structuralist reading of Saussure privileged the notion of language and, by extension, other semiological systems, as systems of signs. It gave emphasis to the ontological claims of a *langue*-based system of differences. Yet, Saussure, as I noted earlier, gives equal weight to the notion of 'groups of signs'. This shows the importance of grammar, and the theory and description of grammar, in Saussure's overall conception of the language system. The structuralist and post-structuralist readings of Saussure have little, or nothing, to say on this important aspect of Saussurean thought.

Grammar, understood as the synchronic description of a given linguistic system, is not a closed and autonomous system of forms *per se* (Chapter 3, section 2). Instead, Saussure quite explicitly affirms that grammar is meaning-making (*CLG*: 185; Chapter 13, section 1). This accords perfectly with Saussure's stratal conception of the sign. In other words, the value-producing distinctions which are internal to the grammatical organization of the language system are meaning-making. I shall have more to say about this in Part VI of this book.

On the whole, Saussure's commentators have taken up and focused on only the first of the five distinctions discussed here. This has been at the expense of a more holistic account. Consequently, signs, in spite of Saussure's claims to the contrary, tend to be talked about as things-in-themselves, rather than as both the product and the process of the practices of social meaning-making in some community. This has had the unfortunate consequence of hindering a truly social-semiological account of how signs are made and function in social life. In the remaining chapters I shall focus on these questions.

Chapter 10

The symbolic character of the sign

1 THE POSITIVE CHARACTER OF THE SIGN AS A WHOLE

Thought and sound, as I have already pointed out, are analogue domains of, respectively, perceptual experience and bodily process. Crucially, Saussure argues that the phonic and conceptual terms which comprise the two orders of difference in *langue*$_1$ have no positive value. He points out that 'the language system comprises neither ideas nor sounds which pre-exist the linguistic system, but only conceptual differences and phonic differences stemming from this system' (*CLG*: 166). How, then, can an analogue continuum of pure differences give rise to 'ideas' and 'sounds'? Ideas and sounds, as Saussure defines them, have positive value. They do not pre-exist the language system; rather, they emerge from it by virtue of the selective combining of the two orders of difference in the making of signs. There has been a good deal of misunderstanding on this point. As I argued in Chapter 3, section 4, *langue*$_1$, as a system of pure values, is a system of contextualizing relations for the making of signs. What matters are the ways in which these values are distributed in the combining of the two orders of difference. In this way, as Saussure argues, the system of values is the constitutive link between signifier and signifed in the sign (Chapter 9, section 2):

> But to say that everything is negative in the language system, this is only true of signified and signifier taken separately: *when the sign is considered in its totality, one is in the presence of a positive thing in its order.* A linguistic system is a series of differences in sounds combined with a series of differences in ideas; but this putting together of a certain number of acoustic signs with corresponding cuts made in the mass of thought gives rise to a system of values; and it is this system which constitutes the effective link between the phonic and psychic elements on the interior of each sign. Although signified and signifier, taken separately, are purely differential and negative, *their combination is a positive fact*; it is indeed the only kind of fact that the language system consists of, since the distinctive characteristic of the linguistic institution is precisely to

maintain the parallelism between these two orders of difference.

(*CLG*: 166; my emphasis)

The sign, 'considered in its totality', is a *positive*, rather than a negative, fact because it represents the combining of selections of terms from the two orders of difference in response to some specific contextual requirement. The terms themselves may be selectively combined and re-combined in new ways in many different contexts. It is the overall system of values which entrains and co-ordinates the cross-coupling of the two orders. The act of selectively combining negatively defined terms from the two orders of difference means that the analogue continuum is digitalized as a positive distinction in the making of a sign. This is why the sign in its totality has positive value:

> When one compares signs among themselves – positive terms – one can no longer speak of difference; the expression would be inappropriate, because it is only correctly applied to the comparison between two acoustic images, for example, *père* ['father'] and *mère* ['mother'], or to that between two ideas, for example, the idea of 'père' and the idea of 'mère'; two signs each comprising a signified and a signifier are not different, they are only distinct. Between them there is only an *opposition*. All of the language mechanism, which will be discussed below, rests on oppositions of this sort and on the phonic and conceptual differences that they implicate.
>
> (*CLG*: 167; emphasis in original)

The fixing of a value in a particular combination of terms from the two orders of difference in the making of a sign means that a digital opposition, or a boundary, is introduced into the analogue continuum of pure difference. Let us consider this question from the conceptual point of view with respect to the signs *man* and *woman* in English. From the conceptual point of view, these two signs may be seen as the selecting and combining of the following sets of conceptual terms:

> *man*: [THING; ANIMATE; HUMAN; MALE; ADULT]
>
> *woman*: [THING; ANIMATE; HUMAN; FEMALE; ADULT]

The terms in each of these two conceptual series are associated according to the principle of taxonomic hierarchy. This is based on a paradigmatic principle of classification. Any given term may freely combine with other terms to form some other sign: for example, the conceptual term [MALE] combines with other terms in the word *stallion*, [FEMALE] in the word *mare*, and so on. Analogously, each of these words selects for different combinations of phonic terms to form their signifiers. The point I wish to make here is that terms such as [THING], [FEMALE] and so on are purely negatively defined differences that have no positive value as such. The convention I have adopted in this book of using square brackets and small capital letters is nothing more than a means of providing linguistic glosses on these otherwise ineffable analogue differences. These glosses should not be confused with the actual words *thing*, *female*, and so on in English.

A given sign is always a selective combination of terms, as illustrated by the words *man* and *woman* above. These two signs are distinguished from each other on the basis of the opposition between [MALE] and [FEMALE]. If the terms belong to the analogue continuum of pure difference, then the combining of terms in the making of a given sign, or linguistic form, constitutes a digitalization of this continuum. That is, the fixing of the conceptual series [THING; ANIMATE; HUMAN; MALE; ADULT] in the linguistic form (the sign) *man* introduces a digital distinction into this continuum. It introduces, to borrow an expression from Wilden (1980 [1972]: 174), 'a desired closure' into the analogue continuum of difference. Saussure's point is that value is the operative principle – the contextualizing principle – which enables a given combination of signifier and signified to arise. The selective combining and re-combining of the two orders of difference in the making of signs entails a selective orientation to and an intervention in the analogue domains of both perceptual experience (thought) and bodily process (sound). For example, the intersection of the terms [THING; ANIMATE; HUMAN; MALE; ADULT] in the sign *man*, when used to index some 'object' in the purview (real or imagined) of the speaker–listener, co-ordinates the speaker–listener's orientation to the phenomena of perceptual experience in some specific ways rather than in others. This depends on which terms are selectively combined, in which signs, when and how. I am not saying, however, that the terms constitute pre-linguistic information which is attached to the phenomena of perceptual awareness, and which language form then re-processes as data to be computed by the individual's cognitive machinery. This would be to assume (1) that the terms are non-linguistic constituents of prior perceptual experience and (2) that the phenomena we perceive are already categorized in some pre-semiotic way. Saussure, in my reading, assumes neither of these theses. My point is that the form itself (the sign), in selectively combining terms from the two orders of difference, entails both a selective re-construal of perceptual experience *and* a selective intervention in it.

The above examples serve to show that the terms are not intrinsic to any particular sign *per se*. The value of a sign is a result of the particular combination of terms that are intersected in it. Here is how Saussure formulates the relationship between 'simple terms' and grammatical facts:

> that which is commonly called a 'grammatical fact' corresponds in the final analysis to the definition of a unit, for it expresses above all an opposition of terms; this opposition alone is particularly significant [*significative*], for example the formation of the German plural of the type *Nacht* ['night'] and *Nächte* ['nights']. Each of these terms which is made present in the grammatical fact (the singular without the umlaut and without final -*e*, opposed to the plural with the umlaut and final -*e*) is itself

constituted by an entire play of oppositions within the system. Taken in isolation, [there is] neither *Nacht* nor *Nächte*, they do not exist: therefore everything is opposition. In other words, the relation *Nacht* : *Nächte* can be expressed by an algebraic formula *a/b*, where *a* and *b* are not simple terms, but each results from an ensemble of relations.

(*CLG*: 168)

Value is not intrinsic to any given sign as such, however. Words such as *man* and *woman* are what Saussure variously refers to as linguistic 'units' or 'grammatical facts' (*CLG*: 168). As such, they are signs of varying degrees of complexity. These are not reducible to 'simple terms' such as [MALE], [FEMALE], and so on. To illustrate this, Saussure refers, in the above quotation, to the systematic contrast between the simple terms [SINGULAR] and [PLURAL] in the German type which is illustrated by the lexical pair *Nacht* ('night') : *Nächte* ('nights').

2 VALUE AND SIGNIFICATION ARE NOT SYNONYMOUS

There has been a great deal of confusion concerning the distinction Saussure makes between value and signification. This confusion is easily cleared up by examining the above distinction in the light of a further distinction that Saussure makes: viz. the principle of arbitrariness in relation to the two-way link between signifier and signified in the sign (Chapter 9, sections 1–2).

Saussure points out that value and signification are not synonymous (*CLG*: 158–9). However, the order of exposition in *CLG* somewhat obscures the various logical steps in this argument. For instance, the chapter on the sign precedes that on value, and this may create the impression that Saussure attached more importance to the notion of the sign *per se*, than he did to value. It may also suggest that the principle of arbitrariness refers, above all, to the internal link between signifier and signified in any given sign. A careful logical re-construction of the various steps in Saussure's argument results in a somewhat different conception. I believe that this will help to clarify the importance that Saussure attaches to the distinction between value and signification.

Godel (1957: 246) points out that the order of exposition in *CLG* may give the impression that the sign, seen in isolation, is primary. Yet Saussure points out that it is a mistake to isolate the sign from the system which gives rise to it. Saussure's starting point, as we saw in Chapter 3, is not the isolated sign *per se*, but the system of *langue*. The second step in Saussure's argument is that the language system is defined purely differentially: it is not comprised of signs as such, but of the conceptual and phonic differences that stem from the system. In the two orders of difference, abstracted from specific signifying acts, there are only negatively defined differences among terms. It is the relation of any given term to all the other terms in the system which defines the value of each and every term in that system (*CLG*: 158–9; Chapter 3, section 3).

Any reasoning about value must be made on the basis of the terms that lie behind the linguistic forms (signs), rather than the forms *per se*. The signified is, in actual fact, a metalinguistic gloss on the particular configuration of conceptual terms that intersect in a given sign. I shall now try to illustrate this point more concretely with reference to Saussure's discussion of the difference between the French word *mouton* and the English words *sheep* and *mutton* (*CLG*: 160) that I initiated in Chapter 8 (section 5).

The French word, as Saussure points out, may have the same signification as the English *sheep*, but its value is different. Now, in order to establish just what this means it is necessary to look behind the signification of these words to the conceptual terms that are combined in them in the two languages. First, the French *mouton*: this word is assignable to two distinct series of conceptual terms in *langue*, as in Figure 10.1. In English, on the other hand, the two series of conceptual terms proposed above, both of which refer to two distinct systems of taxonomic classification, are distributed across two distinct lexical items. In the case of the French word, I have used numerical subscripts, viz. *mouton*₁ and *mouton*₂, to indicate the two conceptual series to which this word is assignable. Which series is activated will depend on which interplay of systemic and contextual factors is relevant in any given instantiation.

Figure 10.1 draws attention to the importance of the terms which lie behind the linguistic forms. It shows how a given sign selectively combines terms from the hierarchies of contextualizing relations in the conceptual order of difference. The fact that I can compare the French *mouton* with the English *sheep* and *mutton* occurs on the basis of the terms that combine in

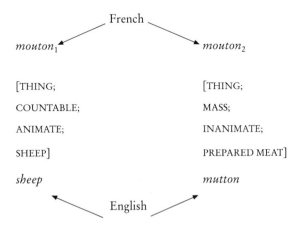

Figure 10.1 Assignment of conceptual terms to French *mouton* and English *mutton* and *sheep*

these forms. Again, this point has often been misunderstood.

One example of the kind of misunderstanding which arises is shown in Holdcroft's (1991: 52–3) discussion of the distinction that Saussure makes between the signifieds of 'ox' in French and German (*CLG*: 100). According to Holdcroft, Saussure does not free himself of the very nomenclaturist assumptions that he critiques at the beginning of this same chapter. After introducing the notion of the arbitrariness of the sign, Saussure offers the following example by way of preliminary discussion:

> Thus the idea of '*sœur*' ['sister'] is not linked by any interior relationship with the sequence of sounds *s-ö-r* which serves as its signifier; it could just as well have been represented by some other sequence: witness the difference between language systems and even the existence of different language systems: the signified '*bœuf*' ['ox'] has as its signifier *b-ö-f* on one side of the border, and *o-k-s* (Ochs) on the other.
>
> (*CLG*: 100)

Saussure refers to the signifieds of the French and German words, which he glosses as *bœuf* ('ox'), and which he takes as shareable by the two language systems. In both cases, the signified *bœuf* ('ox') is in fact a metalinguistic gloss on the conceptual values, or some specific weighting of these, which are combined in the two signs in their respective language systems. In this way, the signified is a metalinguistic means of construing the values of the conceptual terms that are combined in a given sign in one's own language, or in some other language. In other words, the comparison between signs belonging to two different language systems always takes place on the basis of the terms that lie 'behind' the forms themselves.

An analogous situation also applies to the signifier. It is not the material sounds of the language that have values, but, as Saussure points out, 'the phonic differences that allow one word to be distinguished from all the others' (*CLG*: 163). Material sounds as such do not belong to the language system. Only the values pertaining to the phonic terms do (*CLG*: 164). Speaking of the signifier, Saussure makes the following observation:

> in its essence, it is not in any way phonic, it is incorporeal, constituted, not by its material substance, but uniquely by the differences which separate its acoustic image from all the others.
>
> (*CLG*: 164)

The signifier, just like the signified, functions as a metalinguistic (metaphonological) gloss on the phonic terms that combine to form any given signifier. It is this which enables speakers to make categorical judgements as to the conformity or otherwise of a given material sound uttered by someone to the phonological values which a given combination of phonic terms represents in the phoneme (*CLG*: 164). That is, the speaker–listener construes a given material sound as belonging to this or that phonemic type category on the basis of metalinguistic judgements concerning the phonic terms which are relevant to the interpretation of that sound in the spoken chain. In other words, the signifier does not have a phonological value as such (see also Godel 1957: 248; rather, it represents a judgement as to which combination of phonic terms is relevant to the phonological interpretation of a given material sound.

3 INTERSTRATAL SYMBOLIC CONSTRUAL: EXPLAINING THE RELATION BETWEEN SIGNIFIER AND SIGNIFIED

I shall now try to clarify the nature of the internal relationship between signifier and signified in the sign. In my view, this is another area in which there has been considerable misunderstanding of Saussure's position. In particular, this concerns the principle of the arbitrariness of the sign (*CLG*: 100–2; Chapter 9, section 2). Saussure proposes this principle in order to explain the essentially *systemic* nature of the relations which give rise to signs. That is why, as Saussure points out, 'arbitrary' and 'differential' are 'correlative qualities' (*CLG*: 163). The arbitrariness principle does not make sense if it is reductively taken to refer to the internal relationship between signifier and signified in any given sign, taken as an isolated unit (Chapter 9, section 2). Unfortunately, this is the way in which Saussure's principle has generally been understood. With this problem in mind, I shall now attempt to explore the nature of this link.

Much confusion arises when naturalistic arguments are implicitly invoked in order to show that, in Saussure's account, there is no natural link between 'sound' and 'idea' in the sign. I do not think that these arguments represent the more essential point that Saussure is making. 'Sound' in the sense that Saussure intends this term does not refer to a material and perceptual event. There is nothing physical about the signifier, which is a component of language form. Nor does Saussure's conception of the sign entail a formal conception of meaning. The signifier is neither an 'empty' form which acts as the neutral carrier of a pre-linguistic content or idea, nor is there a fixed or 'literal' correspondence between signifier and signified. Speaking of this problem, Saussure provides the following example of the grammatical categories of tense and aspect in the Slavic languages and French:

> The Slavic languages regularly distinguish two aspects of the verb: the perfect represents the action in its totality, like a point, outside of all becoming; the imperfect shows it in the process of becoming, and on the time line. These categories create difficulties for a Frenchman, because his language system is unaware of them: if they had been predetermined, this would not be so.
>
> (*CLG*: 161–2)

If the 'correlative qualities' 'arbitrary' and 'differential' (*CLG*: 163) both refer to a given sign's position in the overall system of *langue*, then how can the two-way and reciprocal link between signifier and signified be defined? I shall argue that this link is intrinsically motivated, or *symbolic* (see also Langacker 1987: 76–86). The importance of these two correlative qualities has to do with Saussure's radically *contextual* and *relative* theory of the language system. The system is neither formal nor autonomous (Chapter 3, section 3). This fact serves to underscore the importance which Saussure attaches to his critique of correspondence theories of the word–object relation. It is only when we grasp the contextual and relative character of Saussure's conception that we can fully appreciate the systemic and internally stratified nature of the sign. This claim may come as a surprise to those who, like Holdcroft, remain convinced that Saussure is a closet nomenclaturist. According to Holdcroft, Saussure

> does retain a relic of nomenclaturism in the assumption that a sign is a 'double entity' in a surprisingly uncritical way, and that one of the more difficult things he has to do is to explain why, if each sign has a double aspect, neither of the aspects can exist independently of the other.
>
> (Holdcroft 1991: 50)

Holdcroft fails to understand two crucial points. First, there is not, in Saussure's theory, a separate 'entity' called meaning which corresponds to the signified (see the above quotation from *CLG* and discussion). Second, he does not appreciate the stratified nature of the relation between signifier and signified. Such misunderstandings would not arise if the contextual and relative implications of Saussure's theory were properly understood. One linguist who has, on the other hand, appreciated this is Louis Hjelmslev, as can be seen in his discussion of the minimal units that comprise the English word *inactivates*:

> When, for example, the analysis of an English word like *in-act-iv-ate-s* is carried though in this way, it can be shown to contain five distinguishable entities which each bear meaning and which are consequently five signs.
>
> In suggesting so far-reaching an analysis on a conventional basis, we should perhaps draw attention to the fact that the 'meaning' which each such minimal entity can be said to bear must be understood as being a purely contextual meaning. None of the minimal entities, nor the roots, have such an 'independent' existence that they can be assigned a lexical meaning. But from the basic point of view we have assumed – the continued analysis on the basis of functions in the text – there exist no other perceivable meanings than contextual meanings; and thus also, any sign is defined relatively, not absolutely, and only by its place in the context.
>
> (Hjelmslev 1969 [1943]: 44–5)

This helps us to clarify two questions. First, arbitrary and differential refer to the *systemic* context of a given sign: that is, to its place in relation to the system of differences, rather than to its instantiation in text. Second, the system itself is still a context because it shows the relations of any given term to all the others in the same system. A systemic context is a formal means of specifying the meaning potential of the term in this relative sense (Chapter 3).

How does this relate to Saussure's insistence on the two-way and reciprocal nature of the link between signifier and signified? It is at this point that the epistemological claims that Saussure makes about language form come to the fore. Signs are necessary conditions for social action and experience (Chapter 2, section 9). It follows from this that such activities and experiences as are possible in a given social-historical formation depend, in part, on the internal organization of the social-semiological resource systems which members have available to them. Sounds and thoughts *per se* are pre-semiotic (Chapter 7, section 4). They have no efficacy independently of semiotic form and social activity. The epistemological relativity of Saussure's position means that all values and, hence, all signs are socially produced. Human agents are not simply thinkers in any abstract and absolute sense. What can be thought and meant depends on the linguistic and other semiotic forms that are deployed in a given culture. Now, Saussure's epistemological relativity, which simply means that linguistic values are produced in determinate social and historical circumstances, should not be confused with ontological relativity (Bhaskar 1979: 73). This last, which asserts that all values are equally good or valid, leads to irrationalism, and to a specifically post-modern appropriation of difference as an *ontological* category (Chapter 8, section 6).

I have already claimed that Saussure sees the internal link between signifier and signified as a symbolic one. I shall now extend the earlier discussion of this important point. After discussing the French word *juger* ('to judge'), Saussure sums up what he calls the 'real interpretation' (*CLG*: 162) of this two-way relation as follows:

The real interpretation of the schema of the sign can now be seen. Thus

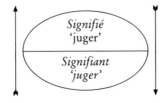

means that in French a concept *juger* ['to judge'] is united to the acoustic image *juger*; in a word *it* [the sign] *symbolizes the signification*; but it is to be understood, of course, that there is nothing prior about this concept, that it is only a value determined by its relations with other similar values, and that without them the signification would not exist.

(CLG: 162; my emphasis)

Saussure points out in the above passage that this symbolic relation refers to the sign as a whole. Only the sign in its entirety 'symbolizes the signification'. The *symbolic* nature of this relationship is one which is being increasingly recognized in modern linguistics as fundamental to the intrinsic design features of language form. For example, Langacker (1987: 81) claims that 'grammar is inherently symbolic', however unorthodox this may sound to those linguists who remain attached to the idea of the autonomy of both syntax and the language system. In my view, it can be straightforwardly shown that the internal relation between signifier and signified is symbolic in character. I shall now consider arguments in support of this position. In so doing, I hope to draw attention to the real importance of Saussure's radical and pioneering account of the sign.

It is quite mistaken, in my view, to assume on the basis of the two-way relation between signifier and signified that 'arbitrary' means, above all, that the relation between signifier and signified is neither 'natural' nor 'inevitable', as Culler (1976: 19) puts it (see also Hawkes 1977: 25). It is not so much that Culler is wrong, but that he misses the more fundamental point at issue, which is the inherently symbolic nature of the internal link between signifier and signified. This does not in any way contradict the systemic basis of the arbitrariness principle that I discussed in Chapter 9, section 2. Culler expresses his point of view on this issue as follows:

> What does Saussure mean by the arbitrary nature of the sign? In one sense the answer is quite simple. There is no natural or inevitable link between the signifier and the signified. Since I speak English I may use the signifier represented by *dog* to talk about an animal of a particular species, but this sequence of sounds is no better suited to that purpose than another sequence. *Lod, tet*, or *bloop* would serve equally well if it were accepted by members of my speech community. There is no intrinsic reason why one of these signifiers rather than another should be linked with the concept of a 'dog'.

(Culler 1976: 19–20)

Culler implicitly appeals to naturalistic criteria to argue that any sequence of sounds would serve equally well as the signifier of the concept 'dog'. But this recourse to naturalistic criteria misses the point of Saussure's argument. The conventional nature of this relation is based on the historical and social dimensions of language. Thus, in English, one cannot say *pen* to designate the concept conventionally designated by the word *table* except in an abstract, dehistoricized and quite vacuous sense, for the concrete reality is that both among and within all speakers of a given language there is an historical dimension which guarantees the conventional (i.e. arbitrary) nature of the relationship between signifier and signified (Coseriu 1973: 16–17).

Saussure is not talking about objectified material sounds 'out there' in the world of perceivable acoustic events. To do so would be to reproduce the phonological equivalent of the nomenclaturist fallacy. Culler assumes that the signifier of 'dog' 'refers' in a direct or unmediated way to sequences of sounds in the real world. The real point is that the signifier is itself a layer or stratum of symbolic organization which symbolically construes the conceptual layer of the signified. Signifiers have their basis in the order of phonic differences and, hence, in the phonological system of a particular language, rather than in physical sounds *per se*. Signifiers are not comprised of sequences of sounds. The signifier, rather than a 'sequence of sounds' is a structured sequence of phonemes which constitutes a layer of symbolic organization which is internal to language form.

Saussure's own discussion, and the examples he provides, are concerned, above all, with lower-level grammatical units such as morphemes, simple words, compounds and simple phrases. If language form is inherently symbolic, then the relative size of the unit should not obscure this fact. Unfortunately, the kind of argument used by Culler renders this point less accessible than it really is. Culler treats both the signifier and the signified of his chosen example, *dog*, as if they were single unanalysable units. In so doing, he fails to reveal the symbolic work which is invested in the internal structure of this particular sign.

In order to illustrate this point in some detail, I shall refer once more to the word *boy*. If we simply claim that the sequence of phonemes /bɔɪ/ signifies the concept 'boy' then we are failing to capture the most important aspect of the two-way link between signifier and signified. The word *boy* is a single-morpheme instantiation of the grammatical class 'noun'. It is also a portmanteau, or one-to-many, realization of the conceptual terms [THING; ANIMATE; HUMAN; MALE; YOUNG]. This means that on the stratum of the signified the noun *boy* is internally complex, and in ways that are not made obvious by the one-to-many nature of the interstratal relationship. That is, the conceptual complexity of the noun *boy* is opaque with respect to the single morpheme which realizes this particular configuration of conceptual terms. The fact that this word is not further analysable into morphemic constituents tends to obscure the relative conceptual complexity of this grammatical form. As the analysis into its conceptual terms reveals, it is rather misleading to say that the morpheme in question simply signifies the unanalysable concept 'boy' (or 'dog', as in Culler's example).

Nor is it very revealing simply to say that the sequence of phonemes /bɔɪ/ signifies the concept 'boy'. This is merely tautologous and tells us nothing interesting about the principles of symbolic construal that Saussure discusses in the passage cited earlier. In order to understand this relationship it is necessary to prise apart the internal workings of even deceptively simple linguistic units such as *boy*. That is, it is necessary to show how both the

signified

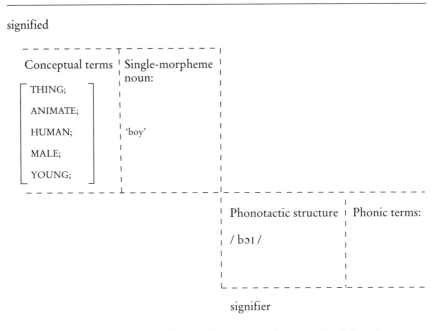

Figure 10.2 Stratification of single-morpheme noun *boy*, showing internal
stratification of signifier and signified

signifier and the signified are themselves internally stratified. Figure 10.2
illustrates the internal stratification of both signifier and signified in the case
of *boy*. It also shows how both layers of organization in the sign relation do
not derive from a pre-existing order of categories or material sounds in the
physical world. Instead, both signifier and signified are layers of symbolic
organization which are determined by systems of values deriving, respectively, from the phonic and conceptual orders of difference. Rather than raw
physical sounds, the signifier has a particular phonotactic structure, comprised of phonemes and possible combinations of these, in the English
language. The real point is this: particular combinations of phonemes that are
permitted by the system of English phonology symbolically construe the
conceptual structures in the grammar of the English language. There is, then,
no direct link between simple, unanalysable 'concepts' and 'sounds' in the
sign. Even a very simple example such as *boy* shows, on the other hand, that
this relationship is always mediated by a two-way relationship of symbolic
construal between a phonological or graphological structure and a lexicogrammatical structure, both of which are constitutive of, and internal to,
language form in Saussure's theory of the sign.

The preceding discussion shows how the units and structures on any given
stratum in the sign symbolically motivate the units and structures on the
strata which are 'above' and 'below' it. Compare this to Culler's analysis.

According to the logic of Culler's own analysis, it is simply a question of a non-natural or non-essential relationship between an unanalysable concept and an unanalysable sound. But neither signifier nor signified are unanalysable. As the example of *boy* shows, even a single-morpheme exponent of the grammatical class 'noun' is *internally* complex on the strata of both signifier and signified. Instead of talking in terms of 'sounds' and 'concepts', it is more revealing to talk in terms of the ways in which the phonological (or graphological) units and structures in the signifier symbolically construe grammatical and conceptual relationships in the signified, and vice versa. Put simply, the phonology and graphology of English function to symbolize the lexicogrammar and semantics of English, and vice versa. The two perspectives are analytically, but not constitutively, separable parts of a single, unified process of meaning-making. The fact that *boy* may be translated as *ragazzo, garçon* and *Knabe* in, respectively, Italian, French and German in no way alters this fundamental point. In each of these languages it is the tactic relations of the phonological or graphological structures of the words in question which symbolize the corresponding conceptual structures in their respective languages.

Now, the relations between the units and structures on any given stratum do not stand in a one-to-one relationship with those on any other stratum. If they did, then it would be harder to demonstrate the symbolically motivated nature of these interstratal relationships. As I have shown, both signifier and signified are internally structured. In the case of *boy*, for instance, a composite phonological structure, viz. /bɔɪ/ symbolically construes a composite conceptual structure: [THING; ANIMATE; HUMAN; MALE; YOUNG]. It is the symbolic integration of these two layers of structure through the interstratal relation of symbolic construal that gives rise to the sign *boy* (see also Langacker 1987: 58).

The integration of these two layers of structure is the 'two-way' link discussed in Chapter 9, section 1. It is in this sense that a given stratum 'calls up' or 'invokes' the other (*CLG*: 99). I shall now explore this in more detail. The basic point may be expressed as follows: (1) in English the signified [THING; ANIMATE; HUMAN; MALE; YOUNG] is signified by the signifier /bɔɪ/ at the same time that (2) the signifier /bɔɪ/ signifies the signified [THING; ANIMATE; HUMAN; MALE; YOUNG]. That is, each stratum in any given sign of a given language system predicts or redounds with the other. The two-way nature of this relationship means that the interstratal relationship of symbolic construal is a symmetrical one of 'metaredundancy', as already explained in Chapter 9, section 1.

There is no causality involved in this relationship. That is why it is misleading to suggest that a signifier 'stands for' a signified. This kind of formulation may too easily suggest that the relationship between the two strata is a one-to-one or causal one. A causal relationship of this kind is the very antithesis of the semiological character of the interstratal relation which links signifier and signified. Causality would imply the very kind of non-semiotic reflectionist view of language that Saussure refutes:

> If words were charged with representing concepts given in advance, each one would have, from one language system to the next, exact correspondences for their sense; yet this is not the case.
>
> (*CLG*: 161)

Such a view assumes that it is possible to postulate a univocal causal or 'standing for' relationship between the internal sense relations of language forms and the extralinguistic concepts which pre-exist these 'out there' in the world. The stratal theory of semiotic organization which Saussure's theory of the sign inaugurated has been re-theorized in the work of Jay Lemke (1984d) as a system of redundancies among the various levels in the given system of relations (see also Halliday 1992; Chapter 9, section 1). In the case of our earlier example, the redundancy relations between the two strata of the sign *boy* may be expressed as follows: the composite conceptual structure [THING; ANIMATE; HUMAN; MALE; YOUNG] redounds not with the single morpheme noun [BOY], but with the redundancy of this grammatical form with the composite phonological structure /bɔɪ/. Thus:

([THING; ANIMATE; HUMAN; MALE; YOUNG]) ⌄ ([BOY] ⌄ /bɔɪ/),

where the downwards arrow, '⌄', is simply a notational convention meaning 'redounds with'.

In this formulation, the perspective is that of the signified. However, this perspective is reversible, as implied by the symmetrical nature of meta-redundancy relations (Chapter 9, section 1). Therefore, from the perspective of the signifier, it is more appropriate to say that the signifier /bɔɪ/ signifies the symbolization of the conceptual structure [THING; ANIMATE; HUMAN; MALE; YOUNG] in the grammatical form BOY. Thus:

([THING; ANIMATE; HUMAN; MALE; YOUNG] ⌄ [BOY]) ⌄ /bɔɪ/

Whichever perspective is adopted, the relationship between strata is not one of causality or of equivalence (see also Hjelmslev 1981 [1948]). It is, as I have shown, a relationship of symbolic construal, or redundancy (Chapter 9, section 1). Rather than saying that a signified is signified by a signifier, or vice versa, which implies causality, it is more accurate to say that conceptual structures are symbolically construed by the symbolic construal of grammatical form in phonological structure. There is much more at stake here than a terminological distinction. A causal relation between signifier and signified would entail a closed and determinate relationship between language form and its outside. This is the problem Saussure addresses in the brief passage quoted above: viz. all languages would causally reflect the same non-linguistic concepts. But the whole point of Saussure's notion of value is to show that the language system does not stand in any such fixed or determinate relationship with its outside. Instead, the language system is a meaning-making potential – a system of contextualizing relations – which is interfaced on both sides of its stratal organization by the material–phenomenal domains that Saussure calls 'thought' and 'sound' (Chapter 7, section 4). 'Thought' and 'sound' are the two dimensions of the environment with which language engages in complex exchange transactions both systemically at the level of the entire speech community in historical time, and instantially, at the level of the single act of *parole*.

'Thought' and 'sound', considered separately, are simply two 'amorphous' and 'indistinct' masses (*CLG*: 155). The point is that in a given language system the phonological structure is symbolically motivated *in relation to* the conceptual structure, and vice versa. As Saussure's little 'thought-experiment' shows, if the symbolic relationship which motivates the relationship between the two strata is taken away, so to speak, then there is nothing but undifferentiated thought and sound (see also Hjelmslev 1969 [1943]: 50; Langacker 1987: 85).

The same is no less true of individual morphemes, taken on their own. In such cases, the criteria for establishing symbolic motivation may be seen to be maximally opaque. Consider, for example, the conceptual term [PLURAL] in English. It might be thought that this is a good example of a one-to-one relationship between signifier and signified, as in the plural morpheme in the noun *boys*. However, matters are more complex than this, and the same general principles outlined above still apply. The first complication arises because the conceptual term [PLURAL] in the English noun may be realized by four different possibilities of wording (morphemes), along with their corresponding phonemes. The following contrast sets illustrate the four possibilities: *sheep/sheep*; *child/children*; *man/men*; *boy/boys*. Thus, there are four main morphemes in the grammar of the English noun which may signify the conceptual term [PLURAL].

Yet it would be misleading to suggest that the conceptual term [PLURAL] only ever occurs on its own as a single isolable unit outside grammatical structure (Chapter 11, sections 2–3). This would only be true of the purely formal and systemic context that pertains to the order of conceptual differences in *langue*$_1$. In the plural noun *boys*, for example, it is, of course, possible to segment this word into its two morphemic constituents – the base noun and the plural suffix – and, on this basis, to argue that the essentially symbolic nature of the relationship between the signifier (the phoneme) /z/ and the signified (the conceptual term) [PLURAL] is reducible to a simple one-to-one relationship, as shown in Figure 10.3. This figure, in actual fact, presents a *reductio ad absurdum* or a caricature of the true nature of interstratal symbolic construal. In actual fact, no such sign relation exists, or could exist, in language. The reasons why will be further explored in the next paragraph.

It is misleading to assume that in the composite sign *cats*, for example, the

[PLURAL]
$-\ -\ -\ -\ -\ -$
/z/

Figure 10.3 Stratal relation between conceptual term [PLURAL] and phoneme /z/, as in the plural noun *boys*

concept [CAT] is signified by the phonological sequence /kæt/ and the concept [PLURAL] by the phoneme /s/. It is more accurate to say that the composite phonological structure /[kæt] + [s]/ signifies the composite grammatical form [[LEXICAL BASE NOUN: CAT] + [PLURAL SUFFIX]]. In turn, the symbolization of the plural noun by the phonological structure symbolizes the conceptual structure [[THING; ANIMATE; FELINE] + [PLURAL]]. The phonology or graphology does not directly construe the conceptual level. Instead, the stratified nature of the sign means that the units and structures on the phonological or graphological level are re-construed as units and structures on the lexicogrammatical level at the same time that the redundancy relationship between the phonology (or graphology) and the grammar is in turn redundant with the conceptual level.

Both the phonology or graphology and the lexicogrammar are levels of pure form which construe the two orders of difference in the making of signs. On the other hand, the phonic and conceptual orders of difference represent the two interfaces between the sign as a whole and (1) the processes of phonation or audition (sound) and (2) the phenomena of perceptual experience (thought). The sign is, necessarily, a form which is freed from direct, unmediated dependence on either of these interfaces (Halliday 1992: 23). With reference to the composite sign *cats*, the relationship between the internal organization of the sign and the two orders of difference may be modelled as in Figure 10.4.

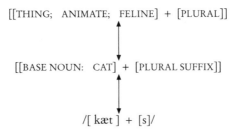

[[THING; ANIMATE; FELINE] + [PLURAL]]

[[BASE NOUN: CAT] + [PLURAL SUFFIX]]

/[kæt] + [s]/

Figure 10.4 Stratal organization of the sign *cats*

4 LINEARITY OF THE SIGNIFIER AND SYMBOLIC MOTIVATION

In his discussion of 'Absolute arbitrariness and relative arbitrariness' (*CLG*: 180–4) Saussure provides numerous examples of the ways in which the syntagmatic integration of lower-level units into larger, more complex units gives rise to motivated signs that are more complex than their constituent parts, considered separately. For example, he claims that the French *vingt* ('twenty'), which comprises a single morpheme, is unmotivated whereas *dix-neuf* ('nineteen') is relatively more motivated on account of the symbolic integration of the two morphemes which combine in this form (Chapter 12). Among the various examples which Saussure discusses, I shall select for more detailed commentary the observations he makes on the English plural noun *ships*:

> The English plural *ships* 'navires' evokes on account of its formation the entire series *flags*, *birds*, *books*, etc., whereas *men* 'hommes', *sheep* 'moutons' do not evoke anything.
>
> (*CLG*: 181)

In my view, Saussure's claim that the French *vingt* and the English plural nouns *sheep* and *men* are entirely unmotivated is not accurate. In the paragraph which follows the one I have just quoted Saussure offers the following qualifying remarks on his analyses: '[motivation] is always more complete when the syntagmatic analysis is easier and the sense [*le sens*] of the sub-units is more obvious' (*CLG*: 181). In other words, a distinction must be made between transparency of motivation, when the integrative function of the syntagm is most obvious, and motivation which is less evident, as in cases such as *vingt*. In the second case, the syntagmatic integration is less obvious. However, I would say that by Saussure's own criterion, as he shows in the above passage, even single-morpheme words such as *vingt* show some degree of syntagmatic integration and, therefore, of symbolic motivation. The arguments that I applied to *boy* in the previous section are no less valid here. That is, the syntagmatic integration of phonemes on the stratum of the signifier in single-morpheme words such as *vingt* symbolically construes the signified of the word in question. In such cases, a composite phonological structure symbolically construes a given signified.

Syntagms such as *vingt* require a minimal amount of what Langacker calls 'constructive effort' (1987: 157) in order to motivate the symbolic relationship between the two strata of the sign. That is, less syntagmatic integration means minimal constructive effort or less interpretative work in order to symbolically motivate the relationship between the two strata. In such cases, the symbolic relationship is standardized or conventionalized, to the extent that it has become a fully 'automatized' relationship, to use Prague School terminology.

No constructive effort would only apply to those signs where no syntagmatic integration occurred. Arguably, this would be the case when both signifier and signified are unanalysable wholes (Langacker 1987: 58). However, this is only ever the case from the point of the view of the systemic context of the system of pure values in *langue*$_1$. In *langue*$_1$ 'arbitrary' and 'differential' are the only criteria which operate. There are, then, no syntagmatic or associative solidarities among the terms that comprise the two orders of difference. Outside of this systemic context of pure values the conceptual term [PLURAL], for example, is always syntagmatically integrated into some larger whole, as in the case of nouns like *ships* and *men*.

Signifier and signified are unanalysable wholes only in cases such as that shown in Figure 10.3 above. However, the plural morpheme of nouns in English does not occur as a single isolated unit. It is *always* syntagmatically integrated with the base noun with which it combines. Take, for instance, the plural nouns *dogs* and *cats*. On the stratum of the signifier the first of these comprises the phonological structure /[d] + [ɒ] + [g] + [z]/ and the conceptual structure [[THING; ANIMATE; CANINE] + [PLURAL]] on the stratum of the signified. Likewise, *cats* comprises the phonological structure /[k] + [æ] + [t] + [s]/ and the conceptual structure [[THING; ANIMATE; FELINE] + [PLURAL]]. In both of these words, a phonological structure comprised of the syntagmatic integration of three phonemes symbolizes the base noun. In turn, this is integrated with the phonemes /s/ and /z/, which occur after voiceless consonants and voiced consonants, respectively, to signify the plural morpheme suffixes in the two nouns in question. In English, the plural morpheme of nouns has a number of allomorphs, with their various phonemic realizations: viz. /z/, /ɪz/, /s/, /n/, /ʊ → iː/, /æ → e/ and ∅, as in *dogs*, *horses*, *cats*, *children*, *feet*, *men* and *sheep*.

Thus, words like *men*, no less than *ships*, *flags* and so on, to go back to Saussure's own examples, may be seen to be motivated by processes of both syntagmatic integration and association on both strata of the sign relation. Take, for example, *men* in Figure 10.5. In this figure I wish to show that the seemingly opaque (unmotivated) plural noun *men* is symbolically motivated in Saussure's terms by both the syntagmatic integration and the associative 'evocation' of terms from the two orders of difference.

The processes of syntagmatic integration and symbolic construal mean that some linguistic work, however minimal, has been expended in order to assemble the unit in question. Further, the values which are so assembled in the making of the whole are never the same as the mere sum of the values of the constituent parts, taken separately (Chapter 11, section 2). The value of the whole, no matter how conventional, always embodies a residual trace of the social work which motivated its construction. This rests on the fact that the entire system of *langue* is a socio-historical product of the social work that agents have invested in the continual making and re-making of the whole system of values. This raises the question as to the links between this

Conceptual series

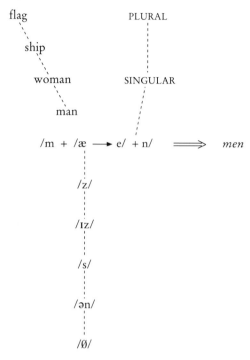

Phonic series (phonemic realizations of plural only)

Figure 10.5 Integration of syntagmatic and associative relations showing symbolic motivation in the plural noun *men*

product and the material practices of sign-making in social life. In the following section I shall refract Saussure's reflections on the sign through the Soviet semiotician, V. N. Vološinov's critique of Saussure with this in mind.

5 IS A SAUSSUREAN THEORY OF SIGNS IN SOCIAL LIFE POSSIBLE?: VOLOŠINOV'S CRITIQUE

Saussure, as we have seen, locates his conception of the sign in *langue* as a socially made system of signs. Ruqaiya Hasan (1987a) has discussed how this makes it difficult for Saussure to deal with indeterminacy, or variation, in the relations between signifier and signified. Consequently, it is often thought that Saussure's notion of *langue* cannot admit of variation in the relations between the two components of the sign. For example, Terence Hawkes (1977: 25) argues that the 'very arbitrariness of the linguistic sign protects it from change'. Saussure appears to see the matter differently:

> A language system [*une langue*] is radically powerless to defend itself against those factors which shift from one moment to the next the relationship between signified and signifier. It is one of the consequences of the arbitrariness of the sign.
>
> (*CLG*: 110)

An attentive reading of *CLG* will show that the source of the presumed homogeneity in *langue* is not, however, located in the link between signifier and signified, as Hawkes supposes. Instead, it is located in the typical systems of social practices that regulate the social making of meanings.

> Among all the individuals thus linked by language [*le langage*], a sort of mean will be established: all will reproduce – *doubtless not exactly, but approximately* – the same signs united to the same concepts.
>
> (*CLG*: 29; my emphasis)

The first point to make is that Saussure identifies the heterogeneity and variability of *langage*, rather than *langue*, as that which links individuals. *Langage*, as I pointed out in Chapter 5, section 3, is Saussure's term for the concrete reality of language as individuals encounter it in social life. This relation has its basis in what Saussure refers to in the following paragraph as 'this social crystallization' (*cette cristallisation sociale*, *CLG*: 29). It is this 'social crystallization' which Saussure takes to be the source of the typicality referred to above. But even here, as the above quotation shows, Saussure does not overlook the 'approximate' nature of this. Saussure is aware of the fact that it is the methodological requirements of his theory of *langue* which tend to play down variation and heterogeneity. The theoretical impetus for this may derive from Durkheim's notion of the 'crystallized' forms of 'well-defined' social organizations (Durkheim 1982 [1902]: 52). This does not mean, however, that variation and heterogeneity cannot be explained, as Saussure's own notion of idiosynchrony clearly demonstrates (Chapter 4, section 4).

Commentators such as Hawkes and Culler short-circuit the whole problem by continuing to talk as if language were simply comprised of a collection of words. The word, as an abstract type, isolated from the grammar, may be said to be maximally arbitrary. But this way of thinking perpetuates the dichotomous reading of *langue* and *parole*. The writings of the Soviet semiotician, V. N. Vološinov, in the 1920s and 1930s, provide an insightful and roughly contemporary critique of the problems which this thinking poses. Here is Vološinov's own formulation of the 'arbitrariness' of the word:

> The word is not only the purest, most indicatory sign but is, in addition, *a neutral sign*. Every other kind of semiotic material is specialized for some particular field of ideological creativity. Each field possesses its own ideological material and formulates signs and symbols specific to itself and

not applicable in other fields. In these instances, a sign is created by some specific ideological function and remains inseparable from it. A word, in contrast, is neutral with respect to any specific ideological function. It can carry out ideological functions of *any* kind – scientific, aesthetic, ethical, religious.

(Vološinov 1973 [1930]: 14; emphasis in original)

The word, as a 'pure' and 'neutral' sign, is not dissimilar to the arbitrariness principle. Vološinov argues that the 'pure' and 'neutral' sign is abstracted from any 'ideological function': that is, from social use. Vološinov locates meaning and variation in meaning in those ideological and social functions, without which the word is no more than an abstract potential for making meanings. On the other hand, Saussure is concerned to establish the theoretical and methodological premises necessary for the study of the internal design features of language as system, rather than *parole*, or language in use. Vološinov's account of the sign takes the 'utterance' (cf. *parole*) as its principal object of study.

By the same token, Vološinov does not reject the systemic basis of word meaning. However, his emphasis is quite different. He is concerned to relate what he called utterances (cf. texts) to their socially stratified conditions of production and reception. Vološinov's account does not include a theory of the lexicogrammatical resource systems (cf. *langue*) which makes this possible, although his theory does provide for the internal nature of the relationship between lexicogrammatical form and social context. Vološinov critiqued what he called the 'abstract objectivism' of Saussurean linguistics (1973 [1930]: 45–63). In my view, a theoretically adequate account must be able to relate the resource systems of the language to their social uses in a unified way.

Vološinov (1983: 115) has proposed an integrated schema for relating signs

Table 10.1 Some parallels between Vološinov's and Saussure's theories of social meaning-making

Vološinov	Saussure
1 The economic organization of society	*Langue* as system of values arising from the totality of social–linguistic work
2 Lexicogrammatical form; the neutral sign	Syntagmatic and associative solidarities in *langue*$_2$
3 Social communication; speech genres	Habits, rules, conventions; typical patterns of discourse
4 Utterance	*Parole*
Speech interaction	Discourse

to concrete social life. It may be surprising to some, but there are a number of interesting parallels between the proposals of Vološinov and Saussure, in spite of the substantial differences of emphasis between their respective theoretical projects. I have made some suggestions along these lines in Table 10.1. Paradoxically, it is the attempt to refute naturalistic criteria which hinders efforts to understand the inherently social-semiological, or symbolic, character of the relation between signifier and signified. The processes of both syntagmatic integration and interstratal symbolic construal show, as I pointed out in Chapter 9, that the sign is both the product and the process in and through which meanings are socially made. There is no fixed or pre-given relation between signifier and signified. The point is not so much that this has no necessary naturalistic basis, however correct this may be, but that these relations are themselves constantly made and re-made whenever signs are used in discourse. The sign implies a praxis in which means (the resources of *langue*) and ends (*parole*) are unified. Signs are not fixed and closed entities; they are open and dynamic processes. It is their adaptability to changing contextual factors which ensures the constant renewal of the relations between language users and system.

With these questions in mind, the three chapters in Part VI will explore how Saussure's social-semiological theory may be related to concrete acts of social meaning-making in social life.

Part VI

Sign, discourse and social meaning-making

Chapter 11

Dimensions of contextualization
The mechanism of *langue*

1 SYNTAGMATIC AND ASSOCIATIVE RELATIONS

This chapter will explore the relevance of Saussure's conception of *langue* for a theory of how meanings are made in particular instances of signs-in-use. In particular, I shall focus on Chapter 4 of *CLG*, which is entitled 'Mechanism of the language system'. It is important to point out from the outset that the perspective which Saussure adopts in this chapter, as its title suggests, is that of the system of *langue*, rather than specific instances of language use. Saussure begins this chapter by referring to the distinction he had made in the previous chapter between syntagmatic and associative relations. It is worth while quoting this passage in full:

> The ensemble of phonic and conceptual differences which constitute the language system [*la langue*] result then from two kinds of comparison: relations are both associative and syntagmatic; the groupings of one or the other order [of difference] are, in large measure, established by the language system; *it is this ensemble of usual relationships which constitutes and which presides over its functioning.*
>
> (*CLG*: 176; my emphasis)

There are two important points that I should like to emphasize here. First, both associative and syntagmatic relations are 'established by' the language system. This important point needs to be emphasized because there is a widespread tendency to misread Saussure's distinction between 'syntagmatic' and 'associative' as corresponding to that between the instance and the system perspectives, respectively. Both syntagmatic and associative relations are part of the essential workings of the language mechanism in *langue*. Saussure points out that it is only through the simultaneous operation of both syntagmatic and associative relations that the two orders of difference in *langue*$_1$ give rise to the signs of a language. That is, the two orders of difference are organized into regular syntagmatic and associative patterns, or 'groups', in the language system.

Second, Saussure also points out that *langue* is constituted by what he calls this 'ensemble of usual relationships'. The key word here is 'usual'. *Langue* is a systemic potential for making meanings. In the first instance, it is concerned with the 'ensemble of phonic and conceptual differences' in the two orders of difference. However, these are constituted as regular syntagmatic and associative relations. 'Usual' means typical or regular. The emphasis is on the typical, rather than specific, groupings or patternings of syntagmatic and associative relations. These belong to the order of the system, rather than to specific uses in *parole*.

Thus, both syntagmatic and associative relations are constitutive of *langue*. In one oversimplified reading of Saussure, language is a system of differences *per se*. In actual fact, Saussure emphasizes that *langue* is a system of both differences *and* groups. If *langue* were no more than a system of differences *per se*, then this would imply that the phonic and conceptual terms which belong to the two orders of difference would be distributed with equal probability across all of the typical syntagmatic and associative relations that can be modelled in the language system. Theoretically speaking, this could only be possible of the most schematic representation of *langue*$_1$, where the terms from the two orders are not combined with each other in any specific groupings. However, the typical patternings of syntagmatic and associative relations mean that not all combinations occur with equal probability. Some combinations rather than others typically occur in a given language system. In other words, the equilibrium values of the patterns of difference are not equiprobable: they are skewed or biased according to system-internal probabilities into some patterns and not others. There is not, then, an equal probability that any given difference will combine with all others in an equiprobable way.

Saussure points out that it is the 'usual' or typical syntagmatic and associative groups that constitute *langue* and which 'preside over its functioning'. What exactly does this mean? The language system is a resource which enables social agents to make meanings in determinate acts of *parole* (Chapter 3). Therefore, if all differences combined with all others with equal probability, then there would be no meaning-making, no social semiosis. This would be equivalent to a totally uniform patterning of differences in which no specific principles of order or construction could be discerned. In actual fact, the possible patterns of difference are constrained – 'presided over' – by the 'usual' or typical principles of both syntagmatic and associative organization. That is, the system of differences in *langue*$_1$ is distributed over the typical patterns of organization of a given language system. They are distributed over the typical groupings of syntagmatic and associative relations in that language system. There is not, then, a global system of differences *per se*.

2 SYNTAGMATIC SOLIDARITIES

Saussure next illustrates the distributed nature of the system of differences by means of a simple example. He shows how the French *désireux* ('desirous') is comprised of two subunits, viz. *désir* + *eux*, which combine to form a larger-scale *syntagmatic solidarity*. The notion of a syntagmatic solidarity is Saussure's term for explaining that a given combination of units to form some larger whole is not simply the sum of the individual parts which are so combined. Saussure's example shows how the smallest units of grammar combine to form larger-scale units. For example, the smallest-scale grammatical units, or morphemes, in languages such as French and English combine to form larger-scale units such as words at the next-higher level of grammatical organization. However, Saussure does not simply divide words into their constituent parts. In the case of *désireux* he comments:

> The suffix, taken in isolation, is non-existent; that which confers it its place in the language system is a series of usual terms such as *chaleur-eux* ['warm', 'fervent'], *chanc-eux* ['lucky', 'fortunate'], etc. In its turn, the root is not autonomous; it only exists in combination with a suffix; in *roul-is* ['roll(ing)'], the element *roul-* is nothing without the suffix which follows it.
>
> (*CLG*: 176–7)

In this passage, Saussure emphasizes the functional value which the parts have in relation both to each other and to the whole to which they belong. This value is not intrinsic to the part, seen in isolation from the whole. It arises only as a result of the particular function the part plays in the overall structure to which it belongs. According to Saussure's analysis, each of the parts into which he segments the syntagm is identified on the basis of two criteria. These are: (1) the given subunit may be replaced by others of the same general type which are co-classified as belonging to the same associative series; and (2) each subunit has a functional value in relation to the whole to which it belongs. These two criteria are closely related to each other. They indicate that the syntagm is not mechanically segmented on the basis of purely formal criteria. That is, what counts as a particular subunit in relation to the whole is in some way *motivated* by the functional value which the given part has in relation to the whole. A given grammatical unit is subdivided into its parts on the basis of the functional value which each of the parts has in relation to the higher-order unit in question. Saussure does not, in my view, advocate an unmotivated segmentation of a given unit into as many subunits as possible. Instead, he advocates fairly parsimonious criteria of segmentation. According to Saussure, the segmentation of linguistic units should only take place on the basis of *functionally motivated* criteria. Saussure does not advocate purely formal criteria *per se* for the segmentation of linguistic structures into their constituent units (Chapter 3, section 2).

The same basic principle applies to units at all levels in the grammar. Take the following examples of the nominal group (noun phrase) in English and Italian: *a backward step, a notable difference, un esempio valido* ('a valid example'), *una descrizione esauriente* ('an exhaustive description'). Each of these examples may be segmented into three parts on the basis of the criteria specified above. That is, each of the three parts in these nominal groups has a functional value in relation to the larger whole to which it belongs. This is another way of saying that the nominal group has its own internal grammatical structure and that the parts which comprise the whole are defined in relation to the whole. This principle is illustrated in Figure 11.1. In each of these examples, Saussure's criteria, as discussed above, may be applied. Each of the three subunits may be replaced by others of the same general type in a given associative series. For example, words such as *step, difference, solution, reader* and so on are all of the same general type; they are all instances of the grammatical class of common noun. On the basis of this shared feature, they are all potentially assignable to the same associative series. The nominal groups under discussion here are constituted by a particular configuration of functional values on the syntagmatic axis. This is exemplified by the structural–functional configuration Deictic^Epithet^ Thing. The labels Deictic, Epithet and Thing refer to the functional values the

a	backward	step
a	notable	difference
Deictic	Epithet	Thing

un	esempio	valido
una	descrizione	esauriente
Deictic	Thing	Epithet

Figure 11.1 Functional values in the nominal group in English and Italian

three constituents have in this particular syntagmatic solidarity. Note that this is at least partially independent of the sequential ordering of the grammatical items which realize these values. In English, the structural–functional configuration [Deictic; Epithet; Thing] is realized by the following sequence of formal items: determiner^adjective^noun. In Italian the sequence is determiner^noun^adjective.

In the above examples, I have applied precisely the same principles of analysis which Saussure demonstrated in his analysis of the French word *désireux* into its two constituent morphemes. Saussure sums up the basic principles at the conclusion of his analysis as follows:

> The whole has value through its parts, the parts also have value in virtue of their place in the whole, and here is why the syntagmatic relation of the part to the whole is just as important as the relation among the parts.
>
> (*CLG*: 177)

In this passage, Saussure lays down what he calls 'a general principle' (*CLG*: 177) which can be seen to govern all kinds of syntagms. The basis of the general principle is *functional*, rather than formal. In other words, he is establishing the fundamental principles of the structural–functional analysis of language form. His notion of *syntagmatic solidarities* may, therefore, be taken to refer to some configuration of functionally related items in some structure. The nominal group constitutes a syntagmatic solidarity in this sense. The syntagm provides the means whereby a linear sequence of grammatical forms, viz. determiner^adjective^noun in the English nominal group, may be re-construed as a configuration of functional values. The above examples illustrate this general principle: the whole (the nominal group) is defined, or has its value, only by virtue of the relations among the parts which comprise the whole. Further, the assignment of functional values to each of the parts in the whole also means that the assignment of values to the respective parts occurs because they are related to a whole of a certain type. For example, *a backward step* and *a notable difference* both constitute syntagmatic solidarities of a certain general type, or grammatical class, in languages such as English and Italian, viz. the nominal group.

Saussure's point is that the spatio-temporal extension of the syntagm provides the material means whereby language units are put into particular value-producing relationships or syntagmatic solidarities with each other. However, these relationships are not reducible to the spatio-temporality of the syntagmatic sequence *per se*. Of syntagmatic solidarities, Saussure observes:

> almost all of the units of the language system depend on either what surrounds them in the spoken chain, or on the successive parts of which they themselves are composed.
>
> (*CLG*: 176)

The syntagm is, then, the spatio-temporal means of bringing linguistic units into a specific value-producing relationship. It does so by arranging the units in a determinate sequence. However, the values which are assignable to the units in the sequence are not reducible to the linear sequence of formal items *per se*. I shall illustrate this point through the example of *a backward step*. This nominal group is a linear sequence of three distinct classes of grammatical item, which I earlier identified as determiner, adjective and noun. These labels are said to be formal class items because they refer to the general class of grammatical item, independently of any specific structure and, hence, of the functional values that are assignable to the items in some syntagmatic solidarity. That is, formal class labels refer to the structure-forming potential that particular instances of these grammatical classes have in the grammar of English. On the other hand, the functional values of which Saussure speaks are only assignable to formal items by virtue of some larger syntagmatic context in which these grammatical units function. In order to describe the functional values these items have in particular syntagmatic contexts, it is necessary to specify a higher level of analysis, one which construes the sequence as a particular configuration of functional values, rather than as a sequence of formal items *per se* (Chapter 3, section 2). In the examples considered above, the nominal group is the higher-order context in which the functional values [Deictic; Epithet; Thing] are distributed across the units in the structure of these nominal groups, as shown in Figure 11.2. Saussure goes on to point out that this general principle of syntagmatic solidarity applies to 'larger units, themselves composed of smaller units, the one and the other being in a relationship of syntagmatic solidarity' (*CLG*: 177). A given unit, such as the nominal group, may in turn have a functional value in some still larger-scale structure. Typically, nominal groups form part of the structure of clauses in precisely this sense. I shall now consider this

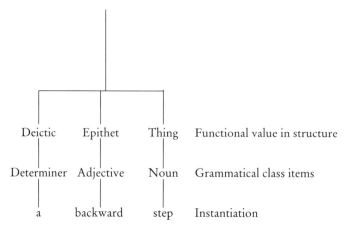

Figure 11.2 Functional values in the nominal group

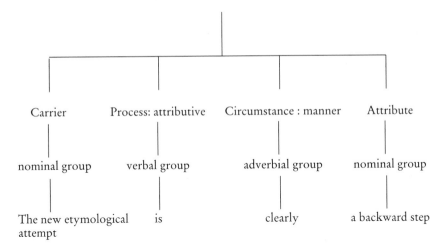

Figure 11.3 Functional values in attributive *be*-clause

question in relation to the clause from which the nominal group *a backward step* is taken. This clause is as follows: *The new etymological attempt is clearly a backward step*. The nominal group *a backward step* is, accordingly, assigned a functional value in the higher-order structure of the clause in which it occurs. The clause as a whole may be analysed as in Figure 11.3 which shows that it comprises four grammatical class items, viz. the sequence nominal group^verbal group^adverbial group^nominal group. The clause as a whole is an attributive *be*-clause. Consequently, the four formal items that enter into the structure of this clause are assigned their respective functional values on the basis of their participation in a clause of this type, rather than some other, in the grammar of English. Consider, for example, the clause *John took a backward step*. In this clause, the nominal group *a backward step* may be assigned a different functional value on account of the quite different syntagmatic solidarity which is constituted by the relations among the three formal items (the grammatical constituents) that form the structure of this clause. In this case, the sequence of formal items proper noun^verb^nominal group signifies the following configuration of functional values: [Actor; Process: Material; Range]. In this clause, the nominal group *a backward step* is construed as having the functional value Range (Halliday 1994: 146–9).

The specific clauses I have discussed here are, of course, particular instances of language-in-use. As such, they belong to *parole*. Yet, we have seen how Saussure opens his discussion of 'the mechanism of the language system' by referring, not to specific instances, but to the 'usual', or typical, syntagmatic and associative relationships which constitute a given language system and its overall functioning. What, then, is the connection between the language system and specific instances of language-in-use? The functional values which are assignable to the various units-in-structure in the above examples are the result of two kinds of contextualizing relations, which Saussure refers to as syntagmatic and associative relations. It must also be borne in mind, when referring to the notion of contextualizing relations in this sense, that Saussure's theoretical perspective is that of *langue*, rather than *parole*. Specifically, the level of abstraction corresponds to that of *langue*$_2$ (Chapter 3, section 5).

The notion of a syntagmatic solidarity refers to the way in which the parts which comprise some larger whole have functionally differentiated values in relation to the whole. Take the sequence of phonemes /k/, /æ/, /t/ and /s/ in the phonological structure /kæts/. Each of these phonemes has a functionally differentiated phonological value in the overall structure to which they belong. The four phonemes in /kæts/ form a syntagmatic solidarity of the part–whole kind. According to Saussure, these tend to satisfy two criteria. First, they are locally compact (Lemke 1985: 287). That is, the units which constitute the structure are syntagmatically integrated into some specifiable whole. Second, structures of this kind have a definite beginning, middle and end. Thus, the integration of /k/, /æ/, /t/ and /s/ in the phonological structure /kæts/ takes place on the basis of the fact that the four phonemes follow each other in a determinate sequence (Langacker 1987: 83). In other words, the four phonemes do not occur randomly in separate words. Saussure's principle of the linearity of the signifier expresses this fact. Consider, in this regard, the following sentence: 'The next day she *c*arried her secret we*a*pon *t*o school in her satchel' (Roald Dahl, *Matilda*, p. 139). The three graphemes, *c*, *a* and *t* which I have italicized in this sentence do not enter into a locally compact structure in this sense. They do not form the word *cat*, for instance. Each of the three graphemes in italics is syntagmatically integrated into the words *carried*, *weapon* and *to*, respectively. In the example, the three graphemes I have focused on are not locally compact in the sense defined above. They do not, therefore, constitute a structural unit in the graphology of the sentence in question.

From this point of view, a given unit of lexicogrammatical form, such as the nominal group or the clause, is a group or a clause of a given type. In order to be recognizable as a given type of grammatical structure, it must be able to be contextualized along two specific dimensions. That is, it may be contextualized as being a syntagmatic solidarity of functional values which correspond to some 'usual' or regular pattern in the language system. It may also be contextualized as being a member of some more general class. These are the two dimensions that Saussure calls syntagmatic and associative relations, respectively.

In this way, it is possible to say that the following three clauses are all tokens of the more general class of attributive *be*-clauses:

Carrier	Process: attributive	Attribute
1 The sense of self	is	an experience
2 The ability to use your eyes	is	a bit like the ability to use your hands.
3 Lyn Young	is	a teacher who has worked for many years with older inexperienced readers in outer-western Sydney.

In spite of individual differences in wording, these three clauses are all assignable to the same general type, viz. the attributive *be*-clause. This fact reflects the two dimensions of contextualization – the syntagmatic and the associative – that come into operation whenever we assign meaning to a given act of *parole*. Along the syntagmatic dimension, the functional values [Carrier; Process: attributive; Attribute] are assignable to the three formal items that I have identified in these syntagmatic sequences.

3 ASSOCIATIVE SOLIDARITIES

The construal of this particular pattern also occurs in relation to a system of possible alternative selections. The meaning of the three clauses is defined, in part, in relation to a system of contrasting alternative selections. However, Saussure's notion of associative solidarities is more than just a system of contrasting alternative selections. In this connection, Saussure adds the following observation to his prior discussion of the principles concerning the formation of syntagmatic groups:

> Among syntagmatic groups, so constituted, there is a tie of interdependence; they condition each other reciprocally. In effect, the coordination in space contributes to the creating of associative coordinations, and these in their turn are necessary for the analysis of the parts of the syntagm.
>
> (*CLG*: 177)

The various analyses proposed above illustrate, above all, how it is that the spatio-temporal co-ordination of units in the syntagm contributes to the formation of some larger structural whole. How, then, does this syntagmatic co-ordination lead, in turn, to what Saussure calls 'associative coordinations'? In other words, what does it mean to say that syntagmatic contextualization necessarily and reciprocally also entails associative contextualization? Saussure illustrates this second dimension of contextualization with a first example, as follows:

> Take the compound *dé-faire* ['to undo']. We can represent it on a horizontal ribbon corresponding to the spoken chain:

dé-faire →

But simultaneously and on another axis, there exist subconsciously one or more associative series comprising units which have an element in common with the syntagm, for example:

dé-faire →

décoller	faire
déplacer	refaire
découdre	contrefaire
etc.	etc.

(*CLG*: 177–8)

Saussure notes that associative relations enable connections to be made between two or more units on the basis of associative series which have something in common with the particular unit which actually occurs in the syntagm. His example of *défaire* shows how two such associative series may be established in relation to the two morphemic units which combine to form the compound word in this syntagm. However, it would be a mistake to think that the associative series comprising, for instance, *décoller, déplacer, découdre* and so on only refers to the morphemic prefix *dé-*. Similarly, it would be wrong to think that the series *faire, refaire, contrefaire* and so on only refers to -*faire* in Saussure's example.

Importantly, Saussure does not claim that the common element in any given associative series is uniquely linked to just one component of the overall syntagm. For example, the common element, which is shared by all members of the postulated series, is the prefix *dé-*. His point is that the various associative series which are relevant to the contextualization of any given syntagm construe a tie among the various units in the syntagm as a whole. This happens in the following way. It is the syntagmatic combination of units which itself, in part, establishes the wider associative context at the same time that the associative context classifies and constrains the relations among the individual components of the syntagm. The syntagm 'indexes' or 'evokes' the wider associative contexts which are relevant to its interpretation. It is not the case that a given associative series contextualizes just one part of the overall syntagm, and another series some other part. Instead, the combination of units into some larger syntagmatic whole is globally contextualized in relation to all of the potentially relevant series. In other words, both series in Saussure's example become relevant to the contextualization of the whole. They enable criteria of relevance or salience to be assigned to it. At some level of abstraction, *dé-* and *faire* in this syntagm are members of both series. That is why, as Saussure says, they share 'common syntagmatic elements'.

Saussure's own analytical practice slightly simplifies this last point. In establishing the iterative nature of the various associative series, he does not show clearly enough how these, in so far as they are established on the basis of some 'common element', are abstractions from actual syntagmatic combinations. My point is that a given syntagmatic combination *enacts* the relevant system of associative relations, rather than vice versa. For example, Saussure shows that when *dé-* occurs, then one or more associative series are potentially relevant to its interpretation. Of course, *dé-*, as a morphemic prefix, does not occur on its own. It only ever occurs in syntagmatic contexts of a given type, as exemplified in Saussure's analysis. It follows that the combination of *dé-* and *faire* in this syntagm implicates that all of the associative series relevant to *dé-* and to *faire* are potentially relevant to the meaning of the whole syntagm, rather than to each of its constituent parts taken separately.

Saussure's own analysis of *défaire* also demonstrates the dialectical duality of the system and instance perspectives in the making of meanings in discourse. The starting point for his analysis is the temporal unfolding of the spoken chain in *parole*. This is also indicated by the graphic convention of the rightward-pointing arrow, which is iconic to the temporal flow of the spoken chain, in his diagram. On this basis, Saussure then proceeds to re-constitute, analytically speaking, the two dimensions of contextualization from the perspective of the language system, or *langue*. This shows his awareness of the fact that it is only in and through the real-time enactment of semiosis in acts of *parole* that (1) the *langue*-based system of syntagmatic and associative relations is maintained and renewed; and (2) this same system may be analytically re-constructed by the linguist.

4 EFFECTIVE AND VIRTUAL DIMENSIONS OF CONTEXTUALIZATION

Langue designates a systemic order of linguistic facts which exist outside space and time. That is why *langue* is said to be 'virtual'. For this reason, this order of facts is not reducible to statements about concrete instances of language use; rather, *langue* comprises 'two forms of our mental activity'. Saussure refers to these with the terms 'syntagmatic' and 'associative' relations, respectively (*CLG*: 170). They are the two dimensions of con-textualizing relations which characterize the operations of *langue* in relation to *parole*. This important point needs to be clarified from the outset in order that the theoretical nature of the relation between *langue* and *parole* may be understood.

Saussure (*CLG*: 171) argues that syntagmatic relations are '*in praesentia*; [they] rest on two or more terms equally present in an effective series'. By contrast, associative relations 'unite terms *in absentia* in a virtual mnemonic series' (*CLG*: 171). I shall now focus on the distinction which Saussure makes here between 'effective' and 'virtual'. 'Effective' does not, in my view, equate with 'actual'; rather, the *langue*-based principle of linearity in syntagmatic relations is not the same as the real-time enchaining of concrete elements in discourse (Chapter 5, section 4). Instead, the former is able to be projected onto the latter. It is in this sense that it is 'effective'. An 'effective series' is one which is able to be activated in discourse. As such, it is 'effective' in the assignment of values to the concrete sequence of elements which are enchained in actual discourse. The 'effectiveness' of the syntagm as a recognizable contextualizing relation in the language system is necessarily independent of the concrete elements which happen to enact it on a given occasion.

Associative relations, on the other hand, are 'virtual' in the sense that they do not operate in the spatio-temporal dimension of the syntagm. Associative relations intersect with syntagmatic ones according to the ways in which the terms in a given associative series may substitute for the terms in a particular syntagmatic series. Saussure gives the following example:

> Whereas a syntagm immediately calls up the idea of a sequential order and a determinate number of elements, the terms of an associative family show neither a definite number nor a determinate order. If *désir-eux* ('desirous'), *chaleur-eux* ('hearty', 'warm'), *peur-eux* ('fearful', 'timorous'), etc., are associated, one will not be able to say in advance what the number of words suggested by memory will be, nor in what order they will appear. A given term is like the centre of a constellation, the point where other coordinated terms converge, the sum of which is indefinite.
>
> (*CLG*: 174)

In this passage, Saussure illustrates the basic principles of constituent (part–whole) analysis of some types of linguistic syntagms. Each of the words analysed here is segmented into two constituents. This analysis reveals the principle of substitution: in each case both the adjectival stem (*désir-*, etc.) and the suffix (*-eux*) may, potentially, be replaced by other items in the associative series to which they belong. A word such as *désir + eux* is an *effective* syntagmatic series. It has a definite number of elements (two morphemes) and a determinate sequential order. It is effective because it fulfils determinate criteria which are required by syntagms of this type.

By the same token, the associative series which intersect in this syntagm constitute a further order of relations which define the syntagm itself. The 'indefinite' and 'indeterminate' nature of these associative relations means that the syntagm stands in a virtual relationship with a far richer set of relations than those which actually occur in the particular syntagm. Any given word such as *désir* + *eux* stands in a virtual relationship with all of the other words with which it can be associated.

5 SYNTAGMATIC AND ASSOCIATIVE RELATIONS: A TEXT ANALYSIS

I shall now illustrate the principles which I have discussed so far through the analysis of a short piece of text from an American introductory textbook for undergraduate students of psychology:

Aggression
(1) Helping others is a prosocial act of conformity that has clear social benefits. (2) Its opposite, hurting others, has clear social costs. (3) An act that is intended to cause pain is an act of interpersonal **aggression**. (4) The key attribute of an aggressive act is intent: (5) to be considered aggressive, an act must be deliberate – (6) a definition that encompasses verbal attacks, such as insults and slander, as well as physical or material injuries. (7) Unintended injuries are not considered aggressive.

(Richard R. Bootzin *et al.*, *Psychology Today: an Introduction*, p. 674)

Psychology, according to the traditional definition, is the science of human behaviour. Psychologists use a specialized technical language in order to define and describe and, hence, to give structure to and interpret human behaviour according to the requirements of their discipline. The above text makes extensive use of both identifying and attributive *be*-clauses in order to do this.

The technical language used by psychologists often serves to 'translate' the language of everyday experience into the language of scientific discourse. This is especially evident in textbooks, whose function it is to train students of psychology in the technical language of the discipline and its appropriate uses. With these considerations in mind, I shall now turn to the text.

The preliminary analysis of the transitivity structure of the seven clauses in the text is set out in Table 11.1. The analysis will be concerned, above all, with the particular categories of process–participant configurations that are selected by the seven clauses in the text. All seven clauses belong to the categories of either identifying or attributive *be*-clauses.

The text is an instance of the genre of introductory scientific textbook. Some of the lexicogrammatical features which are typical of scientific and technical registers include (1) extensive use of *be*-clauses to define and specify phenomena and (2) nominalization and the use of specialized technical lexis in the organization and classification of the given domain of the technical field. I shall now turn to the text analysis proper.

Clause 1 is an identifying process which works to 'translate' between the everyday and technical ways of talking about the same social domain. Thus, the non-technical term *Helping others* is semantically re-construed in terms of the technical term *a prosocial act of conformity.* The identifying process, *is,* is the means whereby this re-contextualization across domains takes place.

Each of the two semantic participants in this clause also potentially evokes an entire set of latent associations. The syntagmatic structure of clause 1 does not simply 'translate' from one nominal group to the other. More precisely, it creates a new joint context in which the values that are specific to the two associative series, taken separately, are re-combined and consequently re-evaluated. As Saussure points out, the values which result from the combining of parts into more complex syntagmatic wholes 'is never equal to the sum of the values of the parts' (*CLG*: 182). This is true of syntagms of all types – from single words to whole texts. The basic principle is still the same.

Clause 1 begins a process of constructing a *joint* thematic system which attempts to negotiate the differences between the technical and the non-technical ways of talking and their associated values.

Table 11.1 Transitivity structure of clauses in 'Aggression' text

1	Helping others	is	a prosocial act of conformity that has clear social benefits
	Token	Process: identification	Value
2	Its opposite, hurting others,	has	clear social costs.
	Carrier	Process: attribution	Attribute
3	An act that is intended to cause pain	is	an act of interpersonal **aggression**.
	Token	Process: identification	Value
4	The key attribute of an aggressive act	is	intent:
	Token	Process: identification	Value
5	an act	(must) be	deliberate
	Carrier	Process: attribution	Attribute
6	a definition	(that) encompasses	verbal attacks.
	Token	Process: identification	Value
7	Unintended injuries	are not considered	aggressive.
	Carrier	Process: attribution	Attribute

If clause 1 functions to re-define one set of terms in relation to another, clause 2 uses the semantics of attribution for a different purpose. Here, what is at issue is some quality or attribute of the semantic Carrier. Clause 2 specifies an instantial quality of the type category *hurting others*. In so doing, clause 2 introduces a contrasting or opposing set of associative values with respect to those introduced in clause 1. This is explicitly foregrounded by the nominal group *Its opposite*. Clause 2, like its predecessor, also construes a relationship of contrast between the non-technical *hurting others* and the technical *social costs*.

To sum up the situation so far: these first two clauses construe two sets of contrasting values. The first is the contrast between the technical and non-technical registers; the second is the contrast between 'non-aggressive' and 'aggressive' acts. The remainder of the text is a further development and working through of the relations among these contrasting values and the associative series that they implicitly relate to. The overall result is a new, contextually contingent value system which is not the sum of these various associative series taken separately. I shall now return to the text.

Clause 3 is another identifying process. Again, it functions to 'translate' between the non-technical *Any act that is intended to cause pain, damage, or suffering to another person* and the more technical *an act of interpersonal aggression*. Clause 3 is also a further development of the two sets of contrasting associative series that are evoked in clauses 1 and 2. It does so through the introduction of another potentially important thematic element in the lexical verb *intended*. In clause 3, the relevance of the associative series evoked by this verb is less prominent on account of its realization as the Qualifier in the nominal group in which it occurs.

In clause 4, on the other hand, the thematics evoked by *intended* take on a more central role in the text. Clause 4 is a further identifying process in which the noun *intent* is construed as the defining characteristic of both the nominal groups *helping* and *the key attribute of an aggressive act*. That is, *intent* is construed as a defining characteristic of both of the opposed thematic systems which I previously glossed as 'aggressive' and 'non-aggressive' behaviour. In this way, the associative series invoked by *intended* and *intent* in clauses 3 and 4 serves to unify the previously contrasted values of 'helping' and 'hurting' by means of a contingently new value system that is shared by both.

Clause 5 is another attributive process. It further develops the new joint value system that was introduced in clause 4 by specifying what an 'aggressive act' is. It does so by instantiating a specific quality, viz. *deliberate*, of the type category 'aggressive act'. The Attribute *deliberate* may thus be seen as contributing to the further thematic development of *intended* and *intent*, all of which are assignable to the same associative series.

What we see here is the way in which specific *syntagmatic* combinations in texts enact newly relevant systems of values, by construing joint relationships among associative series that were either not previously combined, or not combined in this particular way. That is, the process of syntagmatic combination and re-combination in texts is the means whereby associative series and the values these entail are further developed and renewed.

In the text in question, clause 1 begins by combining in the same syntagm two sets of contrasting values, which I shall gloss, respectively, as [TECHNICAL] and [NON-TECHNICAL]. Clause 2 represents both a further development of this contrast at the same time as it introduces a further contrast. I shall gloss this second contrast as that between [PROSOCIAL] and [ANTISOCIAL]. In the text, this second opposition is articulated on the basis of, respectively, the social 'benefits' and 'costs' of the two thematic systems to which these two words are assigned in the text. Clause 4, in turn, brings in yet another thematic system. It functions to construe a new re-alignment of the previously contrasted series that I glossed as [PROSOCIAL] and [ANTISOCIAL]. These are now more explicitly defined in terms of the contrast between [AGGRESSIVE] and [NON-AGGRESSIVE]. The new alignment which takes place in this clause hinges on the verb *intended* and the associative series it implicity evokes. I shall designate this series with the superordinate gloss [PERSONHOOD].

Both 'helping' and 'hurting' others *qua* intended or deliberate acts are now located in a textual value system which is concerned not so much with social 'benefits' and 'costs' as with issues of personal agency and responsibility. This becomes clearer when an explicit contrast between 'intended' and 'unintended' acts is made in clause 5. Unintended acts such as those mentioned in clause 5 do not entail criteria of personal responsibility in the way that intended ones do.

At the same time as clause 4 initiates this textual re-alignment of associative series and their values, it also functions to weaken the earlier semantic contrast between [TECHNICAL] and [NON-TECHNICAL]. This is evidenced by the 'translation' of the more technical *intent* in this text back into the less technical *deliberate*.

As an introductory psychology textbook, the text does a lot of work negotiating among potentially conflicting social domains and the semantic–thematic resources that are typically associated with these. In this text, the associative series that I glossed as [PERSONHOOD] is critical to this overall process. Items in this series serve, in the text, to mediate between the technical and the non-technical discourses in the process of unifying these in a new jointly shared value system. In so doing, a kind of semantic bridge is constructed between the familiar, everyday ways of talking of the student reader and the less familiar ways of talking of the specialist scientific discourse of psychology.

6 THE DIALECTICALLY DUAL CHARACTER OF SYNTAGMATIC AND ASSOCIATIVE RELATIONS IN DISCOURSE

I have thus far emphasized that the two dimensions of contextualization which Saussure postulates are theorized on the basis of their constitutive role in the functioning of the language system. Saussure also speaks of 'the play of this double system in discourse' (*CLG*: 179). The crucial question here concerns the ways in which this 'double system' is immanent in concrete acts of *parole*. I have already discussed the nature of this double system from the point of view of *langue*. From the point of view of discourse, on the other hand, specific, concrete acts of *parole* are contextualized in and through this 'double system', as I showed in the text analysis in section 5. I shall now consider what this means.

A given act of *parole* does not have meaning in itself; rather, it is always situated at the intersection of these two dimensions of contextualization. These are put into operation whenever a given act of *parole* is performed. In other words, it is this 'double system' of contextualizing relations in *langue* which denotes an act as being of a certain type, rather than some other. This does not mean, however, that acts of *parole* are contextualized in a single or determinate way by a closed system of relations in *langue*. A given act of *parole* may be contextualized by a range of potential, alternative relations in *langue*. Syntagmatic relations tend, as Saussure points out, to present 'an ordered succession of a determinate number of elements' (*CLG*: 174). That is, syntagmatic relations tend to be complete, or completable, structural wholes.

As for associative relations, on the other hand, 'the terms of an associative family present neither a definite number nor a determinate order' (*CLG*: 174). In ways strikingly reminiscent of Wittgenstein's (1989 [1953]) notion of 'family resemblances', an 'associative family' is an open-ended set of possibilities. The indeterminate character of associative relations also reveals the flexible and gradable nature of syntagmatic relations. Rather than conforming to rigidly defined type categories, linguistic syntagms are very often contextualized by a plurality of associative series which contribute to the many dimensions of meaning which interact in discourse. Signs are plurifunctional, rather than monofunctional. This shows the revealing character of Saussure's term 'associative'. That is, the indeterminate and open-ended character of associative relations implicates an entire system of latent associations in the contextualization of any given act of *parole*.

The 'double system' of contextualizing relations proposed by Saussure is relational in character. It is not based on the positive choice of a term in which meaning inheres, but on a whole network of contextualizing relations along the two dimensions under discussion here. That is, *langue* provides the semiotic resources in and through which acts of *parole* are both constituted in discursive activity, as well as recognized and interpreted in relation to a *langue*-based system of types. Saussure makes the following pertinent observations in connection with the French first person plural imperative form *marchons!* ('let's walk!'):

> Our memory holds in reserve all types of more or less complex syntagms, no matter of what kind or duration, and at the moment of using them, we bring in associative groups in order to fix our choice. When someone says *marchons!* ('let's walk!'), he unconsciously thinks of diverse associative groups at the intersection of which may be found the syntagm *marchons!* This figures as a part in the series *marche!* ('walk!' – 2nd Person Singular), *marchez!* ('walk!' – 2nd Person Plural), and it is the opposition of *marchons!* to these forms which determines the choice; on the other hand, *marchons!* evokes the series *montons!* ('let's go up!'), *mangeons!* ('let's eat!'), etc., within which it is chosen by the same procedure; in each series one knows what has to be varied in order to obtain the differentiation which is appropriate to the unit required. If the idea to be expressed is changed, other oppositions will be necessary in order to bring about another value; one will say, for example, *marchez!*, or else *montons!*
>
> (*CLG*: 179)

Saussure makes an important distinction in this passage between the 'types of syntagms' that are held in memory and 'the moment of using them'. Syntagms *qua* types are purely schematic categories. They do not correspond to actual contextual uses of syntagms in discourse. Saussure points out that when a given syntagm is actually used it is contextualized by its connections with a number of associative groups. This means that specific associative patterns are evoked from the virtual associative series that constitute 'an entire latent system' in response to specific contextual contingencies. That is, the justification for a given choice is not made on the basis of ready-made and consciously retrievable plans, intentions, etc., but on the basis of the operations performed on a whole 'latent' system of terms in order to constitute a particular syntagm. Thus, the 'fixing' of a given choice is really a question of how the patterns of interconnections among the terms in the various associative series are stabilized and 'weighted' according to specific contextual factors in a given act of *parole*.

Saussure's analysis of the French first person plural imperative form *marchons!* shows that this form is related to and belongs to a number of associative groups. It does not, therefore, have a ready-made meaning; rather, it is assignable to a number of associative series on the basis of the relations of similarity and difference among the terms in these series. Saussure suggests two such series in the case of *marchons!* The first includes *marchons!*, *marche!*, *marchez!* and so on. In this case, the common factor which relates each term is the base morpheme *march-* of the lexical verb, and the distinguishing factor is the morphemic suffix *-ons*, *-e*, *-ez*, etc., which realizes the categories (the terms) of both [PERSON] and [NUMBER]. Another possible

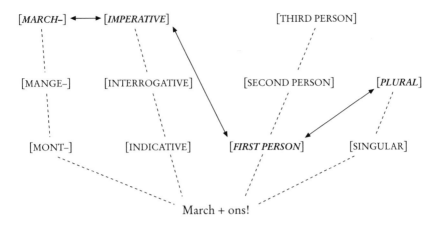

Figure 11.4 Intersection of associative groups to produce the syntagm *marchons*, showing weighted connections among terms

series is *marchons!*, *montons!*, *mangeons!* and so on. In this second case, the common factor is the morphemic suffix *-ons*, which realizes the categories [FIRST PERSON], [PLURAL] and [IMPERATIVE], all of which derive from specific associative groups in the grammar of French. The differentiating factor in each case is the base morpheme which distinguishes the lexical meaning of each of the verbs in question. The associative series which intersect to produce the syntagm *marchons!* are presented in Figure 11.4. This figure shows the intersection of four associative groups to produce the syntagm *marchons!* The use of square brackets and small capital letters indicates that the items in each group are abstract conceptual terms, which belong to virtual associative series, rather than syntagms. The italicized term in each of the four series indicates the specific term which is activated in each group to produce the syntagm *marchons!* The links I have drawn between the italicized terms are meant to suggest the weighted connections that give rise to the syntagm in question.

The 'choice' of a given syntagm is not, however, the result of a positive choice on the part of the speaker. Saussure remarks:

> it is not sufficient to say, in adopting a positive point of view, that *marchons!* is taken up because it signifies what one wants to express. In reality, the idea calls up, not a form, but an entire latent system, thanks to which the oppositions necessary for the constitution of the sign are obtained.
>
> (*CLG*: 179)

Irrespective of what the speaker 'wants to express' in any positive sense, he or she can only do so in and through the social-semiological resource systems of *langue*. Nor are signs, in Saussure's view, simply given by the system of *langue*. What is given is a system of 'oppositions necessary for the constitution of the sign'. Signs are made, or 'constituted', by the intersecting of the two dimensions of contextualization in acts of *parole*. Further, a given selection, so constituted, 'calls up' or evokes its possible meanings in relation to 'an entire latent system' of possibilities which are potentially relevant to the contextualization of any given act of *parole*.

Chapter 12

Arbitrariness and motivation in the sign

1 ABSOLUTE ARBITRARINESS AND RELATIVE ARBITRARINESS

In the final section of the chapter on 'The mechanism of the language system' Saussure turns to the question of absolute and relative arbitrariness. This distinction, he declares, represents 'another angle' (*CLG*: 180) on the mechanism of the language system:

> The fundamental principle of the arbitrariness of the sign does not prevent one from distinguishing in each language system that which is radically arbitrary, that is, unmotivated, from that which is only relatively so. Only some signs are absolutely arbitrary; in others there are phenomena which allow us to recognize degrees of arbitrariness, without removing the notion of arbitrariness altogether: *the sign may be relatively motivated.*
>
> (*CLG*: 180–1; emphasis in original)

As I pointed out in Chapter 9, section 2, the arbitrariness principle has often been taken to refer, reductively, to the internal link between a given signifier and signified *per se*. Saussure makes the following comments on his use of the word 'arbitrary':

> The word *arbitrary* also calls for comment. It must not give the idea that the signifier depends on the free choice of the speaking subject (we will see further below that it is not in the power of the individual to change anything in a sign once it is established in a linguistic group); we mean that it is *unmotivated*, that is, arbitrary in relation to the signified, with which it has no natural attachment in reality.
>
> (*CLG*: 101; emphasis in original)

The individual is not free to choose any signifier for a given signified because the relation between these is *systemic* in nature. From the perspective of *langue*, this relationship cannot, logically speaking, have any natural connection with extrasystemic reality. This system view refers to an abstract system of differences; it is language considered independently of any specific context in which meanings are made. The sign, as an abstract type, is outside meaning-making. In this sense, it is unmotivated.

It is only in concrete acts of *parole* that particular selections and combinations from the system of differences are cross-coupled with and, hence, motivated by their contact with the material world. As I pointed out in Chapter 5, *langue* is, by definition, an analytical abstraction from the 'global totality of language'. It is a conceptual framework for theorizing the social-semiological and transindividual character of the resources which the members of a given culture use to make meanings in regular and socially shareable ways. It is but one constituent, albeit a central one, in a more complex theoretical framework.

In this perspective, signs cannot be motivated by any appeal to criteria which lie outside the province of *langue* for the simple reason that an analytical abstraction *per se* does not have a context-specific meaning. Only actual, concrete uses of signs do. Nor can the individual, by an act of free will or free choice, motivate the systemic relationship between signifier and signified. If this were so, then it would introduce an individualistic principle of anarchy and irrationality into the mechanism of the language system. Carried to its logical conclusion, this would subvert the systemic basis of *langue*. Consequently, no meaning would be possible because there would be no socially shareable criteria for making meaning in and through acts of *parole*.

The notion of arbitrariness means, then, that the relationship between signifier and signified is established by *systemic*, rather than naturalistic, criteria. This means that a given sign type is recognizable as a semiotically salient difference in a given language (or other semiological) system. A signifier which makes a difference in this way has a regular, patterned relationship with its signified(s). That is, it is recognizable and able to be contextualized in relation to a higher-order system of types (Chapter 9, section 2). Neither voluntaristic acts of free choice nor naturalistic connections with 'external' reality can serve as the systemic basis of this relationship. In both of these cases, there would be no specifically social-semiological basis to the relatively stable system of sign types in a given language community. A 'signifier' which does not enter into such a regular pattern according to systemic criteria would, in actual fact, be no more than a potential signifier. That is, it would be a material act of vocalizing, tracing, bodily movement and so on which has not been assimilated to the higher-order system of types in a given social-semiological system.

Langacker (1987: 91) proposes the criterion of degrees of correspondence between the semantic and phonological poles of a symbolic structure (cf. sign in Saussure's terminology) to explain this:

A linguistic symbol involves a correspondence between two structures in semantic space (broadly construed), one of them in the phonological domain. When the two poles of a symbolic structure occupy vastly different regions of semantic space, their comparison for similarity or identity is severely limited; this incommensurability underlies the basic arbitrariness of simple linguistic signs. However, when the semantic pole of a linguistic symbol is itself situated in phonological space, comparison of the corresponding structures is feasible, and we recognize the expression as onomatopoeic when the structures show an appreciable degree of similarity. As a limiting case, moreover, a phonological structure can be put in correspondence with itself and hence be self-symbolizing, as in sentences like (2): *The boy went* [NOISE].

(Langacker 1987: 91)

This implies a continuum of possibilities. There may be maximal correspondence between the two poles, as in the limiting case proposed by Langacker, or minimal correspondence. Those showing 'minimal correspondence' are absolutely arbitrary in Saussure's sense. I would explain Langacker's limiting case in a slightly different way. Langacker's term 'self-symbolizing' suggests an identity relation between tokens such as /NOISE/, in his example, and the original referent situation which the token refers to. Take the following example, in which the speaker, Dion, who is speaking to her husband, refers to the fact that she had been crying earlier in the day:

Dion: (1) I just went back and stuck my head under the shower (2a) sitting there going (2b) /IMITATES CRYING NOISE/ (3) /LAUGHS/ (4) crying (5) it was so hot

(*Sylvania Waters*, Episode 1, ABC Television (Australia), 11 July 1992)

Utterances such as (2b), when speakers imitate some non-linguistic vocalization, clearly have the status of discourse-level moves, or constituent parts thereof, as here. However, they are not conventional lexicogrammatical units. How can they be dealt with? Rather than 'self-symbolizing', I would say that examples such as these are in some ways analogous to direct speech, or quotation. That is, the speaker of the utterance preserves the deixis of the 'quoted' vocalization, rather than construing it through more conventional lexicogrammatical means such as 'I cried' or 'I made a crying noise'. In the latter case, the 'original' vocalization is linguistically reconstrued from the perspective of the speaker. This would make it analogous to reported or indirect speech, which shifts the deictic centre of the speech act to the reporting rather than the reported context.

Quoted vocalizations such as /CRYING NOISE/ are not, of course, identical to the event they purportedly refer to. However, they are construed as closely corresponding to, or iconically 'resembling', the original vocalization. For this reason, they are maximally motivated by the vocalization (the referent situation) that they construe.

This says something quite fundamental about the arbitrary nature of the sign. Vocalizations such as /CRYING NOISE/ are not meaningless. However, they are not full-fledged linguistic units in the language, even though they may be integrated into the quoted frame in direct speech. They have no conventional phonological or lexicogrammatical status in the language system. Nevertheless, they do have meaning. This is so for the following two reasons: (1) they are maximally motivated by an iconic resemblance to some referent situation; and (2) the act of crying, say, is a meaningful act in all cultures. In my view, vocalizations such as /CRYING NOISE/ are instantiations of a type category of culturally recognized vocalization. There is, then, a relationship of iconicity between a given schema and its instantiations. However, such vocalizations have not been 'conventionalized' as symbolic interstratal construal relationships in a *langue*-based system of sign types. That is, it is not possible to specify a structurally stable form on the basis of a regular interstratal relationship between the phonic and conceptual orders. In *langue*, on the other hand, it is always possible to postulate a core decontextualized meaning potential for the terms and the sign types that constitute the system. This is, of course, not the same as the contextualized meaning the form has in *parole*. Nevertheless, this system-meaning constrains the possibilities of the latter. My point here is that it is much more problematic to establish a core, or systemic, value for vocalizations such as /CRYING NOISE/ as these have no formal status as conventional linguistic units in *langue*.

Saussure's own discussion of examples such as the Chinese prostration ritual (*CLG*: 101) as a sign of politeness, or cases of onomatopoeia such as the French *tic tac* (*CLG*: 102), for the ticking of the clock, illustrate this. These become conventional when they fulfil the two criteria referred to above. That is, signs are arbitrary when they acquire the status of general types in a system of value-producing relations. Both phonologically and grammatically they are replicable across many different occasions of use. Sign types do not, therefore, have a one-off status. They are fully generic, both phonologically *and* grammatically. If all potential signs had the status of /CRYING NOISE/, then we would have to invent a new sign for every occasion of use. That is, there would be no stable system of sign types to draw on.

The point is that whereas signs such as /CRYING NOISE/ are motivated by a naturalistic link between vocalization Schema and Instance (occasion of use), this cannot stand as an organizational principle for *langue*. If all signs were 'directly' motivated in this way, then this would mean that the system of *langue* would have no intrinsic organizational properties which are relevant to semiosis. Arbitrariness refers, then, to the ability to 'unhinge' the relationship between the strata of signifier and signified. These are not fixed by naturalistic criteria, but are open to selective re-contextualization.

Onomatopoeia is not really an exception to this general principle. Words such as *tick tock*, *clang*, *buzz* and so on are fully conventional in English.

Linguistically, it is misleading to assume that these are motivated by a mimetic, or naturalistic, relationship with real-world sounds. Clearly, there is a relationship, and this needs to be explained. But first, it must be pointed out that these examples of onomatopoeia, and many others, fully conform to the type categories of both English phonology and lexicogrammar. Saussure has this to say about onomatopoeia:

> As for authentic onomatopoeia (those such as *glou-glou*, *tic-tac*, etc.), not only are they not very numerous, but their choice is already to some extent arbitrary, since they are only the approximate and already half conventional imitation of certain noises (compare the French *ouaoua* ['bow-wow'] and the German *wauwau*). Furthermore, once introduced into the language system, they are more or less entrained in the phonetic, morphological, etc. evolution which other words are subjected to (cf. *pigeon*, from the Latin vulgate *pipio*, itself derived from onomatopoeia): obvious proof that they have lost something of their initial character in order to take on that of the linguistic sign in general, which is unmotivated.
>
> (*CLG*: 102)

In my view, onomatopoeia is better explained as a particular case of the 'de-automatization' of the phonological stratum of the signifier in relation to the signified. Rather than fulfilling their 'automatized' function of construing the signified in an unmarked way, which does not draw attention to its own principles of construction, onomatopoeia draws attention to the constructive role of the phonology itself in the process of construing the conceptual level of the signified. That is, the semiotic potential of the combinatorial contingencies of the phonology itself to construe conceptual order is de-automatized, in the sense that these contingencies are partially freed from the constraints of the combinatorial contingencies in the lexicogrammar. (See Halliday 1982: 135–6, for discussion of this principle in relation to lexicogrammar.)

2 RELATIVE ARBITRARINESS AND LEXICOGRAMMATICAL FORM

Nevertheless, the fact remains that the principle of absolute arbitrariness may be relativized. Saussure does not deny this; nor does he see this as in any way undermining the 'fundamental principle of the arbitrariness of the sign'. Rather than contradicting this 'fundamental principle', Saussure logically extends it in order to encompass motivation within the conceptual framework of *langue*. To understand why, it is necessary to grasp from the outset that Saussure's basis for explaining the relatively motivated character of signs remains that of *langue*, rather than *parole*. I shall now consider more closely what this means.

An 'absolutely arbitrary' sign is a purely *conventional* linguistic unit. It is a part of the systemic resources – the system of differences – which are potentially distributed across *all* possible contexts in which the language system is used to make meanings. At this level of abstraction, the relationships among the terms from the two orders of difference are, theoretically speaking, equiprobable. That is, the potential for the cross-coupling of terms from the two orders is not skewed by factors such as syntagmatic combination, membership in particular associative series, or the contextual contingencies of a particular act of *parole*. Absolute arbitrariness can only refer to the most abstract conception of the language system, or *langue*$_1$, as a system of pure differences, negatively defined. *Langue*$_2$, on the other hand, refers to typical lexicogrammatical units and structures that are assembled from the combining of the two orders (Chapter 3, section 5). The regular patterns in *langue*$_2$ have some positive value (Chapter 10, section 1). Motivation can only occur on the basis of positive principles of pattern and organization.

The fact that *langue* is a meaning-making resource which social agents draw on to varying degrees of standardization or creativity in the making and negotiating of meanings in *parole* means that *langue* does not in and of itself produce or generate utterances. It does not determine or cause linguistic behaviour or 'output'. Instead, it is an open and dynamic system of structured relations and conventions which its users adapt to ever-changing material and semiotic contingencies. *Langue* is both enabling and constraining, but it does not cause acts of *parole*. As Saussure points out on more than one occasion, *langue* is the social product resulting from the historically prior linguistic work of its users. It is, then, an objectification which the language user implicitly takes as a given in the enactment of *parole*. If *langue* simply caused or determined the individual's use of the system, then (1) there would be no room for individual innovation and creativity, and (2) there would be no way of explaining creativity if it were to arise. Most importantly, the fact that *langue* is the collective and evolving product of all the linguistic work which has gone into its maintenance and change provides the necessary framework for understanding Saussure's account of arbitrariness and motivation (Chapter 8).

Importantly, Saussure's account of these two notions and their interrelations hinges on a view of causal agency which he never properly spells out. He claims, for instance, that 'the sign may be relatively motivated', but he does not specify the agency in this passive construction. This brings me to the question: motivated by whom, or by what? I shall begin my exploration of this question by considering some of the examples which Saussure provides of relative motivation:

Thus *vingt* ['twenty'] is unmotivated, but *dix-neuf* ['nineteen'] is not to the same degree, because it evokes the terms of which it is composed and others with which it is associated, for example, *dix* ['ten'], *neuf* ['nine'], *vingt-neuf* ['twenty-nine'], *dix-huit* ['eighteen'], *soixante-dix* ['seventy'], etc.; taken separately, *dix* and *neuf* are on the same footing as *vingt*, but *dix-neuf* presents a case of relative motivation.

(CLG: 181)

Saussure's analysis draws attention to the combined effect of both syntagmatic and associative contextualization on the construction of a given unit. The French *vingt* is an example of an 'unmotivated' or 'absolutely arbitrary' sign because it does not require the language user to reflect on or to be aware of the terms out of which this sign is made. It is a single-morpheme word which requires minimal or no interpretative and/or constructive effort on the part of the language user in order to understand it or to use it (Chapter 10, section 4). As a single-morpheme word, *vingt* has unitary status as a single, unanalysable unit. Its single-morpheme status does not call attention to any internal principles of grammatical construction. On the stratum of the signifier, it is composed of the two phonemes, but the sign which results is near enough, for most practical purposes, to being a single unanalysable whole. That is, the sign as a whole cannot be further decomposed into its constituent grammatical units. A sign which cannot be so decomposed is a purely conventional combination of terms from the two orders of difference. Here I am ignoring the fact that *vingt* may also be analysed as two phonemes, or five graphemes, on the stratum of the signifier.

On the other hand, a two-morpheme construction such as *dix-neuf* is, by definition, decomposable into its constituent grammatical units. It draws attention to its own principles of grammatical construction: the constituent morphemes are transparently combined to form a higher-order unit of meaning. In turn, the two morphemes so combined evoke their respective associative series in a fully transparent way. The composite grammatical structure which results is both motivated by the new, composite meaning which arises from the intersection of the various associative series in this form at the same time as the syntagmatic combination of *dix* and *neuf* itself motivates this meaning, in a constant dialectical duality, involving the two dimensions of contextualization.

Composite structures such as *dix-neuf* require relatively more constructive and/or interpretative work on the part of the language user so as to construe the new joint meaning which results from the combination of their constituent parts (Chapter 11, section 2). In one sense, this means that the values of such forms are motivated by the users of the language. But this is an unsatisfactory formulation as it stands. It does not explain two closely related factors: (1) the systemic basis of Saussure's discussion; (2) *dix-neuf* is itself a standardized or conventional lexicogrammatical unit in $langue_2$. There is nothing striking or exceptional about it to native speakers of French. Therefore, it requires minimal constructive or interpretative effort on the part of the individual to motivate a functional value for the form. Where, then, is the source of the motivation in such cases? This brings me back to the systemic basis of Saussure's discussion.

The fact that *dix-neuf* is a conventional lexicogrammatical unit is a consequence of the accumulated linguistic work on the part of all speakers of French – past and present – which has constituted the French language system. As a conventional unit in French, *dix-neuf* is fully assimilated to the system of lexicogrammatical types in *langue₂*. In this sense, it is relatively arbitrary. It is also, as we have seen, relatively motivated on account of the composite grammatical structure which goes into the making of this form and the particular configuration of functional values it realizes. In other words, composite lexicogrammatical forms in *langue₂* tend to involve, to varying degrees, a complex interplay of both arbitrariness and motivation.

But what of absolute arbitrariness? The phonic and conceptual terms in *langue₁* have no positive value (Chapter 3, sections 3–4). They constitute a purely negatively defined system of differences. It is here that absolute arbitrariness comes into its own. A system of pure differences has no positive values because the 'double system' of contextualizing relations discussed in the previous chapter has not been brought into play. Theoretically, all possible cross-couplings of terms from the two orders of difference are equally probable. However, this most schematic definition of *langue* does not correspond to the way the system is, in actual fact, organized. There are always typical syntagmatic and associative groups that skew the probabilities of the system and its internal organization and patterning in some ways rather than others (Chapter 11, section 1).

If Saussure had limited his conception of the system to *langue₁*, the result would be a case of pure reification. It would be as if the system possessed a life of its own, independently of the ways in which its resources are used in acts of *parole*. Saussure is concerned, on the other hand, with modelling the systemic basis of the ways in which signs are made using these resources. That is why the relationship between 'arbitrary' and 'motivated' is such an important one.

Saussure's analysis of *dix-neuf* and other examples shows that the language system is comprised of stable patterns and relations, rather than an equiprobable distribution of pure differences. His analyses serve to highlight a most important general principle. This may be formulated as follows: which 'usual', or typical, syntagmatic combinations occur, and in relation to which associative series are these typically co-classified? These two questions refer to the dual nature of the typical contextualizing relations in and through which signs are made and have their meaning (Chapter 11, section 1). In this way, signs are systemically motivated.

3 MOTIVATION IN *LANGUE* AND *PAROLE*

What, then, of signs-in-use, or *parole*? Can we talk about 'absolute motivation' in *parole*? Given the theoretical terms of Saussure's framework, the notion of 'absolute motivation' – Saussure does not use this term – is a contradiction in terms. It would amount to the assumption that in *parole* signs are 'absolutely' motivated by extrasystemic factors such as the individualistic and naturalistic definitions that Saussure explicitly rejects. Further, it would assume that *parole* is divorced from, 'external' to or otherwise unrelated to *langue*. In other words, contextualized language-in-use, in such a view, would be extrinsic to, or a mere epiphenomenon of the language system. However, the relationship between *langue* and *parole* is not like this (Chapter 5, section 2).

A given act of *parole* always involves a dialectical interplay of the typical and the unique. In responding to the contingencies of specific material and semiotic circumstances, individuals, in acts of *parole*, necessarily draw on the social-semiological resources of *langue* in order to do so. Social agents do not simply reproduce abstract sign types in a purely mechanical fashion. As Saussure points out, they use their 'will' and 'intelligence' so as to adapt, in strategic ways, the resources of *langue* to specific contextual requirements. Even the most innovative uses of language draw on the resources of the system. This is shown, for instance, in the way in which there is never a simple one-to-one relationship between a sign-in-use and some feature of its situation. Instead, the 'double system' of contextualizing relations in *langue* may potentially cross-classify all of the component parts of a given syntagmatic context both with each other, as well as with all of the associative series to which the parts of the syntagm, and the syntagm as a whole, are assignable (Chapter 11, section 2). This means that in *parole* all of the relevant differences which are co-deployed may potentially contextualize each other in the making and enacting of a specific act of meaning. Such is the specificity of *parole*. However, this specificity is always a complex interplay of both systemic and situational factors. For this reason, 'absolute motivation', which cannot be equated with the specificity of *parole*, is a contradiction in terms. It would imply extrinsic and non-semiotic criteria of motivation which do not explain the 'mechanism of the language system', or its workings, in and through acts of *parole*.

In adopting this perspective, Saussure does not claim that the distinction between 'absolute' and 'relative' arbitrariness is an all-or-nothing distinction. Instead, it is a graded continuum. 'Relatively motivated' in Saussure's discussion means *systemically motivated*. The continuum of possibilities ranging from the absolute arbitrariness of *langue*$_1$ to the interplay of arbitrariness and motivation in *parole* is a consequence of the maximal schematicity of the former in relation to the maximal specificity of the latter. Table 12.1 sets out these relationships. Strictly speaking, absolute arbitrariness can only refer to the terms, rather than to the sign types, that arise from the system of pure values. The phonic and conceptual terms in *langue*$_1$ are schematic categories: they have no grounding in either linguistic form or substance. At this level of schematicity, there are simultaneous, but not combinatorial, contingencies.

The notion of relative arbitrariness, on the other hand, brings in some degree of grounding, or instantiation. This is not, to be sure, the full instantiation that occurs in acts of *parole*; rather, *langue*$_2$ specifies *prototypical* instantiations of syntagmatic and associative solidarities in the lexicogrammatical patterns of the language (Chapter 13, section 8). This is language form which is not cross-coupled with thought and sound. In other words, *langue*$_2$ specifies arbitrary instances of lexicogrammatical and phonological prototypes. Saussure's discussion of *dix-neuf*, and other examples, is a case in point. The notion of relative arbitrariness means, then, relatively grounded in the prototypical syntagmatic and associative solidarities – compare Saussure's 'regular models' – in *langue*$_2$.

Moving further 'down' the proposed continuum in Table 12.1, we have the typical patterns of use of the 'regular models' described in the preceding paragraph. These are specified to particular text types, discourse genres, semantic registers and so on (Chapter 3, sections 6–8). Thus, an arbitrarily chosen set of texts of some type will selectively instantiate the typical patterns of use of the lexicogrammatical and text-making resources of some community.

Finally, *parole* means maximal specificity. *Parole* refers to fully grounded instances of signs-in-use on particular occasions. It refers to the cross-

Table 12.1 Continuum from Absolute Arbitrariness to Relative Motivation in *langue* and *parole*

Degree of arbitrariness	*Maximal schematicity (*langue*)*
Absolute arbitrariness	System of negatively defined terms, or pure values, in *langue*$_1$
Relative arbitrariness	Systems of typical syntagmatic and associative solidarities; sign types in *langue*$_2$
Relative systemic motivation	Systems of typical deployments of sign types in discourse genres, semantic registers in *langue*$_3$
Interplay of factors relating to arbitrariness and motivation	Specificity of contextualizing relations; signs-in-use; intrasemiotic and semiotic/material cross-couplings in *parole*
Degree of motivation	Maximal specificity (*parole*)

coupling of the material and the semiotic domains, which is a necessary condition of all meaning-making. This also entails the cross-coupling of the linguistic and other semiotic modalities. The notion of maximal specificity does not, however, designate that which is totally unique and individual in any individualistic and non-social sense. A given act of *parole* may simply combine conventional units in entirely typical ways, or it may creatively transform these. Whichever, *parole* is never the mechanical reproduction of sign types. *Parole* is always a motivated response to the specific contingencies of particular situations, no matter how standardized these may be.

I pointed out above that the absolute arbitrariness of $langue_1$ entails a system of simultaneous contingencies only. That is, the terms in $langue_1$ do not specify any criteria of either syntagmatic or associative solidarity. There is only the *systemic* solidarity of the reciprocally defining relations among all of the terms in the system of pure values. $Langue_1$ is a purely synoptic system, outside space–time. In $langue_1$, there is neither lexicogrammatical form nor semiotically formed substance.

The relative arbitrariness of $langue_2$, on the other hand, shows that when criteria of syntagmatic and associative contextualization enter the picture, so, too, do system-internal criteria of spatio-temporal continuity (Chapter 5, section 4). This is reflected in the linearity of the signifier, which is a property of *langue*, not *parole*. This is not the same as the real-time unfolding of discourse. My point is that the sequential contingencies of syntagmatic combination in $langue_2$ entail a system-internal space–time which is crucial to the principle of relative (systemic) motivation.

Language has the semiotic potential to construe the phenomena of the world of our experience as events, happenings, actions and so on (Chapter 7, section 4). For example, the experiential grammar of the clause construes the phenomena of experience as particular types of processes, participants and circumstances that are internal to the grammar of the clause itself. The phenomena of experience necessarily have spatio-temporal continuity in order that they may be perceived. Yet the processes, participants and circumstances in the experiential grammar of the clause belong to the linguistic signified. Clause-level configurations of process–participant–circumstance interpret both physical–material and imaginary events as instantiations of the categories internal to language form. The perceived or imaginary events, etc. so construed belong to the domain of signified substance. Nevertheless, clause-level configurations of a process, its participant(s) and circumstance(s) have their own language-internal criteria of spatio-temporal succession. It is only in this way that the phenomena of experience are semiotically construed as particular categories of events, happenings or whatever. This is so irrespective of whether the events are real, imaginary, hypothetical or fictive and so on (section 8 below).

Take the clause *The Delta rocket arrived several weeks before launch* (George Smoot and Keay Davidson, *Wrinkles in Time*, p. 233). This clause construes a particular event as comprising three constituent parts, all of which have a role to play in the overall event. These are the *The Delta rocket* (participant: non-intentional Actor), *arrived* (process: material event), *several weeks before launch* (temporal circumstance). The clause does not directly 'reflect' some real event; rather, in analysing it into a number of constituent parts according to the categories which are internal to the English language, it construes a particular interpretation of the event. That is, language semiotically *re-contextualizes* material happenings, such as the one which this clause indexes, as particular configurations of the functional values internal to language itself.

Now, if absolute arbitrariness held total sway in the language system, then there would only be simultaneous contingencies. There would be nothing more than negatively defined differences constituting an analogue continuum. Language would be without regular and stable patterned relations (cf. Saussure's 'regular models'), without form. Combinatorial contingencies, on the other hand, mean that terms enter into the constitution of particular configurations of functional values, as shown in the example discussed in the previous paragraph.

4 SYNTAGMATIC AND ASSOCIATIVE INTERDEPENDENCIES: TOWARDS A THEORY OF CONTEXTUALIZATION

According to some scholars, Saussure's criterion of an 'internal' linguistics of *langue* detaches the sign from any consideration of the various 'referential', 'indexical' or 'pragmatic' factors which relate the general system of types in *langue* to its contexts-of-use. This view is taken by Lee, for instance, who argues that 'the relation between *langue* and reference is completely severed, and the ontological commitments of *langue* are unspecified' (1985: 113). In my view, Saussure's point is very different from this. I have already dealt with the ontological questions that Lee raises in Chapter 7. In that chapter, I argued that the system of values is itself a system of contextualizing relations which enables language users to construct and enact meaningful relationships with the world in and through specific acts of *parole*. Context is not something which simply impinges on language and other semiotic forms from the outside; it is construed by these. In this section, I shall examine the implications of the following passage for a theory of contextualization in the Saussurean perspective.

> the notion of relatively motivated implies: 1. the analysis of the given term, hence a syntagmatic relation; 2. the appeal to one or several other terms, hence an associative relation. This is none other than the mechanism in virtue of which any term whatsoever lends itself to the expression of an idea. Up to this point, [linguistic] units have appeared to us as values, that is, as elements of a system, and we have considered them above all in terms

of their oppositions; now we recognize the solidarities which link them; these are of the associative and syntagmatic kind, and it is these which limit arbitrariness. *Dix-neuf* ['nineteen'] is solidary associatively with *dix-huit* ['eighteen'], *soixante-dix* ['seventy'] etc., and syntagmatically with its elements *dix* and *neuf* (see p. 177). This dual relationship confers on it [i.e., *dix-neuf*] a part of its value.

(CLG: 182)

This is a key passage. A number of critically important implications may be derived from the arguments that Saussure presents here. Most importantly, Saussure shows how his theory of language form and function is a *contextual* one. However, context is not extrinsic to *langue*. Instead, Saussure draws attention to the context-building resources that are intrinsic to the language system. I shall now explore this notion further (see also Chapter 11).

The notion of relative motivation means that both syntagmatic and associative solidarities, in so far as the linguistic units concerned are no longer defined as pure values in a system of negatively defined differences *per se*, do not refer exclusively to a system of pure values in *langue*$_1$. Why, then, does Saussure say that it is this dual relationship of syntagmatic and associative solidarities which 'confers a part' of the given unit's value? The point is this. The sign takes some of its value from (1) the typical syntagmatic and associative relations that constrain it and (2) its *potential* relations to the world. The dual system of contextualizing relations maps functional values onto the sign. Only in this way can the sign 'lend itself to the expression of an idea' in the world.

Now we can see more clearly what it means to say that associative and syntagmatic solidarities 'limit arbitrariness'. These solidarities refer to potential uses of sign types in some context. They refer to (1) the ways in which a given sign type can be used to construe a meaningful relationship with the world and (2) the complex and multiple ways in which language forms are functionally motivated in relation to the meanings of various kinds which they realize. In other words, the issue of 'motivated' signs pushes Saussure's theory to its limits. Once it is admitted that motivation occurs, then we are in the realm of the functional relations between signs and their contexts. Signs are not contingently 'in' a context which is extrinsic to the sign (Thibault 1994); rather, the multiple functional values which are mapped onto semiotic forms construe and enact various dimensions of the relevant contextualization relations. In this way, there are multiple metaredundancy relations between the forms and the wider situation in which these occur.

Signs are *made* in and through their syntagmatic and associative 'solidarities'. They do not exist ready-made, waiting to be used. The 'units as values' or 'elements of a system' are not fully made signs. They are the systemic resources in and through which signs are made according to formal, discursive and social constraints and practices. Once it is understood that the relationship of function to form is a 'solidary', rather than an arbitrary, one, then it should be clear that the functionally motivated nature of this relation involves multiple functional 'solidarities' between the syntagmatic and associative dimensions of contextualization in the making of signs. That is, different kinds of functional 'solidarities' act upon each other in the making and motivating of signs. The mapping of multiple associative series onto a given lexicogrammatical form shows that a given form is always motivated by a plurality of functional values. Language also entails intrafunctional solidarities.

5 IDEAS, NOT VALUES

The passage discussed above is also interesting for the shift in emphasis from the notion of value to that of *idea*. Whereas values are differential and systemic, ideas arise from the interdependence of syntagmatic and associative solidarities. Saussure says that the mechanism of this dual system of contextualizing relations 'lends itself to the expression of an idea'. What, then, does Saussure mean by an 'idea'? It should be clear that he cannot be referring to any kind of pre-semiotic and purely psychological notion (Chapter 7, section 4). This would directly contradict the very semiotic basis of the mechanism which expresses ideas in his explanation. Yet he limits himself to saying that this mechanism 'lends itself to the expression of an idea' (see above). That is, it is *potentially* able to do so. However, the systemic basis of Saussure's discussion means that he cannot go beyond this point because the focus remains that of *langue*. But what, then, is an idea, if not a pure value?

In my view, an 'idea' refers to signified thought-substance. That is, thought that has been semiotically re-construed, or re-contextualized, by signified form as a signified substance. I am assuming that thought-substance and signified substance, which are my own terminological glosses, are synonymous notions. Signified substance refers to the phenomena of experience in the world that the signified contextualizes in and through the categories internal to language form. The 'double system' of contextualizing relations in *langue* is the mechanism by which ideas are expressed in *parole*. An 'idea' is, then, a contextually specific conceptual meaning that results when signified form redounds with 'thought' to produce a specific signified substance in some context.

6 LIMITING ARBITRARINESS

The 'double system' of typical contextualizing relations in *langue* also functions to limit arbitrariness. It is this 'limitation of arbitrariness' which is, Saussure argues, the 'best possible basis' for the study of the language system (*CLG*: 182). Now, if arbitrariness is the foundational principle of the system of pure values, is not this a somewhat paradoxical conclusion to reach? I do not think so. Before clarifying the reasons why, here is how Saussure develops his own point of view on this question:

> In effect, the entire language system rests on the irrational principle of the arbitrariness of the sign, which, applied without restriction, would lead to utter chaos; but the mind [*l'esprit*] manages to introduce a principle of order and of regularity in certain parts of the mass of signs, and that is the role of the relatively motivated. If the mechanism of the language system were entirely rational, one could study it in itself; but as it is only a partial correction of a naturally chaotic system, one adopts the point of view which is imposed by the nature of the language system itself, in studying this mechanism as a limitation of arbitrariness.
>
> (*CLG*: 182–3)

The 'irrational principle of the arbitrariness of the sign' would lead to chaos because, logically speaking, the unrestricted arbitrariness of purely simultaneous contingencies in the system of pure values would give rise to no discernible patterns and constraints on the possible syntagmatic and associative solidarities in the system. Without such constraints, there can be no pattern, no order. Meaning would be impossible. Meaning is only possible when the possibilities of combination of the two orders of difference are limited by regular and typical patterns. Meaning entails order, pattern, regularity.

Saussure says that the mind introduces such principles of 'order' and 'regularity' in a partial way into the 'mass of signs'. It is not entirely clear what Saussure intends by the concept of 'mind'. It is difficult to read this as referring simply to individual mind. The principles of 'order' and 'regularity' that Saussure mentions are systemic regularities. They are not projections of individual mind. By the same token, it is crucial to the functioning of the mechanism of the language system that individuals are able to infer and learn its principles of ordering in order to be able to use the system for the expression of ideas in *parole*.

These principles of order and regularity are only ever partial, rather than total. An entirely rational order would mean that all possible contextualizing relations are determined in advance or pre-fabricated. *Langue*, in this scenario, would be a fixed order of things. That is, it would be a closed, purely self-regulating system.

Yet the 'naturally chaotic' or irrational basis of *langue* also means that there are system-internal principles of both 'order' and 'chaos'. The 'naturally chaotic' refers to the system's own latent potential for construing patterns and connections between patterns that do not conform to the principles of 'order' and 'regularity' of the language mechanism. The system may change when the reserve potential of the 'chaotic' and the 'irrational' alters the regular patterns of syntagmatic and associative solidarities in the system itself. It is this constant synchronic and diachronic dialectic between absolute arbitrariness and relative motivation which explains the dynamic of stability and change, order and chaos, homogeneity and heterogeneity in the system.

7 RE-DEFINING MOTIVATION: SEMIOLOGICAL CRITERIA

Psychologists who work in the experimental and behavioural paradigms define motivation in terms of the various factors that 'energize, maintain and direct behaviour toward goals' (Bootzin *et al.* 1991 [1975]: 376). The language which psychologists in these traditions use to describe motivation refers to observable physical phenomena, physical stimuli and physical forces, or to internal drive states. These may be physical, physiological or social in character and origin. In all cases, however, it is the language of physical cause-and-effect that is associated with the Newtonian paradigm (Chapter 4, section 10) that tends to inform psychologists' explanations of motivation.

Saussure's rejection of naturalistic criteria for explaining the relationship between signifier and signified needs to be understood against the background of these considerations. Saussure's psychic conception of the sign entails (1) a selective and intentional orientation to perceptual phenomena and (2) a conscious awareness of the self as the one who so construes the phenomena of experience (Chapter 6, section 4). The psychic and and the semiological are closely related notions in Saussure's theory. The dually psychic and semiological character of the sign entails higher-order, or linguistic, consciousness on the part of language users (Edelman 1989). This is only possible through a socially shared system of signs such as language.

Semiotic motivation is not adequately describable in the language of mechanical cause and effect. A signifying act is a psychic orientation to some 'object'. It is not an 'output' which is proportional to its 'input'. Psychic acts are acts of higher-order consciousness. They are self-generated, or autopoetic, orientations to the world through an appropriation and re-working of the meaning-making resources of the system. There is no necessary relation between utterance and response. Semiotic motivation does not entail causal necessity.

Any attempt to understand the phenomenon of motivation in semiosis needs to take these factors into account. Saussure's rejection of specifically naturalistic criteria means that the physical world, the physiological processes of, say, articulation and audition, and subjective psychological (not psychic) states cannot constitute the basis of a social-semiological theory of the sign. That is, these factors cannot explain the motivated character of particular signifying acts. All of these various factors may, of course, be construed by signs, but they are not constitutive parts of language form; rather, they belong to the pre-semiotic physical–material realm. This may, in turn, be construed as a semiotically formed substance. This does not mean, however, that Saussure rules out the motivated character of the sign in acts of meaning-making. Instead, he rules out specifically naturalistic criteria as a basis for explaining the very different question of *semiotic* motivation. This calls for a very different approach – one which starts with the intrinsic nature of semiotic forms themselves, rather than with extrinsic factors, based on substantive and naturalistic criteria.

Seemingly paradoxically, Saussure's starting point for explaining semiotic motivation is the principle of arbitrariness. The point is that meaning-makers appropriate and adapt the resources and conventions of the system in order to construct meanings which are relevant to specific contexts. This is, of course, the instantial perspective of *parole*. However, *parole* is neither random nor accidental (cf. Holdcroft 1991: 32); rather, it refers to the patterned deployment of the resources of the system in the making of an occasion-specific meaning. *Parole* refers to the ways in which the meaning-making potential of the system is specialized to particular uses. Acts of *parole* are always mediated by the systems of meaning-making practices that I designated as *langue*$_3$ in Chapter 3. This means that there is no direct specification leading from the terms in *langue*$_1$ to *parole*. This further entails that motivation is an intrinsic part of the workings of the system, albeit not at the most schematic level of the terms which constitute the system of pure differences in *langue*$_1$. Systemic motivation does not preclude instantial motivation. The point is that in a given signifying act language users always appropriate and adapt the resources of the system in the service of their own purposes and intentions in specific contexts. *Parole* is, then, the point where the psychic and the semiological come together.

In my view, misunderstandings have tended to arise when the principle of arbitrariness is erroneously de-located from the theoretical domain of *langue* and re-located in *parole*. This has led to a great deal of confusion and misinterpretation of the overall place of both arbitrariness and motivation in Saussure's social-semiological theory. Researchers as diverse as Givón (1989: 94–6), Holdcroft (1991: 52–5) and Kress (1993) all put forward arguments in support of the view that the sign is motivated, rather than arbitrary. In all three cases, however, the perspective adopted in order to do so is that of *parole*. This leads to the kind of misunderstanding that I referred to above. Above all, it leads to a failure to assign the principle of arbitrariness its rightful place in Saussure's overall theory. Let me affirm, however, that I take it as axiomatic that signs-in-use are always motivated. This follows from the fact that in specific acts of *parole* the values that the terms have in *langue*$_1$ are re-combined in complex patterns. In this way, the values that the terms have in the system of pure differences are necessarily altered and re-weighted in response to specific contextual factors. Nevertheless, the resulting motivation arises from the resources which the system itself affords language users. The central question for Saussure is not why speaker x said something to speaker y at time z, but how the internal design features of the system itself make motivated acts of meaning possible.

8 MOTIVATING THE SIGN: THREE TEXTUAL ANALYSES

Textual analysis I

Consider the following textual transcription of a segment taken from a radio talk-back programme:

LYNNE: (1) my husband and I were both are very capable responsible people (2) in retrospect I think that we could have done both most effectively

OLLE: (3) and how does your husband feel?

LYNNE: (4) pardon?

OLLE: (5) husband feel the same?

LYNNE: (6) ah well (7) he doesn't get greatly involved in it (8) because ah it was I took the decision (9a) and ah I stayed home (9b) and he continued with his career.

(*The World Today*, ABC Radio (Sydney), 4 November 1988)

Prior to the excerpt, Lynne had spoken at length about the reasons why she left her career to raise children and her subsequent regrets about not having combined the two activities. The excerpt begins with the first mention of her husband, which prompts the programme presenter, Andrew Olle, to ask her the question in clause 3. I shall focus on clause 3 in the brief illustrative text analysis which follows.

In clause 3, there is no consistent selection of terms from a single associative group in the language system. Instead, there is a selective re-combining and re-weighting of terms from a number of different functionally organized associative groups in the grammar. For example, clause 3 is not simply specifiable as a clause with the following mood selection: [INDICATIVE; INTERROGATIVE; WH-]. Instead, the mood selection combines with a number of other options which originate from distinctive associative groups in the grammar of English. These include the fact that the clause selects a Mental Process of Affect (*feel*) in connection with the experiencer of this (*your husband*), who is the focus of the question in clause 3. A further salient feature is the use of the paratactic conjunction *and*, which serves to foreground the syntagmatic integration of Olle's question with the preceding discourse at the same time that it seeks to orientate the interaction in a specific direction. That is, Olle attempts to focus the discussion, at least temporarily, on Lynne's husband, rather than on Lynne. However, this is not taken up at any length by Lynne in her response, which begins in move 6.

The main point of this brief analysis is to show that clause 3 selectively combines selections from a plurality of associative groups in the grammar of English. There is no one-to-one relationship between a stimulus and a response. The selective adaptation of the resources of the system to the contingencies of the situation is non-deterministic; rather, language users strategically deploy the resources of the system in the making and negotiating of meanings in discourse.

Textual analysis II

I pointed out above that the sign is maximally motivated when the interpretative and/or constructive effort that is required so as to construe a symbolic relationship between signifier and signified is greatest. Lewis Carroll's famous poem, 'Jabberwocky' in *Through the Looking-Glass*, provides us with a good example. Here is the first stanza:

'Twas brillig, and the slithy toves
Did gyre and gimble in the wabe:
All mimsy were the borogroves,
    And the mome raths outgrabe.
(Lewis Carroll, *Through the Looking-Glass*, p. 126)

This poem poses a series of interpretative problems for the reader. In Saussurean terms, this might be formulated as follows: how can we construe an interstratal symbolic relation between the two orders of difference in words like *brillig*, *slithy*, *toves* and so on? Compared to the noun *cats*, which is a prototypical instantiation of a purely conventional unit in English grammar, items such as those mentioned here require a disproportionate amount of interpretative work in order to motivate them as signs in the English language. With this problem in mind, I shall now consider some selected aspects of the first stanza of the poem.

On the stratum of the signifier, the printed text combines units (graphemes, etc.) from English graphology so as to form composite graphological structures such as *brillig* and so on. Analogous observations can be made in connection with English phonology, should the text be read aloud. These sequences of graphemes (or phonemes) are syntagmatically integrated so as to form composite graphological structures which fully conform to the patterns of combination of graphemes into orthographic words in the system of written English.

Take the case of the item *toves*. The syntagmatic integration of the graphemes in this visual–graphic signifier forms a syntagmatic solidarity which results from the combination and integration of the individual graphemes, as follows: $<[t + o + v + e] + [s]>$. As in the case of more conventional units such as *cats*, this syntagmatic solidarity among the graphemic units of the graphic signifier evokes the possibility of a corresponding syntagmatic solidarity on the stratum of the signified (Chapter 8, section 4).

Initially, the resulting signified may be schematized as follows: [[THING] + [PLURAL]]. Like *cats*, the word *toves* instantiates a regular morphological pattern in English for the formation of plural nouns. However, and unlike *cats*, there are no specific terms in the conceptual order of differences which can be combined with the sequences of graphemes (or phonemes) in the word *toves*. This means that the symbolic relationship between the two strata is made problematic. There are no *specific* terms in the conceptual order which are conventionally associated with this particular combination of graphemes. In the case of both *cats* and *toves*, the most schematic representation of the conceptual terms of these plural nouns may be glossed as follows: [[THING] + [PLURAL]]. However, such highly schematic categories are not specific instantiations as such (Chapter 3, section 4). In the case of *cats*, it is possible to specify a fully conventional instantiation of the more schematic terms referred to above: viz. [[THING; ANIMATE; FELINE] + [PLURAL]]. As for *toves*, it is not possible to specify any such conventional instantiation of the specific terms, beyond a certain point in the taxonomic hierarchy: viz. [[THING; ANIMATE; ?] + [PLURAL]]. The question mark simply indicates the non-availability of a more specific conceptual term for this word. The word *toves* has schematic but, beyond a certain point, no specific conceptual content. Coming down to the grammatical level, on the other hand, presents no problems: both items are prototypical instantiations of regular syntagmatic patterns in the formation of plural nouns in English. The relevant syntagmatic model is the following: [[BASE NOUN] + [PLURAL MORPHEME SUFFIX: S]].

There are, then, no available conceptual terms in English which construe the graphic sequence <[t + o + v + e] + [s]> in an unproblematic way. The reader must construe a conceptual meaning which is, in some sense, both non-prototypical, as well as resistant to exact categorization. Lewis Carroll's poem calls our attention to two most important aspects of the stratified nature of semiosis. First, the signifier is not a form which 'carries' a meaning; rather, all of the various levels which are involved in the organization of the sign each contribute a layer of meaning and organization to the overall structure of the sign (Chapter 9). Second, it is not the case that the linguistic sign is a simple bistratal relationship between the phonic or graphic and the conceptual orders. Signs are not simple, fixed relations between a signifier and a signified. Instead, there are combinatorial contingencies on *both* strata. The syntagmatic integration of phonemes or graphemes in the signifier is re-construed as the syntagmatic integration of lexicogrammatical and conceptual units and relations in the signified (Chapter 10, section 4). Both signifier and signified show combinatorial contingencies in this sense. It is these combinatorial contingencies on the two strata which intersect motivated combinations of phonic or graphic and conceptual terms in language form.

The interpretative work which is required to motivate the sign *toves* may be taken a stage further. Figure 12.1 displays the various levels at which the combinatorial contingencies of the signified operate. I have already discussed this word at the levels of morpheme and word. Figure 12.1 shows the relationship of these levels to the still higher levels of the nominal group, clause and discourse genre in which the word functions. Each level provides a further layer of contextual motivation for the word in question, even in the absence of exact conceptual specification. Thus, the nominal group in which *toves* occurs assigns it the quality *slythy*. In turn, this nominal group is revealed to be the semantic Actor, or performer, of a material action in the experiential structure of its clause. Finally, the text is assignable to the genre of narrative poem, and this provides further reasons for motivating the clause in question as an action or event in the plot structure of the narrative.

It is at the discourse level of organization that the signified in question can be further motivated in relation to its signified substance. Lexicogrammatical form is not directly motivated by its relationship to the world. This is always mediated by the discourse level of organization. Both the fictive status of the discourse genre and the invented nature of the noun *toves* implicate that the referent world of the text is an imaginary one which both writer and reader

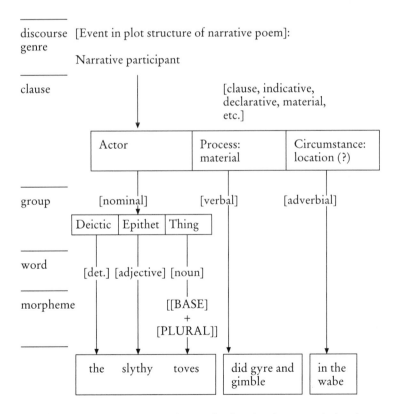

Figure 12.1 Combinatorial contingencies motivating the sign *toves* in Lewis Carroll's poem 'Jabberwocky'; lexicogrammatical and discourse levels of the signified

construe in and through the language forms used. Signified substance can, as here, be that which is simply 'thought' or 'imagined' in and through the semiotic resources of language, rather than a physical entity 'out there' in the material world. 'Thought', in Saussure's sense, can be semiotically motivated and construed as signified thought-substance, whether it materially exists 'out there' in perceptual experience or not.

The conceptual stratum functions to construe the phenomena of thought in and through lexicogrammatical form. The conceptual is an interface between the possibilities for meaning in thought and the possibilities for expressing this in the lexicogrammatical forms of the language. This relationship between form and thought results in a signified substance.

Textual analysis III

Consider now the visual text in Figure 12.2. This text was produced several years ago by a four-year-old around Christmas time in Bologna (Italy). The child's schematic drawing of a Christmas tree no doubt constitutes her response to a salient event in her life at that time. However, the drawing is not a re-presentation of a prior perceptual experience. Instead, it is a semiotic orientation to salient objects in the world of the child. Kress points out, with reference to his own analysis of a drawing of a car by a three-year-old, that such drawings reflect the child's developing interests, and that it is these interests that motivate visual, linguistic and other semiotic forms (1993: 173). Nevertheless, I would want to emphasize here that the child's selective and intentional orientation to the world in and through signifying acts of all kinds also depends on his or her developing command of the resources of a visual or linguistic grammar. That is, on the relevant meaning-making conventions and principles of grammatical organization in the two systems. In both cases, the child must infer systemic regularities from his or her experience of the two systems on many different occasions of use, and learn to adapt these to his or her own purposes.

In the drawing of the Christmas tree in Figure 12.2, the child selectively attends to only some of the most salient features. Detail is conspicuously absent. Even so, the drawing illustrates a number of ways in which the child is learning an emerging grammar of depiction. These features are not unique to this picture. They are systemic regularities in the European tradition of visual composition. They include the following schematic principles of organization in the grammar of the visual:

1   *Equilibrium*. There is a distribution of visual elements that produces an overall effect of balance and equilibrium. That is, the form, the direction of the lines and the way these connect are all seen as reciprocally defining in ways that convey a sense of 'inevitability' of the parts in relation to the whole. There is syntagmatic integration of the parts in relation to the

Figure 12.2 Child's schematic drawing of a Christmas tree

whole. The overall effect is one of stability.

2   *Weight*. The centring of the visual image on the vertical axis, the absence
of other visual elements, and the relative dominance of the tree with
respect to the star at its apex confer an overall feeling of centrality and
weight to the tree.

3   *Direction of movement*. Visual forms create axes. In turn, these create
lines of force which are orientated in a certain direction. In the present
case, the narrowing of the tree as one progresses from base to apex
creates a line of force which suggests an 'upwards' movement.

4   *High–low*. The greater distribution of weight at the base of the visual
image anchors this in relation to the vertical axis.

5   *Rhythm.* Visual compositions have rhythm. This is usually signified by the 'repetition' of lines, colours, forms and so on. In Figure 12.2, the repeated 'zig zag' effect of the margins contributes to the effect of a progressive vertical orientation.

6   *Symmetry.* The simple bilateral symmetry of the composition has the effect of making all its elements seem to be distributed in 'equal' fashion around the vertical axis.

7   *Perspective.* The simple bidimensional perspective, which is typical of this phase of children's drawings, indicates that the grammar of (three-dimensional) perspective in the western tradition has not been acquired at this stage.

The various principles of visual organization that I have outlined above are schematic to their instantiations in particular texts, such as the one shown in Figure 12.2. From this schematic point of view, they are unmotivated by specific combinatorial contingencies. They are, therefore, arbitrary in the sense defined above. It is only when they enter into actual visual compositions that their combinatorial contingencies may be said to be motivated.

9 MOTIVATING SOUNDS: SYSTEMIC AND CONTEXTUAL FACTORS

Saussure recognizes that a given sound event which occurs in the acoustic flux can be 'imaged', or categorically construed, as being an instance of a phonological type which belongs to a given language system. In other words, such an instance is construed as a sound event which makes sense in the speech practices of some community, or for which it is possible to imagine or construct a sense.

In English, the configuration of phonemes /bɔɪ/ is able to be construed as an event which makes sense in the system of English phonology. In the case of the word *toves*, in Lewis Carroll's famous poem, the problem differs from the first example only in degree, not in kind. Both sequences are regular patternings of phonemes of the English language. Both sequences have the potential to make sense in the speech practices of a given language community. It is not the case that *boy* is meaningful and *toves* is not, or only peripherally so. There is no need to have recourse to dichotomies such as standard vs. deviant phonological forms, or sense vs. nonsense strings. Nor is it the case that configurations of phonemes simply 'contain' or 'convey' their conceptual meanings. Instead, both of these configurations of phonemes, in so far as they correspond to, or instantiate, regular phonological patterns in the sound system of the English language afford an open-ended set of actual and potential meanings. These meanings are adduced on the basis of the categorical judgements which language users make concerning whether a particular instance either fully or partially conforms to the requirements of the higher-order phonological or other schema (Langacker 1987: 158).

In other words, if language users can construe even partial conformity to the essentially systemic requirements of schematicity, then it is possible to *motivate* a sense for a given configuration of phonological units. The basis on which specific motivations are adduced always occurs in relation to particular formal, generic and intertextual relations and conventions. These contextual factors will skew the motivation of the configuration's meaning potential in certain ways rather than others. With respect to any specific language system, phonological form and phonic substance are not dichoto-mized. There is a continuum of possibilities in which such motivation may take place. In Figure 12.3, I have suggested, albeit informally, one possible way of thinking about such a continuum. In this case, the two 'outer' extremes are those of 'non-animate natural sounds' and 'sounds from other (non-English) phonological systems'. Figure 12.3 proposes a continuum of possibilities which cluster around the phonological system of English, as indicated by (7) in Figure 12.3. The main purpose of Figure 12.3 is to show that motivation refers to the ability of language users to assign a sense to material events of all kinds, as shown by the continuum of possibilities suggested in the figure. The phonological units and structures of, say, English are, synchronically speaking, relatively stable structures that function to construe lexicogrammatical and conceptual structures and relations. These

1	non-animate natural sounds
2	animate natural sounds
3	non-criterial or semiotically non-salient vocalizations
4	laughter, crying, etc.
5	she went /CRYING NOISE/
6	onomatopoeia
7	prototypical phonological units (e.g. /bɔɪ/)
8	non-prototypical phonological forms (e.g., *toves*)
9	'nonsense' strings (aphasic speech, children's games)
10	non-English phonological units assimilated to English phonology
11	non-English phonological systems

Figure 12.3 Motivation and sound events

structures provide the stable phonological context types on the basis of which grammatical and conceptual relations are construed. That is, these phonological contexts specify which lexicogrammatical and conceptual meanings and relations occur, and when. This means that a given sequence in the spoken chain of the signifier is contextualized by the relations it has with the conceptual level of the signified. It is the *langue*-based system of phonological types which enables us to relate particular spoken events to their signifieds. It is the stable meaning system of a community which establishes the typical ways in which particular sound sequences become mutually contextualized by their relations with certain conceptual signifieds, and not others, in a given language system. In this way, language users have a systemic basis for knowing that there are only *some* kinds of arbitrarily defined relations between signifiers and signifieds, and not others. For example, the English word *sang* is comprised of the sequence of phonemes /sæŋ/. This sequence of three phonemes comprises the overall phonological shape of the word in question. The three phonemes in the sequence are syntagmatically integrated as functional values in a still larger structural–functional configuration. Such global configurations comprise the phonological patterns which constitute the sound system of a given language. They are regularities of phonological form which differentially construe categorical distinctions on the stratum of the signified. Each phoneme is a local category. Phonemes are discrete categories of phonological form. Further, each phoneme displays possibilities of combination with other such local categories in specifiable distribution patterns. In this way, it enters into more global configurations. Such global configurations of phonological form are structural–functional relationships which provide local criteria of coherence on the basis of which still higher-order contextualizing relations may be construed on the stratum of the signified. Arbitrariness, in other words, provides a systemic basis for motivating a productive relationship of signification between signifier and signified in and through the regular higher-order contextualizing relations in *langue* (Chapter 9, section 2).

But what of those more peripheral cases of sound events which may not be assimilated to a *langue*-based system of contextualizing relations? The system of *langue* tells us that certain patterns, and not others, are globally consistent in a given speech community. The sequence of phonemes /sæŋ/ is a case in point. But the further one moves away from the stable system of types, the more semiotic work has to be done in order to motivate a sense for the otherwise 'meaningless' sound event. That is, a given sound event can always be assigned a meaning, albeit not a phonological one, by the motivating of a context for it. As I showed in Chapter 9, section 5, the motivating of a conceptual meaning for a given phonic sequence is, then, the first stage in the building of the larger contextual wholes in which meanings are made. This question is central in the final chapter.

Chapter 13

Making and motivating signs in discourse

1 FORM AND FUNCTION IN GRAMMAR

Saussure calls into question the distinction that traditional grammarians have made between morphology, syntax and lexis. In Saussure's conception, the study of morphology, syntax and lexis are not separate studies; instead, they refer to different levels of organization and their corresponding units and structures in one unified object of study: viz. the grammatical system of a given language. This is more than simply an argument against a fragmented study of language form and function. It follows logically from Saussure's social-semiological conception of the linguistic sign. Morphemes, words, phrases, sentences and so on are constitutive units and levels in the grammar of some types of languages. They are all signs, or sign types, of varying size and complexity.

Saussure also argues that grammatical form and function are 'solidary': they are not independent of each other (*CLG*: 186; Chapter 9, section 6). This follows from his view of *langue* as a 'system of means of expression' (*CLG*: 185) for the making of meanings. Grammar, as he says, is the study of this system. Saussure does not provide an explicit definition of the notion of function. However, it is clear that both grammatical form and function, in his theory, are intrinsic to the language system:

> this distinction [between morphology and syntax] is illusory: the series of forms of the substantive *phúlax* only becomes a flectional paradigm through the comparison of the functions attached to the different forms; reciprocally, these functions are only justifiable by the morphology if a determinate phonic sign corresponds to each of them. A declension is neither a list of forms nor a series of logical abstractions, but a combination of these two things (see p. 144): forms and functions are solidary, and it is difficult, if not impossible, to separate them. Linguistically, morphology has no real and autonomous object; it cannot constitute a discipline distinct from syntax.
>
> (*CLG*: 186)

In speaking of the paradigmatic basis of grammatical form and function, Saussure argues that *both* lexis and morphology are functional. It is only recently that a number of linguists have begun to take this important principle seriously (Hasan 1987b; Silverstein 1987: 20). In stressing a unified approach to lexis and morphology, Saussure draws attention to the ways in which these mutually restrain each other in the assignment of functions to the various forms in a given paradigm.

This is so in two ways. First, the paradigm establishes a systematic set of oppositions among its members. In providing a systematic and principled basis for comparing the functions 'attached to' the forms in a paradigm, this avoids the problem of a random list of forms which are not systematically related to specifiable functions. Second, it shows that distinctions in meaning have a systematic basis in the contrasting form–function relations which the linguist can represent as paradigms of options which are internal to *langue*.

If grammar is a means of expression for signifying meanings, and if form and function are mutually defining, then this brings us to the question of the role of the system of *langue* in the making of meanings in specific contexts-of-use. Can Saussure's social-semiological theory of language form and function bridge this apparent gap? The answer to this question is, in my view, an unqualified 'yes'. Furthermore, the means of doing so are built into the system of *langue* itself. They are not extrinsic to it. In the various traditions of functional linguistics which developed after Saussure, there is a broad consensus regarding the relationship between language function and the uses to which language is put in specific contexts. This relationship has been formulated in a variety of different ways. From one point of view, functions are 'extrinsic' to language form and exert pressure on it from the outside. From another point of view, the functions are built into the intrinsic design features of language form itself. There are many positions in between these two points of view. Nevertheless, a general consensus exists as to the fundamental importance of the functional connection between language form and its uses in context.

Saussure himself suggests that the functions of language forms are intrinsic to the systemic organization of *langue*. The question then arises as to how the intrinsic functional values of the regular syntagmatic and associative groups in *langue* relate to specific acts of *parole*.

2 GRAMMATICAL FORMS ARE MEANING-MAKING

Saussure's theory of the sign outlines a number of fundamental concepts which are crucial to the construction of a truly social-semiological explanation of language form and function. These concepts, which I take to be intrinsic characteristics of *langue*, are outlined as follows:

1   The sign is inherently dialogic in character. That is, it is always orientated

to the other in jointly constructed and enacted signifying acts. There is, then, an interactional dimension to the sign, as revealed in Saussure's discussion of the psychic character of this in the speech circuit (Chapter 5, section 1; Chapter 6, section 9).

2   Signs are intrinsically categorical. That is, signs construe, or interpret, the world of 'thought' and 'sound', respectively, as contextually significant thought-substance and phonic substance. They do so by means of the categorical distinctions – the conceptual values – which are internal to the language system. The sign does not reflect a pre-given order of things (Chapter 7, section 4).

3   Signs are syntagmatically integrated into larger, more complex signs as particular configurations of functional values (Chapter 11, section 2). Syntagms, so defined, may range from the smallest-scale grammatical units to entire occasions of discourse. A given configuration, however abstract, must also be concretely enacted. This means that the syntagm also functions to create or to enact context; it is not simply contained by an already-given context which is 'extrinsic' to it. In this sense, the syntagm has a dual function to play: (i) it is the concrete means of enacting a given configuration of values; and (ii) the resulting material unit is not, however, defined independently of 'the sense, the function' which it bears (*CLG*: 191).

4   The unifying principle which is at the basis of the grammatical system of a given language, rather than an *ad hoc* division into a separate morphology, lexis and syntax (*CLG*: 187), is the 'double system' of syntagmatic and associative contextualizing relations (Chapter 11). The resulting relationship of solidarity between grammatical form and function constitutes the means by which meanings are 'expressed', or made, by the users of a given language.

All of these characteristics are intrinsic to the grammatical systems of language. Syntagmatic and associative relations are the very basis of grammatical organization in *langue* (Chapter 11). Grammar is a system of potential signs. The system itself provides the semiotic means for relating signs to the world of human action and interaction. In this chapter, I shall explore and develop the implications of this claim further.

3 *LANGUE* AND THREE FUNDAMENTAL DIMENSIONS OF MEANING-MAKING

It is the mechanism of *langue* which provides the necessary conceptual framework for relating the instantiations of the system in *parole* to the system of *langue* in a systematic way (Chapter 11). Three additional concepts may be added to the above list. These are outlined below and will be discussed and developed in the remainder of this chapter. These are:

5   synchronic identity, schematicity, and prototypicality;
6   interstratal symbolic construal and systemic self-reference;
7   the contextual grounding of signs.

In the next three sections, I shall argue that 5, 6 and 7, respectively, provide the basis for a theory of three fundamental constituents of all acts of social meaning-making: viz. INTERTEXTUALITY, METASEMIOSIS, and GROUNDING (INDEXICALITY). As we shall see, all of these are built into the internal design features of *langue*.

4 SYNCHRONIC IDENTITY AND SCHEMATICITY

In Saussure's theory, the identity of a given type of linguistic unit is established on the basis of stable and invariant features which distinguish this unit from others in the same language system. These invariants are independent of material variations in phonic substance and in the subtle variations in meaning the unit may have in a given context. This is the principle which Saussure calls *synchronic identity*:

> When, in a lecture, one hears the word *Messieurs!* ['Gentlemen!'] repeated several times, one is aware that it is the same expression each time, and yet the variations in delivery and intonation present it, in its various passages, with very appreciable phonic differences – as appreciable as those which serve in other respects to distinguish different words (cf. *pomme* ['apple'] and *paume* ['palm'], *goutte* ['drop'] and *je goûte* ['I taste'], *fuir* ['to shun', 'avoid'] and *fouir* ['to dig'], etc.). Moreover, this feeling of identity persists, in spite of the fact that from the semantic point of view there is no absolute identity from one *Messieurs!* to the next, just as a word can express quite different ideas without its identity being seriously compromised (cf. '*adopter* une mode' ['to adopt a fashion'] and '*adopter* un enfant' ['to adopt a child'], 'la *fleur* du pommier' ['the flower of the apple tree'] and 'la *fleur* de la noblesse' ['the flower of the nobility'], etc.
>
> (*CLG*: 106–7)

The problem is this: how may the synchronic identity of a given linguistic unit be established in spite of the material and semantic variations it may display across many different contexts of use? In other words, what features are criterial to the synchronic identity of the unit in *langue*, and what are merely contingent, situational features in *parole*?

Synchronic identity depends on the dialectic of identity and difference (*CLG*: 151; Chapter 8, section 3). For Saussure, the establishment of correspondence relations between elements in the spoken chain and their concepts is different from the question of synchronic identity (see the above quote). This shows that for Saussure synchronic identity may not be established on the basis of the two-way interstratal symbolic construal relation that holds between signifier and signified. Synchronic identity poses a different kind of question: viz. how is any given instance in *parole* related to the more general type which defines its systemic identity in *langue*? This may be explained in terms of the varying degrees of correspondence which are evidenced between the general type (schema) and its instantiations (instance).

In spite of the many specific differences – both phonetic and semantic – which may distinguish any given use of, say, *Messieurs!* ('Gentlemen!') from one occasion to another, there is a core set of criterial features which remain the same from one occasion of use to another. The criterial features are schematic to any given instance (Langacker 1987: 58). The former are less specific than the latter. Synchronic identity establishes degrees of equivalence between Schema and Instance. The 'persistence' of this feeling of identity in spite of many material and contextual variations in its use is explainable by the fact that the criteria for establishing the identity of a given linguistic unit are always irreversibly mapped in one direction, that is, from Schema to Instance. Only the criterial features belonging to the Schema can define a given Instance as conforming to this or that type. This relationship is not reversible: individual and contextual variation-in-use is not criterial for the establishment of synchronic identity, however relevant this may be in a specific act of *parole*.

5 SYNCHRONIC IDENTITY: THE ANALYSIS OF A CONVENTIONAL UNIT

Consider the following example: *Animal tests pose dilemmas* (*Times Higher Education Supplement*, 11 February 1994, p. 3). In this brief, illustrative discussion, I shall focus on the noun *tests*. This word has a fully established synchronic identity in the lexicogrammar of English. In spite of the many different phonic, graphic and semantic variations in its use, it is possible to postulate a decontextualized formal or systemic value which remains invariant across the many different contexts in which the word is used. This is so irrespective of the semantic variation in instances such as *animal tests*, *driving tests*, *cricket tests*, *blood tests*, *English tests*, *eye tests* and so on. Synchronic identity means that it is possible to define a set of criteria to which a given occurrence will conform to a greater or lesser degree. Saussure's identity–difference dialectic means that a given instance may be fully identical to these criteria, or it may differ to some extent. The extent to which it differs is a matter of degree.

The notion of synchronic identity refers to the way in which the conventional specification is both more general and more abstract than its specific instantiations. This is the relationship which Langacker has defined as the Schema–Instance relation (1987: 166–8; Chapter 7, section 6; Chapter 8, section 3). Synchronic identity entails a categorizing judgement as to whether a specific instance conforms to, or is identical to, the criteria which are embodied in the higher-level Schema. Thus, it is possible to propose a higher-level [TEST] Schema which would be schematic to its instantiations, such as those referred to above. The Schema is both sufficiently general and sufficiently abstract to be able to define properties and attributes which are shared by all members of the category in question. The [TEST] Schema, for example, may be glossed as [CRITICAL EXAMINATION OF A PERSON'S OR THING'S QUALITIES AND PROPERTIES]. The Schema specifies the criterial features which are common to all of the uses cited above.

Langacker (1987: 68) rightly emphasises that the categorizing judgements which are entailed in the Schema-Instance relation are both a 'matter of degree' and of 'speaker judgement'. This is exactly Saussure's point in the quotation discussed above. This further entails that a given instance may, with respect to its Schema, be fully or partially in conformity with the criteria established by this. In the following section, I shall further illustrate this principle by focusing on a unit which only partially conforms to its Schema.

6 SYNCHRONIC IDENTITY: THE ANALYSIS OF A NON-CONVENTIONAL UNIT

Consider the following sentence from *Finnegans Wake*:

> Let us now, weather, health, dangers, public orders and other circumstances permitting, of perfectly convenient, if you police, after you, policepolice, pardoning mein, ich beim so fresch, bey?
>
> (James Joyce, *Finnegans Wake*, p. 113)

In particular, I shall briefly consider the syntagm *if you police*. Unlike *tests*, this is a non-conventional unit. It is maximally distinct from the criteria established by its schema. The syntagm in question does not meet fully the specifications of the schema on account of the non-conventional occurrence of the lexical item *police*. The schema may be glossed as follows: [IF + YOU + MODAL VERB]. Unproblematic, or fully conventional, instantiations of this schema, include *if you please*, *if you will*, and so on. The categorizing judgements entailed in these relations may be represented as in Figure 13.1. Following Langacker (1987: 68), the horizontal arrows going from left to right indicate the degree of conformity to the schema.

There is also an important link between synchronic identity and the notion of associative relations. I shall now explore this link in the lead-up to the discussion of intertextuality that I anticipated earlier.

7 ASSOCIATIVE RELATIONS, GRAMMAR AND SCHEMATICITY

Figure 13.1 shows that there may be more or less typical instantiations of a given grammatical category. Instantiations such as *if you please* are *proto-*

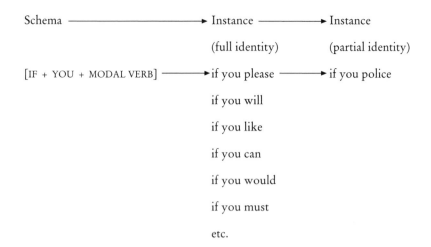

Figure 13.1 Synchronic identity and schema–instance relation

typical. A prototypical instantiation of a schematic category is one which can be referred to that category without ambiguity. That is, it fully conforms to all of the criteria established by the higher-order schema. Saussure's notion of associative relations is founded on this same principle. The indeterminate character of associative relations means that there is no absolute criterion for assigning a given linguistic unit to a given associative series. Again, the criteria for establishing membership of a series are graded.

The 'element common to all the terms' (*CLG*: 173) in a given associative series is the most schematic category on the basis of which a given instance may be assigned to a given series, or not. The common element refers to those features which all the terms in some series have in common, in spite of individual differences among the terms. That is, the individual members of a given series may conform to the schematic criterion to varying degrees. The 'family' basis of associative relations implicates that there is no definite or absolute boundary between one term and another (Chapter 11, section 4).

Importantly, the assignment of a given term to a particular associative series requires some criterion of co-classification. This is where associative relations make contact with grammar:

> To associate two forms is not only to feel that they have something in common, it is also to distinguish the nature of the relationships which govern the association. Thus, subjects are aware that the relationship which links *enseigner* ['to teach'] to *enseignement* ['teaching'] or *juger* ['to judge'] to *jugement* ['judgement'] is not the same as that which holds between *enseignement* and *jugement* (see pp. 173ff.). It is in this way that the system of associations is linked to that of the grammar. It may be said that the sum of the conscious and methodical classifications made by the

grammarian who studies a state of the language system without letting history intervene must coincide with the sum of the associations, conscious or not, which are brought into play in *parole*. It is these associations which establish in our mind word families, flectional paradigms, formative elements: roots, suffixes, declensions, etc. (see pp. 253ff.).

(*CLG*: 189)

It is necessary, as Saussure points out, to specify the nature of the relationships which govern a given associative series. This is where grammar comes in. Thus, if any two (or more) terms, A and B, are, at some level of schematicity, both members of the same associative series, then they are both members of the same schematic category. That is, they both have in common some classifying feature, x, which is common to all of the terms potentially assignable to the same series. A given term may, as Saussure points out (*CLG*: 174), belong to more than one series, simultaneously. In one sense, an associative series may be seen as a typology. Type feature x is the superordinate, or schematic, term in a taxonomic hierarchy. In relation to A and B, x is a higher-level term in the sense that it is both more general and more abstract than the lower-level terms that are defined by it (Chapter 3, section 3).

8 DEFINING PROTOTYPICALITY: A RE-ANALYSIS OF SAUSSURE'S EXAMPLE *DÉFAIRE*

Saussure's discussion of *défaire* (*CLG*: 178; Chapter 11, section 3) demonstrates the principle of classification referred to in the preceding paragraph. As Saussure points out, *défaire* is analysed from the point of view of the associative series which intersect in this particular syntagm, seen from the point of view of the spoken chain in *parole*. For this reason, his analysis reveals that *dé-* and *-faire* are the two 'common elements' in the two associative series that come into play in this syntagm. However, this does not in itself reveal the schematic categories, or terms, which lie 'behind' the various members of the two series. In the series defined by *dé-*, for example, all the members – *défaire, décoller, déplacer* and so on – are *prototypical* instantiations of the schematic category that defines the series.

The notion of prototypicality should not be confused with the different, though related, notion of schematicity. The point is that the individual members of the series referred to are all prototypical instantiations of the still higher-level schematic category. That is, they all unambiguously conform to the criteria of the schematic category. The prototypical does not, therefore, refer to that which is most abstract and general. That is the province of schematicity. Instead, prototypicality refers to a more specific level in the overall categorizing hierarchy. *Défaire* is a prototypical instantiation of its higher-level schematic categories. The notion of prototypicality is cognate with *langue*$_2$: it refers to the 'usual' or typical grammatical patterns in the language system. That is, *langue*$_2$ refers to the prototypical instantiations of the higher-level schemata of *langue*$_1$ as regular grammatical models. This is why Saussure is at pains to point out from the start that the mechanism of the language system is concerned with syntagmatic and associative *groups*, rather than with the schematic terms – phonic and conceptual – of *langue*$_1$ *per se* (Chapter 11, section 1).

Saussure's decision to use a concrete syntagm such as *défaire* in order to illustrate his point may have a sound pedagogical purpose; however, it does somewhat hinder the attempt to grasp the various levels of schematicity that are involved in the analysis. This is so in the sense that he uses a concrete unit such as *défaire* to refer to both prototypical instantiations as well as to concrete units in the spoken chain. Consequently, the various levels of schematicity that are involved in his analysis are not sufficiently distinguished. I shall now re-construct the schematic categories of which *défaire*, *découdre* and so on, are prototypical instantiations.

The linguistic unit *dé-* is a morphemic prefix which functions as a premodifier of the verb stem. As attested by a very large number of verbs in French which have this prefix, it functions to negate the meaning of the lexicalized verb stem: for example, *défaire* means to 'undo', *découdre* 'to unpick', *détacher* 'to untie' or 'to loosen', *déplacer* 'to displace' or 'to transfer', *décoller* 'to unstick' and so on. The schematic categories or terms which intersect in *dé-* may be glossed as follows: [MORPHEMIC PREFIX: PREMODIFICATION OF VERB STEM: NEGATION].

The verb stem *faire* is a little more complicated. This French verb may, depending on context, signify either that something was done to an already pre-existing entity, or that something which did not previously exist was creatively brought into existence. In English, this distinction is lexicalized by the difference between *do* and *make*. Consider, for example, the difference between *He did his homework* and *He made a cake*, where *do* is intentional and *make* is causative. I shall distinguish between *faire*$_1$ and *faire*$_2$, in this sense.

Saussure's analysis shows that it is the 'do' meaning of *faire*$_1$ which is relevant to his example. This is evidenced by the various instantiations he proposes. Thus, *défaire* means 'to undo', 'to take down', 'to dismantle', 'to unpack', 'to unfasten', etc., *refaire* 'to do again' or 'to redo', *contrefaire* 'to imitate', 'to mime', 'to disguise', 'to counterfeit' and so on. In all of these verbs, it is the intentional 'do' meaning that comes to the fore. The focus is on the agent who intentionally performs an action on something which already exists. These verbs do not designate the causal or creative bringing into existence of something which did not previously exist. This is reinforced by the presence of the negative prefix *dé-*. All of these compound verbs refer to the negation of some already-existing state of affairs. Something has to exist already before it can be untied, undone, dismantled, imitated, forged and so on. Thus, *faire₁* may be glossed as follows: [MORPHEMIC VERB STEM; AGENT: INTENTIONAL; MODALITY: REALIS]. By way of contrast, *faire₂* may be glossed as [MORPHEMIC VERB STEM; AGENT: CAUSATIVE; MODALITY: IRREALIS].

In French, as in English, the most schematic category in the experiential grammar of the clause is the effective two-participant structure which is realized by the configuration of functional values [AGENT^PROCESS^ AFFECTED]. In the case of material action clauses, this high-level schematic category is instantiated by lower-level 'transitive' and 'ergative' structures. The transitive model is realized by the configuration of values [ACTOR^PRO-CESS^GOAL]; the ergative model by the configuration [INSTIGATOR^PRO-CESS^MEDIUM]. Both of these categories are further differentiated into still more specific categories. It is at this lower level that the prototypical instantiations are found (Davidse 1991: 14). In French, *faire₁* instantiates the transitive prototype. This refers to the intentional acting-on-that-which-already-exists, in order to achieve some goal: for example, *J'ai fait ma valise* ('I have packed my suitcase'). *Faire₂* instantiates the ergative prototype, which is concerned with the causal bringing-into-existence of some pre-viously non-existent state or process: for example, *Le professeur fera lire les élèves* ('The teacher will make the pupils read').

To return to Saussure's analysis of *défaire*, we may now specify the higher-level schematic terms in relation to their prototypical instantiations, as in Figure 13.2.

9 ASSOCIATIVE RELATIONS AND INTERTEXTUALITY: A TEXTUAL ANALYSIS

Associative relations can fully accommodate the taxonomic relations entailed by schematicity. Yet the fact that associative relations necessarily make contact with the grammar of the language if they are to be enacted in *parole*

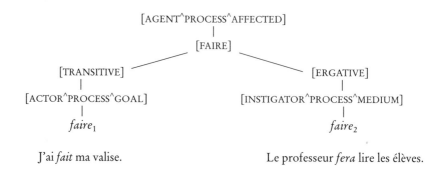

Figure 13.2 Transitive and ergative instantiations of *faire* in relation to higher-order schematic categories in *langue₁*

somewhat broadens this perspective. The basic question is the following: what are the typical ways in which the various associative relations and groups are formed in the language system? In *langue*, the members of any given series constitute an arbitrary set. But in particular texts, these typical relations are deployed in ways which specify how the items in a given textual syntagm are relevant to each other's interpretation. This is already clear enough in Saussure's analysis of lower-level syntagms such as *défaire*. Social agents draw on and deploy their knowledge – conscious or not – of typical associative relations in order to contextualize the specific items which occur in syntagms of all sizes. To illustrate this, let us consider the following text:

> (1a) Cosmic strings are one example of a topological defect in the cosmos, (1b) and certainly the most famous. (2a) The concept of topological defects concerns symmetry, (2b) and how it is sometimes broken. (3) Water is a good example: (4a) If you are submerged, (4b) water looks exactly the same in all directions; (4c) it has no structure. (5a) When water freezes into ice, (5b) it has a different symmetry. (6a) Ice consists of long crystal lattices of atoms (6b) that are oriented in specific directions. (7a) The water's degree of symmetry is related to its temperature, (7b) and at certain temperatures water undergoes 'phase transitions' (7c) when it turns from liquid into ice.
>
> (George Smoot and Keay Davidson, *Wrinkles in Time*, p. 167)

This short text is a paragraph from a book about the authors' experimental research on the 'big bang' theory of the origin and evolution of the cosmos. It aims to present modern theories of cosmology to the scientifically informed lay reader.

Most of the clauses in the text are relational clauses. The exceptions are the material processes in clauses 5a, 7b and 7c. Relational clauses link two grammatical entities in the clause in a logical relation of *elaboration*. One linguistic entity further specifies or describes (elaborates) the other entity. Typically, in English the copula verb *be* is the means of construing the logical relation of elaboration between the two entities. However, a large number of other verbs are also involved (Davidse 1992). There are two main subtypes of relational processes: (1) attribution and (2) identification.

In attributive clauses, a quality or attribute is assigned to an entity, as in *We were ready for flight*. Here, the quality or attribute *ready for flight* is attributed to *We*. In so doing, it further specifies, or semantically 'elaborates', *We*. Semantically, *We* is the Carrier of the Attribute, *ready for flight*.

In identifying clauses, two co-referential entities are logically equated with each other in such a way that one entity provides an alternative semantic gloss on the other. Consider *In 1978, the thirty-one-year-old Alan Guth was a research fellow at Cornell*. In this clause, the two entities, *the thirty-one-year-old Alan Guth* and *a research fellow at Cornell* refer to the same referent. The second entity provides an alternative semantic gloss on the first.

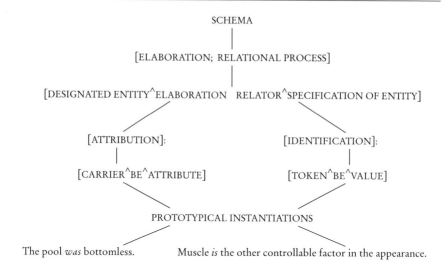

Figure 13.3 Schematic categories and prototypical instantiations of elaborating relational clauses

Semantically, the second assigns a semantic Value to the first (the Token). The Value is a semiotic re-interpretation of the referent entity (the Token) (Halliday 1994: 124–38).

Prototypically, attribution and identification are instantiations of the same higher-order schematic category. This relationship of prototypical instantiation is represented in Figure 13.3. The link that Saussure makes between associative relations and grammar is based on functional criteria concerning the values which different forms may have in common:

> But does association only emerge from material elements? No, not at all; we know already that it relates words linked only by their sense (cf. *enseignement* ['teaching'], *apprentissage* ['apprenticeship'], *éducation* ['education'], etc.); it must be the same in grammar: take the three Latin genitives: *domin-i* ['of a master'], *reg-is* ['of a king'], *ros-arum* ['of roses']; the sounds of the three declensions afford nothing in common which may be taken as the basis of an association; but they are, however, linked by the awareness of a common value which imposes an identical use; this is enough to create an association in the absence of any material support, and it is in this way that the notion of the genitive in itself takes root in the language system. It is through an entirely similar procedure that the flectional declensions *-us, -i, -o,* etc. (in *dominus, domini, domino,* etc.) are linked in consciousness and that the more general notion of case emerges. Associations of the same kind, but more general in scope, link all substantives, all adjectives, etc., and determine the notion of the parts of speech.
>
> (*CLG*: 189–90)

This makes it possible to specify the associative relations belonging to *langue* and those that are relevant to the interpretation of a single text according to the same principles. That is, it is not just words that form associative relations, but also, and more importantly, grammatical relations. A continuum from text-specific to *langue*-based associative relations may be postulated. That is, the particular grammatical relation in a given text is also a typical selection of the same relation in a given wider intertextual system (Lemke 1983). For example, clause 2a in the text on page 313 is an identifying relational process. In this clause, one grammatical entity, *The concept of topological defects*, is semantically re-construed or re-defined in terms of a second entity with which it is co-referential: viz. *symmetry, and how it is sometimes broken*. Here, it is the verb *concerns*, rather than *be*, which construes the logical–semantic relationship. There is no need to multiply the examples here. The point is that the use of linguistic selections such as relational processes to specify and define abstract theoretical entities, abstract lexical taxonomies, and nominalization are all typical of this semantic variety of English, as well as in many other languages (Halliday 1988).

The lexicogrammatical choices in a given text do not simply contribute to the syntagmatic construction and integration of that text. They also serve to index the typical systems of associative relations which this particular text has potentially in common with many others in some wider intertextual set (Lemke 1983). This is another way of saying that the grammatical choices of the single text index its relations to a wider system of intertextual relations in a given speech community. Associative relations are, then, inherently INTERTEXTUAL. This is so in two interrelated senses: first, the making of signs in texts depends, in part, on the associative relations that are specific to that text (Chapter 11, section 5); second, these text-specific associative relations are always assigned their meaning and value in relation to still wider, typical systems of relations, which form part of a given intertextual set in a particular community. In this way, we see how the stable core values of the language system, as represented in its schematic categories and their prototypical instantiations, are deployed as contextually specific meanings in the making and re-making of these resources in acts of *parole*.

10 SCHEMATICITY AND VISUAL SEMIOSIS

The principle of synchronic identity, or schematicity, also operates in the grammar of the visual. In the semiotics of depiction, lines and connections, junctions and intersections of lines constitute a fundamental signifying resource. On the level of the signified, these are re-construed as specific types of visual forms which realize, among other things, a visual semantics of 'equilibrium' vs. 'dynamism'. The grammar of this particular area of the visual semiotic is comprised of orientated lines of tension. It may be represented as an associative group of schematic categories, as shown in

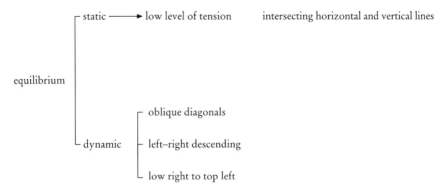

Figure 13.4 Associative group of visual schema; static vs. dynamic equilibrium

Figure 13.4. Depiction, which includes drawing, painting, photography and so on, is not a record of sense data perceived by the observer. It is, instead, a record of informational invariants which are extracted from the optic ambient array (Gibson 1986 [1979]: 273–4). Depiction is not, then, a mere description or re-presentation of the sense impressions received by the observer; rather, it is a textual record of invariants in the optic ambient array, relative to a point of observation (Gibson 1986 [1979]: 284). The person who draws, paints, photographs or whatever uses the schematic resources of the visual grammar. It does not matter whether the drawer or painter actually experienced the scene or simply imagined it. As with the linguistic semiotic, the visual schemata we are considering here are conventional units in a grammar of visual forms. They are higher-order visual categories in the sense that they are both more general and more abstract than their specific instantiations in actual drawings, paintings and so on. Visual schema, no less than their linguistic counterparts, specify the criterial, rather than the specific, features of the visual categories in question.

Consider now the visual text in Figure 13.5. This figure shows the child's ability to synthesize and co-ordinate a number of invariants that are *typical* of the objects depicted. Forms and colours are simple, regular and symmetrical. The scene is depicted with a minimal number of structural elements of visual forms, which are, nevertheless, co-ordinated to form a composite visual text. The text is not, however, a copy or a replica of some act of perception. At the time this drawing was made, the child, who is the author's daughter, was attending the first year of elementary school in Bologna, Italy. Part of her previous experience included a period of living in Sydney, Australia. The house depicted in Figure 13.5 is not typical of the kinds of dwellings normally seen in Italian cities, but more typical of those seen in the suburbs of Australian cities.

Whatever the factual basis of the child's picture, it is not a copy of a perception. The picture in Figure 13.5 shows that the child has acquired the basic principles of a more abstract visual grammar. This is evident not only in the bilateral symmetry of the house and the tree, but also in the spatial relations which connect the various objects in the picture to each other in a co-ordinated spatial frame of reference. Sky and ground are schematized as horizontal lines of blue and green, located respectively at the top and bottom of the visual frame.

The abstract grammatical schema which prevails in Figure 13.5 is a grid based on horizontal and vertical lines, as shown in Figure 13.6. The internal equilibrium is one of harmony. It is orientated to the maximum level of stability, as shown by the use of the grammatical schema in Figure 13.6. The scene depicted in Figure 13.5 is primarily based on this schematic principle of the visual grammar. This accounts for its harmonious and symmetrical characteristics.

On the other hand, a picture which uses the schematic principle of oblique lines, as in Figure 13.7, produces a different type of equilibrium. This is no longer static, but dynamic. In the child's picture of the robot, which formed part of a narrative text composed of pictures and words, there is an interplay of diagonals which intersect in the middle section of the robot. The symmetry of the middle section contrasts with the diagonal lines that are

Figure 13.5 Child's schematic drawing of a house
Source: Ilaria, age 5.0

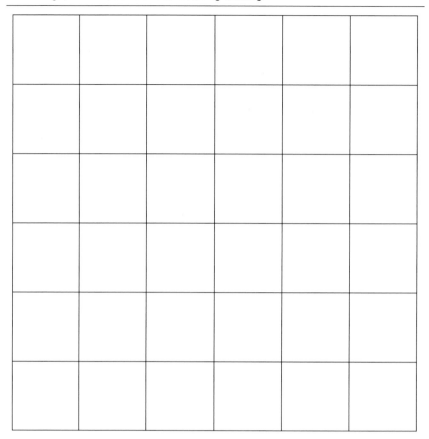

Figure 13.6 Grammatical schema; static equilibrium

projected from the prominent legs of the robot. The diagonals are counter-posed to the horizontal–vertical lines of the head and torso. It is this counterpointing of stability and dynamism which creates the dramatic appearance of the robot. The grammatical schema at work here is shown in Figure 13.8. A further illustration of the use of diagonal lines to create dynamism is shown in the photograph which is reproduced in Figure 13.9. In this case, the abstract schema is as shown in Figure 13.10. In this figure the convergence of the diagonal lines of force, projected from the eyes of the various participants to the incipient handshake between former US President, John F. Kennedy, and former Soviet Premier, Nikita Khruschev, highlights the dynamism and the dramatic significance of the scene.

All of the categorical visual schemata that I have referred to here constitute part of the grammar of the (western) visual semiotic of depiction. That is, they constitute some of the available visual resources for making meanings in and through visual texts. Like the grammar of language, the visual

Figure 13.7 Child's picture of a robot, showing use of oblique lines
Source: Ilaria, age 5.0

grammar, seen from the system perspective, is arbitrary in the sense discussed in Chapter 12. That is, the abstract schemata are non-specific and are not grounded in specific textual instances. They are schematic categories of visual forms. By definition, these type categories of visual forms are both more general and more abstract, hence less detailed, than actual instances. They are conventional visual forms and, for this reason, are arbitrary. It is only when these forms are selected and combined in the making of actual textual meanings that they are motivated. Figures 13.11a and 13.11b are line drawings of the 'same' scene. They are taken from a textbook used in Italian elementary schools. I shall focus on a single feature in the depicted scene: that is, the direction in which the river flows in Figures 13.11a and 13.11b. The person who drew these line drawings has used a series of oblique lines which

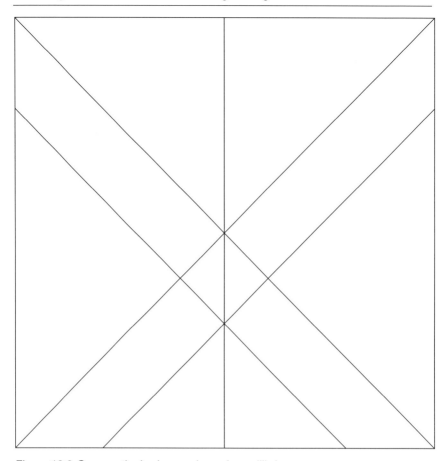

Figure 13.8 Grammatical schema; dynamic equilibrium

function to construct a preferred viewing perspective. These lines, or vectors, invite the viewer to direct his or her gaze from the lower right of the frame, which appears to be nearer to the viewer's own point of observation, towards the top left of the frame. This constructs the visual perspective of the river, which is construed as flowing away from the viewer and in the direction of the distant horizon. The impression of the river which moves obliquely away from the observer is constructed by the artist and re-construed by the viewer on the basis of a particular semiotic convention concerning the use of lines. In the visual grammar, the most schematic way of recording this invariant is a series of oblique lines 'moving' from the bottom right of the frame to the top left, as shown in Figure 13.12. Figure 13.12 is proposed as a schematic representation of this particular type category in the grammar of visual forms. Figures 13.11a and 13.11b, on the other hand, are instantiations of the schematic category. Both Figures 13.11a

Figure 13.9 Photograph showing use of diagonals to create dynamism
Source: Il Manifesto, 9 October 1994, p. 25

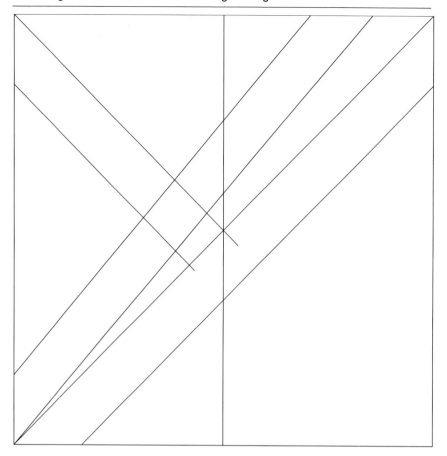

Figure 13.10 Grammatical schema; converging diagonals

and 13.11b may be said to be fully schematic with respect to the particular visual category in question: that is, they fully conform to the criteria specified by the schema. The fact that there are obvious differences of detail between the two drawings does not alter this fact. In Saussure's sense, this means that there is a relation of synchronic identity between these two instances and the schematic category shown in Figure 13.12. That is, the drawings in Figures 13.11a and 13.11b are both prototypical instantiations of the same schematic visual category.

11 STRATIFICATION, SELF-REFERENCE AND METASEMIOSIS

The stratified nature of semiosis hinges on a specific issue: a given order of difference – phonic or conceptual – in the language system is used to act on and construe the other order. Language is inherently self-referential in this

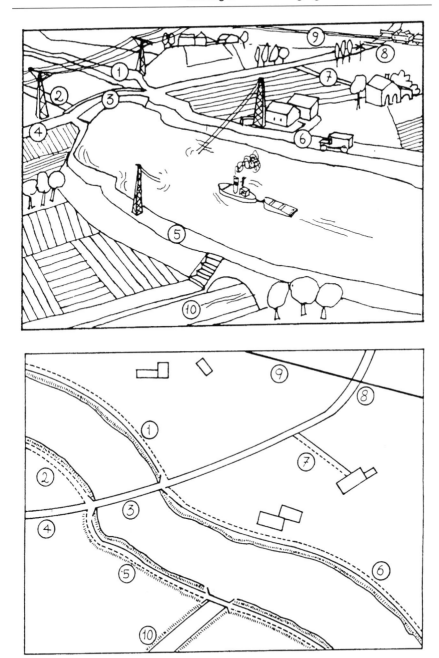

Figure 13.11 Use of oblique lines to create perspective
Source: Danieli, *Quaderno di lavoro 5*, p. 13

Figure 13.12 Grammatical schema; oblique lines to create perspective

sense: one order 'translates' the other. The two-way nature of this process means that it is possible to look at it from the perspective of either the phonic or the conceptual orders. Whichever perspective is adopted, the conclusion is the same: a social-semiological system such as *langue* necessarily includes self-reference as one of its properties. The construal of one order of difference by the other embodies a principle of semiotic order. In other words, the 'two orders of coordination', as Saussure (*CLG*: 171) designates the dual system of syntagmatic and associative relations in *langue*, are the means by which the system self-reflexively acts upon and construes itself. Saussure also points out that the dual system of syntagmatic and associative relations 'preside[s] over' the functioning of the mechanism of *langue* (*CLG*: 176). The 'two orders of coordination' provide the metasemiotic resources for self-reflexively acting upon and imposing order on the 'ensemble of phonic and conceptual differences'.

This may appear to lock us into a closed circle. There is, however, a way out of this seeming impasse. As we saw in Chapter 2, Saussure is concerned to 'show the linguist what he does'. What the linguist does is to formalize instances of *parole* in order to re-construct, analytically speaking, the social-semiological system of *langue*. By the same token, *langue* is the metatheoretical means by which the linguist reflects on and analyses acts of *parole*. This is abundantly clear in the many analyses which Saussure provides in the chapter entitled 'Mechanism of the language system': in any given analysis, the linguist always starts with concrete words, phrases and so on in the spoken chain of *parole*.

Nevertheless, Saussure's praxis as a linguist also means that he can use, analytically speaking, the 'two orders of coordination' in order both to reflect on and to act upon the 'ensemble of phonic and conceptual differences' (*CLG*: 176). *Langue*, as I pointed out in Chapter 3, has a dual status as both analytical construct and systemic resource. Saussure points out that this 'ensemble' is the result of 'two sorts of comparison': syntagmatic and associative relations. Now, 'comparison' is a process noun; it implies an act of comparing and, therefore, an agent who performs this act. The linguist is one such agent. The linguist is interested in re-constructing the system in the way referred to above. Saussure's discussion of the ways in which linguistic units are delimited in the spoken chain is a concrete demonstration of this (Chapter 9, section 5). In that discussion, he shows how the two strata of the sign relation are not pre-given; rather, the phonological units and structures in the spoken chain of the signifier are re-construed as grammatical units and structures on the stratum of the signified. This shows how the linguist self-reflexively uses the resources of the system both to act on and to reflect on the system in order to analyse it.

12 STRATIFICATION AND THE MAKING OF MEANING IN DIALOGUE: THE PRAXIS OF THE LANGUAGE USER

The linguist is not the only person to have this experience of language. These same processes of interstratal construal and re-construal also occur in the negotiation of meaning in dialogue. Here is a short example, taken from a much longer conversation between two female speakers:

SPEAKER A: (1) does that bother you?
SPEAKER B: (2a) yeah (2b) it really does
SPEAKER A: (3) that's when you know it's time to get out
SPEAKER B: (4) right

This brief exchange is transcribed from a documentary film about a brothel in Texas. The transcribed text is part of a very long conversation between two of the prostitutes who work in the brothel. The conversation takes place shortly after speaker B has announced her intention to quit working at the brothel.

I shall focus on the mood selections in the above dialogue. Mood is a grammatical category (Chapter 3, section 7). In the grammar of English, the system of mood contributes a layer of meaning to the negotiation of speech act moves in discourse. In the analysis, I have designated each move with a number. A speech act, on the other hand, is a semantic interpretation of some co-patterning of lexicogrammatical and other selections at, say, clause level in discourse. There is, however, no fixed or one-to-one correlation between grammatical form and function. Saussure's notion of 'solidary' does not imply this. A mood category such as 'declarative' may very often be straightforwardly interpreted as a Statement. However, the often complex meanings of speech acts may not be derived on the basis of a one-to-one fit between any given grammatical choice and the meaning the speech act has in discourse. In discourse, a number of selections from different associative groups in the grammar may be relevant to the meaning of the speech act (Chapter 12, section 8, text analysis I). Language users interpret the grammatical selections in clauses and other units with respect to the functional role they play in the making and negotiating of meanings in discourse (Martin 1991: 115; 1992: Ch. 2; Thibault and Van Leeuwen 1996). For this reason, the signified is itself internally stratified as 'two meaning making levels' (Martin: 1991: 114; see also Figure 13.14 below). That is, there is, in the signified, (1) a layer of co-patterned lexicogrammatical units and relations deriving from various associative groups in the grammar of the language and (2) their interpretation according to the semantic functions that are attributed to these in discourse (Chapter 9, section 5). Let us see how this works in the brief exchange under consideration here.

Move 1 selects interrogative mood. A more delicate analysis will reveal that it is more than just a question, or a demand for information. The lexical verb *bother* constructs a particular axiological, or modal, orientation, which the speaker invites the addressee to identify with. This axiological dimension becomes clearer if one thinks of the quite different modal stances which alternative selections, such as *please*, *anger*, *irritate*, *worry* and so on, in some associative series would entail.

Line 2 comprises two submoves. Each of these could have occurred on its own as a satisfactory response to move 1. However, the occurrence of both of these follows a typical pattern in spoken discourse: each responds to and negotiates a particular strand of the meaning potential which is co-patterned in the previous speaker's move. Thus, move 2a responds to the mood selection in move 1, which is [INTERROGATIVE: POLAR]. In so doing, it resolves that strand of the meaning potential of move 1 which requires a yes/

no type response. Move 2b, on the other hand, takes up and negotiates a further dimension of the meaning potential of move 1. Specifically, clause 2b responds to the modal orientation in the lexical verb *bother*. The speaker of 2b, in selecting the modal adjunct *really*, indicates a high degree of subjective commitment to the axiological orientation expressed by *bother* in the previous speaker's move. Again, this is clearer if contrasted with alternative modal values, such as *possibly, regrettably, probably* and so on. All of these would express a different axiological orientation from the one selected.

Move 3 is a complex form comprising a number of levels of embedded structure. I shall concentrate on the outermost (non-embedded) level. Here, *that* carries the semantic feature Token, to which its speaker assigns the semantic Value *when you know it's time to get out* (section 9 above).

Move 3 may be glossed as a Response Statement to Statement. The speaker, having attained the previous speaker's assent to the modal orientation proposed in move 1, now orientates the exchange towards a specific course of action. In other words, the speaker of move 3 implicitly recommends or prescribes a course of action that her interlocutor should follow. But note that move 3 selects declarative mood. Semantically, recommendation and prescription are subtypes of Command. Typically, a command selects for imperative mood, as in the clause *Get out!* Commands may, however, be realized in a variety of ways other than by imperative mood. In actual fact, move 3 may be construed as both a Statement and a Command. In this case, the Command interpretation is deeply embedded in the clause as the non-finite verb *to get out*, which is hypotactically dependent on the noun *time*. Dependent clauses such as *to get out* do not independently select for grammatical mood. That is the task of the independent clause, such as *that's when* ... etc. in our example. This means that the semantics of the Command are presented by the speaker as non-negotiable: that is, a command to act in a certain way is 'dressed up' as a Statement. This is only one possible interpretation, though it seems a highly likely one here. The speaker of this move, it should not be forgotten, is not the one who is 'getting out'; she will continue to work in the brothel. From this point of view, she is stating her commitment to a certain re-evaluation of her addressee. In effect, her addressee is being subtly re-classified as an outsider – one who no longer shares in the norms of this particular interpersonal moral order by virtue of her decision to quit.

Move 4 can be interpreted as Response Statement to Statement. Again, this does not go far enough. The modal adjunct *right* expresses the speaker's modal orientation to the previous move. She not only agrees with the propositional content of move 3; she also assents to the modal 'rightness' of the particular course of action which has been proposed. In agreeing that it is time to 'get out', she has implicitly separated herself from the interpersonal moral order of the brothel.

A move contributes to the negotiation of meaning on the discourse stratum. It is a re-construal of the meaning-making potential of the lexicogrammatical forms which speakers select and co-pattern in the real-time negotiation of meanings in discourse. In discursive interaction, language users selectively attend to the meaning potential of lexicogrammatical form. Meaning is not already fixed in these. This is a consequence of the process of re-interpreting the stratum of lexicogrammatical form in relation to the functional values these have on the discourse stratum. However, speakers and listeners do not do this on the basis of isolated features of language form. Instead, it is particular co-patternings of lexicogrammatical, and other semiotic, forms which are interpreted as signifying this or that move, and are responded to accordingly. That is, a given syntagmatic solidarity is attributed its functional value in relation to its role in the making of text (Chapter 12, section 8).

Discourse functions are not, then, alien to the forms that speakers and listeners jointly deploy and interpret in discourse. The goals, plans, intentions, attitudes and so on of language users do not pre-exist discourse or push it along from the outside. Instead, they are an aspect of the signified substance which speakers and listeners attribute to each other in and through the semiotic forms with which conversation is jointly constructed and negotiated. The relation between language form and function is an open and adaptable one. Rather than emphasizing a closed and autonomous language system with fixed or 'literal' form–function correspondences, Saussure's social-semiological theory of language allows a different kind of question to be put: viz. what functions does language have in its typical contexts of use, and what are the forms which express these?

13 STRATIFICATION AND THE PRAXIS OF THE LINGUIST

In the examples which Saussure analyses, we see the concrete application of this principle in the re-construction of the syntagmatic and associative relations and interdependencies which give rise to particular linguistic units. In the case of *défaire* and other examples, Saussure shows how the starting point of the analysis is 'a horizontal ribbon corresponding to the spoken chain' (*CLG*: 178). But, Saussure continues, it is only on the basis of the associative series which can be established in relation to the spoken chain that linguistic units 'can be decomposed into subunits, or in other words, are syntagms' (*CLG*: 178). Neither associative relations nor syntagms are simply given. Saussure's analysis of *défaire* illustrates the principle that a stratum of signified form – the two morphemes comprising this word – can be construed in the 'horizontal ribbon of the spoken chain'. The latter is, of course, the phonological stratum of the signifier. The signified is not simply already given in the lower-level stratum. It is only in relation to the dual system of contextualizing relations in *langue* that phonic differences in the spoken chain are re-construed as conceptual differences. That is, the system of contextualizing relations is used to construe a given phonic event as an instance of a sign of a given type.

It also includes the praxis of the language user who deploys, consciously or not, these same resources so as to impose semiotic order on the ensemble of phonic and conceptual differences in the process of making and negotiating meanings in discourse. As Saussure's analyses show, a scientific theory of language must go beyond our everyday perception and understanding of language in use (Chapter 5, section 4). The linguist is required to develop high-level abstractions and categories which do not remain limited by our conscious awareness of everyday language use and our explanations of it.

14 THE STRATIFIED NATURE OF LINGUISTIC AND VISUAL SEMIOSIS

In both linguistic and visual semiosis, a full-fledged tristratal principle of semiotic organization is evidenced. The stratum of the signified is internally stratified so that a level of grammatical organization is inserted between the semantic and phenomenal–material levels of the prior system.

In the visual semiotic, the stratum of the signifier corresponds to the phenomenal–material level of the object which is seen. This is a treated surface which comprises a certain number of regions with differing rates of absorption and reflection of the incident light rays. Such a surface gives rise to the modulation of the light in which the information concerning the chromatic and spatial structure of the surface is contained. On the phenomenal–material level of that which is perceived, the visual signifier comprises a number of regions which are distinguished in clarity and colour, as well as being separated by margins that indicate the transition from one type of informational invariant to another (Kanizsa 1991: 84). These volumes are related to other volumes by distributed lines of tension, or vectors, which interact both with each other and with the frame to create an effect of equilibrium or dynamism (Lazotti 1990: 103). The resulting grammatical schemata constitute the basis of the visual structuring and construing of the experiential world of phenomena. As in language, the experiential grammar of the visual organizes the world of experience into culturally specific classifications of happenings, events, doings, the participants who take part in these, and the circumstances that pertain to them. These visual signifieds, no less than their linguistic counterparts, do not directly 'refer' to the real world; rather, they construe culturally salient visual categories for acting on and interpreting the world.

Theoretically speaking, the situation is analogous to language itself. If the visual semiotic were no more than a reflection of external reality, it would mean that any given visual image would have to be uniquely tied to some referent situation. That this is not the case testifies to the fact that the principles for the making of visual meanings are internal to the visual semiotic itself. That is, there is a grammar of visual forms which may be

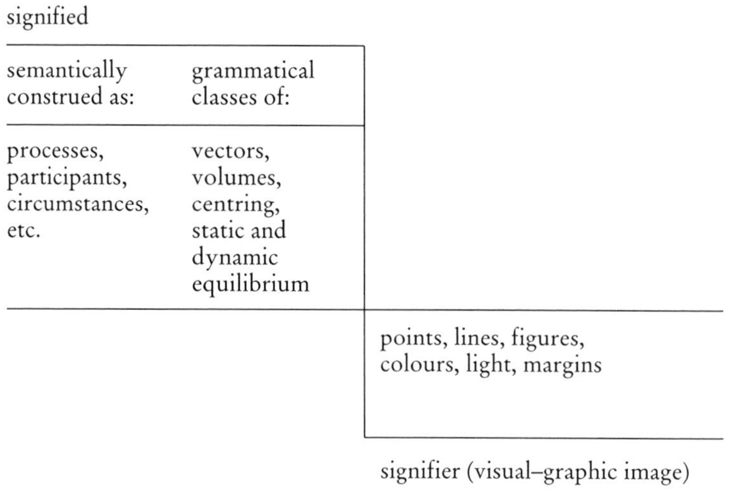

signified

semantically construed as:	grammatical classes of:
processes, participants, circumstances, etc.	vectors, volumes, centring, static and dynamic equilibrium

points, lines, figures, colours, light, margins

signifier (visual–graphic image)

Figure 13.13 Tristratal organization of the visual–graphic sign; experiential meaning only

specified systemically according to the metasemiological principles which Saussure sought to establish for language (Kress and Van Leeuwen 1990, 1996; O'Toole 1994).

The tristratal organization of the visual and linguistic semiotic may be compared, as in Figures 13.13 and 13.14. In the case of depiction, the visual grammar is comprised of visual forms such as vectors, lines of tension, volumes and principles of symmetry and asymmetry, which enter into structural relations with each other in the visual image. It is a particular configuration or distribution of such visual forms which establishes a dynamic pattern of tensions within a frame or border (Kanizsa 1991: 186). It is on the basis of such patternings of visual forms that the viewer–reader produces the meaning of a given visual text (Lazotti 1990: 103).

Visual forms have a semantic potential in the visual semiotic. Just as nominal groups tend to realize various types of semantic participant (Actor, Goal, etc.) in the clause grammar of the linguistic semiotic, so, too, do principles of volume and the relations between volumes tend to realize analogous semantic participants in the visual semiotic (Kress and Van Leeuwen 1990: 63–87).

In the linguistic grammar, the nominal group is a grammatical class item. It has a certain structural–functional potential, depending on the particular clause-level configuration of process–participant relations that it takes part in. Similarly, a volume is a form in the visual grammar. It has a structural–functional potential which depends on the particular configuration in which it occurs: for example, the configuration of a volume with a vector in the visual grammar realizes the visual analogue of the semantic relation

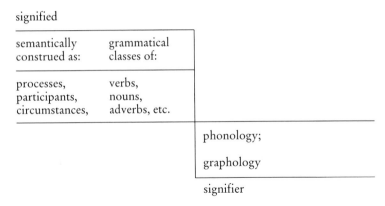

Figure 13.14 Tristratal organization of the linguistic sign; experiential meaning only

Actor^Process. Figure 13.15 illustrates this relationship. The group of soldiers form a single volume, as indicated by the homogeneity of size, shape and density of lighting with respect to the other visual regions which are distinguished (the deck of the aircraft carrier, the jet fighter, etc.). Their rifles form a single vector, or a line of force, which extends from the soldiers and may extend to a second volume, or not. Volumes are visual forms that signify semantic participants of various types. Vectors signify semantic processes. The configuration of volume (the soldiers) plus vector (their rifles) in Figure 13.15 signifies a visual semantic structure of the type [ACTOR^PROCESS: MATERIAL: INTENTIONAL]. This is a one-participant actional process.

Figure 13.15 may be compared with Figure 13.16. In this figure, the vector extends to a second volume, which is the recipient of the action signified by the vector. Figure 13.16 signifies the visual semantic structure [ACTOR^PRO-CESS: MATERIAL ACTION^GOAL]. It signifies a two-participant actional process.

In the two photographs in Figure 13.17, on the other hand, the close-up of the face in each of these two photographs signifies the visual equivalent of a *mental* process. These have been little studied in the visual semiotic (but see Guterres 1992: 131–2). Mental processes consist of the semantic configuration [Senser^Process: Mental^Phenomenon]. The 'worried' expression on the face, the position of the hand and the absence of an outwardly extended vector from the eyes to some object in the field of the participant's vision suggest a focus on 'inner' subjective states of consciousness.

How, then, do we explain the stratified nature of the linguistic sign? The language system is a stratified reality which produces meanings in and through the interactions among the various levels of its organization, as well as the ways in which these interact with the world. At the same time, it is also the metasemiotic means for analysing the stratified reality of language itself.

Figure 13.15 Military exercise on an American aircraft carrier in the Adriatic; configuration of volume and vector to realize the Actor^Process relation in the visual image

Source: Il Manifesto, 30 May 1995, p. 4

Figure 13.16 Configuration of volumes and vector realizing the Actor^Process^Goal relation in the visual image

Source: *Time*, 2 January 1995, pp. 56–7

Figure 13.17 'Clean Hands' judges; Mental Process in the visual image
Source: Il Manifesto, 7 June 1995, p. 10

Saussure's social-semiological theory of *langue* shifts the focus away from positivistic conceptions of the 'real' object world which pre-exists semiosis, to our social-semiological resources for attempting to know and act on this. The stratified reality of language is the means by which language form and the 'external' world of thought and sound are selectively incorporated into a still wider system of contextualizing relations. Signified thought-substance and sound-substance are not given 'in' the world; rather, they emerge progressively from the analogue flux of thought and sound. This occurs through a process of selective contextualization according to the multiple possibilities afforded by the language system in and through the exchange transactions with the world that take place in acts of *parole*.

The arguments I have proposed in this section suggest how in social semiosis the sign is motivated along a second important dimension. I shall refer to this as the METASEMIOTIC dimension. Stratification is METASEMIOTIC for two reasons: first, it shows how one order of difference selectively construes pattern and meaning in the other order; second, it constitutes the principle whereby this same system of differences, or some part of it, may be selectively deployed so as to act and reflect on the system, on the way it is used and on our relationship to it as users and theorists of language.

15 THE CONTEXTUAL GROUNDING OF SIGNS

We have seen that Saussure's notion of an 'idea' refers to signified substance, rather than to a value in signified form (Chapter 12, section 5). This is an important distinction. The signifieds of the language system refer to their type classes, or their prototypical instantiations, in $langue_2$. In the speech circuit, Saussure adopts the terminology of concept and acoustic image to draw attention to the psychic basis whereby interactants construe material events (e.g., vocalizations) as instances of this or that sign type. Neither of these perspectives in itself shows how signs are 'grounded', to use Langacker's term, in specific acts of *parole*.

Langacker (1987: 126) uses the term 'ground' to explain how a *langue*-based system of types can be used in ways which are specific to a given situation. In my view, this is a third dimension along which signs are motivated in *parole*. Grounding is also called 'indexicality' in some traditions. It refers to the ways in which deictic and other semiotic forms function to 'ground' an expression in a specific context-of-use, or to specify otherwise the contextual relevance of some feature of the situation. That is, grounding specifies how linguistic and other semiotic forms, material events and objects and so on are mutually relevant to each other's interpretation in the construction of the larger whole – the context – to which they belong. In Saussurean terms, it is concerned with how signified substance (an idea) is related to signified form, which is internal to the sign.

The resources for grounding a sign in contextually specific ways are internal to *langue*; they are not outside it. A 'pragmatics' of language-in-use need not be opposed to the system view. The two are complementary perspectives on the same phenomenon. For example, the grounding of the noun occurs through the grammatical resources of the nominal group (noun phrase). It is only through the resources of the nominal group that nouns can index entities in the world. Langacker points out that the difference between a noun and a nominal group lies in the fact that a noun is a type specification of some entity, whereas a nominal group construes a given thing as an instance of the type. A parallel argument also applies to the verbal group. Non-finite verbs designate a type specification of a given process. A finite verb, on the other hand, instances the process as a 'finite' proposition relative to a given speech event (Davidse 1991: 195n.).

Acts of *parole* are not simply motivated in relation to the contingencies of the specific situation. They are also *systemically* motivated through the contextualizing mechanism of *langue* (Chapter 12, section 4). In this way, acts of *parole* are not merely contingent and *ad hoc* happenstances which are outside the social-semiological regularities of *langue*. If this were not so, then a given vocalization, say, would have no situationally specific meaning or relevance for the participants in the speech event. In order to be semiotically grounded in the situation, acts of *parole* must also be grounded in a *langue*-based system of types.

There are a number of more specific types of grounding which are specified in *CLG*. These are:

1   Signified form (the signified) cross-couples with thought to form a contextually specific signified substance. This clarifies Saussure's claim that *langue* is 'a system of signs for expressing ideas' (*CLG*: 33). An 'idea' is another term for signified substance.

2   Signifying form (the signifier) cross-couples with sound to form a contextually specific phonic substance. In this way, the signifier grounds the signifying act in the bodily processes of the speaker.

3   Language form cross-couples with other semiotic modalities to form composite texts of, say, verbal and visual forms.

4   Acts of *parole* are grounded in relation to the 'personal thoughts' the speaker wishes to express (*CLG*: 31), to his or her locally perceived goals, intentions and purposes in the interaction. Signifying acts are 'psychic' in this sense.

5   The systemic linearity of the signifier (*CLG*: 103), rather than filling in an abstract and empty Newtonian space–time, constitutes the very basis of the interactional space–time and its rhythms in which subjects feel they are participating during the course of discursive interaction. This is qualitatively different from the mechanical clock-time of the Newtonian paradigm.

6   The ability to hear oneself speak is the indexical ground of one's consciousness of the self–other dialectic (*CLG*: 98).

7   A given act of *parole* does not transmit 'encoded' information or content. Rather, it indexes the speaker's orientation to the unfolding speech event; it does not specify in advance what the orientation of the hearer is. An act of *parole* is a localized grounding of the meaning potential of the system, or some restriction of this.

I prefer Langacker's term 'ground' to the better-known term 'indexicality', because the former captures a most fundamental aspect of any act of meaning-making. The ground is the earth–air interface. It is both the reference point for our perception and behaviour, and the material support of our bodies when we enact socially meaningful acts (Gibson 1986 [1979]: 16). Signifying acts are always grounded in bodily processes and corporeal schema in relation to this interface (Thibault, forthcoming).

In the next section, I shall examine a short piece of spoken discourse in order to investigate how diverse semiotic modalities are co-deployed in order to ground the discourse, dually, in interactional space–time and bodily process.

16 THE GROUNDING OF DISCOURSE IN EMBODIED SPACE–TIME: A TEXTUAL ANALYSIS

The text which I shall analyse in this section is transcribed from a television documentary concerning the life of a family in Sydney (Australia). The transcription is taken from a longer episode in which the two interactants, Laurie and Noeleen, who are husband and wife, argue about Laurie's inability to make any of the pens he is trying to write with work. The exchange takes place in the kitchen–dining room area of their home.

N: (1) this is the one you had
/picks up same blue pen that Laurie had been using/(Picture 1)

L: (2) well I picked up one of those **first** (Picture 2)
/he picks up another pen from the pen rack on his right; while uttering clause 2 his right hand, still holding the pen just picked up, makes a sharp downstroke, which coincides with the tonic accent on the word 'first'/

   (3) and I said that's the **third** one (Picture 3)
/repeats gesture referred to above; this time coinciding with tonic accent on 'third'/

   (4) didn't you hear me say that?
/returns pen in hand to rack on his right/

N: (5) but there's nothing wrong with that one
/said while leaning over to take same pen back from rack/

   (6) look
/said as she writes with the pen on the piece of paper in front of Laurie/(Picture 4)

L: (7) there probably was never anything wrong with it (Picture 5)
   (8) it wouldn't write when I wanted it to write
   (9a) if you leave it for a while and *play* with it
   (9b) it will probably work
/iconic gesture of scribbling with hand on word *play*/

Grounding refers to the way in which language form cross-couples with thought and sound in acts of *parole* in order to produce contextually specific signified substance and phonic substance. Acts of *parole* are, then, dually grounded in relation to (1) the phenomena of the world which are selectively contextualized as signified substance and (2) the bodily (kinetic) processes of phonation and gesticulation which are selectively contextualized as signifying substance. In the specifically linguistic sense, this may involve the use of deictics or indexicals to specify the relevance of particular entities, events and so on to the interaction, as well as particular bodily and affective states of the speaker–listener.

Picture 1

Picture 2

Picture 3

Picture 4

Picture 5

Clause 1 indexes a particular object – the blue pen in question – in this sense (Picture 1). However, this is not an unmediated act of 'referring' to something real 'out there'. The use of the demonstrative pronoun *this* derives its semantic value from a system of contrasts with other linguistic forms in an associative group comprising *the, that* and so on. Further, clause 1 is an identifying process (section 9 above). The demonstrative pronoun *this* is the concrete Token which is semantically re-construed as having a certain Value: viz. *the one you had* from the point of view of the speaker of clause 1. It is not the case that *this* 'refers to' a given object (the pen), but that the pen has been globally re-construed as a signified substance by the entire clause, relative to the interactional perspectives of speaker and listener. In this case, the language form used selectively re-contextualizes a given object in the spatio-temporal purview of the interactants as having a particular kind of semiotic Value in the interaction itself. The spatio-temporal purview is an analogue continuum of perceptual experience which language form selectively intervenes in.

Clauses 2 and 3 are uttered in synchrony with a particular gestural movement which Laurie makes with his right arm and hand while holding the pen (Pictures 2 and 3). In both cases, this is a sharp downward movement of his right arm, the endpoint of which coincides with the tonic accent in its function as the unmarked position for information focus at the end of these two clauses. These examples draw attention to the ways in which bodily processes cross-couple with language form.

In the present example, this is so in three main ways. First, Laurie's gestures directly participate both in the assigning of informational prominence in the two clauses. Second, they also assign boundaries to these two moves in the discourse. Third, Laurie's gesture is a visual–gestural prosody which is iconic to his affective investment in the assertions he is making here. This particular phase of the interaction is completed in clause 4, which synchronizes with a particular bodily movement: that of leaning to his right to place the pen back on the rack.

Clause 5 is a presentative clause. Noeleen introduces a new discursive entity into the interaction. This clause functions to negate the prior expectations established by Laurie, that is, that something is wrong with the pen. It is uttered in synchrony with a particular bodily movement: Noeleen, who is directly opposite Laurie and leaning across the table to face him, reaches to her left and takes the same pen that Laurie had placed back on the rack. This clause constitutes a specific challenge to Laurie's point of view. Clause 6 takes this a step further. Importantly, the uttering of this clause cross-couples with the material act of Noeleen using the pen to write on the piece of paper in front of Laurie (Picture 4). The use of imperative mood in clause 6 dialogically focuses both participants on the material act of Noeleen's writing with the pen. Unlike its predecessors, which select declarative mood, clause 6 does not make a proposition about a given state of affairs. In this sense, clause 5 is part of the ongoing argument between the two speakers as to whether something is wrong with the pen(s) or not.

Clause 6 has quite a different illocutionary value. Semantically, its interactive purpose is to focus Laurie's attention on the material act of writing, thereby providing concrete proof of the assertion made in clause 5. That is, it seeks to constitute Laurie in a particular kind of interactive relationship to a simultaneously semiotic and material event. Clause 6 cross-couples with a particular material action, but it does not in any way represent that event. Its function is to co-ordinate dialogically the two interactants in relation to the material action of Noeleen's writing with the pen.

There is one final feature I shall mention here. Clause 9a cross-couples with the iconic gesture of Laurie's performing a scribbling movement with his hand while uttering the word *play* (Picture 5). Overall, clauses 7–9b constitute a re-evaluation on Laurie's part of the prior situation – especially given the material evidence that Noeleen has just placed before his eyes. In this case, the gestural sign is iconic to a particular kind of material action. For that reason, it has experiential value. That is, it construes a particular kind of material activity, viz. the material act of writing with pen and paper.

What is the function of this spatial syntagm in relation to the spatio-temporal flow of the speech event? As part of an overall response to the preceding interaction, this iconic gesture does more than simply co-pattern with clause 9a. It is also a bodily response to Noeleen's previous act of writing on the piece of paper. In other words, Laurie's response to Noeleen takes place in both the linguistic and the gestural semiotic modalities. It is a dialogic response both to what he has heard and to what he has seen. It grounds the hypothetical status of clause 9a in Laurie's embodied participation in and re-evaluation of the nexus of semiotic and material events which have constituted the interaction up to this point.

17 TOWARDS A THEORY OF SIGNS IN SOCIAL LIFE

Throughout this study I have emphasized the rich and in many ways unexplored potential of Saussure's social-semiological metatheory. It is now time to take stock of these considerations. I have tried to show how these continue to provide viable alternatives to the sterile and decontextualized formalisms and the mechanistic metaphors that have characterized so much recent theorizing about human social meaning-making.

Winfried Nöth locates Saussure at the beginning of the 'road of linguistic semiotics' (1977: 22), which leads straight from Saussure to Hjelmslev and on to the French structuralists such as Roland Barthes. Certainly, that is the road down which Saussure's thought has, for the most part, been taken. According to Nöth, this road leads, in the work of Roland Barthes (1967 [1964]), to the view that 'non-linguistic semiotics' should be considered 'a second-order language', which does not exist 'independently of language' (Nöth 1977: 22).

In Nöth's view, Barthes reverses the usual hierarchy so that semiology is subsumed by linguistics. Similarly, Eco claims that Barthes' translinguistics 'examines all sign systems with reference to linguistic laws' (1976: 30). In my view, Barthes' point is somewhat different:

> though working at the outset on non-linguistic substances, semiology is required, sooner or later, to find language (in the ordinary sense of the term) in its path, not only as a model, but also as component, relay or signified. Even so, such language is not quite that of the linguist: it is a second-order language, with its unities no longer monemes or phonemes, but larger fragments of discourse referring to objects or episodes whose meaning *underlies* language, but can never exist independently of it. Semiology is therefore perhaps destined to be absorbed into a *trans-linguistics*, the materials of which may be myth, narrative, journalism, or on the other hand objects of our civilization, in so far as they are *spoken* (through press, prospectus, interview, conversation and perhaps even the inner language, which is ruled by the laws of imagination). In fact, we must now face the possibility of inverting Saussure's declaration: linguistics is not a part of the general science of signs, even a privileged part, it is semiology which is part of linguistics: to be precise, it is that part covering the *great signifying unities* of discourse. By this inversion we may expect to bring to light the unity of the research being done in anthropology, sociology, psycho-analysis and stylistics round the concept of signification.
>
> (Barthes 1967 [1964]: 10–11; emphasis in original)

In the first instance, Barthes notes that non-linguistic semiotic modalities often do not exist independently of language, but may take language as a 'component, relay, or signified'. This does not mean that such non-linguistic modalities are necessarily secondary in status. To say that these are not independent of language does not automatically lead to the conclusion that linguistics subsumes semiotics. Instead, Barthes points out that linguistic and non-linguistic modalities of semiosis are co-deployed in discourse. On any given social occasion of discourse, many different semiotic modalities will, typically, be simultaneously orchestrated. Language may be a 'component' in a discourse in which linguistic and non-linguistic semiotic modalities interact; it may be a 'relay' in the sense that it specifies the relevant cultural references through which some other semiotic system which it accompanies (e.g., the visual) is to be interpreted; and it may be the 'signified' of some other semiotic system in so far as it 'individuates' the meanings of some other system (Barthes 1967 [1964]: 10).

Barthes also seeks to extend the definition of language beyond that of the boundaries (phoneme, morpheme, sentence) fixed by the linguistics of his day. The 'larger fragments of discourse' which Barthes refers to, correspond to our present-day notion of text. In my view, Barthes does not propose a simple inversion of Saussure's proposal to subsume linguistics under a general theory of signs in social life. This does not account for Barthes' admittedly programmatic reference to a 'trans-linguistics'. Instead, Barthes denies a privileged place for either in his attempt to re-synthesize the two in a still broader study of discourse and the role it plays in an interdisciplinary study of social meaning-making. The resulting 'trans-linguistics' is concerned with all kinds of texts (linguistic and non-linguistic) and the wider cultural meanings which 'underlie' them. Barthes perceives very clearly that these meanings are made in and through '*great signifying unities* of discourse' – composite semiotic action texts – and in ways which are not independent of the lower-level linguistic and other signifying units out of which these unities are assembled and made.

Far from saying that linguistics subsumes semiology, Barthes argues that the latter 'is part of' the former. This is so in the sense that a linguistics which confines itself to the levels of phoneme, morpheme and sentence is inadequate for the study of the wider cultural meanings which language and other semiotic systems realize in the form of cultural texts. Being 'a part of' does not mean that one is necessarily subsumed by, or subordinate to, the other: the 'parts' can be re-constituted, theoretically speaking, in the development of a still wider 'semiological knowledge'.

We need a semiotic description which is able to provide a record of the composite semiotic action texts – the socio-discursive events – in and through which meanings are made and interpreted. This brings me to two key dimensions of semiosis which have received all too little attention. These may be summarized as follows:

1   The semiotic–discursive practices of a community are *strongly cross-coupled* with the physical–material domain (Lemke 1993: 249–51).
2   The linguistic semiotic is *strongly cross-coupled* with the various other semiotic modalities in social semiosis.

Language has usually been seen as only weakly cross-coupled with the two dimensions referred to here (Lemke 1993). As a consequence, we have the theoretical fiction (1) that language is form, but not substance and (2) that it is an autonomous system, not systematically related to other modalities of social semiosis (Chapter 2, section 13). Now, Saussure recognized that the 'concrete real' is only meaningful when cross-coupled with the contextualizing relations of *langue* (Chapter 2, section 9). Hjelmslev also recognized that substance is 'semiotically formed' (1954: 173), yet this insight has not been systematically developed. Semiotic form and substance co-evolve, both synchronically and diachronically, through the impact of the one on the other in countless acts of *parole*. Semiotic substance does not exist independently of a system of semiotic forms. It is only through the latter that the former emerges as the culturally salient phenomena of human action and experience.

Point 1 highlights the way in which a social activity-structure type is constructed in and through the joint deployment, by the participants in it, of the available semiotic *and* material resources in order to enact a regular, repeatable activity-structure of a given cultural type. The semiotic–discursive resources are deployed in ways which co-ordinate and entrain physical–material states and processes. Furthermore, social activity-structures are themselves semiotic–material performances. Just like the texts which they produce or enact in determinate ways, social activity-structures themselves deploy semiotic resource systems in regular and repeatable ways. These may include all the semiotic resource systems which may not be included in a verbal transcription, or may be so but only marginally. Thus, actional, paralinguistic, kinesic, somatic and other semiotic modalities have hitherto been seen as merely 'contextualizing' the linguistic text, which is seen as having primary status (Thibault 1994). This now brings us to the importance of point 2.

I said that language is strongly cross-coupled with the other, non-verbal semiotic modalities. In other words, there are strong *inter*semiotic cross-couplings. This has a number of important consequences, viz. language has both co-evolved with and is *always* co-deployed with other semiotic resource systems (Lemke 1993: 249–51). There are no exceptions to this, including the seemingly emblematic case of the written text. Written language always *simultaneously* co-deploys both visual and linguistic semiotic modalities in the making of texts (Kress and Van Leeuwen 1990; Thibault 1994). This brings me back to the relevance of Barthes' attempt to steer the Saussurean legacy in the direction of a more comprehensive theory of social meaning-making than that envisaged by structural linguistics.

Barthes is both realistic and honest enough to point out that his 'trans-linguistic' project, at the time he wrote, was heavily reliant on 'linguistic knowledge'. Yet he is also aware of the need to analyse non-linguistic semiotic systems (1967 [1964]: 11). In my view, this reliance has now been substantially, if not entirely, superseded by more recent developments in the study of the dynamics of signs in social life.

Postscript

Social life entails the lived experience of meaning-making, rather than the abstract system of types in *langue*. That is, social life is the domain of *parole*. It is the domain where specific historical–biographical individuals jointly enact and interpret signifying acts on specific occasions. It is the domain where lived human experience, biography, personal psychology, corporeality and the phenomena of experience in the material world come together. It would be a mistake, however, to oppose this perspective to the higher-order system of types in *langue*. The relationship between the two perspectives is not a dichotomy. The dichotomous reading can only put the relation between *langue* and *parole* and between society and individual, in a straightjacket. *Langue* is an open-ended and historically changing resource which the members of a society draw on in concrete acts of *parole*. It is social life, rather than *langue*, which is the source of the individual's 'will', 'intelligence' and 'personal thought', as manifested in the innumerable acts of *parole* that individuals engage in with others. Social life is the point of contact where a discursively informed 'social psychology' can specify the links between the speech practices that individuals engage in in *parole* and the meaning-making resources of *langue*. The latter can both enable and constrain these possibilities; however, their concrete working out and further development can only occur in and through the making and re-making of signs in social life. *Parole*, as the point of contact between individual and social-semiological systems, is the means by which both the individual and the system are renewed in and through the signifying acts that are the very material of social life.

Appendix

PUTTING IN THE RIBBON

1   Check that the printer is not connected to the power supply.
2   Take off the dust cover.

Warning:
The power must be off when you move the print head, otherwise you can damage the printer mechanism. If the printer has been used just before changing the ribbon, allow the print head to cool before you remove the old ribbon.

---

3   Gently but firmly move the print head to its middle position.
4   Tighten up the ribbon by turning the feeding knob in the direction of the arrow marked on the cartridge – this will make it easier to insert it into the printer.
5   Push the cartridge firmly into position, making sure it fits over the ribbon feeder knob. To find the knob, look down into the printer: it is an upright black plastic knob, towards the left.
6   Use a pencil, paper-clip or your fingers to guide the ribbon between the print head and the ribbon mask, making sure that the ribbon is not creased or folded.
7   Check that the ribbon is tight by turning the feeding knob anti-clockwise.
8   Move the print head backwards and forwards along the carriage to check that the ribbon is installed correctly.

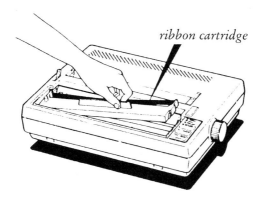

ribbon cartridge

REPLACING THE RIBBON

When your printouts become too faint, you need to fit a new ribbon cartridge.

Warning:
Always use replacement ribbons designed specifically for the Epson LX-800 or the FX-800 printer (#8750). Do not use ribbons from other printers. They will be unsuitable. Do not try to re-ink your ribbon: you may block up the print head and corrode its pins, and replacing the print head will cost you far more than buying a ribbon.

To replace the ribbon, grip the cartridge by the plastic tab at the top, and pull the cartridge out. You can then install a new ribbon by following the steps described on the previous page and above.

(*Source: User's Guide. Epson LX-800 9 Pin Dot Matrix Printer*, Seiko Epson Corporation, Japan, pp. 12–13)

References

PRIMARY TEXTS

Godel, Robert (ed.) (1957) *Les Sources manuscrites du Cours de linguistique générale de F. de Saussure*, Geneva and Paris: Droz & Minard.

Saussure, Ferdinand de. (1957) 'Cours de linguistique générale (1908–9). IIe Cours. Introduction', ed. Robert Godel, *Cahiers Ferdinand de Saussure* 15: 2–103.

——— (1959) *Course in General Linguistics*, trans. Wade Baskin, New York and London: McGraw-Hill.

——— (1961 [1894–1911]) 'Lettres de Ferdinand de Saussure à Antoine Meillet' (ed. Emile Benveniste), *Cahiers Ferdinand de Saussure* 21: 89–135.

——— (1967) *Cours de linguistique générale*, critical edition in three volumes, ed. Rudolf Engler, Wiesbaden: Otto Harrassowitz.

——— (1971 [1916]) *Cours de linguistique générale* [= *CLG*], ed. Charles Bally and Albert Sechehaye, Paris: Payot.

——— (1983) *Course in General Linguistics*, trans. Roy Harris, London: Duckworth.

——— (1994 [1967]) *Corso di linguistica generale*, introduction, Italian trans. and commentary, Tullio de Mauro, Rome and Bari: Laterza.

——— (1994) *Manoscritti di Harvard*, ed. Herman Parret, Italian trans. Raffaella Petrilli, Rome and Bari: Laterza.

Starobinski, Jean. (1971) *Les Mots sur les mots: les anagrammes de Ferdinand de Saussure*, Paris: Gallimard.

SECONDARY TEXTS

Annibale, Elia. (1978) *Per Saussure, contro Saussure: il 'sociale' nelle teorie linguistiche del novecento*, Bologna: Il Mulino.

Antonelli, Carla. (1978) 'On the Saussurean distinction between *signifié* and *signification*', *Ars Semeiotica* 1, 3: 107–28.

Ashby, W. Ross. (1956) *An Introduction to Cybernetics*, London: Chapman & Hall.

Bakhtin, Mikhail. (1981 [1975]) 'Discourse in the novel', in Michael Holquist (ed.) *The Dialogic Imagination: Four Essays*, Austin and London: University of Texas Press.

Barthes, Roland. (1967 [1964]) *Elements of Semiology*, trans. Annette Lavers and Colin Smith, New York: Hill & Wang.

Bernstein, Basil. (1990) *The Structuring of Pedagogic Discourse*, vol. IV: *Class, Codes and Control*, London and New York: Routledge.

Bhaskar, Roy. (1979) *The Possibility of Naturalism: a Philosophical Critique of the*

Contemporary Human Sciences, Brighton, Sussex: Harvester.

Bierwisch, Manfred. (1970) 'Semantics', in John Lyons (ed.) *New Horizons in Linguistics*, Harmondsworth, Middlesex: Penguin, pp. 166–84.

Birch, David. (1987) 'Expanding semantic options for reading Early Modern English', in David Birch and Michael O'Toole (eds) *Functions of Style*, London and New York: Frances Pinter, pp. 157–68.

Bohr, N. (1935) 'Quantum mechanics and physical reality', *Nature* 136: 65.

——— (1948) 'On the notions of causality and complementarity', *Dialectica* 7–8: 313–14.

Brentano, Franz. (1874) *Psychologie vom empirischen Standpunkte*, Leipzig.

Broca, Paul. (1965) 'On the speech center', in Richard J. Herrnstein and Edwin G. Boring (eds) *A Source Book in the History of Psychology*, trans. Mollie D. Boring, Cambridge, Mass.: Harvard University Press, pp. 223–9. [(1861) 'Remarques sur le siège de la faculté du langage articulé, suivies d'une observation d'aphémie', *Bulletin de la Société Anatomique de Paris* 2, 6: 343–57.]

Chomsky, Noam. (1965) *Aspects of the Theory of Syntax*, Cambridge, Mass.: MIT Press.

Coseriu, Eugenio. (1973) *Lezioni di linguistica generale*, Turin: Boringhieri.

——— (1981) *Sincronia, diacronia e storia: il problema del cambio linguistico*, Italian trans. Paola Mura, Turin: Boringhieri. [Original Spanish-language edition, *Sincronia, diacronía y historia: el problema del cambio linguístico*, Montevideo, 1958.]

Culler, Jonathan. (1976) *Ferdinand de Saussure*, London: Fontana.

Davidse, Kristin. (1991) 'Categories of experiential grammar', unpublished Ph.D. dissertation, Department of Linguistics, Katholieke Universiteit Leuven.

——— (1992) 'A semiotic approach to relational clauses', *Occasional Papers in Systemic Linguistics* 6: 99–131.

Derossi, Giorgio. (1976) *Semiologia della Conoscenza: presupposti e fondamenti del significare*, Rome: Armando Editore.

Derrida, Jacques. (1974/6 [1967]) *Of Grammatology*, trans. Gayatri Chakravorty Spivak, Baltimore and London: Johns Hopkins University Press.

Dewey, John. (1965) 'Against reflexology', in Richard J. Herrnstein and Edwin G. Boring (eds) *A Source Book in the History of Psychology*, Cambridge, Mass.: Harvard University Press, pp. 321–5. [(1896) 'The reflex arc concept in psychology', *Psychological Review* 3: 357–70.]

Durkheim, Emile. (1982 [1902]) 'The rules of sociological method', in Steven Lukes (ed.) *The Rules of Sociological Method and Selected Texts on Sociology and its Method*, trans. W. D. Halls, London: MacMillan, pp. 29–163.

Eco, Umberto. (1976) *A Theory of Semiotics*, Bloomington and London: Indiana University Press.

Edelman, Gerald M. (1989) *The Remembered Present: a Biological Theory of Consciousness*, New York: Basic Books.

Edwards, Derek and Jonathan Potter. (1992) *Discursive Psychology*, London and New Delhi: Sage.

Ellis, John M. (1993) *Language, Thought, and Logic*, Evanston, Ill.: Northwestern University Press.

Fawcett, Robin P. (1982) 'Language as a semiological system: a re-interpretation of Saussure', in J. Morreal (ed.) *The Ninth LACUS Forum 1982*, Columbia: Hornbeam Press.

Foucault, Michel. (1974 [1969]) *The Archaeology of Knowledge*, trans. A. M. Sheridan Smith, London: Tavistock.

Gibson, James J. (1986 [1979]) *The Ecological Approach to Visual Perception*, Hillsdale, N.J. and London: Lawrence Erlbaum.

Givón, T. (1989) *Mind, Code and Context: Essays in Pragmatics*, Hillsdale, N.J. and London: Lawrence Erlbaum.

Godzich, Wlad. (1984) 'The semiotics of semiotics', *Australian Journal of Cultural Studies* 2, 2: 3–22.

Goidànich, P. G. (1938) 'Il mio insegnamento di glottologia', *Archivio Italiano di Glottologia* 30: 1–51.

Guterres, Denise Michelle. (1992) 'The functional visual', unpublished B.A. Honours degree thesis, Department of English Language and Early English Literature, University of Sydney.

Halliday, M. A. K. (1979) 'Modes of meaning and modes of expression: types of grammatical structure, and their determination by different semantic functions', in D. J. Allerton, Edward Carney and David Holdcroft (eds) *Function and Context in Linguistic Analysis: a Festschrift for William Haas*, Cambridge and London: Cambridge University Press, pp. 57–79.

—— (1982) 'The de-automatization of meaning: from Priestley's *An Inspector Calls*', in John Anderson (ed.) *Language Form and Linguistic Variation: Papers Dedicated to Angus McIntosh*, Amsterdam: John Benjamins, pp. 129–59.

—— (1988) 'On the language of physical science', in Mohsen Ghadessy (ed.) *Registers of Written English: Situational Factors and Linguistic Features*, London and New York: Frances Pinter, pp. 162–78.

—— (1992) 'How do you mean?', in Louise Ravelli and Martin Davies (eds) *Advances in Systemic Linguistics: Recent Theory and Practice*, London and Dover, N.H.: Frances Pinter, pp. 20–35.

—— (1993) 'New ways of meaning: a challenge to applied linguistics', in *Language in a Changing Word*, Occasional Paper 13: 1–41, Deakin, A.C.T.: Applied Linguistics Association of Australia.

—— (1994) *An Introduction to Functional Grammar*, 2nd edn, London and Melbourne: Arnold.

Harré, Rom. (1979) *Social Being: a Theory for Social Psychology*, Oxford: Basil Blackwell.

—— (1990) 'Exploring the human Umwelt', in Roy Bhaskar (ed.) *Harré and his Critics: Essays in Honour of Rom Harré with his Commentary on them*, Oxford: Basil Blackwell, pp. 297–364.

Harré, Rom and Grant Gillett. (1994) *The Discursive Mind*, London and New Delhi: Sage.

Harris, Roy. (1987) *Reading Saussure: a Critical Commentary on the* Cours de linguistique générale, London: Duckworth.

Hasan, Ruqaiya. (1987a) 'Directions from structuralism', in D. Attridge, A. Durant, N. Fabb and C. MacCabe (eds) *The Linguistics of Writing*, Manchester: Manchester University Press, pp. 103–23.

—— (1987b) 'The grammarian's dream: lexis as most delicate grammar', in M. A. K. Halliday and Robin Fawcett (eds) *New Developments in Systemic Linguistics*, vol. 1: *Theory and Description*, London and New York: Frances Pinter, pp. 184–211.

Hawkes, Terence. (1977) *Structuralism and Semiotics*, London: Methuen.

Heisenberg, W. (1966) *Fisica e filosofia*, Milan: Il Saggiatore.

—— (1976) 'The nature of elementary particles', *Physics Today*, p. 38.

Hjelmslev, Louis. (1942) 'Langue et parole', *Cahiers Ferdinand de Saussure* 2: 29–44.

—— (1954) 'La stratification du langage', *Word* 10, 2–3: 163–88.

—— (1969 [1943]) *Prolegomena to a Theory of Language*, trans. Francis J. Whitfield, Madison, Milwaukee and London: University of Wisconsin Press.

—— (1981 [1948]) 'L'analisi strutturale del linguaggio', in *Saggi di Linguistica*

Generale, Italian trans. Massimo Prampolini, Parma: Pratiche Editrice, pp. 15–25.

Hodge, Robert and Gunther Kress. (1988) *Social Semiotics*, Cambridge: Polity.

Holdcroft, David. (1991) *Saussure. Signs, System, and Arbitrariness*, Cambridge and New York: Cambridge University Press.

Hunter, Ian. (1984) 'After representation: recent discussions of the relation between language and literature', *Economics and Society* 13: 397–430.

Jameson, Frederic. (1972) *The Prison-House of Language*, Princeton and London: Princeton University Press.

Kanizsa, Gaetano. (1991) *Grammatica del vedere*, Bologna: Il Mulino.

Kant, Immanuel. (1970 [1781]) *Critique of Pure Reason*, trans. Norman Kemp Smith, London: MacMillan.

Kress, Gunther. (1993) 'Against arbitrariness: the social production of the sign as a foundational issue in critical discourse analysis', *Discourse and Society* 4, 2: 169–91.

Kress, Gunther and Theo Van Leeuwen. (1990) *Reading Images*, Geelong, Victoria: Deakin University Press.

—— (1996) *Reading Images: the Grammar of Visual Design*, London and New York: Routledge.

Langacker, Ronald W. (1987) *Foundations of Cognitive Grammar*, vol. 1: *Theoretical Prerequisites*, Stanford, Calif.: Stanford University Press.

Lazotti, Lucia. (1990) *Leggere l'immagine: educazione visiva e processi di apprendimento*, Milan: Franco Angeli.

Lee, Benjamin. (1985) 'Peirce, Frege, Saussure, and Whorf: the semiotic mediation of ontology', in Elizabeth Mertz and Richard J. Parmentier (eds) *Semiotic Mediation: Sociocultural and Psychological Perspectives*, New York and London: Academic Press, pp. 99–128.

Lemke, Jay L. (1983) 'Thematic analysis: systems, structures, and strategies', *Recherches Sémiotiques/Semiotic Inquiry* 3, 2: 159–87.

—— (1984a) *Semiotics and Education*, Monographs, Working Papers and Prepublications of the Toronto Semiotic Circle, Victoria University, Toronto, no. 2.

—— (1984b) 'Action, context, and meaning', in Jay L. Lemke (ed.) *Semiotics and Education*, Monographs, Working Papers and Prepublications of the Toronto Semiotic Circle, Victoria University, Toronto, no. 2, pp. 63–93.

—— (1984c) 'Textual politics: heteroglossia, discourse analysis, and social dynamics', mimeo, School of Education, Brooklyn College, City University of New York.

—— (1984d) 'The formal analysis of instruction', in Jay L. Lemke (ed.) *Semiotics and Education*, Monographs, Working Papers and Prepublications of the Toronto Semiotic Circle, Victoria University, Toronto, no. 2, pp. 23–62.

—— (1985) 'Ideology, intertextuality, and the notion of register', in James D. Benson and William S. Greaves (eds) *Systemic Perspectives on Discourse*, vol. 1: *Selected Papers from the Ninth International Systemic Workshop*, Norwood, NJ: Ablex, pp. 275–94.

—— (1988) 'Towards a social semiotics of the material subject', in Terry Threadgold (ed.) *Working Papers* 2, 1–2: 1–17, University of Sydney: Sydney Association for Studies of Society and Culture.

—— (1993) 'Discourse, dynamics, and social change', in M. A. K. Halliday (guest ed.) *Language as Cultural Dynamic*, special issue of *Cultural Dynamics* 4, 1–2: 243–75.

Lévi-Strauss, Claude. (1972) *Structural Anthropology*, trans. Claire Jacobson and Brooke Grundfest Schoepf, Harmondsworth, Middlesex: Allen Lane, Penguin.

Lichtheim, L. (1884) 'Über Aphasie', *Deutsches Archiv für Klinische Medizin* 36:

204–68 [(1885) 'On aphasia', *Brain* 7: 433–84.]

Lukács, Georg. (1980 [1978]) *The Ontology of Social Being*, vol. 3: *Labour*, trans. David Fernbach, London: Merlin.

McCarthy, Rosaleen A. and Elizabeth K. Warrington. (1990) *Cognitive Neuropsychology: a Clinical Introduction*, New York and London: Academic Press.

Martin, James R. (1991) 'Intrinsic functionality: implications for contextual theory', *Social Semiotics* 1, 1: 99–162.

—— (1992) *English Text: System and Structure*, Amsterdam and Philadelphia, Pa.: Benjamins.

Marx, Karl. (1906 [1867]) Frederick Engels (ed.) *Capital: a Critique of Political Economy*, vol. I: *The Process of Capitalist Accumulation*, trans. from the 3rd German edn, Samuel Moore and Edward Aveling, Chicago: Charles H. Kerr.

Meillet, Antoine. (1921) 'Remarques sur la théorie de la phrase', *Journal de Psychologie Normale et Pathologique* XVIIe Anné 1920: 609–16.

Nöth, Winfried. (1977) 'The semiotic framework of textlinguistics', in Wolfgang U. Dressler (ed.) *Current Trends in Textlinguistics*, Berlin and New York: Walter de Gruyter, pp. 21–34.

O'Toole, Michael. (1994) *The Language of Displayed Art*, London: Leicester University Press.

Pareto, Vilfredo. (1963 [1935]) *The Mind and Society: a Treatise on General Sociology*, vol. IV: *The General Form of Society*, ed. Arthur Livingston, trans. Andrew Bongiorno and Arthur Livingston, New York: Dover.

Parret, Herman. (1994) 'Introduction', in Herman Parret (ed.) *Manoscritti di Harvard*, 3–5, Italian trans. Raffaella Petrilli, Rome and Bari: Laterza.

Peng, Fred C. C. (1994) 'Language disorders and brain function', *Acta Neurologica Sinica* 3, 3: 103–30.

Petitot-Cocorda, Jean. (1990 [1985]) *Morfogenesi del senso: per uno schematismo della struttura*, Italian trans. Marcello Castellana, Mario Jacquemet and Francesco Marsciani, Milan: Bompiani.

Ponzio, Augusto. (1977) 'Linguistica saussuriana ed economia politica: per una critica dell'approccio marginalistico alla comunicazione sociale', in his *Marxismo, Scienza e Problema dell'Uomo*, Verona: Bertani, pp. 163–82.

Potter, Jonathan and Margaret Wetherell. (1987) *Discourse and Social Psychology: Beyond Attitudes and Behaviour*, London and New Delhi: Sage.

Prakasam, V. (1987) 'Aspects of word phonology', in M. A. K. Halliday and Robin Fawcett (eds) *New Developments in Systemic Linguistics*, vol. 1: *Theory and Description*, London and New York: Frances Pinter, pp. 272–87.

Prampolini, Massimo. (1994) *Ferdinand de Saussure*, Teramo: Giunti Lisciani Editori.

Prigogine, Ilya and Isabelle Stengers. (1985) *Order out of Chaos. Man's New Dialogue with Nature*, London: Fontana.

Reddy, Michael J. (1979) 'The conduit metaphor – a case of frame conflict in our language about language', in Andrew Ortony (ed.) *Metaphor and Thought*, Cambridge and New York: Cambridge University Press, pp. 284–324.

Rosch, Eleanor. (1977) 'Classification of real-world objects: origins and representations in cognition', in P. N. Johnson-Laird and P. C. Wason (eds) *Thinking: Readings in Cognitive Science*, Cambridge and Melbourne: Cambridge University Press, pp. 212–22.

Rossi-Landi, Ferruccio. (1977) *Linguistics and Economics*, The Hague and Paris: Mouton.

Sartre, Jean-Paul. (1969) *Being and Nothingness: an Essay on Phenomenological Ontology*, trans. Hazel E. Barnes, London: Methuen.

Sebeok, Thomas A. (1977) 'Ecumenicalism in semiotics', in Thomas A. Sebeok (ed.) *A Perfusion of Signs*, Bloomington and London: Indiana University Press, pp. 180–206.

Shannon, Claude E. and Warren Weaver. (1949) *The Mathematical Theory of Communication*, Urbana: University of Illinois Press.

Silverstein, Michael. (1981) 'The limits of awareness', *Sociolinguistic Working Paper* 84, Austin, Tex.: Southwest Educational Development Laboratory.

——— (1987) 'The three faces of "function": preliminaries to a psychology of language', in Maya Hickmann (ed.) *Social and Functional Approaches to Language and Thought*, New York and London: Academic Press, pp. 17–38.

——— (1992) 'The indeterminacy of contextualization: when is enough enough?', in Peter Auer and Aldo di Luzio (eds) *The Contextualization of Language*, Amsterdam and Philadelphia: John Benjamins, pp. 55–76.

Simone, Raffaele. (1992a) *Il sogno di Saussure*, Bari: Laterza.

——— (1992b) 'La linguistica come assiomatica in Saussure', in Raffaele Simone, *Il sogno di Saussure*, Bari: Laterza, pp. 159–73.

——— (1992c) '"Montrer au linguistique ce qu'il fait"', in Raffaele Simone, *Il sogno di Saussure*, Bari: Laterza, pp. 174–96.

Small, Edward. (1987) 'Semiotic referentiality: Saussure's sign and the Sanskrit *Nama-Rupa*', *The American Journal of Semiotics* 5, 3–5: 447–59.

Sperber, Dan and Deirdre Wilson. (1986) *Relevance: Communication and Cognition*, Oxford: Basil Blackwell.

Thibault, Paul J. (1986) 'The cognitive hypothesis: a critical comment', in *Text, Discourse, and Context: a Social Semiotic Perspective*, Monographs, Working Papers and Prepublications of the Toronto Semiotic Circle, 3: 26–42. Victoria University, Toronto.

——— (1991) *Social Semiotics as Praxis: Text, Social Meaning Making, and Nabokov's "Ada"*, ed. Wlad Godzich and Jochen Schulte-Sasse (Theory and History of Literature, 74), Minneapolis and Oxford: University of Minnesota Press.

——— (1994) 'Text and/or context? An open question', in Paul Bouissac (ed.) *The Semiotic Review of Books* (Toronto), 4, 3 (May): 10–12.

——— (in press a) 'Structuralism', in Paul Bouissac (ed.) *The Encyclopedia of Semiotics*, New York: Garland.

——— (in press b) 'Code', in Paul Bouissac (ed.) *The Encyclopedia of Semiotics*, New York: Garland.

——— (forthcoming) *The Signifying Body*.

Thibault, Paul J. and Theo Van Leeuwen. (1996) 'Grammar, society, and the speech act: renewing the connections', *Journal of Pragmatics* 25: 561–85.

Trevarthen, Colwyn. (1978) 'Modes of perceiving and modes of acting', in Herbert L. Pick and Elliot Saltzman (eds) *Modes of Perceiving and Processing Information*, Hillsdale, N.J.: Erlbaum, pp. 99–136.

Van Dijk, Teun A. (1992) 'Discourse and cognition in society', to appear in David Crowley and David Mitchell (eds) *Communication Theory Today*, Oxford: Basil Blackwell.

Vološinov, V. N. (1973 [1930]) *Marxism and the Philosophy of Language*, trans. Ladislav Matejka and I. R. Titunik, New York and London: Seminar Press.

——— (1983) 'The construction of the utterance', in Ann Shukman (ed.) *Russian Poetics in Translation*, vol. 10: *Bakhtin School Papers*, trans. Noel Owen, Oxford: Holdan, pp. 114–38.

Wernicke, Carl. (1977) 'The aphasia symptom complex: a psychological study on an anatomic basis', in Gertrude H. Eggert (ed.) *Wernicke's Work on Aphasia: a Source*

Book and Review, vol. 1: *Early Sources in Aphasia and Related Disorders*. The Hague and New York: Mouton, pp. 91–145. [(1874) *Der Aphasische Symptomencomplex: eine psychologische Studie auf der anatomischer Basis*, Breslau: Cohn & Weigert.]

Whitney, William Dwight. (1979 [1875]) *The Life and Growth of Language*, New York: Dover.

Wilden, Anthony. (1980 [1972]) *System and Structure: Essays in Communication and Exchange*, 2nd edn, London: Tavistock.

——— (1981) 'Semiotics as praxis: strategy and tactics'. *Recherches Sémiotiques/ Semiotic Inquiry* 1, 1: 1–34.

Wittgenstein, Ludwig. (1989 [1953]) *Philosophical Investigations*, Oxford: Basil Blackwell.

Wundt, Wilhelm. (1896) *Grundriss der Psychologie*, Leipzig.

SOURCE MATERIALS FOR TEXT ANALYSES

Bootzin, Richard R., Gordon H. Bower, Jennifer Crocker and Elizabeth Hall. (1991 [1975]) *Psychology Today: an Introduction*, 7th edn, New York and London: McGraw-Hill.

Carroll, Lewis. (1965 [1872]) *Through the Looking-Glass and What Alice Found There*, in *The Works of Lewis Carroll*, Feltham, Middlesex: Hamlyn, pp. 111–219.

Dahl, Roald. (1988) *Matilda*, Harmondsworth, Middlesex: Puffin.

Danieli, Sergio. (1981) *Quaderno di Lavoro 5*, Florence: Giunti Marzocco.

Joyce, James. (1975 [1939]) *Finnegans Wake*, London: Faber & Faber.

Smoot, George and Keay Davidson. (1995 [1993]) *Wrinkles in Time: the Imprint of Creation*, London: Abacus.

Worrell, Eric. (1963) *Reptiles of Australia*, Sydney and London: Angus & Robertson.

Name index

Subject index